D0394290

EMILE ZOLA

EMILE ZOLA

A Biography

Alan Schom

Henry Holt and Company
New York

Copyright © 1987 by Alan Schom
All rights reserved, including the right to reproduce this
book or portions thereof in any form.
First published in the United States in 1988 by
Henry Holt and Company, Inc., 115 West 18th Street,
New York, New York 10011.

Library of Congress Cataloging-in-Publication Data
Schom, Alan.
Emile Zola : a biography.
Bibliography: p.
Includes index.
1. Zola, Emile, 1840–1902—Biography.
2. Authors, French—19th century—Biography.
I. Title.
PQ2528.S36 1988 843'.8 [B]   87-35583
ISBN 0-8050-0710-5

First American Edition

Printed in the United States of America
10 9 8 7 6 5 4 3 2 1

ISBN 0-8050-0710-5

To My Daughters—Sarah and Emma

'*Dans le grand calme de ma solitude, je vis enragé.*'

Zola to Fernand Labori,
19 August 1898

'*Quelle folie de croire qu'on peut empêcher l'histoire d'être écrite.*'

Zola, '*Lettre à la France*',
6 January 1898

CONTENTS

Eight pages of photographs follow page 160.

ACKNOWLEDGEMENTS

A great number of people and institutions aided and abetted my research efforts and in particular I should like to thank the following: Dr B.H. Bakker, Director of the Research Programme on Zola and Naturalism, University of Toronto; the Houghton Library, Harvard University; the Sterling Memorial Library, Yale University; the Bancroft Library, University of California at Berkeley; the Bodleian and Taylorian Libraries of Oxford University, whose librarians have gone to considerable trouble to meet my needs over a period of years; the Musée Carnavalet, the Bibliothèque de l'Arsenal, and especially the Bibliothèque Nationale — all of Paris; the Research Foundation of the City University of New York and The American Philosophical Society. I am grateful to the Département des Manuscrits at the Bibliothèque Nationale for permission to quote from the letters they hold, and to the University of Toronto for permission to quote from *Emile Zola, Correspondance,* ed. B.H. Bakker, 5 vols, (1858-1886), (Presses de l'Université de Montréal/Editions du CNRS, 1978-1985). The quotations from Zola manuscripts held at Harvard appear by permission of the Houghton Library.

I should also like to thank the following individuals: the late Thornton Wilder; Professor Eugen Weber, of UCLA; Professor Albert Salvan, of Brown University; Professor Henri Mitterand, of the Sorbonne; Dr Graham Falconer, of the University of Toronto; Dr A.W. Raitt, of Magdalen College, Oxford University; Dr François Emile-Zola, Mme Simone Le Blond-Zola, and M. Bernard Le Blond-Zola; Barbara Tuchman; Judge Jacques Defos du Rau; and lastly, Dr Bruce McCully.

PREFACE

As a historian my attention was first seriously drawn to Emile Zola as a result of questions asked by my students during a course of lectures I gave on nineteenth-century France. I was startled both by their general ignorance of the man and by their willingness to assume that he was just a cheap, publicity-seeking writer. As a rule they knew of him as the author of *Nana, Germinal* and the *J'accuse* letter of January 1898, while quite ignoring the obvious implications of these works, especially of the latter, somehow dismissing them and instead reverting to the image that Zola's detractors had for decades succeeded in foisting upon the public, namely that of a pornographic writer. I told the students to seek all the biographical information they could find, but, alas, they were to be disappointed.

Zola, himself, had never published or written a full autobiography and the two important biographies written by men who knew him, Robert Sherard and Ernest Vizetelly, were published before or just after the turn of the century and had many enormous gaps in them. They were only supplanted by Matthew Josephson's popular but thin and unscholarly work, in 1928. In addition to some purely literary studies, more recent works have since appeared. Only one of these (published in 1954) made a really fresh attempt at looking at Zola's life, not simply repeating most of the old information, and that was Armand Lanoux's *Bonjour, Monsieur Zola*, although it was weakened considerably by the inclusion throughout of fictional conversations. Hence the need for a totally new biography of Zola remained, one which would endeavour to undertake a more thorough study of his letters and manuscripts, in order to permit a more complete and balanced assessment of the man, while at the same time putting his life in historical perspective.

Before I began writing this book eleven years ago, I had been considering quite a different work: a series of biographical studies of writers who had suffered exile and pain as a result of their beliefs, and originally Zola was just the first of those to be included. As the result of some conversations and correspondence with Thornton Wilder, who also felt a new, more complete and honest biography of Zola was badly needed, as well as my students' dilemma, I looked more closely into Zola's life, becoming more fascinated by the man as I did so. Thus I gradually decided to put my book on exiles aside and concentrated instead on Zola alone. Little did I realize how many years I would be at this task and to what an extent, almost to the point of obsession, that novelist would claim a place in my own life. He was not a man who left acquaintances impassive. One either liked him, or did not.

There is no such thing as a definitive biography any more than there can be a definitive history of a nation. There are too many valid different ways of looking at the same subject, as any good historian, lawyer, portrait painter or musician can attest. My biography then, which certainly makes no claims at being definitive, does nonetheless attempt to take a more comprehensive look at the major aspects of Zola's life, including some which either have been hitherto overlooked altogether, barely touched upon, or simply ignored. At the same time, by taking advantage of both the vast amount of research published over the past few decades, and the impressive manuscript sources now available, this work also considers not only Zola the journalist and novelist, but the man himself and his values, in an attempt to get to know what sort of person he really was, in as much as one can ever get to know anyone in this manner. This also requires making the times he lived in come sufficiently alive to appreciate why Zola reached many of his conclusions about his society and acted or reacted as he subsequently did. His life was certainly filled with momentous events; it was also complicated by the two women — Alexandrine and Jeanne — who came to play a decisive role in it. These women, both of whom he lived with and claimed to love, posed a dilemma for him, as they both wanted him to choose between them.

In addition to his other writings, he tried his hand at the theatre, and though failing in this endeavour, never fully lost his zest for it and indeed it resulted in the colourful, if totally unexpected, collaboration with William Busnach. He also spent portions of his last years in another collaborative effort, as librettist of Alfred Bruneau's lyric operatic works.

That Zola was a crusader bent on removing, or at least diminishing, some of the social ills of his country, is evidenced in most of his books. The destructiveness of demi-mondaines, abuse of alcohol, ignorance, appalling living conditions and a maltreated working class become central themes. In short, France could not become a better, healthier country in which to live until these problems were tackled. He attacked politicians, he attacked the Catholic Church, he attacked the Army, he attacked cant and hypocrisy whenever possible, but of course his greatest moral crusade ultimately involved his direct role in the Dreyfus Affair, when he literally put his life on the line and by so doing created a myriad miseries for himself and his family.

Lastly, Zola was a husband to Jeanne, and father of their two children, Denise and Jacques, something which meant more to him than all the books in the world.

Begun many years ago at a summer hillside retreat overlooking the tranquil waters of a Wisconsin lake — far removed from the turmoil of nineteenth-century France — when my children were young (but not too young to know the name 'Mr Zola', as they referred to him), followed by years of research, mostly in France, my task now draws to a close.

Alan Schom
Oxford

1

A Panthéon Affair

Dusk was already beginning to settle over the Ile de France by 7 p.m. on 4 June 1908, when the police suddenly appeared in the Montmartre Cemetery in Paris, clearing it of the few remaining visitors, as workmen began to open the vault containing the remains of Emile Zola. Descending into the darkness to remove the coffin, they discovered that, though only six years old, it was too badly decayed to be placed upon a catafalque in the Panthéon for the forthcoming State ceremony. M. Parisot, the Director of Services of the Seine Préfecture, rushed through a telephone call to the Minister of Education, asking permission to transfer Zola's remains to a new coffin, for there was no time to call Mme Zola first. Clearly, the Chamber of Deputies had not authorized the expenditure of 35,000 francs in March of that year for the transfer of the controversial author's remains (despite the vociferous opposition of Maurice Barrès, the influential nationalist and writer), to have the entire schedule now disrupted by something as minor as a rotting coffin. Had Zola been there to witness the event, he would undoubtedly have given one of his rare smiles.

Towards eight o'clock that evening the horse-drawn hearse carrying the immaculate new coffin emerged from the rue Cujas into the place du Panthéon. The bearers lifted the coffin to their shoulders and carried it inside, their footsteps echoing against the marble floor of the eighteenth century neo-Greek building. Until the Revolution of 1789, the Panthéon had served as a church; during the Revolution it was used as a 'temple', where the ashes of the great men of France were interred. During the Restoration and as late as the Second Empire, it was again used as a church. But with the establishment of the Third Republic, it became once more a memorial to the great men of the nation, whose remains were placed in its cold subterranean vault. Its vast, upper sunken floor was usually completely devoid of any furniture or statuary, looking more like an empty Roman bath than a shrine, but on this day it was filled with chairs and benches for the ceremonies which were to take place on the morrow.

The place du Panthéon was cordoned off by hundreds of police and troops, as huge crowds pushed, shoved, and shouted. Not all had come to honour Zola, and in the midst of shouts of, 'Long Live Zola!' there could be heard cries of, 'Down with the Jews! Down with Zola!' If the

Government officials assembling the next day were coming to honour Zola, such had not been the case just ten years earlier (during his famous trial), and the abusive shouts were an unpleasant reminder that ill-feeling towards the author of *'J'accuse'* was still very much alive in Paris now. When a few carriages with journalists had accompanied the hearse, they were mistaken for officials by the jostling crowds and were booed, as police — on foot and bicycles — and Republican Guards held back the swelling masses. Even so one journalist was caned by a student.

Inside the Panthéon discreet sections of black cloth covered the stone walls lit up by the flickering torches located behind the peristyle. Mme Zola and M. Dujardin-Beaumetz (Under-Secretary of State for Fine Arts), Zola's two children by his mistress, Denise and Jacques, Maître Albert Clemenceau, Major Alfred Dreyfus, his wife, and his brother, Mathieu, Zola's publisher, Eugène Fasquelle, Maurice Le Blond and several others stood on the peristyle, totalling less than two dozen in the otherwise empty monument.

The solemn silence majestically vaulted high above their heads, encircling and entombing this moment of historical reflection. Mme Zola was escorted under the dome to the catafalque where the immense wreaths of flowers sent by herself and her husband's children had been placed. The rear of the huge edifice was hung with folds of the tricolour flag. A large palm plant stood draped in black and violet crêpe, while the columns were covered in black cloth, fringed with gold, bearing Zola's initials, and the chairs were draped in a vivid red velvet. The quiet of the interior was only broken occasionally by whispering voices as the vigil began. Lamps were then lit and placed on the floor of the monument, along the aisle leading to the main entrance. The rich colours disappeared in the encroaching shadows, the grand rounded ceiling now out of reach of the bright torches. The perfume of the flowers filled the air. But while the subdued voices spoke near the catafalque, outside, police and soldiers, swords drawn, kept the tense crowds under control as more shouts pierced and rumbled through the *quartier*. 'Down with Zola! Down with the Jews! Long live Zola!' There were occasional scuffles, curses and forty or so arrests, of which one, a young 'littérateur', was found to be in possession of a pistol. Bands of students roamed along the boulevard Saint-Michel around midnight. Mme Zola had left at about 10 p.m., but still obscenities filled the air. It was like a page out of the *Rougon-Macquart*.

Early the next morning, Friday the fifth, all streets round the Panthéon were again cordoned off as far away as the Jardin du Luxembourg, the gates of which were kept locked. Troops and cavalry units then began to arrive, the cavalry stationing themselves at all intersections, as far away as the place de la Sorbonne and the Medici Fountain. Soldiers were stationed along the pavements of the boulevard Saint-Michel, and cuirassiers stood in a deep column opposite the Panthéon.

Just before nine o'clock the first guests began to arrive in a stream of magnificent carriages led by the members of the Diplomatic Corps in official uniform, members of Parliament, and high dignitaries. In typical French manner, it was the man on the horse, General Dalstein, the Military Governor of Paris, who received the warmest applause. He was followed by General Sauret and his staff.

Next appeared members of the Prime Ministers's Cabinet, MM. Briand, Viviani, Ruau, General Picquart (the Minister of War), and the presidents of the Senate and the Chamber of Deputies, escorted by resplendent cuirassiers. All along the route of the carriages, university students kept up a steady round of cheers or abuse, and there were some more arrests. The President of the Republic, Armand Fallières, accompanied by Prime Minister Georges Clemenceau, arrived in his landau at 9.30 a.m, and Mme Fallières, M. Lanes and the Deputy Chief of Protocol, M. Fouquières, followed in the next carriage. Members of the President's military entourage, Majors Keraudren and Schlumberger, were in a third.

The doors of the Panthéon were to be closed promptly at 10.15 a.m., and carriages which arrived late were to be turned back from the rue Soufflot. The President and the Prime Minister were received at the foot of the steps of the Panthéon by the presiding officers of the Senate and the Chamber of Deputies as well as by all the Cabinet and police officials, MM. Mollard de Selves and Lépine. As they climbed the steps up to the entrance to take their places behind the catafalque facing the main entrance, drums rolled and the bugles played *'Aux Champs'*. M. Antonin Dubost sat to the right of M. Fallières and M. Henri Brisson to his left, cabinet members sitting on either side. The senators and deputies took their places behind them, and they were joined by members of the Conseil d'Etat, the Military Governor of Paris, the Grand Chancellor of the Legion of Honour, the Prefect of the Seine, the Prefect of Police, high army and naval officers, judges, members of the Academy of Medicine, and the Paris municipal council.

Next to the pyramid-shaped base upon which the coffin rested, covered in violet velvet and fringed with gold, stood candelabra at each corner, the intensity of their flames somewhat diminished by the strong stream of white sunlight falling sharply from the narrow windows of the cupola (the only windows of the Panthéon), over 200 feet above.

Municipal guardsmen in full dress uniform, swords drawn, stood to attention round Zola's coffin, and two rows of guardsmen stood along either side of the main aisle from the nave to the entrance. To the right of the catafalque sat the university professors, deputy mayors of the city, members of the Chamber of Commerce, and the famous writers of the country. To the left were various military personnel. Next to Madame Zola stood Denise and Jacques, Mme Jeanne Rozerot (Zola's mistress), M. and Mme Eugène Fasquelle, M. and Mme Dutar, M. and Mme Alfred Bruneau (the composer), M. and Mme Fernand Desmoulin, and M. and Mme Larat.

As the President of the Republic took his place before the catafalque, the *'Marseillaise'* was played by the orchestra and sung by the choir of the Société des Concerts du Conservatoire, followed by the prelude to Bruneau's *Messidor,* the Funeral March from Beethoven's *Eroica* Symphony, and the *Chant du Départ.*

Then Gaston Doumergue, Minister of Education and Fine Arts, addressed the assemblage in his powerful voice, acknowledging that by granting the honours of the Panthéon to the ashes of Zola, Parliament wished to honour the memory of a great citizen. In typically rhetorical style he held forth on Zola's role in the events that had shaken France in the years preceding his death:

No doubt the nation still trembles from passions aroused by these events, but must national recognition be late in order for it to be warranted? On the contrary, is it not this very spontaneity which shows the measure of its greatness, and won't those who come after us see in our eagerness to glorify [Zola] most conclusive evidence of the intensity of our emotions?

How could posterity be surprised that we honour this citizen who, in a distressing and tragic time in our history, did not hesitate to sacrifice his peace of mind, his well-being, his freedom and his life, to perform (with praiseworthy and steady courage), the compelling civic duty prompted by his conscience, which thirsted for truth and justice, unlike so many of his fellow citizens . . . A strange, incomprehensible fear, which verged on terror, came over us . . . And then there was that countless band of blind and guilty who rashly followed and applauded without thinking, those who are accustomed to scorn truth, those eternal enemies of all social justice.

Alone, a few men of great and lofty conscience, stooping neither to fear nor to lies, whose courage was only increased by the general fear and widespread blindness, threw themselves into the foray to serve as defenders of justice . . .

There were very few of them when Emile Zola took his place in the first rank. Outwardly, there seems to be no reason for his stand . . . He lived outside, and far away from, the scenes where this drama originated; he did not know the actors. He was not involved in politics. He probably had more friends among those who were to become his implaccable foes, than with those he chose to join.[1]

Zola, continued the Minister, was completely devoted to literature and art, and even his detractors were respectful of his hard work and his profound belief in the social value of his writing. The panegyric went on:

And then, suddenly, this solitary and timid man abandoned his ivory tower, his books, his work, in order to throw himself into the political mêlée, into the midst of that crowd of which he had a kind of instinctive apprehension.

He did so not to flatter it nor to arouse it in order to serve his own passions, but in order to hurl himself head first to resist it and gather all his forces to stop its injuries, anger, violence and attacks. Thus he came heroically into the streets, confronting with relentless courage and stubborness the battle of the pretorians and the wrath of the misguided masses.

Ironically, in the light of subsequent events, Doumergue went on to say that such honour was in no way bestowed upon Zola with the intention of provoking his enemies. Those who persisted in upholding wrong instead of right should be pitied, and the nation would emerge stronger and purer as the result of such battles and divisions.

It was Zola's firm conviction which sustained him during the anguished hours, which kept him from becoming discouraged when mists obscured the image of truth. It is to his heroism that we come to pay homage; we can assure you in all conscience that the future will reap a harvest of goodness, equity and infinite hope which he helped sow and in which we share today.

At the end of the ceremony, at 11 a.m., the President rose to leave. Maître Demange, the Dreyfus family lawyer, was standing next to Mathieu Dreyfus with Major and Madame Dreyfus behind him. The President of the Republic had got up to go to the square outside, to assist as the troops marched past, and according to Demange he had told them to stay in their places until the troops began to file out. Just then, a gentleman and a lady, both unknown to Demange, tried to squeeze past him. There was a somewhat muffled revolver shot and a second shot followed about fifteen seconds later. Demange realized that the shot had been fired very close to him, and he turned round and saw Major Dreyfus looking slightly pale, his right arm across his chest. When the shot was fired the Major had instinctively raised his arm and it was this quick movement which prevented his being wounded more seriously, for otherwise he would have been shot right in the chest.

Mathieu Dreyfus had spun round and seized the would-be assassin's arms and Demange led the wounded man to the offices of the Deputy Mayor of the fifth *arrondissement*, located across from the Panthéon.

Thus the 'unappeased resentment' of some Frenchmen, referred to by M. Doumergue not a quarter of an hour before, was given vent to even within the Panthéon during Zola's memorial ceremony. The violent and bitter reactions to the causes Zola chose to support, often at great personal danger to himself, followed him even in death and beyond.

2
Childhood and Youth

'I plunged my body into the waters of the Seine, from one bank to the other, then right down to its deepest depth,'[1] wrote a slender, eighteen-year-old Emile Zola to his old schoolfriend, Paul Cézanne. He was writing from his desk at the Lycée St Louis, overlooking the boulevard Saint-Michel, where he had transferred as a student from the Collège d'Aix. He was studying for his baccalauréat in science, in preparation for a university course in engineering.

He had only been in Paris a few months and was homesick for his friends — Cézanne, Roux, Valabrègue, Baille, Marguery and Solari. Here they laughed at his southern accent, just as in Aix his schoolmates had poked fun at his 'Parisian' accent. He never seemed to fit in, and in Paris, rather than attempt to make new friends, he relied upon his fellow collegians left far behind in Aix.

'Paris is large,' he explained, 'full of interesting things to do, monuments, charming women,' whereas Aix was small and even 'monotonous' in comparison, though 'filled with women . . . (God help me from casting aspersions on the women of Aix!). And in spite of that, I prefer Aix to Paris.'[2] What he really missed was the familiarity of the place that had been his home most of his life, though he had been born in a flat on the Right Bank of Paris at 10 bis, rue St Joseph on 2 April 1840. He missed the cold, limpid waters of the Rivers Arc and Torse where they used to swim, fish and dream, and even the 'arid gorges' with the pervading redolence of the *maquis*. It all seemed so utterly far from the soot-covered stone buildings, dank cobble-stone streets and the penetrating dampness which left the Jardin de Luxembourg so inordinately green, but a youth from the Midi so dreary.

Emile's father, François Zola (or Francesco Antonio Giuseppi Maria Zolla), a native of Venice, was in Paris in 1840 on the umpteenth of many attempts to convince Louis-Philippe's governemnt to adopt his engineering projects, including one involving a major renovation of the Marseilles harbour facilities, a new fortification plan for Paris, and another plan for the building of the Aix (or Zola) Canal. It was from his father and his Venetian ancestors — a long line of army engineers — that Emile inherited his imaginative faculties and his great thirst and drive to create. From his mother, Emilie Aurélie Aubert, who was some twenty-five years younger than her naturalized husband, a native of Dourdan and daughter of a glazier, he inherited his name, his love and understanding of France and a strong sense of family.

Christened Emile Edouard Charles Antoine, it seemed only appropriate that the registration of his birth at the town hall of the third *arrondissement* on 4 April 1840, should be witnessed by Emilie's father, Louis Aubert (who looked very much like a wise old peasant), and a local greengrocer, Norbert Lecerf. But by 1843 the Zolas were in Aix, renting a middle-class dwelling in the old city — first in the Cour Ste Anne, then in the Impasse Sylvacanne — in order that François Zola might continue to prepare plans for the Zola Canal, work on which was to begin shortly.

François Zola (to give the spelling he adopted in France), like his older brother, Marco Alvise Zolla, as well as his father, his two uncles and grandfather, had begun his career as an officer in the Venetian army. But the Zollas were not a fortunate family when it came to career advancement or the accumulation of wealth; both eluded them with astonishing constancy. François Zola's own career proved to be a series of disasters, which ultimately were to leave his wife and son in a state of near destitution upon his sudden death in a Marseilles hotel in March 1847.

Having successfully completed his studies at the Military School at Pavia, François received his commission in the 26th Infantry Regiment serving in Austria. Later he was granted special leave for two years in order to study mathematics and engineering, first at the University of Padua, then at the Academy of Padua. Due probably to poor prospects and pay, François Zola soon resigned his commission to take up more challenging and profitable work as a civil engineer on new railways in Austria. He became deeply involved in the work, and in a company created to fund such projects. Revolution in 1830 saw the disappearance of funding for railways, however, terminating his career abruptly. At the age of thirty-five François left for greener pastures in the Paris of Louis-Philippe and within a year he had accepted a commission in the recently created Foreign Legion, and was posted to Algeria. Alas, that career too proved abortive when, according to Philip Walker, a recent biographer of Zola, he was involved in the temporary disappearance of 1500 francs of regimental funds, the money being returned before he resigned.

He thus began the last phase of his life, once again as a civil engineer, this time in Marseilles. Thereafter his visiting card read 'Engineer Architect Topographer'. It was while in Paris in 1839, submitting plans to government engineers and officials, that he met and married Emilie Aubert on 16 May. They settled in Aix in 1843 where François had concluded contracts with the city for the building of their canal. Later, in 1846, a very small Emile Zola stood proudly at his father's side as the first shovelful of earth was excavated marking the beginning of the canal which would one day bear his name. Unfortunately, shortly after, François was struck down by a respiratory ailment, and less than a week before his seventh birthday, a bewildered Emile stood by another recent excavation of earth, now in the Aix Cemetery, as his father disappeared from his life.

If life had been fairly difficult until this point, for the next two decades it was a recurring nightmare, as Emilie Zola tried to keep a roof over her young son's head. At first she was helped in part by the shared resources of her parents who had moved to Aix, and then when she moved to Paris, her son supported her whenever he could. Meanwhile the 150-franc pension Emilie received each month from the canal company was her main source of revenue until 1852.

Emile was generally a recalcitrant and spoilt child and he avoided figures of authority, especially teachers, whenever possible. It was hardly surprising then that at the age of seven the boy still could not read or write his own name. Thanks to a scholarship, he was finally admitted to the Collège d'Aix (or Collège Bourbon), where he took courses in the sciences rather than classical studies. Although he was hardly an outstanding pupil in general, in his third year, for the first and last time in his life, he won most of the class prizes. Nicknamed 'Frenchy' because of his slightly Parisian accent, young Emile's impoverished circumstances made neither the college nor the city pleasant places to be. The stammer which he developed was to remain with him throughout his life, later leading him to decline most speeches and public appearances. When his maternal grandmother died in 1857, another source of revenue dried up and thus in February 1858, after four and a half years at the college, his mother suddenly ordered him to pack his single suitcase and join her at their new flat in the Latin Quarter of Paris.

The Lycée St Louis where he was to remain to prepare for his baccalauréat in science till the age of nineteen, was a cold place so far as friendship was concerned, while the teaching and examination standards were considerably higher than those he had experienced at Aix. It was hardly surprising that by June 1858 an unhappy Emile was longing for Aix and his old friends, a homesickness which lingered on till the following spring. 'I happened to be looking out of the window of my study today and saw a cloudless sky, a veritable Provençal sky. I thought about the delightful uproar which the sparrows used to make in the evening in the plane trees of the Collège d'Aix.'[3] Although he could spend a few weeks there in the summer, the poverty he had known in Aix had left such a bad taste in his mouth that soon references to such homesickness disappeared almost completely. There was, after all, nothing to go back to other than a handful of schoolfriends. There was no family or family property — his father and grandmother had died there, and Grandfather Aubert was to die soon after in Paris. As for his friends, they were now beginning to make their way to Paris. He had to study, to prepare for a profession, as his mother was saving literally every penny she could to put him through the prestigious Lycée St Louis. But his heart was no longer in his studies, and his mind wandered. He wanted to be a poet, he insisted, an *'homme de lettres'*.

It was, however, only in French composition that he distinguished himself, his papers considered models to be shown to the class. But as for his career in engineering, it was not quite so alluring as the sirens of poetry began to intrude more and more into his world. 'I am no longer the same Zola who used to be so hardworking, who loved science,' he admitted to another former classmate, Louis Marguery, a year after arriving in Paris. 'I have become a lazy lout, to the extent that algebra gives me a headache while geometry fills me with horror, and I have only to see a simple triangle and it sends shivers up my spine. That's the way it is, what can one do?' He had to admit a most painful possibility now facing him: 'I am going to fail my bachot.'[4]

A year later the literary bug had bitten even more severely. All he wanted to do was write, though by now approaching his nineteenth year and also the final examinations which he had to pass if he wished to obtain any important civil service post or matriculate for university. He was experiencing the timeless adolescent frustrations:

> The education I receive at college is perfectly useless: a little theory, nothing practical. What is the answer?. . . I am not concerned with the everyday world. On the one hand, I shall never become a millionaire, for money holds no attraction for me . . . all I want is a little peace and quiet and a modest income.[5]

Zola had considered leaving school on more than one occasion. In a letter to Jean Baille he was both firm and irresolute, struggling to reach a balanced decision:

> In my last letter I informed you of my intention of [leaving school and] getting a job immediately in an office some place; that was a desperate, an absurd idea . . . Fortunately, I've been brought back to my senses just in time . . . Life is a struggle, I tell myself, let's accept that struggle, giving it our all, regardless of the difficulties and pitfalls we might encounter . . . I can pass my final examinations for my B.S. . . . Yet don't do that, a little voice tells me. If labour is to bring about good results, it must be rewarding work. But without the right credentials — diplomas — there is no chance of success; they are the keys to all professions. Back to work, then, to work my fine fellow! Let's get back to our studies . . . As for my B.S., I won't give up now.[6]

Thus in 1859 he girded his loins for a battle he really wanted to lose. The examination duly took place, consisting of an oral and a written part.

Emile passed on the written, but failed the oral, placing Charlemagne's reign in the sixteenth century while providing unique, if unappreciated, analyses of classical French writers.

He had failed and thus burnt his proverbial bridges. He could neither apply for a good government post nor enter a university, as so many of his classmates were doing. He was literally on the street, without prospects, with only his dreams and genius to sustain him. His mother was shattered, and though only thirty-nine years old, already looked fifty. She had such high hopes for the boy: he would do well, get a good post and repay her for her extraordinary faith and efforts. She had boasted to her friends and family of her brilliant son but, alas, those hopes were not realized and when Emile went down to Marseilles to resit his exams later in 1859, he failed both the written and the oral parts. No, there was no turning back, and that was the way he wanted it.

He was still very slender and beginning to nurture a beard by early 1860. Although happy to have bypassed university work, he was not pleased with his personal life which, in fact, he found greatly discouraging and depressing. The Muse of poetry, as he referred to it, teased him remorselessly. He ached to write, and produced both poems and short stories, but they had no literary merit and he knew it. Consequently he grew more discontent and impatient with himself.

Zola's first job was as an assistant clerk in the customs office at the *Docks Napoléon* in the rue de la Douane along the Seine. Here state, municipal and import taxes were collected on goods entering Paris via the St Martin Canal. He earned only fifteen francs a week, which did not even suffice to meet his humble needs, and as for the work — 'I am not at all happy at the Docks,'[7] he confided to Paul Cézanne in May, after completing his first month there, referring to his office as 'that miserable shop'. 'My new life is quite monotonous. At nine o'clock I go to the office. I register customs declarations until four o'clock, I transcribe correspondence . . . or sometimes I read my newspapers, or just yawn and pace back and forth . . . sad but true.' More and more he daydreamed, escaping from an existence he already found stultifying and intolerable. 'All I really desire is a cave high upon a mountainside. There I'll dwell like a hermit, dressed in a frock coat . . . '[8] But he could not escape for long, as he acknowledged: 'What stops me, of course, is that I am responsible for my family . . . It is like a damned maze. I start off on my way, separate myself from others, but somehow always end up where I started.'[9]

This was the loneliest time of his life. 'The extent of my follies,' he told Cézanne, 'is to light the fire every morning, smoke my pipe and think about what I've done and what I have yet to do.'[10] He walked for hours through the medieval streets, along the quays, in the nearby Jardin du Luxembourg or in the Jardin des Plantes, and read enormously. Yet he found it almost impossible to start on his own serious writing, which he found maddening, as the only career he really wanted or considered now was that of literature. How could he earn a living writing stories and novels if he had nothing to submit to publishers?

Youth has little time for compromise and Zola the idealist soon found existence in the customs office utterly unendurable. Unfortunately, when he decided to leave a few months later, he had no other job to go to, and as he had no cave readily available for retreat, once again he had to rely upon his mother's help. He needed work, to be sure, if only to replace the sixty francs a month he no longer received, but even knowledge of his mother's hardship could not speed up the maturation process for the cautious, dreamy and confused Zola. 'What I am looking for is simply the first job I find,' he insisted, 'as I am not entering an office to make a career of it. It really does not matter what that particular office happens to be so long as I have 1200 francs a year, that is all I need . . . such a job for me will be merely a means of keeping me alive,'[11] he told Jean Baille. Nevertheless, he did not take the first job to come along, nor the second, nor the third.

He was groping aimlessly, trying as best he could to find himself, but instead found that he was more and more isolated. He was entering a period of intense introspection: 'I find I have been left all alone; my mother, my friends have disappeared practically before my very eyes, and I cry about this isolation. I ask myself what is the purpose of this suffering and wonder why I was ever born.'[12] Such feelings were only normal for an intelligent young man, particularly as he had no father to reassure him, and his mother was a total stranger to the world he was about to enter. What was unusual, however, was that within a few years he would be out of this period of uncertainty and well on his way to the career of his choice. 'I really could use some encouragement,' he confided to Baille, 'I am young and the last few months have brought me plenty of trouble and disillusionment, plenty of pain, and yet in spite of everything this has not succeeded in stifling the poetry in me.'[13]

He was not physically alone, however. He met his friends occasionally and on rare occasions had a young woman to share his bed, if not his world. He could find neither affection nor love and he was unable 'to communicate' with any of the young women — chiefly uneducated shop girls — with whom he was in contact. The possibility of never meeting the right woman sometimes frightened him, for he was not a man who could easily dwell alone. 'My soul despairs of its immense solitude and becomes sadder and sadder still,'[14] he recorded in March 1861. 'Life shows itself to me with frightening reality and with an unknown future. There is no one I can lean on . . .'[15] He had only himself to rely upon, and he knew it.

Zola was questioning many things for the first time now and he was taunted by the concept of 'true love'. He had contempt for his friends who flitted constantly from woman to woman.

As I have often said about love, the body and soul are intimately linked, true love being incapable of existing without that intermingling. For it is impossible to love only with the mind, as ultimately it will surely lead to bodily love, and that is quite natural. But a polygamous life entirely excludes love with the soul, and therefore real love. One cannot possess the soul of another person the way one possesses a body: the prostitute sells you her body, not her soul . . . Truly happy couples are indeed rare, that's quite true.[16]

It was inevitable that the nineteen-year-old Zola — so serious about life and love — should contemplate marriage. He believed that true happiness — bodily and spiritual — could be found within marriage provided the husband took pains to educate his wife. 'Simply sleeping together is not enough; two people must also think the same. If not, sooner or later, the marriage will fail.'[17] (Over the next several years, as he gained greater experience of life, he was to change many of these views, and his thinking was particularly influenced by studying inherited genetic qualities and abilities.)

Zola's views of the perfect mate were tempered by the reality he had known. He accepted disillusionment with love as part of youthful experiment, and the inevitable price of 'experience'.[18] Writing at length on this subject to his friends in Aix, he analysed the ideal woman from yet another persepective: what sort of woman would he select as a lover? Would she be a girl of easy virtue, a widow or a virgin? Sometimes he fantasized about picking up a prostitute and eradicating her debauched past with tenderness and love, but then he declared that this would be impossible. 'Without any education, devoid and incapable of any fine sentiments, she is a person without a soul,' and he concluded that such a young woman 'would be incapable of appreciating a generous and loving man'.[19]

He could not speculate about widows because he did not know any, but he was wary of them in any case. As for virgins and virginity, he had plenty to say.

It's a very poor joke to talk to me about physical virginity when all I am really concerned with is moral virginity. . . What I am really looking for is the chastity of the soul, love of the grand and the beautiful, one capable of complete freedom of action, without which one only ends up either with hypocrisy or vice. There is no such thing as a virgin; she is like a perfume under three protective seals which we are only allowed to possess if we swear to keep her forever. Is it so astonishing then that we hesitate to choose so blindly, fearful of making a terrible mistake? My ideal virgin is above all, free — free from any cant, free of all pretence; . . . only then could I find her appealing, and love and respect her.[20]

In other words one cannot tell much about a young woman whose character and values have not been fully formed, someone who has not yet lived in the world. To Zola, such a woman was uneducated and unprepared for reality, and one could not know how she would turn out until after marriage and much time had been spent together — but by then it was too late, one was 'choosing blindly'.

> That for me is the unpleasant reality of the thing: the fast woman is beyond consideration, the widow frightens me, the virgin is non-existent. You then think that I am denying love, renouncing the possibility of ever finding a lover anywhere on earth. But I do not deny love, and I am not despairing of anything . . . it is just that I am waiting for some good angel, some rare exception to the rules I have just discussed . . . I know perfectly well I am daydreaming, that my wish may perhaps never be fulfilled.[21]

He turned out to be quite right, for he had to wait till he was forty-eight years old before he met Jeanne Rozerot, and even she was far from fulfilling his definition of the 'good angel'.

Meanwhile Zola was willing to accept what the reality of the Latin Quarter had to offer. 'All I now ask of any mistress is to love me while I hold her in my arms. And yet in truth I find this vulgar reality hideous. How I prefer my dreams and moments of hope!'[22]

He also admitted to Paul Cézanne that his view of life was somewhat more jaded than usual because he had experienced disappointment in love. However, he had learned something from the affair: 'I've gained fresh views on it which will prove most useful for the book I intend to write one day.'[23] Writing was beginning to concern him more and more, but inspiration was unpredictable and his Muse often proved elusive.

If by 1861 the Muse stood lurking in every shadow, peering over his shoulder when he wrote, hovering about his dreams, following him wherever he went, physical poverty was diverting his efforts and sapping his energies. As Paris lay wrapped under a fresh mantle of snow, he wrote in bed in order to keep warm. 'It's the same old story,' he apologized to Cézanne, 'if my stove were lit, I could work so well.'[24]

When he did have a little spare change in his pocket, his energies and desires were sublimated in other directions, as he announced with some hesitation. 'I have become an awful gourmand . . . food and drink, I long for it all and find as much pleasure in devouring a tasty morsel as in possessing a woman.'[25] Over-eating was in fact to prove a serious problem for Zola who, after his marriage, was to eat and eat for the next twenty-eight years until he weighed nearly fifteen stone.

But even at twenty-one there were the first real signs of something exciting, something tantalizing in his writing. 'I have been thinking long enough; now is the time to start producing. An entire book is already forming in my head, episode by episode, chapter by chapter. . . '[26] and in 1862 he would begin the first sketches of what was to be his first published novel, *La Confession de Claude* (Claude's Confession). The creative urge, combined with fresh experience of the world, was increasing and as the months passed this new-found confidence grew, building up momentum. 'I believe and hope that I have regained faith in myself,' he told Cézanne excitedly in the autumn of 1862. 'I have really begun to work; every night I close myself in my room and write and read until midnight. The best of it is that my old gaiety has returned once more . . . and I have already written three short stories.'[27] The three stories would appear in 1864 in *Contes à Ninon* (Stories for Ninon). He rejoiced with schoolboy delight: 'I simply couldn't feel better. I laugh and no longer feel bored in the slightest!'[28]

If he was finally beginning his writing career, nevertheless he still had to earn a living — a problem not so easily resolved as there were old debts to pay, while he was contracting yet others. His mother borrowed from a money-lender on his behalf, and even later when he had a regular salary at Hachette's, money worries continued to plague him. Such precoccupations had become routine ever since the death of his father and would continue to be the bane of Zola's existence for several more years.

On 6 July 1864 Zola jubilantly informed Antony Valabrègue (and all his friends in Aix) of the moment he had been long awaiting: acceptance of his first manuscript (*Contes à Ninon*) for publication. He was delighted and felt that he was at long last on the threshold of success. It was a great achievement for a young man of his age, with no family contacts and neither fame nor fortune (nor even his 'bachot') to help pave the way. He was to be published by Lacroix — no back-street name in the book world: Victor Hugo was his best-selling author. Zola had every right to burst with pride and joy, but alas, the first several books he was to produce did not pay off any debts, barely covering the cost of the champagne bought in celebrating them.

By November he was apologizing to Valabrègue for not replying sooner: 'First I had to correct the proofs and that, let me tell you, is not a very pleasant task and, what is more, it is exhausting.'[29] In truth the task was hardly onerous or exhausting, but it sounded good to say so. He signed his letter, 'a poor man who is expecting his first child'.[30]

As soon as the book appeared he sent review copies to everyone of influence in Paris, and even his friends to review in local papers in Provence. He never did rely on 'luck', believing that if one achieved something, it was because vigorous steps had been taken to ensure its success.

3
Early Days

Later in life, having achieved fame and financial success, Zola looked back upon his early twenties as good years, whereas in reality they were quite the opposite. He was miserable, penniless and constantly moving from one bed-sitter to another; in fact, between 1858 and 1867 alone he moved thirteen times. Paul Alexis, fellow novelist and friend of Zola, accurately describes the writer's existence between 1860 and the end of 1861 as '*une vie affreuse*'. In April 1860 Zola moved from 241, rue St Jacques to a seventh-floor flat at 35, rue Victor, and the same year moved again, to the rue Neuve St Etienne du Mont.[1] In 1861 he moved to 11, rue Soufflot, and in the spring of 1862 to 7, impasse St Dominique, thence to 62, rue Neuve de la Pépinière (overlooking the Montparnasse Cemetery).

During the winter of 1861 Zola was in such dire straits that he had to sell most of his clothes, including his coat, forcing him to remain in his unheated flat. He ate bread which he dipped in oil (when he could afford it) and reportedly roasted sparrows he occasionally trapped on the window sill. 'I wrapped myself in a blanket, covered myself as well as possible, and took such exercise as I could in my room, in order to prevent my limbs from stiffening. When anybody came to see me, I jumped into bed, pretending that I was indisposed,'[2] he related to Guy de Maupassant decades later. When he did hear of a job and applied for it, he was invariably turned down. 'I gathered that people thought me too shabby. I was told, too, that my handwriting was very bad; in brief, I was good for nothing . . . I had grown up dreaming of glory and fortune and now awoke to find myself sunk in the mire.'[3]

Finally a break came, in February 1862, when a certain Dr Boudet got Zola a job with Louis Hachette's publishing firm. It was in the packing department, which was not quite what he had been hoping for. Although his pay was poor (100 francs a month — barely enough to keep him alive), he came to consider this opportunity as the chance of a lifetime. 'I felt myself saved,' he later reminisced. 'I had a foothold and I could say goodbye forever to Bohemia.'[4] In reality, of course, it was neither quite so obvious at that time nor so easy, for working ten hours a day, six days a week, left very little spare time for the aspiring novelist.

Zola was pinning all his hopes on a literary career, but what if he failed?

Up till now, at the age of twenty-two, he had concentrated almost entirely on poetry. But he was positive that he would succeed financially as a writer of prose, and his extraordinary determination and equally extraordinary self-confidence were going to prove themselves, in spite of all the hurdles before him. He could use his position at Hachette to pave the way for a literary career. As a man of ideas — an unending flow of ideas — he could force his career forward if it did not advance of its own accord. After several weeks he was promoted to the advertising department where he began to come into contact with Hachette's authors. He had to check and read the publicity notices as well as the book reviews which appeared in French papers. Some writers dropped into the office, including the former professor of French literature at Aix, Prévost-Paradol, by now a famous journalist in Paris. It was here that he met Edmond Duranty, the author of *Le Malheur d'Henriette Gérard* (The Misfortune of Henriette Gérard), whose literary future looked so promising, but who ended up forgotten and broken. Zola much admired Duranty and later considered him one of the first of the naturalist writers of France. With a fairly good classical education behind him, Zola now began his real education in earnest, reading the works of the men whom he occasionally caught a glimpse of in the offices: Taine, Guizot, Lamartine, Michelet, Littré, Duruy and Edmond About. To further his education he attended evening lectures on literature held at the Salle des Conférences in the rue de la Paix. Taine, the critic, who was preparing his formidable *Histoire de la littérature anglaise* (History of English Literature), had a great influence on Zola. He stopped occasionally to chat with the young man and they corresponded thereafter.

Now that he had found his world and his stride, he had a chance to study French journalism and the business world. He was both a quick learner and an assiduous worker. He was also audacious and, in fact, owed his promotion to the advertising department as a result of his having left a manuscript of one of his long poems, *'L'Amoureuse comédie'* (Amorous Comedy), on Louis Hachette's desk. The poem was not published, nor did Hachette take up Zola's idea of publishing a series of novels by unknown writers, but this brought him to his employer's attention and resulted in a salary rise. Eventually Hachette did commission him to write a children's story for a periodical, but the story he produced, *'Sœur des pauvres'* (Sister of the Poor), was rejected as unsuitable.

By 1863 Zola was beginning to relax a little, so far as his immediate financial status was concerned. When his maternal grandfather (Aubert) had died in 1862, leaving his mother a little money, she and her son moved into a larger apartment at 278, rue St Jacques, near the military hospital, Val de Grâce. Now Zola could begin to think of something more than daily work and devote more time to his projected writing career. He considered two phases of writing and immediately undertook both: fiction and journalism.

Journalism was a rough and tumble world in France in Louis Napoleon's Second Empire when Zola decided to enter it. There was strict censorship of the press, resulting in the demise of a great many newspapers, not to mention the imprisonment of many publishers, editors and journalists. Less than a month after his *coup d'état* of 2 December 1851, Louis Napoleon, or Napoleon III, as he now styled himself, had decreed new restrictions on the press, namely the Law of 31 December 1851. This abolished trial by jury for journalists and required newspapermen, when convicted and fined, to pay their fines within three days. Should a newspaperman or publisher be found guilty in a law court twice within a two-year period (as a result of prosecutions relating to journalism), the editor-in-chief of the paper concerned had to be fired by the publisher and could not be rehired by him for a period of three years. In fact, a French newspaper reporting on politics (the press being divided by the government into papers which did and those which did not), would merely have to receive two warnings from the Ministry of Police in Paris (or to be more precise, by the Director General of Printing, Publishing and the Press, within the Ministry of Police),[5] or by the local prefect of police in the provinces, without having ever been legally charged by the public prosecutor. The result of two such warnings was automatic suppression of the offending newspaper for two months.[6] Such a suspension adversely affected the circulation of any newspaper and meant the doom of many, as their subscribers left them for a more permanent and reliable paper. By another decree, that of 17 February 1852, each newspaper had to deposit a substantial bond with the government before it could be published, and newspapers had to receive prior authorization from the Ministry of Police before being permitted to publish political news. Furthermore, newspapers had to pay a 'stamp-tax', the amount varying, depending upon whether the newspaper concerned was for or against Louis Napoleon. What is more, no unofficial account of parliamentary debates could be published, thereby ensuring complete censorship of all political matters.[7]

Charges brought by the government were heard in a special court in Paris — the Sixth Criminal Chamber of the Court of the Seine — a court with an extremely crowded calendar. Authors as well as journalists were prosecuted by the Ministry of Police in this court. For example, in 1857 Gustave Flaubert was brought to trial on moral grounds, unsuccessfully as it turned out, as a result of the publication of his *Madame Bovary*. Charles Baudelaire was not so fortunate when he appeared before the same court. The Ministry of the Interior forced the publisher of *Le Figaro* to fire the contributor Henri Rochefort, in 1867 and just about every paper was fined at one time or other (except, of course, those semi-official and pro-imperial newspapers). This led an exasperated Jules Favre, a Republican politician and consistent opponent of Napoleon III, to declare, 'In France, there is only one journalist, and that journalist is the Emperor.'[8]

Censorship naturally affected every aspect of writing, including the works of playwrights, and in 1863 the Minister of Police closed down a play by Sardou because of the following line: 'An idiotic colour! . . . Blond is pretty washed out; treason, lies, cats; nothing striking in that colour!'[9] Louis Napoleon's policemen felt Sardou was obviously trying to attack the Emperor (as both the Empress and the Emperor's mistress were blondes).

The loss of the most outspoken newspapermen, and the forfeiture of bonds and subsequent fines, ruined many newspapers permanently, while those which survived were forced to look over their shoulder constantly, which also led to what Roger Bellet, in his book on journalism and the press during the Second Empire, refers to as auto- or self-censorship. Once newspapermen or authors were found guilty on some count, they were usually sent to one of three prisons, Sainte-Pélagie, Mazas, or the Conciergerie, the inmates of which included, at one time or another, Pierre-Joseph Proudhon, Emile de Girardin, Charles and François-Victor Hugo, Auguste Vacquerie, Paul Meurice, Jules Vallès, Victor Noir, Jules Lermina, Eugène Pelletan, Lucien-Anatole Prévost-Paradol, Pierre-Jean Béranger, and of course the raucous Henri Rochefort.

A change for the better did take place, however, when a new press law went into effect on 10 July 1868, which put an end to the prior authorization requirement and also reduced the stamp-tax on newspapers, but there was still no trial by jury and a substantial bond still had to be deposited (*Le Figaro,* for example, had to put down 60,000 francs). What is more, journalists were now required to sign each article in an attempt to reduce the amount of defamation then so common in French newspapers. On the other hand, the Ministry of Police could no longer force newspapers to publish only the government's version of parliamentary debates, although that Ministry did retain the right to intervene directly and alter the content of any article on politics. The government also retained the right not only to compel newspapers to print government notices with regard to the Corps Législatif, but also verbatim reports of parliamentary proceedings (as opposed to the official summary of events previously issued by the government, which was no longer required).[10] In short, if the law of July 1868 was considered far more liberal by the French press then, it hardly appears so now, though the result was the surprising appearance of well over one hundred new newspapers in the country between 1868 and 1869.

The presence of Zola in Louis Hachette's advertising department in 1862 was skilfully and successfully manipulated by the resourceful young man to prepare the way for himself as a member of the Parisian press.

Throughout the nineteenth century, French writers and journalists were to be found at their favourite haunts: the Maison d'Or, the Café de Paris, the Café de Buci, the Café de Madrid, the Boulevard, the Café Voltaire, to name but a few. Zola got to know these cafés and the newspapermen who were to be found at each, and he made it a point to meet as many of these men as he could. But despite his aggressiveness, Zola did not go out of his way to ingratiate himself with these men, nor did he attend many of the salons where numerous reputations were made and unmade, although he later attended a few, including those of Madame Paul Meurice, Jules Michelet and Edmond de Goncourt. On the other hand, if he had not made the most of his contacts directly through the advertising offices at Hachette, his literary and journalistic careers would have been delayed by years, for then as now, one could not easily succeed without the right contacts to open a few doors. Zola liked talking shop and at this stage enjoyed being in the company of his colleagues and cohorts, although he did not share their general interests in women, heavy drinking and duelling, all of which he considered a waste of precious time.

Duelling played an ostentatious role in the world of journalism at this time, and, although quite illegal, was nonetheless much the rage. That Zola was never involved in a duel must be attributed to a combination of his own common sense and a quirk of fate. Even Manet and Duranty were involved in a duel, which must be described as the most unlikely event in the annals of the world of arts and letters.

Zola's first published work was humble enough, a poem entitled *'Le Canal Zola'* (The Zola Canal), which appeared in the weekly Aix newspaper, *La Provence*, in February 1859. The same year saw the appearance of two more poems, and at the end of December the first instalment of his first short story, *'La Fée amoureuse'* (The Amorous Fairy), the final instalment appearing in January 1860. But nothing else by the eager young man was printed that year, and indeed between 1861 and 1862, only one poem (set to music by Louis Marguery) was published. Thus during his first four years in Paris, only five separate titles of his appeared, four of these being poems. This was hardly an auspicious beginning, and indeed, were he to compare his early career with that of Victor Hugo, he would suffer all the more, for by the same age Hugo was already famous.

Although Zola did not have to subsidize the publication of his first volume, *Contes à Ninon* — a rare privilege for an unknown author in those days — by the same token he was to receive no royalties. Yet its publication on 24 October 1864 was a very happy day for him. A published volume provided Zola with his first literary credentials, and the book, though not a big seller, was at least a *succès d'estime*. Though he continued to work six long days a week at Hachette, he spent more and more time on journalism (which nicely doubled his monthly income), and yet he somehow made time for his prose. Both plays he wrote in 1865, *La Laide* (The Ugly Woman) and *La Madeleine* (Shame), were refused by Parisian theatres, however. Zola's first real literary achievement came on 25 November 1865, when Lacroix published his novel, *La Confession de Claude*. The 1500 copies of it sold brought him real satisfaction, not to mention his first royalties as a novelist — 450 francs (based on a 10 per cent royalty agreement). The book was quite well received, when it was noticed, and Zola now had the satisfaction of being a twenty-five-year-old writer with two published works behind him.

It was Zola's job in the publicity offices of Hachette which began to make a more immediate difference to his fortunes. There he was soon corresponding with newspapers and journals across the country, placing copy with them for forthcoming works by Hachette. It was through the advertising offices that he started corresponding, for instance, with Géry Legrand, the founder of *L'Echo du Nord,* as well as being the publisher of *Le Journal Populaire de Lille* and *La Revue du Mois,* all three periodicals emanating from Lille. It was Legrand who gave Zola his first task at journalism, to which he quickly became addicted. Of the seven pieces which appeared in 1863, six did so in Legrand's publications. These included two short stories, *'Simplice'* (one of Zola's pen-names), and *'Le Sang'* (Blood) and four critical pieces. The only other work published that year was a book review in the *Athenaeum.* The following year five more reviews appeared, as well as his short story, *'Celle qui m'aime'* (She Who Loves Me), published in a Parisian periodical, *L'Entr'acte.*

But Zola's real start as a working journalist began in earnest in 1865 and he explained to Antony Valabrègue why he had decided to spend more and more time on journalism:

> The question of money is in part a factor in all this; but at the same time I also consider journalism to be such a powerful lever that I am not at all upset at being able to use it to produce a fair number of readers for me one day. It is this consideration which will explain my entry in *Le Petit Journal.* I am well aware of the low literary level of this paper, but I also know that it quickly develops a popular reading public for me . . . As for *Le Salut Public,* it is one of the better provincial newspapers; I enjoy great freedom in it and am given considerable space in which to treat important literary questions and thus I am quite satisfied to be able to publish in it.[11]

Although Zola had published only thirty-four articles, reviews and stories in 1865 (in *Le Petit Journal, Le Courrier du Monde* and *Le Salut Public),* in 1866 he decided to make journalism his chief source of income. Nevertheless, even now he was already looking forward to the day in the distant future when he could leave journalism behind to dedicate himself to his true love: 'I have an almost ecstatic feeling as I gradually leave the crowd behind, and a sort of anguish when I wonder if I'll have the necessary ability, and if I'll have the stamina to last at the level I want. I'm no longer bored, rest assured. I await most impatiently the day when I'll feel myself strong and forceful enough to leave everything behind in order to devote myself entirely to literature.'[12]

In fact, by November of 1865, and probably earlier, Zola knew he was going to be leaving Hachette, for his employer informed him he would soon be fired. He was tactfully told that his employer thought he could earn far more as a journalist than as head of the publicity department at a mere 200 francs a month. He probably would not have left such a secure job had he not been forced to do so, but it was agreed that 31 January 1866 would be his last day at work with Hachette.

The apparent reason for Hachette's decision was twofold: Louis Hachette, who had hired Zola in the first place, had died in 1864, removing Zola's key support in that firm. More importantly, Zola was having difficulties with the law, especially with the public censor (the office of the Director General of Printing, Publishing, and the Press). The subject in point was Zola's recently published work, *La Confession de Claude,* which *Le Figaro* had begun to serialize in the autumn of 1865. When Zola (and consequently, Hachette & Co.) were investigated by the public prosecutor's office, Hachette (always a conservative firm), decided it did not want to risk being involved with a man whose latest work was described by critics as shameful, degrading and filthy. Although no charges were brought against him in November when the 'investigation' was concluded, his employer decided not to risk another clash with the law and gave Zola his notice.

4
Double Apprenticeship

By the beginning of 1866 the young author-journalist had to anticipate an annual loss of income of 2400 francs, and find work with newspapers to replace it. As it turned out, this was no easy task, and required many months of effort. He took the offensive, making full use of the contacts he had so sedulously acquired and all the information he had gathered on the workings of Parisian journalism. Zola, never a subtle man, took the bull by the horns.

There exist two excellent examples of how he tackled this problem, the first concerning *Le Figaro* and the second, *L'Evénement.*[1] On 11 April 1865 he wrote to Alphonse Duchesne of *Le Figaro*:

Dear Sir,
Allow me to introduce myself, as I have no one to do this for me, and I prefer not to make you mistrustful by assuring the protection of someone else.

I have recently published a volume of short stories which has had some success; I write a literary review for *Le Salut Public* and contribute articles to *Le Petit Journal.* Such are my credentials.

I wish to increase and surpass them as soon as possible. I first thought of your newspaper as the one which could attract attention most quickly. I hope you do not mind my speaking candidly. I take the liberty of enclosing a few pages of prose, and ask you in complete candour: Is that all right? If my humble personality displeases you, let's not discuss things any further; if it is only the enclosed article which does not, I could send you others.

I am young and, I must admit, I have faith in myself. I know that you like to try out people, to create new contributors. Try me, invent me. You can always fire me later.

Please consider my offer and let me know your decision, either by publishing the article in *Le Figaro,* or by asking me to come and collect it at your office.[2]

Although Duchesne did not hire Zola at this time — his first regular articles did not appear in *Le Figaro* until May 1866 — that did not stop the intrepid author. But despite his perserverance over the next several months,

Christmas of 1865 came and went without any sign of success, and it was a pretty desperate young man who saw in the New Year.

Finally, on 22 January 1866, one week before he would be out on the street without a job, Zola wrote to Gustave Boudin of *L'Evénement* (a paper owned by Villemessant), reiterating what he had explained to Duschesne, but now developing his ideas in greater detail. Although he was leaving Hachette, he said, he would be writing three books for them (though this project was never brought to fruition). He offered to write a bibliographical column containing short book reviews, several times a week, for as he put it, 'today's public wants brief notices, liking the news nicely served out in little dishes'.[3] He assured the editor that from a business viewpoint the inclusion of such reviews would increase the amount of advertising book publishers would place with *L'Evénement*. This letter was typical, for not only was he offering his literary services to a publisher, but also explaining how and why a publisher could ill afford not to follow his suggestion. They were there to make money, first and foremost, while reporting news to the public was only of secondary importance. He was wiser than most young men his age and was well aware of the harsh realities of getting ahead with few illusions to sidetrack him, but he still maintained his personal ideals and would never abandon them. By applying for this position in this manner, he was at least partly reflecting the philosophy he espoused in an article written about this time in which he said: 'The heroes of our time are men of action, those who fight for what is true and right. As for the whimperers, for those who seek the ideal and break their necks in ditches, they are simply marionettes of another age whom we must let sleep quietly in the dust.'[4] As Zola saw it, one had to be a man of action in order to survive the times, and one also had to be practical.

As for Villemessant, he knew a good thing when he saw it and himself announced in *L'Evénement* of 31 January 1866 that a new man was joining his staff . . . 'If my new tenor succeeds, so much the better. If he fails, the situation is simple enough. He himself has informed me that in such a case, he will cancel his engagement with us and I shall cross his name out as a contributor. I have spoken.'[5] This was a crude way of introducing the young writer, but Zola was willing to accept this reality if it meant a push in the right direction, and it was a significant step forward having his by-line in such an important paper. The timing, of course, was perfect, leaving no unemployed gap between departing from Hachette and joining *L'Evénement*.

Between 1 February and 7 November, when the agreement ended, Zola produced a staggering total of 119 articles. He had suggested book reviews and that is what he was hired to do, his column, *'Livres d'aujourd'hui et de demain'* (Books of Today and Tomorrow), appearing between two and six times weekly. During the same year he also turned out fifty articles for *Le Salut Public* of Lyons, and an occasional one for *Le Figaro*.

However, this was no labour of love, for he had to read far too many books and yet never write more than a few lines about each. In fact, initially he had tried writing longer reviews for *L'Evénement,* but as a result so many complaints reached Villemessant that he ordered him to shorten the articles while including more titles. He grumbled quietly but obliged his boss. He would review between three and five books daily, which meant a vast amount of reading each week, averaging about thirty-one books per month, or a total of 312 reviewed during the ten-month period in 1866. Because of the colossal number of books he was required to digest, he usually retired about 10 p.m. rarely extinguishing the candle on his nightstand before one or two o'clock in the morning. Nevertheless, when rereading those reviews today, one is struck by the depth and perception of his analyses. Although such reading was hectic, indeed frantic, Zola undoubtedly did learn a great deal about the current state of French literature, yet he somehow managed to find time to attend the theatre regularly (several times a week), to receive his friends every Thursday evening, and to write his own fictional works.

Zola's one outlet for longer literary analyses, similar to Sainte-Beuve's celebrated *'Les Causeries de lundi'* (Monday Chats), was in *Le Salut Public* of Lyons where he published his column, *'Revue littéraire'* (Literary Review), up to three times monthly throughout 1866 (with the exception of the month of March when he wrote nothing). It was in those columns in the provincial press that he began to expound some of his literary ideas and ideals. He would usually take one book and discuss all aspects — for instance, Jules and Edmond de Goncourt's *Germinie Lacerteux,* which he reviewed on 4 February. In this long analysis (and many of Zola's were more than a dozen printed pages in length), he was careful to note and praise the realism of the work, a criterion he was never to abandon. As a reviewer, of course, he had to cover many books on religion, philosophy, science and history, about which he had little or no knowledge. But Zola would not admit his ignorance and did surprisingly well, for example, with Drury's *Introduction générale à l'histoire de France* (General Introduction to the History of France) — rather ironic, as Zola had failed to receive his baccalauréat partly as a result of getting the date of Charlemagne's death wrong by 600 years. He also tackled de Lanoye's *Ramsès-le-grand* (Rameses the Great), Renan's *Les Apôtres* (The Apostles), Beauregard's *Les Divinités égyptiennes* (Egyptian Deities), and Flaux's *La Régence de Tunis au XIXe siècle* (The Regency in Nineteenth-century Tunis). Zola wrote on nearly every conceivable subject, considering all books worthy of his comment. But now, in *Le Salut Public,* too, his readers called for more book reviews (preferably shorter) and the editor, Max Grassis, instructed Zola to substitute increasingly often a new column, *'Correspondance littéraire'* (Literary Correspondence), in which he was obliged to cover several books at once. Thus on 21 March he reviewed *eleven* different books (which was probably a record even for him), though six or seven was more normal. His final article in *Le Salut Public* appeared in January 1867.[6]

On 27 April 1866, Zola published in *L'Evénement* the first of seven critiques on art, entitled, '*Mon salon*' (My Salon). Most of these articles were aimed at the 'jury' of establishment art specialists who were to select exhibits for the annual government-sponsored art show in May. Zola, of course, attacked the jury incessantly, addressing the twenty-four members by name, and declaring most of them to be incompetent and unqualified to judge real art. After all, they had just refused to accept entries which he personally liked, by Cézanne and Manet, to mention just two of the newer painters. Even before meeting Manet for the first time on 7 May 1866, in the artist's studio in the rue Guyot, Zola had been much taken by his work. But he was not now taking up the cause of Manet and Cézanne for *raisons d'art,* as he frankly admitted in *L'Evénement* of 20 May 1866: 'I have defended M. Manet[7] as I shall defend throughout my life any new and honestly different individuals who may be attacked . . . There is an obvious struggle between indomitable spirits and the crowd. I back such spirit and talent and attack the crowd.'[8] These were sentiments he was to reiterate and support throughout the rest of his life.

But Zola's campaign backfired, for so many complaints reached Villemessant's desk, that even that bull-necked publisher had to acknowledge that 'Claude' (as Zola signed his art columns) had to go. The ill-will of some readers followed Zola in various journalistic endeavours for quite a time, and was intensified as a result of his attack on the Romantic School of literature; writers of this genre were often men of considerable influence, especially under the Second Empire.

Zola continued to meet his artist friends on Friday afternoons at the Café Guerbois, then located at 11, grande-rue des Batignolles, nowadays at 9, avenue de Clichy. Here he could talk with Pissarro, Renoir, Manet, Bazille (until his death in 1870), Cézanne and Monet (when they were in town), but these meetings became less and less frequent as Zola grew more and more preoccupied with his own journalistic and literary endeavours. As he had no deep-seated love of art, he was not to remain an *habitué* of this group, though he maintained his friendship with several of its members throughout his lifetime.

Zola continued to write occasional articles and reviews for *Le Figaro,* most of them appearing between November and December 1866, and a few the following year. The total of his contributions, including those published in *L'Evénement* and *Le Salut Public,* amounted to over 160 articles in 1866. But, having roused the ire of a good many readers that year, he was forced to conceal his identity with increasing frequency by the use of various pseudonyms, such as Claude, Simplice and Alceste, but he gradually found fewer and fewer editors willing to print his copy.

The result was seen the following year when he published a total of only nineteen articles.

There remains one general misconception about Zola as a critic, especially of literature, which must be laid to rest once and for all. He often came out strongly against a particular book or school of thought, but he did not attack the authors in a personal manner, and separated clearly the author's professional work from his personal life. In short, Zola was an objective reviewer as a whole, and even when he reviewed the works of friends and colleagues, he did not omit the weaknesses he found in their works. One example of Zola's critical abilities is seen in a review he wrote of *Supplice d'une femme* (A Woman's Suffering), by Emile de Girardin and Alexandre Dumas (*fils*). The review appeared in *Le Salut Public* the day after the opening at the Théâtre Français in April 1865. Girardin, the owner of *La Presse* and *La Liberté,* was a powerful force within the Parisian press, but was not known as a writer. In light of this, Zola's review was refreshing and reached an unexpected conclusion, especially when one considers that he was on good terms with Dumas *fils*:

> Here it is in a nutshell, at least as I see it: on the one hand we have an innovator, a thinker, who has no experience on the boards, and who makes an attempt to introduce the brutal and implacable truth, the drama of life with all its developments and audacities. On the other hand, we have a dramatic author of merit, a master who has achieved real success, an experienced and clever man, who declares that the attempt [to introduce brutal reality] is awkward, that harsh and implacable truth are impossible to bring to the theatre, and that one cannot truly show the drama of life on the stage. Now I must say flatly that I am, a priori, for the thinker and innovator . . . It is a question of knowing whether one can apply to theatrical scenes this love of analyses and psychology which are presently giving us a new generation of novelists.[9]

Perhaps unknowingly the young author expressed his view that the world had changed, and that literature — regardless of its form — had to abandon the Romantic School (to which Dumas belonged) and adopt the Naturalist or Realist School, of which Zola was soon to be a leading exponent.

Zola's critical objectivity is best seen in a series of very long articles written in 1865 at the age of twenty-five, for *Le Salut Public*, and *La Revue Contemporaine,* under the title *'Mes haines'* (What I Hate). 'Hatred' is a strong word, and with the exception of the preface[10] to the volume of these collected articles (also bearing the title *Mes haines*), the word 'hatred' is totally inappropriate. The articles within those periodicals were well thought out, balanced pieces on literature and dealt not with hatreds, but more frequently with what he liked, covering, amongst others, the following topics: Proudhon and Courbet, *'Le Catholique hystérique'* (The Hysterical Catholic), Barbey d'Aurevilly (whom Zola did in fact detest), Eugène Paz (journalist and author), the Goncourt brothers, Victor Hugo, Eugène Pelletan, Hippolyte Taine, and Louis Napoleon's *Histoire de Jules César* (History of Julius Caesar).

These articles include topics which Zola had been attacking and would continue to attack throughout his journalistic and literary career. 'Hatred', he said, 'is sacred.'

> It is the indignation of strong and powerful hearts, and the militant scorn of those who are angered by stupidity and mediocrity. To hate is to love, it is to express its own warm and generous soul, it is to live fully but scorning shameful and unpleasant things.
>
> Hatred assuages, hatred brings about justice, hatred makes greatness. I feel younger and more courageous after each of my revolts against the platitudes of our age. I have made hatred and pride my two hosts; I am glad to isolate myself, and in my isolation to hate that which wounds what is just and true. If there is one thing I value today, it is that I am alone and that I hate.[11]

In this youthful, unguarded tone, Zola becomes more specific, mentioning several categories falling within his firing range. He found the 'empty and the weak' anathema, they 'who deny the present, who are stagnating . . . It is high time that men of courage and energy now have their '93[12]: the insolent royalty of the mediocre has exhausted the world, the mediocre must be thrown into the place de la Grève.'[13] He hated those who bound themselves to a single, narrow dogma and followed it blindly, closing their minds to any other viewpoint. He hated 'the pernicious scoffers, the young people who sneer, unable to imitate the overbearing gravity of their papas'. And there was another sort of weak and foolish person whom Zola hated — the one who cried out 'that our art and literature are dying'.

> I scarcely worry about beauty and perfection. I laugh at the great centuries. I only worry about life, and its struggle and fever. I am at ease with our present generation . . . There are no more artistic masters, no more schools. We are in a state of anarchy, and each of us is a rebel who thinks for himself, and who creates and fights for himself . . . We are on the threshhold of a century of science and reality, and we are tottering, so to speak, like drunkards, before the great struggle ahead of us. We are working, preparing the way for our children; we are about to carry out the necessary demolition . . . Tomorrow the edifice will be rebuilt . . .

He did not want some appointed arbiter of 'taste' dictating what he should create in his art and precisely how it was to be done — according to a specific manner and style. Art and its genius had to be free and unconstrained, in order to develop and create.

The ideas reflected in this preface at once reveal the author's unrestrained youth and his ideals, but three decades later he would be fighting just as outspokenly against unrestrained capitalism, organized religion, and corruption within military and political circles. Above all, perhaps, his principles continued to support the dignity, rights and place of the individual in society.

A great many questions have been raised by Zola's biographers about the author's personal life, but attempts at answering them have revealed a dearth of information. Unlike his wife, Zola rarely alluded to his personal life and problems in his correspondence with friends. Nor did he have the time or, it seems, the inclination to write a diary, which is all the more disappointing.

We know that, with the exception of food, Zola was quite abstemious by nature, both in his youth, and later. He might drink ale or wine occasionally and smoke a pipe (in his twenties), but there exists no record of his ever having been drunk, or even of any heavy drinking on his part. If he had worries, they generally appeared at night, as evidenced by his continued complaints of insomnia, and as he always followed a rigid, self-imposed schedule, his continued loss of sleep could not be made up by sleeping late the following day. His interests revolved round the multifarious aspects of writing, but rarely extended beyond them. Perhaps oddly, he showed little interest in the works of foreign authors (exceptions being such towering figures as Cervantes, Shakespeare and Dante), nor did he like to collect books; he never had a large library. His world was relatively myopic, and he evinced little or no interest in visiting foreign countries, though later in life his work and exile took him to England on two occasions, as well as to Italy.

His home life, on the other hand, was extremely important to him. He also enjoyed frequent visits to the theatre and the homes of his close friends. His fame and wealth never went to his head, and he was always an easy man to approach though he could usually see through a fraud without trouble. He was a very intense person and had very little sense of humour.

Nor is much known about his slightly plump, dark-eyed future wife, Eléonore-Alexandrine Meley, who, when Zola met her in 1864, went by the name of Gabrielle. She was born in Paris on 23 March 1839.[14] Her parents never married, and indeed, her father, Edmond Jacques Meley, who practised several trades — printer and hosier among them — left Gabrielle's mother, Caroline Louise Wadoux, about the time of his daughter's birth and was rarely seen again (though he apparently consented to his daughter's marriage to Zola later on). Gabrielle's grandparents or family took in the mother and child until June 1849, when Caroline Wadoux (then a florist), married a man by the name of Louis Charles Deschamps, though she died shortly after.[15] Gabrielle's family took her in once again and they appear to have maintained close ties with her even after she moved to Paris.

There is no precise information on the first meeting of Zola and his future wife. They may have been introduced at Cézanne's Paris studio in 1864, though she soon grew to dislike that artist very much. It is thought that she was earning a living at that time as a florist in the place Clichy.[16] Zola and the dark-haired Gabrielle took an immediate liking to each other and within a matter of a year or so were sharing the same apartment, to which Madame François Zola apparently gave her blessing, as she later moved in with them. Gabrielle and Zola were not married till 1870; it is not altogether clear why they did not marry earlier. It seems he was accepted by her family and kept up a steady correspondence with them which continued till the time of his death in 1902. Numerous family photographs attest to fairly regular visits, especially after the purchase of a house at Médan.

There remains to this day much conjecture about the relationship between Zola and Gabrielle. Their eventual marriage was probably one of convenience, both young people wanting to settle down, despite their differences, however ill-matched the years proved them to be. (Gabrielle, for example, was deficient in all but the most elementary education, though she could read and write and had a knowledge of basic arithmetic.) Marriage meant security, and this was essential to both of them. As it turned out, Gabrielle could not have children and Zola was greatly disappointed about that, for he very much wanted to be a father, and furthermore, strongly believed in the necessity of reproduction, as is seen in various writings, especially his novel *Fécondité* (Fruitfulness). As for his wife, she directed her maternal instincts to the children of her cousins, the Labordes.

Zola's insomnia never ended, and his wife soon developed all sorts of chronic illnesses, most particularly bronchitis. She would remain bedridden for weeks at a time, which over the years must have become extremely trying for Zola, a man almost always in perfect health. However, he too became more and more of a hypochondriac — probably a psychological defence to compensate for the lack of love and sympathy between the couple.[17] It is possible that the unfortunate woman was afflicted with allergies: her recurring bouts of bronchitis sound suspiciously like allergies, which in those days would not have been diagnosed as such.

Zola and his wife were to remain together, however, despite continued clashes and growing friction, and he seemed to feel a special responsibility towards her. He knew that she had been jilted by a former lover and that she had been abandoned by her father as a baby. Zola appeared to feel an obligation to make up for all this. The fact that he himself had been brought up by one parent may have also influenced his attitude. In return, Gabrielle cooked and cleaned the house diligently until they could afford a cook and servants, and even then took an unusually strong interest in everything which concerned their home. She willingly, even proudly, entertained Zola's friends over the years, and their Thursday night salons became a regular event over the next few decades.

By August 1867 Zola's name, as well as his articles in *L'Evénement, Le Salut Public* and *Le Figaro,* had become anathema to a great many people because of his critical attacks on the accepted values and institutions of his times. No more articles by him were published between September and December 1867, as his editors had become wary of this *'enragé'.* This year marked a nadir in his journalistic career. He was nearly penniless, and probably reassessing, if not doubting, his abilities and values.

With the vast amount of reading and writing required of him for his journalistic work, it is surprising that Zola found any time for his prose, but his unflagging determination to succeed as an author would not allow him to rest and, inevitably, the results were uneven. In conjunction with Marius Roux, for instance, Zola wrote a less than adequate novel, *Les Mystères de Marseille* (Marseilles Mysteries),[18] which was serialized in the Marseilles newspaper, *Le Messager de Provence* between 2 March 1867 and 1 February 1868. As Zola admitted, he and Roux wrote this joint work (the only novel he was ever to write as a co-author) for one purpose only: to pay for room and board. However, another novel which he began to write in 1866, and which he considered to be excellent, originally called *Un Mariage d'amour* (A Marriage of Love), appeared in *feuilleton* form[19] in Arsène Houssaye's *L'Artiste* in 1867, and the author received 600 francs in payment.[20] As usual, a controversy of sorts arose over the publication of the novel, and Empress Eugènie herself (if Houssaye is to be believed), asked Houssaye to have the serial version expurgated. Zola had no choice in the matter. However, when Lacroix published this same book under the title of *Thérèse Raquin* in the autumn of 1867 in unexpurgated form, it caused a minor sensation. If Louis Ulbach denounced this book as decadent, Sainte-Beuve on the other hand, though criticizing it in part, claimed it to be 'remarkable and conscientious'. It remains to this day a powerful and compelling work. Inspired by the partial success of *Thérèse Raquin,* Zola took out the manuscript of his previously rejected play, *La Madeleine,* and did something he would never do again: he transformed it into a novel, naming it *La Honte* (Disgrace). Henry Bauer (the illegitimate son of Dumas *fils*) agreed to publish it in *L'Evénement,* but once again so great were the complaints of that paper's subscribers, that it was withdrawn before completion. When Lacroix published it in 1868, as *Madeleine Férat,* the book sold fairly well. Throughout this period, Zola was developing the ideas and concepts about fiction which would change his life and give his literary career depth, purpose and cohesion; he began to outline in his mind the *Rougon-Macquart* series.

If bad luck plagued Zola in the field of journalism till the end of 1867, the New Year was to see a change in his fortunes. An acquaintance of his, Mille-Noé, was establishing a new newspaper in January 1868, *Le Globe*, and Zola was given an opportunity to review books for it in a column again entitled *'Les Livres d'aujourd'hui et de demain'*, as well as to contribute occasional literary essays. His articles, which began appearing on 16 January, ended abruptly, however, on 13 February 1868, when Louis Napoleon's Ministry of Police seized its press. Zola appeared to be under a jinx which extended to his friends as well as himself. Now in absolutely desperate financial straits, he was forced to borrow 600 francs from Edouard Manet in the first week of April as poverty continued to dog his every step.[21] And even he began to express a strong dislike of fickle journalism, as he declared in an article in *Le Gaulois*: 'Today, it isn't possible for poor young devils to become artists. Men who live by their pen are wretched workers producing articles for consumption just as a shoemaker does a pair of boots; there is no art in this branch of commercial enterprise.'[22] Privately, however, though depressed after being fired from *Le Salut Public* at the end of 1866, followed by the Government's suppression of *L'Evénement*, and blaming journalism for his financial woes, he nonetheless continued to attest to its usefulness: 'Journalism,' he wrote to Valabrègue back at the end of 1866, 'is treating me unusually badly. Nothing seems to be working out . . . But I hope I shall never have to give up journalism altogether; for it is the most powerful lever I know of.'[23]

As it turned out, something far more promising developed when Henry Bauer created a new non-political periodical, *L'Evénement Illustré*. On 20 April 1868 Zola's first article appeared, as did his new literary *'Chronique'* (Chronicle) a few days later, which consisted of a series of essays on art, literature, society, and Paris, among other subjects. Although Zola only contributed to this new illustrated paper until September 1, he found his fellow-collaborators, such as Arsène Houssaye, Edmond Duranty, Marius Roux, Jules Favre and Edouard Lockroy, far more well-disposed than those of *Le Globe*. During his brief stay with this paper, Zola published at least five dozen articles, for which he was handsomely paid.

In mid-June, while contributing almost daily to *L'Evénement Illustré*, Zola joined the staff of yet another newly-founded newspaper, *La Tribune* (which in reality was the amalgamation of *Le Globe* and *L'Intérêt Public*), which Pelletan, Glais-Bizoin, Lavertujon and Théodore Duret had just created as a joint venture. Zola was welcomed and praised by Pelletan when an agreement between the paper and Zola was reached. 'You can count on *La Tribune*,' wrote Pelletan, 'just as *La Tribune* is counting on you, and I proudly feel that for you, as for the paper, this will prove to be mutually profitable.'[24]

Zola had asked to contribute more than one article a week and even had hopes of receiving a monthly salary of 500 francs so that he could devote himself 'entirely to this paper', but he was still limited to his single weekly column, *'Causerie'* (Chat). He made his appearance (the first of twenty-seven articles) in the first issue of *La Tribune,* on 14 June 1868. This weekly paper was strongly republican, equally anti-clerical, and hence stood squarely against Louis Napoleon's Second Empire, attacking both the Emperor's demands for excessive military budgets, as well as his past foreign military intervention in such places as Italy and Mexico. Zola could write on just about any subject, and thus one comes across articles on promenades along the Seine at Gloton, belief in the devil, the Corps Législatif (as the Chamber of Deputies was then called), the birds of Paris, the death of Sainte-Beuve, Flaubert's *Education sentimentale* (Sentimental Education), contemporary poets, state art prizes, and Offenbach. He greatly enjoyed these discursive pieces, though he continued to feel that he was not being given sufficient opportunity to contribute.

Taking advantage of the outspoken political leanings of the paper's editorial staff, Zola expressed his own growing discontent with Louis Napoleon's Second Empire in article after article. At times he would openly attack something specific, such as the overly crowded tenements in the rue Saint-Antoine (a sociological problem which Zola felt Haussmann had deliberately ignored). Alternatively, he penned his biting criticism behind a sarcastic façade, which was to make his name anathema to the Emperor's Ministry of Police. The following example appeared on 22 November 1868: 'I feel that France has never shown a more joyful *insouciance.* There is nothing but hunts, balls and concerts. During the day the gentlemen go for strolls in the woods; at night the ladies show off their shoulders and diamonds. One must indeed be perverse not to state that everything is happening for the best in the most beautiful possible of courts.'[25] All in all he was writing far more creatively now, while producing far fewer reviews than in previous years. 1868 turned out to be an excellent year for him.

Zola's column in *La Tribune* continued to appear throughout 1869, although the young journalist now began to write regularly for *Le Gaulois* as well, once again reintroducing his column, *'Les Livres d'aujourd'hui et de demain',* albeit much against his will. He continued his attacks in his weekly *'Causerie'* and also in *'Coup d'epingle'* (Pinprick) and *'Choses et autres'* (This and That).

Zola's attacks on the Second Empire were stepped up when he gained access to *Le Rappel,* though Paul Meurice was reluctantly forced to return at least one piece to him in June, as national elections were about to take place and both the name of Zola and *Le Rappel* were on the police black list. Indeed, had Zola's article been published, he would undoubtedly have been arrested with other contributors and editors of *Le Rappel* when they were seized and arrested in a police raid a few days later.[26]

Zola's pen may not have been dipped into quite the same acid, but it did continue to level attacks at the Empire, and the number of them increased by 1870. Of his twelve articles on various aspects of Louis Napoleon's dictatorship, five appeared in *La Tribune* and *Le Gaulois* in February 1869, criticizing, amongst other things, the French Army, Rouher, Louis Napoleon's military *coup d'état* of 2 December 1851, and the Emperor's official parliamentary candidates for the Corps Législatif. Zola warned ominously, for instance, that 'a nation of workers is rising up . . . who will pacify the earth, and in doing so avenge the treatment they had received at the hands of the nation's political and industrial leaders,' sentiments echoed many years later in *Germinal.* Corruption had thrived under the Second Empire, argued Zola, and he continued this thematic attack throughout his long *Rougon-Macquart* series later.

Now he claimed that national elections were a farce, that the 'official candidates' were corrupt, yes-men of the Emperor, and that France lacked the most elementary freedoms. Whenever he could review or discuss a book dealing with the military coup of 1851, he did so, which provided him with the pretext for a renewed attack on the government and at the same time, for a warning to the French people. Whenever he could discuss the affluence of the Imperial Court at Compiègne, at a time when there was still so much poverty in the country, whenever discontent arose to be harshly suppressed by the government, Zola would point it out.

But it was during the first seven months of 1870, in *Le Rappel* and *La Cloche,* that he really began to hit out at the Empire of Napoleon III and his militarism. By June and July of that year he was intensifying his campaign. In *La Cloche* of 7-8 June, he chastised Emile Ollivier, a Republican who became prime minister in January 1870 and who came under steady fire from Zola for having sold himself out to his Caesar, Louis Napoleon; on 14 June in the same paper he denounced the trickery of the Corps Législatif, and on 29 June, under the guise of reviewing Houssaye's book *Les Courtisanes du monde* (Courtesans of the World), Zola attacked the immorality of the Court. On 11 July, once again in *La Cloche,* he denounced militarism, discussing it in context with the French role in the Crimean War and in the Italian Campaign of 1859, exhorting Frenchmen not to fight in the armies of their Emperor. Such talk was treason, and had the Emperor not been so preoccupied with his forthcoming declaration of war on Prussia, Zola would certainly have ended up in prison.

Although he was taking greater and greater risks with his accusations and opinions, he was not stopped by the government. 'I should like to have a voice today . . . which would describe the panic of the crowds, the forced marches of exhausted troops, the horror of insane killing',[27] read his column of 18 July. On the following day Napoleon III declared war on the Germans. On 5 August he pointed out that a large portion of the French Army had voted 'no' in Napoleon III's recent plebiscite, but ironically they were now forced to go to war and stake their lives for that very man. But he concluded in this article entitled *'Vive la France'* (Long Live France):

> At this very hour there are 50,000 soliders along the Rhine who said 'no' to the Empire. They wanted no more war, no more permanent standing armies, no more of that terrible power which puts the fortunes of the entire nation in the hands of one man . . . The Republic lies over there, along the Rhine, it is made up of 50,000 heroes; it will be victorious. And we will acclaim it, because they are certainly among the most brave.[28]

In the last article Zola wrote in 1870, appearing on 17 August in *La Cloche* and entitled *'Les Nerfs de la France'* (The Nerves of France), he finally acquiesced, calling France a sensitive and artistic country which was called upon to fight 'brutal' Germans, and saying he had complete confidence in a French victory.

Looking back on Zola's years of apprenticeship in the French press, one finds most of his articles constructive and exceptionally mature for his years, reflecting a young man's intensity, excitement and dedication. When he looked back over his first years as a journalist, however, he was surprisingly hard on himself. It must be kept in mind that by then he was determined to leave journalism behind, to serve the only mistress he felt worthy of serious attention — literature:

> For ten years — like so many I have known — I have fed the best of myself into the furnace of journalism. Of this colossal effort, nothing remains but a few ashes. Pages thrown to the wind, flowers fallen to earth, a mixture of the very best and the very worst, heaped in the same feeding-trough. I touched on everything and soiled my hands in this torrent of troubled mediocrity which flowed at full force. My love of the absolute suffered, in the midst of all this nonsense, so full of importance in the morning, but so utterly forgotten the same evening. While I dreamt of creating something eternal, in granite, something to last forever, I was merely blowing soap bubbles which the wings of any passing bee could burst in the sunlight.[29]

Zola was also in the midst of completing his literary apprenticeship, *Thérèse Raquin* having proved that he could produce what he set out to do. Plans for his ambitious, twenty-volume *Rougon-Macquart* series, tracing the natural and social history of a family under the Second Empire, now took shape, and he penned the first lines of the first volume.

5
The Beginning at Last

In his youth Honoré Balzac had set himself up as a publisher and had failed, having gone so heavily into debt that, like the Count of Mirabeau before him, he would never again be free of pursuing creditors. Zola's career as a publisher was even shorter than Balzac's, but not nearly as disastrous in the long run. During the early winter months of 1870, Zola and his childhood friend Marius Roux pooled their resources, along with another backer (Alfred Arnaud, publisher of *Le Messager de Provence*), and launched their own newspaper, *La Marseillaise*.[1] And yet what a time to start a business, with so little capital, and with France at war. The German invasion of the north, begun in the summer of 1870, had already proved calamitous for the nation. Perhaps Emperor Napoleon III and the army commission had been right when in 1867 they asked for an extension of military service, greater military reserves and a larger budget, but it was too late now. On 2 September the Emperor himself had been captured at Sedan along with 84,000 men, 2700 officers, 39 generals and Field Marshal MacMahon. The National Assembly reacted by declaring the nearly nineteen-year-old reign of Napoleon III to be at an end, and in its place rose a new republic, the third since the Revolution of 1789.

Gabrielle, Zola and his mother had left Paris for Provence on 7 September and a few days later installed themselves at 12, rue Moustier, in Marseilles. His articles were no longer in demand in the capital; the papers were filled instead with war dispatches and political news. There was no place for a literary man now, and even the publication of his novels had been postponed as a result of the critical situation. There was also the elementary question of safety, and both Gabrielle and his mother insisted upon leaving Paris.[2] Perhaps Zola already saw the hopelessness of the war, for there was no reason why he himself could not have remained. Marseilles was not only far from the fighting, but it was the home of many friends and an uncle of Zola's, a shopkeeper by the name of Louis Lucien Alfred Aubert. By leaving Paris at this time he must have realized that his monthly cheque for 500 francs from Lacroix would be jeopardized, but that did not not stop him. The project with Arnaud had apparently been in the works for a good year and a half, and Zola no doubt felt that the newspaper he and his friends were about to begin would be a very good thing indeed, if it succeeded. Marseilles had always stood out as a centre of radical republicanism, a city openly voting against the Empire just months before, and already many other Parisian journalists had arrived here as well.

As for his writing, Zola had begun *La Fortune des Rougon* (The Fortune of the Rougons) in 1869 after he had signed his somewhat unusual contract with Lacroix's and Verbroeckhoven's Librairie Internationale, which bound him to provide two novels a year for the next five years, in return for a monthly advance of 500 francs. Although the advance was set against eventual serialization fees, Zola signed quarterly promissory notes which committed him to repaying the money if the fees did not materialize. It was a good offer and a good income for a twenty-nine-year-old author with just a few (poor-selling) titles behind him. This arrangement, then, in the spring of 1869 was indeed fortuitous, and when he walked into the office of Albert Lacroix at the corner of the boulevard Montmartre and the rue Vivienne, Zola thought a solid beginning had been established after so many years of toil and of even greater anguish. True, he had to provide two volumes a year, in addition to his journalistic endeavours, but this contract meant recognition, for Lacroix was a highly reputable publisher, and in addition to the monthly stipend, Lacroix would pay a generous 13 per cent royalty on each volume sold (at a retail price of three francs).

Unknown to Zola, however, the publisher's impressive reputation masked growing financial difficulties. It was Lacroix's firm which had already published Zola's *Contes à Ninon* and *La Confession de Claude*, but it was far better known as the publisher of Hugo, Michelet, Pelletan, Quinet, Lamartine and the controversial Proudhon[3] (whose work not only resulted in a heavy fine for Albert Lacroix, but a brief period of imprisonment as well).[4] In theory, Lacroix was ideal for Zola, but they had one major disagreement: Zola could not understand why Lacroix continued to publish the pornographic works of L'Abbé Michon — *Le Maudit* (The Damned), *La Religieuse* (The Nun), and *Le Jésuite* (The Jesuit) among them.

> Disgust arises to our lips when one reads these novels floundering through filth, as vulgar in form as they are in thought, and pandering to the gross appetites of the multitude. One must assume that all this vileness and vulgarity is intentional on the author's part: he has written for a certain public and has served to it the spicy and evil-smelling *ragoûts* which he knows will please it.[5]

What is interesting here is that similar criticisms would soon be written, indeed would be almost the hallmark of his critics, about Zola's own works, from *La Curée* (The Quarry) to *Nana*.

On the strength of his new contract with Lacroix, Zola finally married Eléonore-Alexandrine Meley the following year, on 31 May 1870, when they moved from their old apartment at 23, rue Truffaut, to a more pleasant cottage situated in the garden of premises located at 14, rue de la Condamine, still in the Batignolles district on the Right Bank. They now had a servant girl and Zola's mother had her own room, though quarters were so cramped that when he bought a piano, part of the wall had to be knocked down to fit it in. They had their own little garden which was a source of joy to Zola, with its large plum tree, rose bushes, dahlias, and cabbages; there was also a hutch for his wife's rabbits.

Marriage was very important to Zola, more so than to many of his artist and writer friends. His ambition to succeed as a writer could best be achieved if he was able to devote his energies to journalism and writing, with as few obstacles, distractions and outside worries as possible. Marriage to Zola meant a warm, secure place where he could work in peace. Settling down with a dependable woman was of critical importance, for the married state, as he later put it, 'was to be an indispensable condition for the accomplishment of all good and substantial work'.[6] He and Goethe concurred on this point. 'He needed an affection that would guarantee him tranquillity, a loving home, where he might shut himself up in order to consecrate his life to the great series of books which he dreamt of writing',[7] he recorded in the third person. He found all this apparently in Gabrielle Meley, an orphaned daughter of tradespeople, a penniless girl in Paris, but, he added, she was 'handsome and intelligent'.[8] Unfortunately she was as sombre and humourless as Zola himself.

One looks in vain through most of Zola's youthful correspondence for references to eligible young women. Never does he mention 'proper young ladies' of the bourgeoisie. He may have feared their rejection (and of course their parents'), for he had no solid prospects, had already been evicted from at least one humble bed-sitter for not paying his rent, and could hardly claim to be of *bonne famille*. He did not often come into contact with the bourgeoisie and sometimes claimed to despise them. He had to make the best of a bad situation, and frankly, Mademoiselle Meley fitted the bill. However, she was honest, thrifty, decent and devoted, and certainly respectable by Zola's lights. In the past his biographers have skirted this issue with considerable delicacy, but there was nothing shameful in his existence. Times were extremely hard for a young man determined to make a career for himself single-handed. He rarely received help from anyone, and when he did, it was usually because he had worked feverishly to create the opportunity. By 1869 his efforts appeared to be paying off and his fortunes were on the rise, but new shocks lay in store for him.

The war had ruined everything. There was nothing to be gained by returning to Paris; it was already under siege by the Germans and few of his friends remained (an exception being Corporal Alexis, who was later wounded in the fighting there). Zola could not be conscripted as he was the only son and sole financial support of a widow. In addition he was hardly eager to put on a uniform for Louis Napoleon. Henri Mitterand, who has made an excellent study of Zola's journalistic career, indicates that Zola realized by November that his newly-founded newspaper would fail, due to the changing political climate in Marseilles where his subscribers were returning to the older, well-established papers.[9]

By the end of November 1870 Zola was seeking work once again. He looked feverishly in all directions. Alexandre Glais-Bizoin, now a controversial member of the provisional government in Bordeaux, who had met Zola in Paris years before and was much impressed with his abilities, promised him a 'Préfecture', a most prestigious post for such a young man, but this was a promise he could not keep, as none was available. Would Zola accept second-best — a position as Deputy Prefect somewhere? Lowering his sights, he reluctantly agreed, but it would have to be in Aix, Zola insisted with all the confidence of uncompromising youth. Glais-Bizoin tried, but alas, that was not feasible, and finally, only the deputy prefecture of Castel-Sarrasin (a small town on the Garonne) was found. The papers were duly filed by Clément Laurier, the Director of the Office of Ministry of the Interior, nominating Zola for that position. But now yet another unexpected event checked Zola, for M. Camille Delthil, the present holder of that office, refused to vacate the premises. This was too much for the young author.

About the same time Paris capitulated, however, and Zola felt that he would soon be able to return to the capital and regular newspaper work, so he withdrew his acceptance of this questionable appointment. Unfortunately, he was still unable to communicate with his publisher, Lacroix, who was for the moment lost in the Parisian mêlée, which meant he still could not receive his monthly cheque. To add to his anxieties, the last chapter of *La Fortune des Rougon* had been left behind in the Paris offices of *Le Siècle*, and as if that were not bad enough, the provisional government was confiscating property throughout the city; and of course there was still some fighting. What would happen to his house? What would happen to the manuscripts he had stored there? But what could Zola do in Marseilles? Writing an occasional article for *Le Sémaphore* was no substitute for a steady income.[10] Zola had written to Ulbach, in Paris, asking to write parliamentary reports for *La Cloche* in Bordeaux where the provisional government was meeting, and at long last he received a favourable reply. Then Glais-Bizoin arranged for Zola to work as his private secretary,[11] not only increasing his income, but making him an official government employee.

Zola was still debating with himself about his future; should he turn to a political career, for instance? He was saved from this fate by his own integrity for he had to admit that he did not enjoy politics — it was a waste of time and a bore. He had only his vision of greatness as a master writer of fiction to keep him on the narrow path he had set out for himself. He would be a writer, if only a journalist for the time being, for if he could not write, he had no reason to live.

He had written frantically time and again to Paul Alexis in Paris to discover the fate of his cottage, for Edouard Manet had told him that the municipal authorities had confiscated his property. 'I demand that my house be evacuated as quickly as possible,' snapped Zola in his next letter.[12] It was not long, however, before Alexis could report that the house had not only been vacated, but left in good condition, and Zola's *amour-propre* could be satisfied that his commands had been appreciated in higher quarters. But curiously enough, although he was obviously interested in the fate of his cottage, papers and furniture — 'Has nothing been damaged or stolen?'[13] he had asked Alexis almost incredulously — he seemed more concerned with his garden. From Bordeaux in March 1871, Zola again wrote to Alexis:

> I am sending you a money-order for five francs so that you can have my rose bushes, trees and vines trimmed. In particular, I call your attention to my roses which are in the first box. Don't let anyone touch the earth where various bulbs have been planted, including dahlias, which could be destroyed. I am counting on you. Get the gardener to work immediately, for green shoots are already beginning to appear here.[14]

Zola's preoccupation with his garden seems particularly curious at this time when there was near starvation in Paris, as the city was totally cut off by German troops and the northern half of the country was occupied by foreign troops. His attitude seems even stranger when one considers Zola's later interest in the war years and his resulting work, *La Débâcle* (The Débâcle). Alexis and everyone else in Paris was fighting just to survive, to find enough food on a daily basis, and yet rarely does Zola mention the deprivations suffered by any of his friends or the calamity facing the nation. Perhaps the best way to account for Zola's insensitive preoccupation with his garden is that he felt there was nothing he personally could do about the German occupation, so instead he chose simply to ignore it.

Later in March, Zola, his wife and mother returned to Paris where he not only found everything in order, but even his prized roses watered and trimmed. Perhaps his luck was changing at last, but he was not very confident, for as he later related to Alexis:

> For my part, I imagined that it was the end of the world and that there would be no more literature. I had brought the manuscript of the first chapter of *La Curée* with me from Paris, and occasionally I looked at it as I might have looked at some very old papers which had become souvenirs. Paris seemed so very far away, lost in the clouds; and, as I had my wife and mother with me and no certain prospect of money, I ended by thinking it quite natural and advisable that I should plunge into politics, for which I had felt so much contempt previously — a contempt which speedily returned.[15]

This feeling of contempt was only aggravated later when he and Glais-Bizoin were arrested upon their return to Paris, first by the 'government' of the Commune (probably on 21 March), and after being released, by Thiers' 'Gouvernement de la Défense Nationale' in Versailles. Fortunately, he was not held long either time, being released in the last instance when Gustave Simon (the journalist son of one of Thiers' more famous Cabinet officers, Jules Simon) came to his rescue, finding the irate, if dumbfounded, Zola being held prisoner in the Orangerie at Versailles. Zola's thoughts after being arrested by both French governments were very Parisian: 'About the only thing that consoles me at this stage is that there is not yet a third govenment to arrest me tomorrow.'[16] No wonder he took more interest in his rose garden, and considered packing his trunks and leaving Paris altogether.[17]

That Zola could ignore to the degree he did what was happening round him, was nothing short of amazing, for the situation in Paris was by now becoming critical. Although Jules Favre, as Vice-President and Foreign Minister of the Government for the National Defence had surrendered to the Germans at the end of January 1871, Parisians had closed their ancient gates following the subsequent negotiations of Adolphe Thiers, the new head of government, with the Prussian Chancellor, Otto von Bismarck. Thiers was a German puppet, they claimed, as they demanded autonomy for Paris, forming what was to be known to history as the Commune, and arming themselves as they did so. Ironically, it was 130,000 French troops led by Marshal Patrice de MacMahon and under the orders of Thiers (and not a German army under the direction of Bismarck) who now attacked and laid siege to the French capital in May 1871, thereby beginning one of the bloodiest and most destructive battles of the Franco-Prussian War, resulting in enormous hardship and casualties — 4000 French troops were killed and nearly 20,000 Parisians — not to mention the sometimes deliberate torching of much of central Paris by Communard soldiers, or 'Federals', including the Tuileries Palace and the Hôtel de Ville.

The bourgeois in Zola outweighed the rebel in this instance, however, and as much as he disliked violence, he supported Thiers' effort to re-establish order in France and Paris. If the battle against the Communards was over by 27 May, not so the consequences and memories, which were to fester within the French soul and body politic for decades to come, as 30,000 Communards were prosecuted, and 13,000 imprisoned in France or deported to penal colonies in New Caledonia and French Guiana.

Despite this incredible upheaval, Zola somehow settled down to work again, continuing with *La Curée*, and just before MacMahon's attack on the capital, signed a contract with Louis Ulbach for the serialization of that work in *La Cloche*. Ironically, it was Louis Ulbach himself who had earlier described *Thérèse Raquin* as 'putrid literature'. During the last days of September Zola's new work began to appear, while almost simultaneously the first volume of his *Rougon-Macquart* series, *La Fortune des Rougon*, was published by Lacroix. Zola was greatly disappointed in the sales of the book, in which he had for so long placed so much hope.

As if things were not bad enough, he was also summoned before the Public Prosecutor of Paris, and on 6 November 1871 he wrote to Ulbach at the offices of *La Cloche* in the rue Coq Héron, to relate what had transpired. The Public Prosecutor had been very polite, Zola said, and though the official admitted that he had not read any part of *La Curée*, he had received 'a great number of complaints' about this work. 'He informed me that it would be wise to cease serialization, but at the same time left me free to continue with the risk of publication and possible prosecution.'[18] But as much as Zola needed both the exposure of his new work in *La Cloche* and the serialization fee, he knew what this warning meant — a possible heavy fine and imprisonment. He also knew that the newspaper would be embroiled in an unpleasant court case: 'Were I the only party concerned, I would continue with the publication, as I am desirous of learning what crime I have committed and what penalty is reserved for conscientious writers whose task is to achieve art and science.'[19] But he did not want to see Ulbach hurt; he had, after all, been publishing Zola's articles in his newspaper for a number of years. 'It is not the Public Prosecutor therefore, but I who am asking you to suspend publication of my novel.'[20]

What really disturbed Zola about this episode was that the new Republic was censoring his work. What had they to fear by his exposing the corruption and decadence of France under the Empire of Napoleon III? Zola had spent three years researching the book, uncovering shocking information about stolen money, orgies and prostitutes in high places. Did the government not think the French people had a right to know of the great social and moral malaise of the country? As for those who had appealed to the authorities in the first place:

> Well, what do you think of those people who denounced me to the Public Prosecutor? I can guarantee you there was a large number of Bonapartists among them. But for those who are convinced [that Zola has committed a crime], what a strange role they have played in this! A novel wounds them and they immediately call the police . . . Not one of them thought of throwing the book in the fire instead. And I told the Public Prosecutor this is not the way we are going to gain true freedom [i.e. after the suppression suffered under the Second Empire], by calling a policeman over every childish fright.[21]

Although *La Curée* was discontinued in *La Cloche* (in the first week of November), a rival publisher, Catulle Mendès, was not so easily scared off, and he managed to persuade Zola to allow serialization in *La République des Lettres*. When Lacroix brought out the unexpurgated version of the novel in a single volume that December, there was no further talk of legal action being taken by the Public Prosecutor's office. However, the sales of this work were not impressive; Zola was frankly disappointed, and rightly so. He had now published eight volumes of fiction and yet he appeared destined to a peripheral literary existence. He was depressed that his meagre royalties would never support him, and that he would have to rely on journalism for a steady income. What was wrong with his writing? Why did it not sell better? Was it badly written? Was it too realistic and too grim? What Zola did not know at that time was that his next four novels would sell even fewer copies than *La Curée*. Was he foolish to continue trying to win a place for himself in the world of letters? Here, however, the thirty-one-year-old Zola was saved by that uncanny faith in himself which had been with him intuitively since adolescence — but it was to be put to the test again and again.

Albert Lacroix was pinning all his hopes on Zola and when the sales of *La Curée* failed to meet his expectations, Lacroix's firm, which was already on the brink of bankruptcy, collapsed. Zola's main source of income outside journalism dried up overnight. Because of the interruption by the war, his journalistic output was less than adequate by the end of 1871, and he despaired as the police came to seize his few possessions in order to pay off his creditors. It was painful and humiliating. Desperate, Zola literally sold the wool from his mattress in order to buy enough food for a few more days. Somehow he had to hold out, but he felt shattered and once again there seemed little hope for the future. Then at the beginning of 1872 a 'miracle' occurred.

Théophile Gautier, a very popular writer at this time, had heard through his son-in-law, Catulle Mendès, of Zola's desperate situation, and one evening at the Comédie Française, he fell into conversation with Francisque Sarcey (an influential literary critic of the day) and Georges Charpentier (Gautier's publisher). Gautier began talking of the new generation of authors. 'There is one among them who is very unlucky indeed, and yet who is different from all the others. You should take him on as one of your authors, my dear Charpentier. If I am not greatly mistaken he possesses a touch of genius. His name is Emile Zola. Have you ever heard of him?" Sarcey, who would remain a lifelong literary foe of Zola, disagreed with Gautier's estimation. Young Charpentier, however, who was about Zola's age and had just taken over his father's impressive publishing firm, indicated that he would like to meet Zola.

The next day Zola was informed that it might be in his best interests to drop in on Georges Charpentier. But he had sold his last presentable suit for a few francs and now, with the chance of a lifetime before him, had nothing to wear. His mother, with an undaunted faith in her son and realizing the significance of this unique moment, went to the flea market at the Temple where she purchased a black second- or third-hand suit. Zola, his courage up and hope reblossoming, put on that suit and walked all the way from the Batignolles to the River Seine, thence to the offices of Charpentier on the Quai du Louvre. Georges Charpentier's father had had a pretty stern reputation and Zola, half-broken in spirit and famished, was unusually hesitant as he was shown into the publisher's office.

To Zola's amazement Georges Charpentier was an affable and understanding young man. He no longer felt so pessimistic and indeed was quite amazed at what transpired. It turned out that Charpentier had read Zola's last two works and had liked them. As a publisher he was completely familiar with Lacroix's bankruptcy and even knew the details of Zola's contract with him. Would Zola accept a new contract with Charpentier? But surely Charpentier did not know how badly Zola's works were selling. Yes he did, the publisher acknowledged, but nevertheless he agreed with Gautier that Zola was a man of talent with a real future, and unlike Lacroix's firm, Charpentier's was solvent and could afford to take on a relatively unknown writer. An agreement was quickly reached. Over the next five years Zola would produce two books annually, and receive 500 francs monthly — a salary rather than a repayable advance against royalties.[23] In exchange, Georges Charpentier, who was taking considerable risks, was to hold the copyrights to those works for the next ten years, as well as all publishing rights (including serialization and translation rights), but not the dramatic rights. If he was agreeable to these terms Charpentier would have his lawyer prepare the contracts. A humbled, hungry young man, scarcely believing his good fortune, readily accepted without further ado. He would receive 6000 francs a year and his worries would be over at last, or nearly, for he still owed 30,000 francs in back promissory notes to Lacroix, and he would spend the next three years paying them off (with extra income earned from journalism). As for the new relationship with Georges Charpentier, it was to prove unusual, as he would become a staunch friend of Zola throughout his lifetime.

'The works in my new series of novels must vary and strongly differ from one another,' said Zola. Although the characters of the *Rougon-Macquart* series were to be continued throughout the numerous volumes to follow, the same characters were not to appear in each novel. Uniformity and monotony were to be avoided. Thus his new title must be totally different from the elegantly decadent world of the Second Empire seen in *La Curée*, and what could be in greater contrast to Saccard's sumptuous mansion than a butcher's shop in Les Halles? So Zola began work on *Le Ventre de Paris* (Savage Paris).

Although he had escaped prosecution in the case of *La Curée*, he continued to remain under periodic police surveillance. Did he realize that every major step he took was duly reported to the Prefect of Police? Nowhere in his correspondence does he allude to this spying, which the archives of the Paris police attest to, however, so it must be assumed that he remained ignorant of these activities until the time of the Dreyfus case in 1898.

Zola's dedication to his work, his dynamism, self-confidence and single-mindedness of purpose were scarcely to be matched in the Parisian world of letters. As Edmond de Goncourt noted at about this time: 'Hypochondriac and as nervous as he is, Zola works from nine o'clock to twelve-thirty and from three o'clock to eight every evening.'[24] Zola had his own view about succeeding. 'One must want to do so, but do not think I do so of my own free will, for by nature I am weak and lazy. I am driven by an obsession, and if I were to ignore it I would become seriously ill'.[25] This was, in fact, a perspicacious observation on his part, for this childless husband had no other reason for living, knowing in his heart that his marriage had been a mistake. The only warmth and satisfaction he was to find in life over the next several years was in his writing.

Zola certainly tried very hard to keep his new agreement with the Charpentier publishing firm. He would need to duplicate Balzac's efforts and write two novels a year. Indeed, when one includes all his additional journalistic undertakings, he easily produced the equivalent of a couple of volumes, but alas, he was not able to produce the two novels a year, as he sought to earn extra income to pay off the debt to Lacroix.

After preparing his research notes on *Le Ventre de Paris*, he began writing it in his new apartment at 21, rue St Georges. Goncourt was right, Zola was a driven man. He must work harder and longer if he were to succeed, and he was obsessed with one idea — success. If Zola was not yet a household name, at least it was well enough known to bring in sufficient money to meet his monthly bills. Unlike Balzac, his childhood hero, he did not like to leave debts behind him, playing a feline game with creditors. His self-respect and nerves would not allow it. It was bad enough having one's possessions seized by the police and creditors in the past — it must never happen again, and so he worked even harder. Charpentier arranged for the serialization of *Le Ventre de Paris* in *L'Etat*, beginning 12 January 1873. Zola met this commitment and the entire volume appeared on the bookstalls at the end of the third week of April, a second printing following a month later.

Again sales were poor, but they could have been worse, and after all, he was now being acknowledged by his peers as a serious writer and novelist. Even Flaubert had liked Zola's latest work, describing it as only he could: 'an atrocious and beautiful book! I am stunned by it. It is strong! Very strong!'[26] Zola's literary enemies, however, did not like it, the *Revue des Deux Mondes* declaring that his writing was 'contributing to deprave the taste of the public', while critic Paul Bourget echoed similar sentiments. Anatole France's review in *Le Temps* referred to *Le Ventre de Paris* as 'vain, empty, detestable virtuosity'.[27] Hardly the sort of fare to keep up the hopes even of a Zola.

Throughout this period Zola was becoming acquainted with more fellow novelists and had met Jules and Edmond de Goncourt back in December 1868, after years of correspondence with them on literary matters. The Goncourts, in the following year, introduced him to Flaubert who in turn later introduced him to Maupassant.[28] Before 1868 Zola and Alphonse Daudet had occasionally passed each other in the offices of *L'Evénement*, though they only came to know each other in 1872 in the offices of their mutual publisher, Georges Charpentier. A little later he met the mighty Russian, Ivan Turgenev, who did him a very good turn by arranging for him to write well-paid articles for St Petersburg's prestigious journal, *Viestnik Yevropi* (the *European Messenger*), which was to provide him with a fairly steady income for the next couple of decades.

He not only continued to develop his journalistic contacts but began dabbling in drama (see Chapter 8), and went on with his new series of novels, as well as a fresh volume of ten short stories, *Nouveaux contes à Ninon* (More Tales for Ninon), published in 1874. But the second novel promised to Charpentier, begun early in 1873 and scheduled to be the fourth in the *Rougon-Macquart* series, was not ready even for the first serial instalment till the end of February 1874. One of the reasons for this delay was the unforeseen amount of research involved, which included reading several weighty tomes on psychological problems.[29] *La Conquête de Plassans* (A Priest in the House) eventually appeared in the influential Parisian daily paper, *Le Siècle*, between 24 February and 25 April 1874, and was then brought out by Charpentier. It too, proved a dismal failure, sales falling considerably behind the preceding volumes of the series.

This new novel was a study of both religion and insanity. Though never a popular work, it was an interesting and effective study of changes in people's relationships. Zola, of course, was to become famous for the gradual changes and nuances created in the relationships of his characters, beginning with *Thérèse Raquin*, and this unusual ability was to be unimpaired till the end of his career.

Although *La Conquête de Plassans* brought few new readers to Charpentier's publishing house, it was another step forward for Zola. Between 1868 and 1874 he entrenched himself deeply in the world of letters and journalism and from then on he was a force to be reckoned with.

6
First Success

Paris may be pleasant in the spring and delightful in the autumn, but in the summer of 1874 it was dusty and very, very hot; and if in July its citizens were already beginning to escape, by August it was almost deserted.

It was at his latest residence, however, that Zola spent the entire dreadful summer of 1874: another small house in the Batignolles district of Paris (21, rue Saint-Georges), for he had little money, and a novel — *La Faute de l'abbé Mouret* (Abbé Mouret's Sin) begun that spring — to complete. Paul Alexis relates how he followed the author across Paris as he documented this book, first attending early mass morning after morning in the old stone church, Sainte-Marie de Batignolles (where he noted down every detail of the priest's public duties), going to libraries containing religious works, to priests and former priests, and finally to the horticultural exhibition where he studied the plants he would later describe in this book. For Zola, all must be carefully documented, almost as if he were a lawyer preparing a brief.

Unrelenting though the heat was, by midsummer the novel was nearing completion and Zola began worrying about his play, *Les Héritiers Rabourdin* (The Rabourdin Heirs), the production of which he was arranging with Weinschenk of the Cluny Theatre; rehearsals were to begin in the second week of August.[1] Thus Zola wrote, worried and watched with envy as his wife packed her trunks at the end of July to spend several weeks in the relative cool of the countryside. Rarely did he venture out now unless it was to attend a rehearsal at the Cluny. He had avoided most of his friends in order to complete *La Faute de l'abbé Mouret* and would continue to concentrate on it with single-minded determination till its completion in December. (His play was to open in November, but lasted only seventeen performances. Shortly after, Flaubert's play, *Le Candidat*, failed even more abruptly.)

After appearing in the St Petersburg journal, the *European Messenger*, in February and March of 1875, *La Faute de l'abbé Mouret* was published by Charpentier. Sales were not spectacular, but the book sold well enough to make a profit for everyone, and following its publication Charpentier tore up the original contract with Zola. He told him not to worry so much about failing to achieve two novels a year, and even had the cashier pay him an unexpected windfall in royalties exceeding 10,000 francs (not to mention a welcomed increase in the rate of royalties he was to receive in future).[2] The tide finally seemed to be changing and Zola and his wife could celebrate.

The summer of 1875 would be spent along a cool seashore, and in May Zola asked Paul Alexis (his general factotum for many years to come, both in personal and professional matters) to find a summer retreat for them. 'Here is what I need: a little house with a kitchen, dining room, three bedrooms and a garden, right beside the sea, if possible, with suitable places to swim. I should also like the house to be within walking distance of a city, and be furnished, no matter now simply.'[3]

Sitting on a sand dune of the beach at Saint-Aubin-sur-Mer in Normandy, Zola could gaze out at the limitless horizon, or lie back relaxed, soaking up the warm sun. Saint-Aubin was located along the Côte Fleurie, and across from the more fashionable resorts of Deauville and Trouville. Zola found the house Alexis had selected to be '*plus que modeste*', but he was quite content. His wife and mother accompanied him for the two-month sojourn, travelling from Paris to Caen by train and then by carriage to the sea, a journey which had left Zola exhausted, as he told Marius Roux: 'I can tell you, my head still aches. I am not the best traveller in the world, and a change of location upsets my whole way of life. It takes a good week before I can settle down again.'[4]

The sea always had a calming effect on Zola and he would return to it often over the next several years. The following summer he spent with the Charpentier family at Piriac, on the coast of Brittany, and stayed from June till September at a quiet house at L'Estaque, near Marseilles, where he worked until the extreme southern heat of August and the Sirocco left him prostrate, aggravated by the appearance of local reporters who had discovered his hiding place.

The crash of the surf at Saint-Aubin and the turbulent beauty of the English Channel now brought him peace of mind between periods of hard work. He always invited several friends to visit him and this summer was no exception. Alexis came, as did the Rouxs, and even Georges Charpentier's mother. Zola very much enjoyed the company of his friends, who usually stayed for the weekend. Indeed, when he wanted his friends to visit him, he left nothing to chance and prepared detailed instructions for their safe arrival, as here in the case of Alexis.

Your return journey will cost thirty-two francs and a few centimes. The return journey from Caen to Saint-Aubin will cost five francs. You will no doubt spend a few extra francs along the way. Therefore, if you figure a total expenditure of fifty francs, you will be on the high side. You will have no expenses here for either room or board, so don't worry about that.

Fifty francs in ten days, is certainly what you would pay over a ten-day period in Paris. Thus, there is nothing keeping you there. So come along . . . take the 9 a.m. train from Paris. You will reach Caen at three-thirty, and at the railway station there you will find an omnibus which will take you directly to Saint-Aubin.[5]

That summer Zola was preparing a long article for *Le Sémaphore de Marseille* and others for the Russian literary journal (including one on Chateaubriand, and another on Flaubert) and he was also outlining his next novel, *L'Assommoir* (The Drinking Den).

At first all seemed to go well. Zola's wife, who had again been ill in bed for two months prior to their departure,[6] was now much better and swimming almost daily. (When Zola was not swimming, he was to be found fishing for shrimp). Although dissatisfied with the countryside around Saint-Aubin, Zola loved the sea. He took copious notes about its moods, colours and constant changes, but although he filled a notebook with descriptions for future use, he rarely mentioned it in his books, with the exception of *Joie de vivre* (Joy of Life) — rather puzzling considering the unusual attraction it held for him.

> I work a great deal, and surprise myself that I remain at my improvised desk placed before a window. I must tell you that I have a full view of the sea before me. The boats distract me a bit, and I often follow their sails for a quarter of an hour at a time, when my pens falls from my fingers.[7]

A holiday for Zola, meant a change of pace and scenery but not a cessation of work, and despite the distractions he managed to complete all his articles. More importantly on 8 September he could report to Stassulewitch in St Petersburg the completion of his novel, *Son Excellence Eugène Rougon* (His Excellency),[8] which he had begun in November of the previous year. This fascinating study of political life in France under the Second Empire of Napoleon III was certainly one of his finer works, in spite of the neglect it receives today. Stassulewitch immediately agreed to publish it in his journal, *European Messenger,* but it only began appearing in serialized form in *Le Siècle* in January 1876.

Every morning Zola strolled over to the nearby harbour market to watch the fishermen sell their catch, then returned to work on an article and '. . . in the evening I go and sit on the beach in the company of the ladies and watch the sea as the tide comes in. It is stupid and charming. I don't know why this cannot last forever.'[9] This was one of the happiest periods of his life. But his mood soon changed: most of the tourists had gone, the beach was nearly empty, and Zola — quite unlike Hugo — complained about the howling wind and the 'thundering of this devil of a sea which prevents me from being able to think straight'.[10] There was a magnetism about the sea which held Zola irresistibly, but at the same time he dreaded its violence.

Nevertheless, his spirits had been restored and the indefatigable writer and worker had been able to spend eight relatively relaxed weeks unwinding after months and months of extreme tension and anxiety spent meeting rigorous, self-imposed schedules. His face was now sunburnt, his wife was well and he was ready to leave, for as he put it, he had 'an extraordinary thirst to get back to work',[11] and was excited about the prospects of starting his next book, a work which was to change his position in French literary history and circles. Reaching Paris on 4 October he immediately set to work on *L'Assommoir*. He would never again spend a summer in Paris.

Before *L'Assommoir* was completed, Zola was earning at least 25,000 francs a year,[12] which meant that his combined literary efforts were probably producing an income greater than that received by older, even better-established colleagues, including Edmond de Goncourt and Gustave Flaubert. In later years Goncourt was to complain more and more bitterly about this pecuniary 'injustice' which would place a higher premium on the works of a Zola than on his own.

The publication of *L'Assommoir* was to increase Zola's income astronomically, which meant he could put his money worries permanently behind him. The changes in his standard of living were not at first remarkable. He dressed and ate better, growing more and more rotund, but he avoided fashionable soirées (as he always would) and refused to purchase a carriage, or even a horse. After all, times had been hard before — one must be cautious. But he did move into a new, more spacious third-floor apartment at 23, rue de la Boulogne, in the autumn of 1877.[13]

L'Assommoir, which *Le Bien Public* accepted sight unseen, first appeared in that newspaper — to which Zola had just been appointed drama critic — on 13 April 1876. The publisher and managing editor were soon inundated with complaints that Zola, the so-called 'republican', was vilifying the people, and most of the critics joined in on the attack: Henri Fouquier in *Le XIXe Siècle,* Francisque Sarcey in *Le Temps,* Jules Claretie in *La Presse,* but also critics in *La Revue Bleue, La Revue de France,* and of course Zola's life-long opponent, *La Revue des Deux Mondes* — in short, just about every prestigious periodical in Paris. This was accompanied by a rain of pamphlets aimed directly at the 'immoral, corrupt and disgusting' Zola (including one entitled, 'Zola, Pope and Caesar'),[14] followed in turn by a storm of satirical poems and parodies by Galipaux, Blondelet and Beaumaine. As if this incredible uproar were not enough, his detractors then took to the podium, denouncing him in public lecture halls. Zola was stupefied. What he did not know, however, and would no doubt have hurt him, was that two friends whom he greatly respected, concurred with the critics: 'Are you reading good old Zola's dramatic serial?' Flaubert wrote to Turgenev that October. 'I think he is scuppering himself . . . ' The Russian replied, 'There is skill in it . . . but there is too much stirring of chamber-pots.'[15]

Although the works of Hugo, Mallarmé, France, Flaubert, Daudet, Goncourt, George Sand, Turgenev and Ferdinand Fabre were also found currently on the shelves of Parisian bookshops, it was only Zola's name, it seemed, that evoked such extraordinary attacks and attention. As Ernest Vizetelly, Zola's friend, translator and biographer, put it: 'In the literary annals of France, 1876, 1877 and 1878 must always rank as the years of *L'Assommoir*.'[16]

It is always interesting to study the workings of a novelist's mind and just how a major piece of literature comes to be written. Following the publication of *L'Assommoir*, Zola revealed this process to Edmondo de Amicis:

This is how I do it. In fact, I can hardly be said to 'do it' — rather, it does itself. I can't invent facts, as I completely lack imagination. If I sit down to my table to think out the plot of a story, I remain sitting for three days on end with my head in my hands, racking my brains, and finding nothing. Consequently I have had to give up troubling myself about the subject of my stories. I begin to work on my novel without knowing what events will be described, nor what characters will take part in the action . . . I only know my principal character — my Rougon or my Macquart, male or female, always an old acquaintance. I occupy myself with him alone, I reflect on his character, I think of the family in which he was born, on his first impressions, and on the class in which I have decided to place his life. That is my most important occupation . . . After spending two or three months in this study, I am master of this particular kind of life; I see it, I feel it, I live it in my imagination and I am certain of being able to give my novel the special colour and fragrance of that class of people . . . I have in my head a quantity of types, of scenes, of fragments of dialogue, of episodes, of occurrences, which form a confused story made up of a thousand unconnected pieces. Then there remains the most difficult task of all — to attach to a single thread, as best I can, all these reminiscences and scattered impressions. It is almost always a lengthy task. But I set to work upon it phlegmatically, and instead of using my imagination, I use my reasoning faculties . . . I write a little every day, three pages of print, not a line more, and I only work in the morning. I write almost without having to make corrections because for months I have been thinking it all over, and as soon as I have written them, I put the pages aside and do not see them again until they are in print. I can calculate infallibly the date when my book will be finished.[17]

This is not the traditional, romantic view of the novelist at work, but it is a good picture of the pragmatic Zola.

After so many years of relative failure, Zola, at the age of thirty-six, was rather startled to be made so much of following the publication of *L'Assommoir*. He was amazed at the huge sales of the book, and was no less surprised by the type of criticism he received, for he was being thoroughly misconstrued, he maintained, because his aims were not understood. Although he did not always attempt to defend or explain himself, insisting that his books should do that of themselves, he did so on this occasion. One of the criticisms levelled at him was that he had had the audacity to print working-class slang, an accusation Zola scoffed at, as slang was already commonplace in published works, such as Eugène Sue's *Les Mystères de Paris* (Mysteries of Paris). Zola declared that he was merely recording the language of the people as used in daily life.

> *L'Assommoir* is, without a doubt, the most chaste of my books. Often I have been forced to touch sores far worse. The form alone has frightened people, and the words have aroused anger. My crime is to have had the literary curiosity to collect and cast in a very elaborate mould, the language of the people. Ah, form, there is the great crime! Dictionaries of slang do exist, however; lettered men study it and delight in its freshness, in the candour and vigour of its similes. It is a treat for grammarians, even though I never set out to write a purely philogical work; I consider it to be of strong historical and social interest. However, I do not defend myself. My work will defend me. It is a true book — the first novel about the people which has the true scent of the people.[18]

To a reporter he added,

> If only the public knew the true circumstances of this bloodsucking, ferocious novelist — a worthy bourgeois, a man of study and artistic tastes, living quietly and soberly in his own little corner, whose only ambition is to leave as great and vital a work as possible. I deny no story about me. I simply work and trust to time and to the good faith of the public to find me out at last under the heap of nonsense with which I have been covered.[19]

On 9 September he wrote to a fellow author, Albert Millaud, who had criticized him in print, having failed to understand the theme of Zola's latest work: 'My novel is simple enough. It relates the downfall of a working-class family ruined by its environs; the husband drinks, the wife loses courage, shame and death are the result.'[20] This was, in fact, Zola the moralist and 'reformer' (as Vizetelly referred to him) really revealing himself for the first time as such. When his friend, Yves Guyot, as publisher of *Le Bien Public*, was forced by a flood of complaints to ask the author to withdraw the final chapters of *L'Assommoir* from his newspaper, Zola first protested, then pontificated:

Close down the taverns, open the schools. Drunkenness is devouring our people. Consult the statistics, go to the hospitals, carry out an inquiry, you will see if I am lying. The man who can stamp out drunkenness would be doing more for France than Charlemagne and Napoleon. I will go further: clean up the suburbs and raise wages. The question of housing is a pressing one: the stench of the street, the sordid stairways, the small bedrooms where fathers, daughters, brothers and sisters sleep together, these are the biggest cause of suburban depravity. The crushing workload brutalizes a man, and insufficient wages discourage him and make him want to forget. This encourages the growth of taverns and houses of prostitution. Yes, the people are like that, but only because society allows it.[21]

And yet Zola's plea for help for the working-class — which is what *L'Assommoir* was — decrying the shameful conditions in which society forced them to live and work, was totally misunderstood by the vast majority of readers. To them he was cheap and sensational, a vilifier of the people, a man ready to mock the uneducated classes everywhere. Readers may have misunderstood the author, but they bought the book in ever-growing numbers and Zola had his first runaway best-seller, and also his first masterpiece after nearly sixteen years of professional writing.

Writing from L'Estaque in July 1877, Zola described his new novel, *Une Page d'amour* (A Page of Love), of which he had just completed the first two chapters. 'I am quite happy with it, although the material seems a little pale; but I wanted to reflect this bourgeois ambiance in order to contrast this work with *L'Assommoir*, and I have no complaints.'[22] Although he acknowledged that the book was less gripping, he insisted that the change of tone would add variety to the series, even if it was 'a bit thick, a little Johnny-good-boyish'. Indeed, he thought his reading public would feel they were having 'to swallow a glass of syrup, and that is what decided me on it . . . I like to shock my readers.'[23]

But even as he worked on the first few chapters of *Une Page d'amour* his mind was already wandering elsewhere, as he admitted to Charpentier's wife — 'I have been dreaming here of an extraordinary Nana. You will see. At one fell blow we will slay them, Charpentier and I.'[24]

By now Zola was the unofficial head of a new literary school, that of realism, or 'naturalism', as it was then called. He was fighting the 'capes and swords' of Hugo and Dumas, and as such was bound to rouse the anger of his literary opponents and their supporters in the Romantic camp. From now on much of the criticism levelled at him (and his friends) was aimed not only at a particular book, but at the new cult of Naturalism.

Une Page d'amour began appearing in *Le Bien Public* in December 1877 and was published as a single volume by Charpentier the following April. The critics actually liked this book, which at once delighted and upset Zola. What really pleased and surprised him, however, was Flaubert's praise. 'Despite my advanced age, the novel disturbed and excited me. We want Helen badly and can very well understand your doctor. The double-scene of the rendezvous is sublime. I insist upon that word. The character of the little girl is very true, very fresh. Her burial is marvellous. Your recital held my interest; I read it all in one long breath.'[25]

It was in this volume that the famous *Rougon-Macquart* genealogical tree (outlining the characters to appear in the succeeding volumes of the series) appeared, thereby throwing down the gauntlet to the author himself. He had tasted real success with *L'Assommoir* and thirsted for more.

7
Salon Along the Seine

Zola had left Aix as a boy in his teens, and had left it with a very bad taste in his mouth. His father had not been honoured for his plans and work on the canal which would one day bear his name; furthermore, the young man and his mother had been reduced to humiliating poverty while living there. That could not be easily forgotten. It is all the more surprising then, that he kept in touch with several friends from Aix: Cézanne, Coste, Baille, Roux, Alexis,[1] Solari and Valabrègue. He later said — with a few occasional nostalgic exceptions — that he did not like Aix, a sentiment which he vigourously reinforced by avoiding that city for the rest of his life.

Every Thursday Zola and Alexandrine (as she now called herself), held their humble 'salon', and initially some of the young men who attended were from Aix. To them Zola was a model of success and what they all aimed to be — the unknown provincial achieving renown and wealth in Paris. For Zola his friends' admiration meant a special type of recognition (especially from the Aix which had shunned his parents), and even familial warmth. But this particular clique of young men, whose ranks soon expanded a little, was totally different from the group of successful writers whom Zola met separately on Sundays (including Coppée, Daudet, Flaubert and Turgenev). Though both groups were passionately interested in literature and art, they remained for the most part distinct, separated by age and achievement. Over the years death, illness, petty jealousies and misunderstandings thinned the ranks of the more eminent members, while the younger men tended to go their own way even sooner, chiefly from lack of ability or drive, and in some instances simply overwhelmed by the genius, industriousness and success of Zola himself. He certainly appeared to be driven by demons, whereas Céard, Hennique, Alexis, Huysmans and Maupassant were not. Included among the younger group were Zola's friends who resided in Aix and who therefore rarely attended the Thursday evening salons — Cézanne, Solari, Roux, Valabrègue and Marguery.

Cézanne and Zola were old schoolfriends. They exchanged confidences, addressed each other informally as '*tu*', and enjoyed a mutual interest in the arts, but there the similarites ended. Unlike Zola, Cézanne was an unusually timid and sensitive artist who could not cope with the harsh and cruel Parisian world of the arts. While still a young man he abandoned

Paris permanently for the safety of the Midi and his native region of Aix and Provence. Zola's own interest in art was, at best, superficial and temporary, unlike Cézanne's real and abiding interest in literature. Both men shared the rare premature knowledge (from their school days) that they were destined to dedicate their lives to arts and letters.

Cézanne's sensitivity left him open to wound after wound, whereas Zola, though a master writer and physically sensitive to colour, sound and smell, was not always particularly sensitive to human needs and failings. Zola had hardened himself to the outside world for, unlike Cézanne, he had no rich father to support him in the event of failure. Perhaps subconscious jealousy caused him to reject Cézanne's plight. Zola forged ahead slowly and painfully, but successfully. Cézanne, on the other hand, withdrew, worn down by prolonged hardships. Unlike Renoir, Monet and even Manet, Cézanne's paintings did not sell until very late in his life, leaving him especially vulnerable to a rather thick-skinned, domineering and generally unpleasant father. In his mature years Cézanne had to depend entirely upon his father's allowance to keep alive because he had no other talent than painting. As a young man coming to Paris for the first time, his allowance had been 125 francs per month, and it was hard enough to survive on that amount even then. Twenty years later in his thirties, Cézanne's allowance varied according to the whim of his capricious father. At times he was promised 200 and even 300 francs a month, but in the end it was usually reduced to 100 francs, this at a time when Zola was earning thousands each month.

Cézanne's money problems affected Zola, especially in 1878, the year he published *Une Page d'amour* and purchased his property at Médan. At the age of thirty-nine, Cézanne was again reduced to an income of 100 francs, and yet had to support a common-law wife (Hortense Fiquet, whom he married in April 1886) and a young son. Living in real fear of incurring his father's wrath, he had not told either of his parents about Hortense or the child. He, with his unkempt hair (growing long at the sides) and beard, looked a bit like Karl Marx with his bald, noble head. His heavy walking boots were invariably covered in mud and his trousers never pressed, and what with his ill-fitting jacket and large, brimmed hat, he looked more like a *clochard* than the son of one of Aix's wealthiest bankers. This man, so rough-looking externally, internally lived in fear of many people, including Alexandrine Zola. Even children frightened him, as he noted in a letter to Zola in August 1878. 'The schoolchildren of Villevieille insult me in the streets. I had better cut my hair, it may be too long.' Cézanne was an unusually straightforward and ingenuous person, indeed, transparent, whether one were friend or foe. He lived as he wished (within his narrow monetary constraints), and said what he meant, being quite incapable of *double-entendre* or cruel gossip, and this no doubt was a trait which endeared him to Zola. When his young son, Paul, was quite ill in the spring of 1878, though rather hesitant, Cézanne implored Zola to send sixty francs to the child's mother to cover the cost of medical care. Zola did this. In May, Cézanne again wrote to Zola asking for a similar amount for Hortense, and again Zola sent the sum requested.[2] On 1 June, Cézanne sent another letter to him: 'Here is my monthly request of you. I hope this does not upset you too much, and does not seem too indiscreet. But your offer saves me from a most difficult situation, and thus I must still take advantage of it . . . Kindly send sixty francs to Hortense, though she is no longer ill.'[3] In May, June, July, August, September and November (in this latter case, for 100 francs), similar requests were despatched, which may have been annoying to Zola, but they were respected. One of Cézanne's last requests to Zola was to help find a job for Hortense's brother, who was also in dire straits. It seems particularly ironic in retrospect that the impoverished Cézanne was painting masterpieces which would one day be worth millions.

Although the break between Cézanne and Zola is usually said to have occurred as a result of Zola's novel *L'Œuvre* (The Masterpiece), which was partly based on Cézanne, one can detect a distinct falling out after 1878, and the causes are far more complex than the publication of a single book. Compared with Cézanne, Zola lacked sensitivity and a good example may be seen when comparing their correspondence. Zola rarely took a deep, personal interest in anyone but himself, unless it involved a friend's writing career, in which case he would go out of his way to advise or help get the work published. He rarely displays compassion towards the emotional needs of others; his wife's constant gloom and hypochondria probably did much to encourage this attitude in him. For example, his enquiries about friends' wives and children were frequently perfunctory, being childless himself perhaps explaining this to some extent. The impoverished Cézanne, on the other hand, was most solicitous of his friends and their families. Another reason for the parting of the ways was because Zola spoke less and less of painting in his letters to Cézanne, despite the latter's constant requests that he do so. Cézanne, meanwhile, would supply Zola with Latin quotations from classical writers and frequently discuss books he was reading. Though continuing to write to Zola as '*tu*', he always addressed Alexandrine in the formal '*vous*' and rarely referred to her as anything other than Madame Zola.[4] Alexandrine apparently frowned upon Cézanne, who reeked of failure and did not conform to her notions of bourgeois respectability. It was she who turned Zola against Cézanne, or at least made it uncomfortable for Zola to maintain the friendship. It came to the point where Cézanne was afraid to visit Zola without a firm invitation in hand. Indeed, there were times when he took the train between Poissy and Triel, literally next to Zola's property, but feared to drop in on him without warning. The end came suddenly in 1886, following publication of *L'Œuvre*, when all correspondence between the men ceased. Zola must bear the greater part of the burden for the unhappy close to this long friendship.

Paul Alexis and Henry Céard remained closer to Zola than most of his younger friends, though they were never as intimate as Zola had been with Cézanne. Céard's friendship was severely tried and weakened in later years as a result of Zola's relationship with Jeanne Rozerot and, of course, the appearance of children, although Alexis remained close.

Zola's relationship with Alexis, who was several years younger than he, was unique in several respects. Alexis was always deferential towards him and though his interests were basically literary, he did not excel in writing, despite Zola's constant promptings to make him work harder. In addition Alexis aided Zola by helping him with research on several books (including *Nana*), but also helped in his personal affairs as well, from purchasing writing paper to collecting Zola's trunks at the railway station. Thus Paul Alexis became a close friend of the family, although he always addressed the Zolas by their surname, never using anything but the formal '*vous*'. From Zola's correspondence it appears that he did not think Alexis to be above average intelligence, and his numerous items of news and instructions reflect that. Alexis invariably attended Zola's salons on Thursday evening, along with Hennique, Huysmans, Céard and Maupassant, where the subject of conversation was almost always the arts. Alexis claims that at these weekly *chez lui*, the relationship between Zola and the five younger men was not that of master and pupils.

> It differed in no way from the warm camaraderie which reigned between the five of us. On the contrary, I believe that each of us was less inhibited with him than with the others, and could confide in him. There were never lectures; one simply said whatever one chose, and we frequently differed.[5]

Alexis describes Zola's own relationship with him as that of 'a sort of elder brother'.[6]

During the summer months various friends would meet at Zola's country retreat in Médan where they usually stayed as house guests, and their arguments and heated discussions would take place either in the billiards room or else during picnics on the little island of Paradou in the Seine, directly across from his house. If there was small-talk during these meetings, it was almost always on the subject that ruled their lives — literature. Zola's intensity was contagious. The guest list did not always remain the same either in Paris or at Médan. During this period many others were sometimes in attendance at these salons, including Marius Roux, Antony Valabrègue, Marius Bouchor, François Coppée, the Charpentiers and Philippe Burty.

Zola's relationship with Henry Céard took on different dimensions. Not only were they a bit closer in age, but their conversations and correspondence reflected more intricate thinking on more complex subjects than those between Zola and Alexis. If Alexis acted like a diffident younger man, Céard assumed an equal relationship with Zola from the moment they met (in 1876). Céard was very intense, ambitious and aggressive, though lazy when it came to writing his own fiction, and he did not think twice about criticizing something Zola wrote, if he felt he was right. He, too, often helped Zola, chiefly in literary matters involving research projects, but he was apparently also taken into the confidence of Madame Zola for whom he did many little favours. Zola helped Céard whenever possible in placing articles in Parisian periodicals, and even some in the Russian press.

The young men who attended Zola's 'naturalist' salons were often pilloried and caricatured in the press, referred to as 'literary outcasts . . . feeble imitators . . . presumptuous young men' and Zola's 'lackeys'.[7] They were an important part of Zola's life, however, at least before he settled into his middle years, assuring him a certain warmth, respect and attention he badly needed, but would not again find until his friendship much later with Alfred Bruneau.

If Céard's literary output was unimpressive, so was that of Léon Hennique. But two other members of Zola's little group had considerable talent. Joris-Karl Huysmans, like Zola, was born in Paris, but was eight years Zola's junior. He was a fairly handsome young man with regular features, blue eyes and thinning blond hair. He was introduced to Zola by Céard in 1876 and quickly joined his fellow 'naturalists'. Though as outspoken as Céard, he had much more talent, and is today remembered for several novels, including *Marthe* (Martha), *En ménage* (Husband and Wife), *A vau l'eau* (Downstream), and especially *A rebours* (Against Nature). He was fairly hard working and not only produced fiction, but many articles, which at this stage defended the Naturalist School. In an article entitled '*Zola et l'Assommoir*', Huysmans argued: 'No, we are not sectarians, we are men who believe that a writer, as well as a painter, must represent his own times; we are artists thirsting for modernity; we want the "burial of the cape and sword novels".'[8] This, of course, was an attack against the last of the Romantics. It really summed up the attitude of Huysmans' '*naturalistes*' including Zola himself.

Huysmans, in some respects, was more fortunate than the rest of Zola's group, for in 1877 he inherited his mother's fabric store, assuring him of a solid, reliable income. When Huysmans decided to run the business himself (which he continued to do for the next fifteen years while still retaining his position at the Ministry of Education), Zola felt that he was betraying his real profession, and wrote: 'What are you telling me? Huysmans has let up on his novel in exchange for brocades! What's wrong? Just a lazy spell brought on by the heat? He must work, please tell him so. He is our hope. He has no right to let up on his novel when the entire group needs *œuvres*.'[9] Zola meant it. He thought Huysmans a talented young man. For instance, after reading his novel, *Les Sœurs Vatard* (The

Vatard Sisters), he commented, 'The work has an intense life. It grips you and rouses your passion. It raises up the most irritating questions; it has the warmth of battle and victory.'[10]

In short, Huysmans was very much in Zola's thoughts and good graces (except for his business interests), but this was not reciprocated to the same degree, as Huysmans felt closer to Maupassant as a friend and to Flaubert as a writer. Over the years he fell out with the Naturalist School and later criticized it: 'What I reproach naturalism for is not the whitewashing of its gross style, but the filthiness of its ideas. I reproach it with having made materialism incarnate in literature, and to have glorified the democracy of art.'[11] Interestingly enough, when François Coppée summed up Huysmans' work many years later he found it *'un besoin dépravé'*[12] in certain aspects, but still had to admit that the man had unusual talent.

Guy de Maupassant, another member of the Zola group, was ten years younger than its leader and was always much closer to Flaubert than to Zola. Today he is remembered for some of his short stories, at which he was so adept, including *Boule-de-suif* and a few of his novels, such as *Une Vie* (A Woman's Life), *Bel-ami* (A Fine Fellow) and *Pierre et Jean* (Pierre and Jean). It was Maupassant who has left us with a picture of one of those occasions when the young naturalists spent a few days at Zola's.

We found ourselves all together during the summer *chez* Zola, at Médan. During the long dinners there (for we were all gourmands and gourmets, and Zola alone ate enough for three ordinary novelists), we chatted. He told us of his future novels, his literary ideas and opinions on all sorts of things. Sometimes he would toy with his rifle while talking. He did not use it very skilfully, being rather myopic . . .

Some days we went fishing. Hennique distinguished himself, to Zola's great despair . . . I liked to stretch out in the boat, *Nana*, or I went off for hours while Paul Alexis prowled about with his licentious ideas, Huysmans smoked cigarettes and Céard sat bored stiff, enduring the countryside. That was how our afternoons were spent. But how magnificent the nights were—so warm and filled with the smell of leaves, and every evening we went for a walk on the large island opposite. I would take everyone over there in the *Nana*. One moonlit night we were talking about Mérimée, of whom the ladies said: 'What a delightful story-teller!' Huysmans then added, roughly in these words, 'A story-teller is a gentleman who, not knowing how to write, pretentiously recites twaddle.'

Then we started to discuss famous story-tellers, particularly the great Russian, Turgenev . . . Paul Alexis claimed that creating a story is very difficult. . . Zola declared that it would be a good idea to tell some stories. This struck us as funny, and we agreed that in order to increase the difficulty of our task, the framework selected by the first person would be kept by the others who would use it as the basis for their stories.

We sat down in a comfortable, grassy field beneath a stream of brilliant moonlight and Zola related to us that terrible page of sinister history entitled, '*L'Attaque du moulin*' (Attack on the Mill).

When he had finished, each of us cried out, 'You must write that down.' It was my turn the next day. The day after that Huysmans amused us greatly with his recital concerning an unenthusiastic soldier. Céard told us of the siege of Paris with new explanations, telling us a story filled with philosophy, always lifelike, if not true, but as old as one of Homer's poems. . .

Hennique demonstrated to us over again that men who are individually intelligent and reasonable, infallibly become brutes when they are thrown together in large numbers. It is what might be called the intoxication of crowds . . .

But Paul Alexis made us wait a few days, not being able to find a subject. He wanted to tell us a story of Prussians robbing corpses. Our exasperation made him stop, and he finished by creating an amusing anecdote of a tall lady going to get the body of her dead husband on the battlefield and then letting herself give in to a wretched wounded soldier . . . and this soldier was a priest.

Zola found these recitals interesting and proposed that we write them down for a book.[13]

The book was published a few months later and entitled *Soirées de Médan* (Evenings in Médan). It contained not only Zola's excellent '*L'Attaque du moulin*', but also Céard's '*La Saignée*', Huysmans' '*Sac au dos*', and Maupassant's *Boule-de-suif*, which was the first work by that author to attract a great deal of attention and launched him on his career. As for Zola, there were bigger things in store.

8
Playwright Manqué

'The first time I knocked at a publisher's door, MM. Lacroix and Verbroeckhoven let me in. The first time I knocked at the door of a newspaper, M.de Villemessant answered. The first time I knock at the door of a theatre, will M. Montigny welcome me?'[1]

No, instead Adolphe Lemoine-Montigny, the famous actor-turned-director, heading the Gymnase Théâtre, returned Zola's first full-length play, *La Madeleine,* in March 1866. Refusal followed refusal, the young playwright deciding to change its title to *La Honte,* and ultimately to *Madeleine Férat,* as he converted it into a novel which appeared in 1868. As for the original play, it was packed away so carefully in some trunk or cupboard by its disgusted author, that it was not rediscovered until 1889 when Antoine had it staged at his newly opened Théâtre Libre — unsuccessfully, as it turned out.

Oh, but how he wanted to write for the theatre. It beckoned to him with a force and attraction as no Lorelei could. Zola the theatre buff was smitten by the mid-1860s, and so thoroughly that even after an unparalleled history of failure, he persisted with surprising vigour until the outrageous collapse of *Le Bouton de rose* (Rosebud), after which he foreswore any further active role in the theatre, only reluctantly permitting *Renée* to appear briefly in 1887 and *La Madeleine* two years later. Theatrical fame was to come to him belatedly and unexpectedly much later.

The most powerful and compelling play to be created by his pen was perhaps *Thérèse Raquin* (though others would argue on behalf of *Renée*). It was outlined after Zola's return to Paris in 1871, and completed in final form during the winter of 1872-73. This was the tale of a woman and her lover plotting to kill her husband in order that they might marry, only to find themselves foiled by their own success and, in particular, by Thérèse's conscience.

Zola's fights with his adversaries began even before the first play was produced and they had a very long history, which directly affected his career as playwright. When, for instance, Louis Ulbach withdrew the novel, *La Curée* (upon which the play *Renée* was to be based) from his newspaper, *La Cloche,* calling it obscene, Zola was beside himself with anger. Then when Ulbach pronounced the novel, *Thérèse Raquin* 'putrid literature',

Zola literally shook with rage. But despite such prejudice against his works, his confidence remained strong at the outset of his career as a dramatist. 'At this moment in France,' he wrote, 'an imperishable glory awaits the man of genius who, in taking up the work of Molière, succeeds in painting the true drama of modern society in all its reality as living comedy.'[2] Naturally Zola felt himself to be that very man.

Meanwhile, the theatre had so come to grip his soul (though it drained his finances more effectively than it added to them), that he referred to his dramatic ambitions as an illness, a 'theatre fever'. Invariably he carried his latest play round with him, thinking about it, modifying it, trying to find a theatre for it, while knowing all the time that his latest unfinished novel lay on his desk waiting to be completed and that it was the novel, and not this play or the next, which would pay the bills. 'It most certainly is an illness: and yet one cannot help wanting to see a work performed,'[3] he admitted.

'Are you in Paris at the present time, and would you have the courage to face an evening of insuperable heat to hear my *Thérèse Raquin* which is to be performed at the Renaissance?' Zola asked Edmond de Goncourt less than a week before the play's première, set for 11 July 1873. 'Yes, I am in Paris. Yes, I shall go to the Renaissance and I want to be one of your devoted supporters,' Goncourt replied.[4] As it turned out Zola would need all the friends he could muster, for despite a distinguished first-night audience, the play barely limped through seven performances before folding.

Louis Doré's comments in *L'Avenir National* were fairly representative: 'A horrible subject, an ignoble and hideous drama compared to which the most insidious inventions of true-life criminals are mere child's play.'[5]

Returning home from the première, Goncourt, who rarely had much good to say of anything Zola wrote, sent him his compliments and congratulations. 'You have made a dramatic vehicle from a psychological viewpoint and that is not comfortable.'[6] Marie Laurent, the well-known actress who played the role of Thérèse, wrote to the disconsolate playwright after the premature closing, assuring him of 'our esteem for your young talent. With such a beginning your dramatic career is bound to include many future successes'.[7] Zola replied, thanking her for her letter (sent on behalf of the entire cast): 'It has consoled me after the brusque death which has certainly buried my work for a considerable time to come . . . What most upset me, however, was not to have seen the play stopped, though there was always the possibility of it earning money in the future, but rather to have seen lost forever your effort, your creations, your unique interpretation which went far beyond what the script had to offer.'[8] Marie Laurent was obviously touched by his words for she kept the note for the rest of her life.

Zola was never intimidated by the prestige of a theatre director or the reputation of a theatre itself, and after completing *Les Héritiers Rabourdin* by late 1872, he began hawking it around. Its subject is typical farce material, the story dealing with family machinations as old Rabourdin lays dying, the family manoeuvering to get their hands on his purported wealth, which ultimately proves to be non-existent.

The play first went to the Palais-Royal which refused it out of hand and then to the Ambigu which likewise returned it. 'I have indeed reread your play,' wrote Montigny from his office at the Gymnase on 27 July 1874. 'I have thought it over most carefully. I simply do not believe it will be successful.'[9] He found it too monotonous and lacking in action. This was to be a criticism levelled at most of Zola's later works as well. Zola, however, was in no mood to appreciate such an honest appraisal of his work.

The situation was becoming desperate, so Zola took it to the Cluny Theatre, which had a young, inexperienced troupe and a poor reputation. What could I do? It got the better of me, and for my own peace of mind I had to take it there. It was making me ill thinking of that manuscript just lying at the bottom of a drawer.'[10]

The Cluny's director, Camille Weinschenk, had not only accepted his play, but Flaubert's *Le Sexe faible* (The Weaker Sex), as well. Such was his delight at having his play accepted that Zola initially ignored the weaknesses of the Cluny company. 'It is something very special for me. And I am terribly excited just thinking about the forthcoming winter season.'[11] When, in October (and less than a month before *Les Héritiers Rabourdin* was due to be performed), he was invited to Bougival to spend the day with Turgenev, Zola replied: 'Unfortunately, it is quite impossible for me to come and see you . . . At this very moment I am putting the finishing touches on my play and spend every afternoon at the theatre.'[12] Friendship came second to work, or at least pleasure did. To Gustave Flaubert he wrote, 'If I have not written sooner, it is because I did not want to frighten you unduly, writing under the influence of rehearsals which were simply abominable . . . this troupe really frightens me.'[13] 'I shan't hide the fact that I am scared stiff,' he told Charpentier, 'I sense a real flop in the offing.'[14] Flaubert was also having second thoughts about the Cluny company performing his play: 'Everyone tells me I am demeaning myself by allowing my work to appear in such a lowly music-hall as the Cluny Theatre.'[15] Yet, as Zola had recognized long before, there were certain things one did, certain steps one took in order to succeed and advance, even if they sometimes meant temporary failure and unpopularity. He believed this to be a 'clever' attitude, provoking a reaction rather than waiting for it to happen.

According to Zola the première held on the night of 3 November 1874 was an 'abominable massacre'.[16] 'Have you read all the abusive things they've tried to hurl at me?' he asked Flaubert. 'I have been exterminated. I simply cannot remember having ever seen such fury . . . It's hateful, I am absolutely disgusted by it. These people are as primitive as they are cruel.'[17] The critics had indeed been scathing. In *Le Moniteur Universel* Saint-Victor complained that Zola 'seeks heart-rending turpitude and platitudes', calling the play 'trivial, repetitious and filthy'. The ineffable Francisque Sarcey in *Le Temps* described it as 'a boring comedy'. It was unfortunate, he added, that Zola had been 'bitten by the demon of the theatre'. Zola argued that the critics were not really after him personally, nor even this particular play, but his new 'naturalist' school of writing. 'It is the artist they are trying to kill in me,' he insisted.[18]

Zola had sent out his usual special invitation to Flaubert, Turgenev, Numa Coste, Alexis, Duranty, Daudet and others. The invitation to Alexis was intended to lighten the mood after all the tension surrounding the play. 'M. Paul Alexis is invited to attend the most extraordinary performance of *Les Héritiers Rabourdin* to take place on Tuesday, 3 November 1874. Moreover, he is invited to take a cup of hot chocolate at my flat, at ten o'clock most precisely. If he is even a minute late, He will not get any chocolate:'[19] (Alexis had a child's passion for it.)

When Flaubert asked how things were going at the Cluny after the opening, Zola reported that the place was empty again, and nobody would earn a penny. Nevertheless, Zola was never a man to suffer defeat easily. He decided to write another farce — to show up the critics — and by the beginning of 1878 had completed *Le Bouton de rose*. The plot concerns a husband's anxiety about his wife's fidelity. Although she hasn't been unfaithful, his wife decides to teach him a lesson by allowing him to think she has, and he, of course, only learns the truth at the very end. Zola submitted the play to the directors of the Palais-Royal, Léon Dormeuil and Francis Plunkett, and despite Zola's disastrous record, they took it on. Rehearsals began in March and the première was set for 3 May. Then Zola had second thoughts about the production, especially after hearing some of his friends' unusually frank reservations, and at the last minute he tried to have the piece withdrawn and rehearsals stopped. The attempt was in vain, for the Palais-Royal was committed in writing and financially, and Dormeuil now insisted that the contract be honoured.

'They [the audience] listened to the first act,' the playwright *manqué* afterwards noted, 'they hissed at the second, and they absolutely refused to hear the third.'[20] There was such an uproar by the end that utter pandemonium reigned throughout the theatre. Following theatrical tradition, some actors tried to thank Zola on stage, but the obstreperous audience would not stand for it and hurled abuse and crumpled programmes. 'This was all prearranged,' Edmond Lepelletier felt, 'against the already too famous author of *L'Assommoir*.'[21]

When Zola and Alexandrine joined thirty invited friends at Véfour's restaurant after the opening, a pall fell over the group, which included Goncourt, Daudet, Flaubert, Céard, Alexis and Turgenev. As for Zola, said Goncourt, '. . . he sat with his face white, leaning forward, perfunctorily turning a table knife, blade up, in a closed fist.'[22] Zola continued silently to twiddle the knife nervously as they sat gloomily awaiting the inevitable reviews, drowning themselves in champagne and brandy in an atmosphere of despair and awkwardness. The bad news came in the early hours and, as usual, was best summed up by the Cassandra of Paris, Francisque Sarcey: 'It's bound to be an irreparable failure,' he wrote.[23] Lepelletier, a colleague and friend of Zola, was required to write a critique of the play for his paper, and had to admit that he found it 'rather painful'.[24] Goncourt described the play as 'a disaster' — 'And truly that is only right. It is a bad play . . . lacking originality, humour and wit.'[25] 'The work is simply pitiful,' echoed Flaubert.[26]

In 1878 Zola published his first three plays, *Thérèse Raquin*, *Les Héritiers Rabourdin* and *Le Bouton de rose*, in a single volume entitled *Théâtre*, defiantly announcing that he intended to write twenty in all, then the world would begin to take him seriously as a playwright. However, his next play, *Renée*, also proved to be his last, and as he admitted to Huysmans, '. . . the theatre continues to terrify me. I simply must come to grips with it.'[27]

Renée was written during 1880 and 1881 for Sarah Bernhardt, who had asked Zola for it through the intermediary of William Busnach. It was just one of several plays she was to ask for and ultimately refuse. The piece originally dealt with the taboo subject of incest (between Maxime and his mother, Renée), and was based on Zola's earlier novel, *La Curée*. But so great was the outcry that the plot was modified, making Maxime the step-son of the young and beautiful Renée, who in this version was never anything more than the titular wife of her husband. Louis Ulbach had been forced to withdraw *La Curée* from his paper in 1871, and Zola did not want to face possible government prosecution all over again. What is more, Sarah Bernhardt was now afraid of attempting the play in any form, as she felt it could harm her career. The play, like the book, was intended to denounce 'an exhausted Parisian society'.

Although refused by the Théâtre Français, the Gymnase and the Odéon, *Renée* was finally accepted and performed by the Vaudeville Theatre on 16 April 1887, and it ran for thirty-eight performances, far better than any of Zola's previous plays. This time Francisque Sarcey observed that Zola would have achieved fame and fortune as a playwright if he had only devoted himself to drama before espousing the Naturalist School.[28] Zola's reply was to turn his back on the theatre, thinking he had seen the last of it — but he was woefully wrong, as the unexpected entry into his life of a curious little man was soon to prove.

When William Busnach, an unprepossessing man with an unlikely name, wrote to introduce himself in 1876, Zola little guessed how much it would change his life. A short, plump, excitable man of Jewish-Algerian extraction, he was the nephew of the prolific composer, Fromental Halévy. Neither handsome nor ugly, he definitely inclined towards the latter, thanks to his obesity, a large balding head with tufts of grey hair, and an unruly moustache. Busnach, as Zola was to address him over the next twenty-five years, had no original literary talent and hardly looked a part of Zola's world. He was forty-five and excelled at only one thing — adapting the novels of others to the stage.

The two men met and Zola finally agreed to give Busnach and his partner, Octave Gastineau, permission to dramatize his next novel, *L'Assommoir*. Zola would not permit his name to be associated with the enterprise, and it was agreed he would deny any participation in the venture. To the public he must remain just another spectator, but in reality he was to be the closest of collaborators, first during the writing of the script and then later during rehearsals. He was to receive a substantial portion of the receipts — 4 per cent as opposed to Busnach's 3 per cent. To present a purely working-class subject to the Parisian theatre-going public was considered controversial, but the astonishing success of the novel when it appeared in 1877 seemed to satisfy any qualms anyone might have had. Working-class accents, drunks, prostitutes, brutality, real soap and water splashed about — all the physical reality of the capital's underbelly were to be flaunted before ladies in jewel-encrusted gowns and gentlemen in white tie and tails. As it turned out, Gastineau, whom Zola rarely met, proved to be dying, and was never to see the production of his work.

'The première of *L'Assommoir* is more than a mere theatrical event, it is the biggest Parisian event of the year. No other theatrical, global, literary or even political event could have been awaited with greater eagerness,' wrote Charles Darcours in *Le Figaro* immediately after the opening at the Ambigu on 18 January 1879. 'Anything which might have aroused public passions in the past has been eclipsed by the appearance of the "naturalist" drama.' Neither recent terrible railway accidents, the heavy snowfall, nor the Afghan War, could distract a public fascinated with *L'Assommoir*.

> Indeed, the ministerial crisis itself simply cannot possibly vie for the interest shown in the solemnity of this evening. To be sure, the political question, the support or fall of the current government, all that is important, but it is hardly in the same league as the première at the Ambigu. How can MM. Dufaure, Gambetta, de Marcère and Léon Renault possibly compete with MM. Zola, Busnach and Chabrillat when it comes to capturing the attention of the public?

Latecomers shoved and queue-jumped in an attempt to purchase tickets, even for standing-room, but the house had been sold out long before. Neither snow and ice outside, nor an occasional hiss or catcall within ('Death to the naturalist!' and 'Enough of this smelly stuff!'),[29] could in any way deter or diminish the obvious popular and financial success of the event. The critics were virtually unanimous in their praise, one describing Busnach and Gastineau as 'clever practitioners of their art,'[30] another claiming that it was both 'gripping and frightening . . . a very moral work . . . a very great success'.[31] Meanwhile Edmond de Goncourt bitterly confided to his journal, 'the play is a concoction of old tricks, tirades and sentimental catch-words.'[32]

Everyone in Paris was talking about nothing but the play, which is what every playwright dreams of, and this interest extended to the imminent publication of Zola's new novel, *Nana*. When it became apparent that the play would undoubtedly notch up 100 performances, it was agreed that there should be a public celebration, including a free matinée. It was also decided to hold a big dance and, more reluctantly, to spend a total of 6626F to cover the costs. Zola very much liked to flaunt his triumph before those very critics who in the past had so derided both his novels and plays. Invitations were printed for '*L'Assommoir* Ball' to be held at the Elysée-Montmartre, one of the few dance halls large enough to accommodate several hundred guests.

> On the occasion of the one hundredth performance of *L'Assommoir*, the authors and directors of the Ambigu Theatre have the honour of inviting
> ....
> to the ball which will be given at midnight at the Elysée-Montmartre, Tuesday, 29 April 1879. Refreshments will be served. Men are to dress as labourers, ladies as laundresses. Those who wish to wear different attire will be welcome all the same.

The publicity was superb of course, though Zola, the dignified bourgeois of Médan, appeared in white tie and evening clothes, and Alexandrine in an elaborate black gown. The orchestra hired for the occasion was a success, and the crowd waiting to get in, including an enormous number of gatecrashers, jostled outside in the boulevard de Rochechouart as extra police were summoned to regulate a phenomenal tangle of carriages and hansom cabs, all converging on the same place. The number of the famous defeated even the vigorous efforts of reporters. There were some 1500 to 1800 people present, including such celebrities as Belot, Clairin, Nadar and Coppée, as well as most of the Parisian theatrical world, and some foreign writers, such as the young George Moore and the elderly Ivan Turgenev.[33] The orchestra played till three in the morning as Brébant, the celebrated restaurateur, and his waiters (dressed as labourers and sporting boaters), worked to capacity uncorking hundreds of bottles of champagne and serving a massive buffet.

Anything having the title *'L'Assommoir'* in it seemed to be destined for success, and the Paris run of the play lasted for over 250 performances. (The English version in London, entitled *Drink,* more or less doubled that figure.) So ecstatic was Busnach at its success in England that he declared in his usual ebullient manner, *'L'Assommoir* is the Shakespeare of drink!'[34] The staggering box-office success of the play did pose one serious psychological drawback, however. Its extraordinary, hysterical popularity and general acceptance almost intimidated all future Busnach-Zola collaborative efforts. *Nana,* which was to follow, though a substantial success by the terms of that day, paled in comparison to its predecessor.

What then did Zola make of this dynamic little man, William Busnach? He had never worked so closely with a Jew before, and certainly never with a self-educated man. Nevertheless, Busnach had a reputation for accomplishing things and for surprising feats of industry; he was a compulsive worker who knew neither limited hours nor limited effort, and he was acquainted with everyone in the theatre. Once Busnach began a project he was everywhere at once, talking to theatre directors, interviewing actors and actresses, watching new productions, arranging contracts for performances in Lyons, Rouen, Le Havre, Monaco, Marseilles, London, Brussels, Munich or Geneva, then travelling back and forth incessantly to coordinate everything. On top of this was the enormous amount of time he spent working with Zola and other collaborators, plus his own attempts at novel-writing. In other words he somehow managed to combine the roles of literary agent, business manager, impresario and playwright; he certainly deserved every penny he earned.

Such hard work obviously took its toll. Quite suddenly, with little or no warning, Busnach would come to a complete halt and all but collapse. 'My doctor has ordered me to pamper myself, to do nothing [for a while]. No more paperwork, coffee or women!'[35] he reported to Zola. Sometimes he was laid up for days, but over the years this gradually extended to longer periods, even weeks, when he would flee to the palm trees and balmy sea breezes of Monaco. He pushed himself till stress and overwork left him shattered. (At one time, in December 1892, he definitely thought he was dying and made Zola the executor of his literary estate.)[36] Then slowly but surely he would regain his strength and start once again, resuming the same old pace.

Busnach had no wife or family to rely upon, nor was there anyone for whom he was responsible. He always owned a little dog — as did Zola — and could be seen in the *grands boulevards* with an actress on one arm, his dog in the crook of the other. Both he and Zola were gourmands and enjoyed their enormous repasts, though neither drank much. Busnach had a colourful variety of ills: back, stomach, 'syphilitic throat', eyes, gout.

Most of the time fortunately, the afflictions did not interfere with his writing. 'Are you a neuropath like me?' began one letter to Zola. 'At the present, it is my back and stomach which are torturing me most. I can't eat. I can't sleep. I just suffer . . .'[37] This nervous fatigue has condemned me to temporary inactivity,' he sighed with growing frequency. Or ' . . . I hear trains buzzing round in my head . . . my brain is empty.'[38]

There was something very earthy and affable about the man. He was often humorous and could make the cautious Zola laugh as few others could. ('I have come down with a severe case of galloping laziness,' he announced one day.)[39] Sometimes his actions were so bewildering, however, that Zola did not know whether to laugh or cry, especially when Busnach was in one of his fulminating moods. His periodic cataclysmic feuds with actors, actresses and directors, including Henri Chabrillat at the Ambigu, were already legendary in Paris. At one point he called Sarah Bernhardt (a close friend of long-standing), 'an old cow',[40] the actor Henry, 'a fat-head', and referred to Clevès as 'a scoundrel' and 'that scum'.[41] But it was the celebrated Antoine, director of the Théâtre Libre, who regularly received the rough side of Busnach's tongue. One day after another unprofitable meeting with Antoine about the possible production of *Germinal,* an exasperated Busnach vented his ire by declaring that Antoine was 'as stubborn as a gas-fitter'!'[42]

The insensitive Busnach little realized how frequently he overstepped the mark with Zola, particularly in respect to Antoine, whom Zola was trying to help through a bad patch. 'You must keep going,' Zola wrote to Antoine. 'You know that I have full confidence in you as a labourer and struggler. I now live in a quiet corner away from the skirmishes. But should the occasion arise, you will always find in me the foremost of friends and supporters.'[43] Antoine for his part praised Zola in his memoirs decades after the novelist's death. 'It was thanks to him that we emancipated the theatre,' he noted.[44]

The numerous differences between Zola and Busnach were overcome time and again by the many positive points in their relationship. One factor in Busnach's favour was his apparently genuine fondness for Alexandrine. They were constantly exchanging little gifts, he sending her a box of chocolates, she sending him a hamper of food when he was ill. He was one of the few never to take Alexandrine too seriously, and addressed her humorously as *La Châtelaine* (lady of the manor), generally concluding his letters to Zola with, 'Remember me to your lady.'

Busnach held a deep and sincere admiration for Zola, both as a person and a writer. He would unabashedly praise Zola's latest novel in the most extravagant terms, and mean every word of what he said. 'Bravo, bravo, bravo!' he wrote ecstatically when *Nana* was published. 'It's marvellous!'[45] After an entrancing first reading of *La Bête humaine* (The Beast in Man), he was to declare: 'I see that you are indeed a man of genius . . . It is the finest thing you've written. A real masterpiece.'[46] As for *La Débâcle:* 'I have devoured it . . . The whole thing is superb.'[47] After finishing *Le Docteur Pascal* (Doctor Pascal) he exclaimed, 'That's not a novel. That's a philosophical monument!'[48] Once their collaboration was well established, Busnach confided, ' . . . writing a play with you is not merely financially profitable, which of course is something, it is also a joy for me to find myself working with a man of your talent, which to me is worth much more.'[49] Years after they had ceased to work together, Busnach wrote, 'You are the one man I admire and love more than any other in the world.[50] I congratulated you years ago when you were named a Chevalier of the Legion . . . But what I really congratulate you on . . . is being Emile Zola.'[51] It was hard not to like Busnach.

By July 1880, work on their next joint production, *Nana,* was going well. 'I am posting the fourth scene to you. Read it, and if you have the time, write the scene for Georges and Nana. We'll talk about it on Thursday. I shall bring you the fifth and sixth scenes.'[52] This was typical of the way they worked together, Busnach usually writing the first draft of a scene, Zola then modifying it, if he wished to do so, and in some cases even preparing an initial draft for Busnach to go over. They would write and rewrite each scene, then read aloud the finished product. Sometimes Busnach would make the hour-and-a-half rail journey to Médan several times a month.

The première of *Nana* was held on Saturday, 29 January 1881, and Edmond de Goncourt wrote:

> The public at the Ambigu Theatre were in a good mood, even light-hearted. Following the third scene I paid a visit to Mme Zola who had tears in her eyes . . . and when I took the liberty of telling her that I did not find the public as hostile as she seemed to do, she snapped at me, 'So you find that audience good, do you? Well, I can see you are not very hard to please.' I slipped out of the door.

Following the thunderous applause received after the curtain fell on the last act, even Goncourt had to admit that Zola and Busnach had another success on their hands. 'I then went to see Mme Zola again, who was smiling this time and asked me to forgive her.'[53] They went to join Zola and Busnach in Henri Chabrillat's office and discovered that Zola, who as usual had spent the entire time reading a novel in that room, had not ordered dinner in advance. A superstitious man, he feared the play would fail if he did so.

'Afterwards, everyone, all the Naturalist men and women, walked over to Brébant's, where they supped till four o'clock in the morning . . . ' Later, when Chabrillat, who had been sitting at another table with the cast, came over to see Zola, the latter's first remark to the director was: 'Well, did we manage to break even?'[54]

Parisians seemed to like the play, even though some last-minute prudish changes omitted some highly controversial vocabulary from the script. However, the indefatigable Francisque Sarcey managed to denounce it in his column in *Le Temps,* calling it 'a common melodrama', though even he had to admit that it would probably be a big financial success.[55] Auguste Vitu called it 'a mediocre melodrama', though he felt the play would probably have *'un succès de curiosité'.*[56]

As a grey December of 1881 gave way to a chilly January of 1882, one year after the successful launching of the play *Nana,* a new element was suddenly injected into the authors' relationship, poisoning it permanently. In a letter apparently dating from the first week of January 1882, a snowbound Zola received Busnach's bombshell: 'I expect you've received my letter of last Monday, haven't you, in which I informed you that I spent your royalty payment from Germany, so I now owe you 8596 francs . . . I lost your money at baccarat.'[57] If Zola did not know it earlier, he did so now. His portly collaborator was a compulsive gambler and had lost their joint German royalties, and perhaps much more, at the gaming tables that New Year's Eve. He had informed Zola immediately, however, and was to send him a cheque for a few hundred francs every month until it was repaid, as eventually it was. Although nothing like this ever happened again, Zola felt he could no longer trust Busnach, and their relationship, which hitherto had been quite open and confident, became much more cautious and self-conscious, to the point that Zola hesitated about letting Busnach work on the next play, *Pot-bouille* (Restless House). They had made a lot of money of course and that was a real factor. *Nana* had grossed over 400,000 francs and *L'Assommoir* over 600,000. There was much at stake.

What had all seemed to bode so well had now changed, and Zola's 'disciples', as Busnach caustically referred to them, who disapproved of the working-class Jew, were urging the Master of Médan to break with him. The anti-Semitic Edmond de Goncourt echoed their sentiments, describing him as that 'vile Busnach . . . the caricature of a Jew . . . that wretched type of huckster.'[58] Busnach, for his part, was made quite aware of what Zola's 'disciples' were doing and chided him about it. 'Some stupid or clumsy friends of yours have persuaded you that [collaborating with me] harms you. Success can't harm anyone,'[59] he pointed out with the only logic he understood. Busnach was writing popular plays, not philosophical treatises, but they were accomplishing precisely what he intended them to do: entertain, bring a little fame and earn money. 'You can't argue with success,' he declared. But Zola was wary, and remained aloof at Médan where he was protected by silence and distance. 'Rest assured . . . I shall not ask again to work with you, since that idea so disturbs you', Busnach wrote at the beginning of February 1882. But of course he persisted: 'I admire you. I love you like a brother. Above all, I do not wish to upset you in any way . . . That's why I'm stopping.'[60] But William Busnach, who had had to fight very hard indeed to reach the position he now held in the theatre — that 'notorious profession', as Mallarmé once called it — was not about to give up that easily and he wrote again in March. 'To be able to call myself your friend means a great deal to me, at a time when I may no longer call you — though I hope this is only temporary — my collaborator . . . You are like all highly-strung people,' he said, 'too sensitive about what others say. Just remember that whenever you would like me to come over to work with you again, I'll come running at the first sign . . . Your devoted, W. Busnach.'[61] 'I am *absolutely* counting on our doing play number three by the end of next winter,' he wrote in August 1882. 'All in all, we've succeeded far too well the first two times not to start again.'[62]

For the next several months the relationship remained strained and cool, and it was not until the following summer, at the beginning of August, that Zola finally relented, suggesting that if Busnach were still interested in working with him that he should have a look at his most recent novel, *Pot-bouille*. Had he been able to lift his enormous weight off the ground, the rotund Busnach would undoubtedly have clicked his heels with delight. But, alas, after he began reading the book his mood changed to one of consternation. 'I really can't see a play in it, or at least, not the basic ingredients for a play,'[63] he was forced to admit. Sometimes it just took work, and time. 'I am hacking away at it. It is coming along . . . '[64] Obviously it's going to be quite difficult, but not impossible, no, not impossible.'[65] Then in an unguarded moment of euphoria he promised rather prematurely: 'Not to worry, we'll have a success there!'[66] Although Busnach applied his usual assiduity, he appeared to lack the confidence he had before their falling out. The Ambigu was approached and immediately accepted the as yet unseen and incomplete play. Begun in August 1883, Busnach had copies of a finished script sent over to the theatre by November, as the première was scheduled for 13 December.

'I fear *Pot-bouille* is going to be a disaster after all,' he confided to Zola on 18 December, blaming it on poor acting.[67] The critics had looked forward to the latest Zola-Busnach production with growing relish, for excitement and controversy had always seemed to accompany Zola's name. But this time, they were disappointed, the only thing arousing real interest being the scenery, which had reached a 'miserable state of realistic perfection'.[68] Léon Chapron in *Gil Blas* praised the deft work of Busnach — 'a chap who knows his profession right down to his fingertips' — for turning a difficult book into a semblance of a play. He believed that it would be a great success for the Ambigu, although Alphonse Daudet, considered it 'a heap of rubbish'.[69]

Devoid of any sense of tact or inferiority so far as talent and ability went, Busnach felt no qualms in giving Zola advice regarding his theatrical work. When he knew that Zola was hesitant about what changes to make in a piece, Busnach would suggest the answer and counsel, 'Think it over. Think it over.' In fact Busnach was probably the only colleague to work with Zola who never showed the slightest subservience. He even went so far as to correct Zola's grammar. This was a mistake, not least because Busnach was invariably wrong.

They could dispute scenes, using language Zola rarely did with anyone else. 'You might call me an imbecile . . . but I would never dream of saying that about you,'[70] Busnach protested when heated over conflicts in the stage production of *Nana*. Sometimes there were deep misunderstandings and their work appeared to be on the brink of collapse. 'Your letter has absolutely stupefied me,' Busnach wrote. 'I must be completely insane because the last thing I ever intended to do was to hurt you!'[71] Their disagreements also extended to which of their plays should be performed and where. Thus when Busnach, writing from Brussels, got fed up with arguing with Zola, he replied: 'Show something else then, and let's forget about the whole thing.'[72] And in yet another letter he said he must be blind if 'you have seen such insinuations in my letter . . . It is very cruel of you to doubt me so.'[73] When once Zola apologized, trying to appease a troubled Busnach, the latter replied: 'I gladly accept your apology.'[74]

Zola never took Busnach into his confidence regarding his private life even though he was a frequent visitor to Médan (rarely as an overnight guest). He did not even inform him immediately of his mother's death. Busnach was hurt: 'Believe me how truly grieved I am for you, how deeply I feel the misfortune which has struck you . . . ' But why had he not told him, he asked? 'Our close relationship would have led me to believe that you would have informed me sooner of your affliction[75] . . . I am too much your *confrère* and not enough your friend,' he sighed. 'It is very stupid of me, I expect, but I am very fond of you.'[76]

Busnach's work with Zola was always intermittent. Most of their plays required less than a year's collaboration, and some needed less than three or four months, so Busnach frequently found time to collaborate with others, such as Guy de Maupassant and Jules Verne. When it later came to *Germinal*, however, so much resistance was put up by government censors in 1885, that it took years of work — off and on — before the piece appeared at the Châtelet in April 1888. Other works were considered, and written in part or entirety, including *Une Page d'amour*, *La Terre* (The Earth), *La Faute de l'abbé Mouret* (which Sarah Bernhardt had once wanted so badly), and *La Bête humaine*. Busnach offered to help rewrite *Renée* (again for Bernhardt) for a small percentage of the receipts, and he was even willing to have his name omitted from the billing, but to no avail, for Zola would have none of it. In letter after letter, conversation after conversation, year after year, Busnach assailed Médan for release of *La Faute de l'abbé*

Mouret and *La Bête humaine*, but Bernhardt's interest in those productions — as in others — was always unreliable, even after a requested work was completed and handed to her personally by Zola.

The next play Busnach based on a Zola novel was the author's *Le Ventre de Paris*, which had been published back in 1873. They began work on it in October 1886 and by the week before Christmas Busnach was busy reading the completed script to the cast of the Théâtre de Paris. Céard, who for years had denounced Busnach to Zola and chided him on their collaboration, now asked if he could become a collaborator in the play, demanding as large a share of the receipts as Busnach received. Greed and jealousy, it would appear, had got the better of him. Busnach reluctantly agreed to this, no doubt fearing the loss of Zola altogether if he did not, but Céard finally withdrew from the enterprise without ever having participated in it. The completed five-act play lacked the compelling attraction of the novel, one critic simply referring to it as 'a series of colourful scenes'. Yet it received a relatively favourable press, prompting the jealous Goncourt to call it 'a smelly thing'.[77] The plot included a bastard born to Louise Méhudin after the imprisonment of the child's father, Florent, for political activities following Louis Napoleon's *coup d'état* in December 1851. Sarcey accused Busnach of writing another pot-boiler, a real melodrama. The play, which opened on 18 February 1887, managed to last the season and make some money for its authors, but Zola was never happy enough with it to have it published, despite the fact that he had written much of it himself.

The year 1885, in which Zola and Busnach completed their play *Germinal*, was one of the most tense in the early history of the Third Republic, as both Republicans and the extreme right fought bitterly in national elections in October for control of the Chamber of Deputies and the reins of power, though it was the Republicans who finally emerged the winners. In December, as Busnach continued to challenge the government decision to prohibit the play, the Republicans re-elected Jules Grévy as President of the Republic, who in turn asked Charles Freycinet to form a new government, and Busnach for one believed Freycinet should have felt safe enough now to release *Germinal*. But governments can disappear as rapidly as they appear and there was little relaxation in political circles as Prime Minister Freycinet brought Deputy Georges Boulanger into his government as Minister of War. His reputation was now soaring to new heights of popularity with both the Army and the public in general, particularly for having been denounced so strongly by the right in France, while at the same time in the Reichstag by Bismarck, himself, the latter declaring General Boulanger to be a menace to the Germans! The name of Georges Boulanger was on everyone's lips: the man was a hero. So great was his national reputation by the summer of 1887 that when an Opportunist-Right coalition brought Maurice Rouvier to office as the new Prime Minister, he immediately banished Boulanger to garrison duty at Clermont-Ferrand, though a hysterical mob of admirers, many thousands strong, physically tried to stop the General's train from leaving the Gare de Lyon. Clearly Rouvier's decision was wrong, and the government only compounded their error the following year by forcing the general to retire early, which simply gave the handsome officer on the black horse all the more time to devote to politics.

'Demonstrations on behalf of universal suffrage are being demanded by everyone . . . all hoping for deliverance,' noted *Gil Blas* in April 1888 when Boulanger addressed the Committee of National Protest. All this could lead to revolution, the newspaper insisted, and France 'to the worst possible dangers'.[78] There was no doubt that things were beginning to get out of hand.

It was in the same year that scandal in the Elysée Palace added to the political instability of the day with the discovery that President Grévy's son-in-law, Daniel Wilson, had been selling his influence and honours (for example, the Legion of Honour) to affluent clients. This meant the end of Grévy's political career, but did nothing to stem the growing Boulangism in the country, by now a movement which included a few dozen deputies who supported an unofficial party under the leadership of the General. In the spring of 1888 everyone, it seemed, wanted Boulanger to represent their constituency in the Chamber of Deputies. By the following January, after Boulanger won one of the greatest electoral victories in history, his supporters, indeed mobs, demanded that he march on the Elysée Palace itself and carry out a *coup d'état,* and public feeling was so strong that it seems unlikely that anyone could have prevented it. Fortunately, General Boulanger refused to do so, and within months his political influence began to wane as his opponents so out-manoeuvered him that he fled the country never to return (later committing suicide over the grave of his mistress), which only increased public bewilderment. As if this were not enough, the angered right was still smarting from republican legislation forcing all heads of former ruling houses, including the pretender, the Count of Paris, into exile.

Amidst this background of political flux and hysteria, of wild gyrations from left to right, it was hardly surprising that the long delayed production of *Germinal* — censored by Education Minister René Goblet three years earlier, immediately after its completion, because of its 'revolutionary' character and for showing government troops killing striking miners — should attract large crowds, pulsating with excitement and tension as the doors opened for the première at the Châtelet on 21 April 1888.

Once again Busnach was credited as the sole author of the work, but this time he had converted the book 'into a rapid series of scenes . . . like a photo album'. The play admirably reflected the political reality of the time, including the protests heard at General Boulanger's rallies. The critic, Fernand Bourgeat, was unfortunately alone in finding the play 'deeply moving and intelligently written'.[79] Other critics snapped at the authors' heels and did so with obvious delight, including Auguste Vitu who described it as 'the thinnest of melodramas' and 'deadly boring', even for an admirer of Zola's novels. Sarcey, not to be outdone called it simply 'crushing' and 'soporific'. Albert Wolff proved to be the most assiduous of heel-snappers, however: 'This time the Master cannot hide from us; he attended the rehearsals and squabbled with the cast, he created the scenery . . . It is therefore indeed Zola who is the author of this cumbersome machine.'[80] Why does he let Busnach take all the blame for his own shortcomings as a playwright, he demanded? Wolff described Busnach as 'the little chef of the naturalist pot who picks the potatoes and peels the onions'.[81] Of all the critiques, Wolff's alone stung Zola into action, and to the great glee of all those following the skirmish, the next day in *Le Figaro* Zola made an unprecedented admission: 'I declare that the play is entirely by me, that Busnach did not write a single line of it.'[82] Sarcey no doubt sniggered as Paris clapped its hands in delight. They had finally forced the old bear out of his den. Many years later Busnach admitted that of all the plays he had collaborated on, *Germinal* alone had been a failure because it was simply too gloomy. It failed after seventeen performances and Zola never allowed it to be published.

The embittered Goncourt gloatingly echoed Wolff's attack on what he scathingly called Zola's 'Busnachades': 'That Zola really is a sly old fox. Instead of taking one of his young disciples from Médan as his collaborator, he accepted Busnach who, though he never writes any of their plays, is his partner in the eyes of the public and serves as lightning conductor for the attacks by the press which are really intended for the novelist.'[83]

While Busnach tried time and again to revive his flagging relationship with Zola, the failure of *Germinal* marked the end of ten years' effective collaboration. Then, in December 1895, a despondent Busnach emerged from a fifteen-month prison term as a result of financial problems and again contacted Zola, signing his letter, 'your ex-collaborator'. The letter elicted no response and the years passed. On 29 December 1899 the sixty-seven-year-old Busnach wrote to Zola wishing him good health in the new year and the new century, and expressing the hope that Zola would overcome his fear of having *Germinal* performed again, and that he would remain open-minded enough to let the Ambigu Theatre produce *La Bête humaine*.

Zola adamantly refused to change his mind. *Germinal* had been blasted by the critics, debated in the Chamber of Deputies, denounced by more than one government, and its reception in 1888 had been extremely discouraging. Busnach then wrote in August 1900, still trying to coax his former collaborator to go over the final scene of *La Bête Humaine,* for which he already had another theatre waiting. 'If you give me Wednesday, Friday and Saturday, or likewise Sunday and Monday, that's all the time it will take.'[84] Then accepting the reality of the situation: 'You really do believe it impossible for it to succeed, I know it. But you are quite wrong!'[85] 'The brilliant new production of *L'Assommoir*,' scheduled to appear in Paris that winter, 'will, I expect, bring our old collaboration to the attention of the public once again,'[86] it being Busnach's first play since leaving prison five years earlier, and thus meaning a great deal to him. 'To be broke at the age of sixty-eight, that's a bit difficult . . . I need money most urgently,'[87] Busnach confessed in January 1900, hoping no doubt to arouse Zola's sense of compassion to let the works be staged. Zola refused to extend a helping hand, however, and though the new production of *L'Assommoir* did bring in some badly needed revenue that November, its short run did not help much. Nothing could induce Zola to return to a partnership which had gone stale long before. When waiting for a reply which never came, Busnach whipped off a one-liner to Médan: 'My dear Zola, what has become of you out in your prairie?'[88]

Was Zola just callous, or had he been tried beyond endurance? Things certainly were not the same as they had been in 1879. For one, he was just beginning to recover from the impact of the Dreyfus Affair. Also, he had newer, more important interests, including growing children and a woman who loved him. When his name appeared on a billing now, it was a librettist to Alfred Bruneau's popular lyric operas, and unfortunately Busnach — never the diplomat — told Zola he found Bruneau's music disagreeable. Struggling with chronic illness and poverty, Busnach died alone and forgotten in 1907.

9
Militant Journalist

The year 1870, so nearly fatal for France, was equally so for Zola, who had no articles published after the middle of August. From February 1871, however, his position began to improve, though it again fell into a steep slump between 1873 and 1875, with an improvement in 1876. But never again did his journalistic output equal the productivity of 1871 and 1872. In 1881, he announced in *Le Figaro* that his full-time journalistic career was drawing to an end. He had decided that he could no longer afford to set aside two weeks out of every four for journalism, and in any event he had said all he had wanted to say in the papers. He must now concentrate all his efforts on his novels.

Prior to the débâcle of 1870 Zola had rarely, if ever, written on politics, nor had politics hitherto really interested him, but with the collapse of the country and his subsequent dip in revenue, he was quick to accept work for the daily newspaper *La Cloche*. From February to March 1871 he worked as its political correspondent at the temporary seat of government in Bordeaux, and then until May 1872 at Versailles.

Zola's parliamentary reports were quite unlike those of other political commentators. The number of bills debated and votes taken were of little interest to the iconoclastic Zola, who was more preoccupied with impressions. He felt that France had been betrayed by politicians in the past, and consequently sarcasm oozed from every article. He would then discuss 'political issues' not directly concerned with parliament that day, such as Marshal Bazaine or Louis Napoleon. He also relentlessly attacked the parliamentarians of the right, especially Lorgeril and Belcastel. Following the Franco-Prussian War, the right was strong enough to threaten a takeover, not only of political doctrine, but of France itself, and Zola greatly feared this possibility.

Staunch republican that he was, Zola naturally employed his pen at every opportunity to wage war against the right. He personally would have no objection, he claimed, to the princes of the House of Orléans sitting in the Chamber of Deputies (a plan suggested by a deputy, Jean Brunet), but it would be under one condition: they must be elected just like everyone else, taking their places 'as ordinary citizens, fulfilling their political tasks like the most humble deputy'.[1] But Zola did not really take this seriously, nor did he go so far as to suggest this for the Bonapartes. If the Orléans princes were ever elected to the Chamber, he thought their appearance would be more profitable to the Republicans than to the monarchical right, as they would be shown for what they really were - stupid and fallible. Zola seemed to have forgotten, for the moment, that Louis Napoleon had been allowed to sit in parliament under the Second Republic in 1848, and from there had been able to catapult himself into the presidency and then on to the throne.

Following a long pro-monarchy speech in parliament, Zola wrote that monarchy had not always been in the best interests of France, a declaration that few people had the courage to make in public.

> The story of the lives of some of the kings of France would best not be repeated before the podium. I have often thought that the royalists would be wrong to accuse the Republic of creating only the guillotine and arson. If we counted the stranglings, poisonings, massacres, and all the miseries which have served to fertilize and fatten the monarchy, we could then see that it is the republicans who are the amateurs when it comes to crime, and that a burnt Paris weighs less in the balance of eternal justice than a France pillaged and murdered over the centuries.[2]

Going on to discuss Louis Napoleon, Zola wrote:

> First of all, I am of the opinion that he should be given back the sworn oath which he violated; there is no more room in our museums for such royal bagatelles. We could also exhume the dead of 2 December [1851 — the date of Louis Napoleon's *coup d'état*], of those who died in Mexico [the ill-fated Franco-Mexican War] of the dead of Sedan, and send their bones to him. They are after all his bones, his indeed, and perhaps he could make use of them as wall-trophies for his study.[3]

Zola attacked Louis Napoleon whenever possible and under any pretext. Thus, when theoretically discussing the former emperor's biography of Julius Caesar (mainly researched and written by Victor Duruy and Prosper Mérimée), Zola condemned him for the bloodbath at Sedan, and for leaving a trail of creditors. One of these creditors was Henri Plon, who had published *L'Histoire de Jules César* in a luxurious edition in 1865, the Emperor having contracted to pay the 333,000 francs publication cost, but then reneging on the deal, although he had found the money to purchase Chiselhurst (in the south of England) and Beaulieu House, a splendid estate on the Isle of Wight.

Zola's criticism of Bonaparte and his self-made empire was not limited to politics and foreign affairs, but extended as well to the declining moral values of French society, a subject which concerned him till the end of his days. Gambling, especially the gaming tables of the casinos ('cellars where man becomes a brute'), was constantly attacked by Zola who, unlike Dostoevsky and Tolstoy, was in no way addicted to gambling, although on rare occasions he was known to place a small wager on a horse race at Longchamp.

It was not only gambling, however, which was undermining the health and morality of the country, but also excessive drinking and prostitution. By the latter he was referring to courtesans. Millions of francs were spent annually on these women, often for political purposes, in order that the right women might secure the right political appointments for certain gentlemen. Zola described it as a cesspool rotting away at the heart of the government. 'When a nation has sunk its feet into this mire, it slowly rots; the evil gnaws, progressing relentlessly right to the heart. It is high time that the Republic cuts out this infection if it does not want gangrene to set in.'[4]

Zola returned to the subject of education on several occasions. He believed that many social and moral problems would be solved if more people had access to education. He approved of the new 'lay schools', having been much impressed by what he observed in one such school in Paris. 'Our France and all our children must attend these lay schools so that in thirty years from now we shall have a generation of republicans, conscious of their rights and duties and capable of carrying them out. Only then will we have our revenge on monarchical Europe for Waterloo and Sedan.'[5]

Zola's disdain of most politics and politicians is well documented. He believed that politics were controlled by 'little men' very full of themselves and their selfish inclinations, men rarely sincerely interested in the well-being of their country. He claimed he would prefer passionless eunuchs to the politicians of the present republic. But, surprisingly, there was one politician whom he did admire — Thiers, the Head of the Executive Power of the French Republic. During the trying days of February 1871, Zola hailed Thiers as 'French genius incarnate'. He wholeheartedly endorsed Thiers' suggestion that the government should sign a peace treaty with the Prussians to pacify and reorganize France, and only then decide upon what sort of political structure should replace the empire.

Over the weeks to come, however, it was Thiers who was so instrumental in moving the Assembly from Bordeaux to Versailles, a decision that Zola strongly denounced. Why should the nation's Assembly prefer to sit with the Prussian conquerors (whose headquarters were at Versailles), rather than with Frenchmen in Paris? He called it cowardly, unpatriotic and irrational. The Bordeaux Assembly moved north to Versailles in mid-March 1871, where another decision by Thiers and the Assembly upset Zola immensely — the authorization to send in French troops to quell the Paris Commune. On 23 May Zola noted:

M. Thiers is obviously abandoning Paris, having accused it of not supporting
the government. The delirious Assembly praised him and warmly applauded
his view. M. Thiers declared: 'Paris has given us the right to prefer France
to it, and I don't think the sky will fall in as a result.' . . . It is desertion
pure and simple.[6]

Although there were many issues on which they differed, Zola continued
to support Thiers because he was strong and could hold the Republic
together against royalist attack, and he took the proposal to exile the princes
of Orléans as a sign that Thiers was serious about making the Republic
succeed.

Zola was never a predictable man, as seen when he unexpectedly fought
a bill opposing the private production of firearms. The supporters of the
bill felt the suppression of the private arms industry would reduce the
opportunities for future revolution and leave the government with a
manufacturing monopoly. Zola thought the bill was harmful, however,
because it would 'throw thousands of workers out on the streets'.[7]

When the new government attempted to reintroduce the requirement
that newspapers deposit bonds prior to publication, Zola naturally fought
what he termed 'the first link in the chain, which some hope will curtail
the freedom of the press'.[8] But Thiers supported this measure and the
bond was again required. To Zola it seemed inconceivable that a republic
could introduce such legislation, but he had much to learn about the Third
Republic.

What then did Zola so admire in Thiers, when he opposed him on so
many important issues? He certainly considered Thiers to be an honest
and independent politician — something rare at any time in history. Perhaps
even more than that was Thiers' great skill and finesse in dealing with
delicate or unpleasant matters. A good example of this was seen in the
summer of 1871 when the National Assembly debated the sending of
petitions to the Vatican in favour of military intervention in Italy (a move
supported by the French bishops). Zola described Thiers' handling of the
situation:

He has managed to manoeuvre in such a manner as to rally everyone, and
even defused a meeting of impatient clerics threatening him with the most
terrible implications . . . Despite his attempt to conciliate, he has acted
decisively. He has shown the impossibility of French intervention and has
squarely faced the situation in Rome . . . France, according to M. Thiers,
has just discarded revenge.[9]

Zola, too, was against futile war; he opposed intervention abroad, and
party politics which subordinated national interests to party wishes and
whims. All these things contributed to his backing of Thiers.

But there was more to it than that. Thiers had vitality and tenacity, a good-natured style of speech, and the ability to explain complex issues simply. In short, Zola felt that Thiers personified all the qualities of the bourgeois temperament.

After 1872, Zola rarely touched upon political matters again, until his involvement in the Dreyfus Affair. He had become a parliamentary reporter through necessity and he freed himself from the entanglement as soon as he could. In 1873, however, he suffered a sharp setback, scarcely placing twenty articles (chiefly in *L'Avenir National*); 1874 was worse with only one article, and in 1875 he placed only nine, all in the Russian journal, the *European Messenger*.

Though he was a progressive man and approved of the advances in medicine and science, Zola did not approve of changes in the character of the French press, and he said so in August 1877 in the *European Messenger*. The main problem with the French press, he claimed, was that it penetrated every aspect of life, leaving nothing to the imagination. He felt this was undignified — a reflection of the unprincipled journalists now employed by newspapers, who sought self-advancement at the expense of moral standards.

Zola was constantly changing employers throughout his journalistic career, and between 1873 and 1881 alone he wrote for more than a dozen different periodicals. There were numerous reasons for these changes: he was unhappy with the editorial policy, the editor, the publisher, the content, or the paper's attitude to his own writings and theories. Sometimes he resigned, sometimes he was fired. When working for Jules Laffitte on *Le Voltaire*, for example, Zola published an article called '*La Haine de la littérature*' (Hatred of Literature),[10] in which he said that only mediocrities went into politics (after they had failed in everything else), then politics swept you up and made a minister of you'. That was the last straw for Laffitte, who had many friends in high political office, and probably political aspirations of his own. Zola resigned with aplomb, sending Laffitte one of his famous telegrams: 'So far as I am concerned, you are dead.'

Francis Magnard, editor-in-chief of *Le Figaro* (a conservative, royalist paper in those days), was delighted at Zola's break with *Le Voltaire* (a republican paper), and tried to induce him to write a column for him. Zola may have been angry with Laffitte, but he also had his principles, so it seemed certain that he would reject this offer. Much to the astonishment of literally everyone, Zola accepted, afraid that otherwise the voice of dissent would not be heard at all.

Before leaving journalism permanently behind him, Zola discussed what he would really like to see in French politics. 'I should like to see a republic of superior men . . . I should like to see the nation established scientifically on the solid basis of republican governent, having determined its needs according to race, history and the contemporary milieu.'[11] By this he meant that he wanted to see an end to privilege and rigid class distinction. He went on to praise democracy as the system for the future, warning that it might not be easily achieved, but it would be worthwhile. It was a curious piece to appear in *Le Figaro*.

And then it happened: Zola made his famous decision to end his journalistic career. He sat down on 15 January 1882 and wrote the preface to his latest volume of articles published under the title of *Une Campagne*.[12]

> Today I've retired. I left the press four months ago and I count on not returning to it, although I have not sworn a solemn oath to that effect. I feel really good, a result of my new impartiality, a peace of mind resulting from being able to concentrate on only one task at a time after sixteen years of militant journalism. It seems to me that a little peace has already begun to settle over my books and my name, not to mention a little justice as well. No doubt, when I'm no longer seen in the midst of frays, I will be looked upon quite simply as a labourer engrossed in the solitary effort of his work, and then the idiotic rumours about my pride and cruelty will disappear.[13]

Reflecting on whether his journalistic work had been of any value, he stated that it was not for him to decide. He had always attempted to shed light in order to arrive at the truth, but how he had enjoyed feeling indignant and furious about what he saw as the universal mediocrity of that day.

> To feel the constant irresistible need to cry aloud what one thinks, especially when one is all alone in thinking it; to leave this spoils the joys of life! This has been my passion, and I am splattered with blood as a result, but I love it, and if I have achieved anything, it is thanks alone to this passion. . . . Despite great errors which I have made, my voice was heard because of my convictions . . . Refuse me everything, discuss me and deny me as you will, but nothing has prevented me from trying to disengage the heavy hand of political manipulation from literature. If I have done nothing more than that, if I have existed only to kindle literary quarrels, to awaken people sufficiently to write to me about my battle or even heap injuries upon me, well and good. In that case I feel that every writer, especially the young ones, owe me a little gratitude. At least one is alive when fighting. Passions call forth passion.[14]

Zola had put everything into his journalistic career and felt that by 1881 he had accomplished all that he had set out to do. Secretly, of course, the idealist in him may have been disappointed that he had not converted more people to his way of thinking. On the other hand, he was not renouncing life and retiring to a monastery; he was simply renouncing journalism as the primary weapon in his arsenal. Henceforward he would dedicate himself exclusively to literature.

10
Master of Médan

Zola now weighed nearly 15 stone, and this not only gave him a paunch, making him look shorter than his 5 feet 7 inches, but puffed and distorted his still youthful looking face, which was bounded by a full head of closely cropped hair and an even more closely trimmed beard. His small ears and nose seemed almost incidental to this picture of Zola during his late thirties and early forties. The gourmand in him had gradually altered the once slender young writer. Food was one of his obsessions, though he was not to do anything about his corpulence until 1888 when he suddenly went on a crash diet.

Médan, his house (and also the name of a nearby village of some 200 inhabitants), was crowded with workmen as numerous extensions were added to the house. His square tower had come first, and then another, the first paid for from the proceeds of *L'Assommoir,* the second from advances on *Nana.* The second tower had a modern laundry-cum-sewing room on the first floor and a large sitting-room on the ground floor, which could be converted into a billiards room for after-dinner entertainment.

Zola had discovered Médan in 1877 while travelling along the left bank of the Seine between Poissy and Triel. He wanted to lease a place for the following year when the Exposition Universelle would make Paris too noisy to work in. He needed a place where he could work undisturbed for eight months of the year, but there was nothing suitable. At last he found a small farmhouse for sale, and somewhat reluctantly agreed to pay 9000 francs for it. He was never sorry. In addition to the solitude, the house offered a location where he was the only member of the bourgeoisie, the only educated man in the area for miles, both important factors to Zola.

Immediately after the purchase was completed, he himself designed major changes for the property, employing up to twenty-five workmen at a time. In addition to the new towers, he built a guest pavilion, often occupied by Flaubert, Maupassant, the Charpentiers, the Daudets, Céard, Cézanne and later, the Bruneaus, for Zola liked to entertain his friends at weekends. In the evening the guests spent much of their time in the imposing billiards room, which had large columns on either side of the door and exposed beams across the ceiling. On the other side of the room stained-glass French windows opened on to the original formal garden of the house, with its neat *allées* lined with well-trimmed shrubs, and a goldfish pond in the centre.

Much to the amusement of Goncourt, Zola had Céard look up his family's coat of arms, going back as far as his paternal grandmother's family (that of Nicoletta Bondioli), and which he then had painted on the capitals of the columns in the billiards room. As his daughter, Denise Le Blond-Zola, later said, he wanted the house to have an *air seigneurial* and indeed 'Médan was furnished like a château, with its furniture and tapestries of different epochs'.[1] Luxurious silks and rare objects abounded at Médan (and at the Paris residence as well). Unlike Balzac, Zola did not collect simply for the love of collecting, but for the effect the furnishings would create.

Leaving the house one could turn back to the farm, 'a real model farm', his daughter called it, with its hothouses, poultry-yard, aviaries, small sheds and barns, which provided a constant supply of eggs, vegetables, milk, butter, chickens and rabbits (of which Zola's wife was so fond). The place was always immaculate, inside and out, thanks to the fastidious Madame Zola. On Saturday afternoons she could be found at the long table in the kitchen with her account book and a cash box before her, as each workman queued for payment from her. Meanwhile, Zola strolled with visiting friends along his island (Paradou, as he called it), located in the Seine across from the house. Here they could stretch out and talk or read, or sit in the little Norwegian châlet Zola had built. He even established a cemetery there for his animals.

The proceeds from *L'Assommoir* paid for the original purchase of the property and his large new study occupying the top floor of a three-storey tower. Later books, especially *Nana,* contributed to the further development of the estate, and Zola poured some 200,000 francs into it over the next several years. This was a considerable sum at a time when a workman felt very well off indeed if he received 5000 francs a year.

In Paris in the autumn of 1879 the sandwich-board men (some 200 in all), carried signs through the city — 'READ NANA! READ NANA!' — and large coloured posters were to be seen everywhere along the main streets of central Paris. Zola was furious: he felt that Laffitte was making his serious writings appear cheap, nasty and frivolous. *Nana* was not being written for this kind of treatment. Zola tried to slow down the pre-publication publicity, fearing the public would lose patience if the advertising appeared too far ahead of the novel's serialization in *Le Voltaire*. But nothing deterred Laffitte. As Céard informed Zola, 'A great deal of curiosity has been aroused over *Nana.* The name can be found plastered across every wall in Paris. It verges on an obsession and a nightmare.'[2] In reality Zola was pleased as well as annoyed: after all, it was nice to be recognized and famous, and if he did not exactly approve of the way in which Laffitte was achieving this, well, it was a means to an end.

Laffitte's advertising campaign did not stem solely from confidence in Zola's work; his newspaper was in serious financial trouble, and he desperately needed to sell papers, even if it meant distorting the meaning of *Nana* to do so.

And yet this saturation advertising campaign brought some unexpected results as well. For one thing, there was so much of it that some publishers felt it would be useless even to attempt publicizing their own books at the same time. Another side-effect occurred at the Ministry of the Interior, where the Committee on Publishing (responsible for censorship) convened to decide on what sort of action to take against the publication of Huysmans' most recent novel, *Marthe*: the choice was to forbid its being printed, or to seize the entire edition immediately afterwards. They finally settled on the latter. Céard, then a government employee, related to Zola what ensued: apparently the minister himself had cancelled the order on discovering that Huysmans was a friend of Zola. He feared that the seizure could have grave consequences . . . Such was the power of Zola's wrath at that time. As Céard told Zola: 'It seems your name has almost put the fear of God in them.'[3]

Finally, on 8 May 1879, Laffitte wrote in haste from the offices of *Le Voltaire* at 11, rue du Faubourg Montmartre confirming his verbal contract to publish Zola's next novel, *Nana,* in September or October 1880 for a fee of 20,000 francs, it being understood that this work would be shorter than *L'Assommoir*. Although Laffitte later agreed to increase the amount to 30,000 francs, he was going to run the series earlier than expected and Zola panicked. This was May and he had all summer, but could he get the rest of the book finished on time?

The promotional advertising put great pressure on him and he drove himself harder and harder, rarely leaving Médan. He remained there throughout the summer and did not return to the city in the autumn as he normally did. His aim now was to return to Paris by January 1880, and when Laffitte wrote at the end of October 1879 inviting him to a party he was giving, Zola, of course, had to decline, as he was still deeply entrenched with *Nana*. He was terribly anxious about being able to meet the instalment deadlines because at this time he could spend only two weeks out of every four on the novel, the other two being set aside to meet journalistic commitments.

Laffitte was becoming a decided nuisance, however, or perhaps reckless would be a more appropriate description. He throve on controversy, for that sold newspapers, and in October he decided to stimulate sales once again by printing the following declaration in *Le Voltaire:*

We make no secret of the fact that by publishing the work of such an audacious writer, a newspaper must prove itself to be a little audacious, knowing that it can count on readers of a robust spirit . . . The literary friends and enemies of our collaborator both hope to find something in *Nana*

— the former, much to admire, the latter, much to disparage; we declare that this double expectation will not be disappointed.[4]

Zola did not consider Laffitte entirely trustworthy, for the latter had originally promised never to cut or alter the author's writings for *Le Voltaire,* but he had, in fact, cut a couple of lines from Zola's very first article in that paper. Then numerous other incidents occurred around the time of the premature serialization of *Nana.* Laffitte not only cut the novel in the wrong places for the *feuilleton* publication, but he also deleted what he considered to be some controversial parts, although he did clear such deletions with Zola. Nevertheless, Zola was not at all pleased with the ravaged version as it appeared in print: '*Nana* disgusts me as it is appearing in *Le Voltaire*; I would give a great deal to see its publication ended . . . '[5] In December he wrote from a snowbound Médan: 'Laffitte has been worrying me. He took advantage of me at a time when I was terribly agitated, to make me agree to the suppression of certain passages, by frightening me about the possible consequences.'[6] In all fairness to Laffitte, however, he rightly feared government censorship and in private Léon Gambetta, the famous Republican leader and staunch opponent of Napoleon III, had warned the publisher that *Nana* was 'too strong'. If Laffitte were not to act quickly, he would be fined, his paper stopped, and he could even end up in jail. Consequently each new issue saw more phrases deleted, not all of them strictly necessary, so before the year was out Zola decided to settle things with his publishers once and for all.

He completed the book at Médan on 7 January 1880, and gave a well-earned sigh of relief. But it was not over yet; the mutilated serial continued in *Le Voltaire* as Charpentier prepared the unexpurgated version. Finally, on 15 February the book appeared on Paris bookstalls at a price of six francs. It caused an immediate sensation, and 55,000 copies were sold within a few weeks. Georges Charpentier, a conservative man, ordered another printing of 10,000 copies. The book outsold *L'Assommoir,* and during Zola's lifetime was only surpassed in sales by one other book, *La Débâcle.*

Zola was now really portrayed as an evil man by the moral majority. No one could be more pornographic; no one could appeal to the delights and decadence of the flesh as well as Zola; no one could be more vulgar or more sensational — or so declared his enemies and critics. Laffitte's advertising scheme was paying unheard of dividends for Zola, whether he liked it or not. In addition to the 30,000 francs from *Le Voltaire*, the author received another 220,000 francs from the initial book sales. His earnings made him the envy of the literary world. He was inundated with mail from all over Europe, including Scandinavia and Russia. Much of it was crude, however, and much of it anonymous. Women invited Zola to share the pleasures of the flesh with them; reformers and priests wrote denouncing him as the most immoral and destructive man in French society. Few, it would seem, understood that he simply wanted to show as vividly as possible how evil and corrupt women of the Parisian *demi-monde*, such as *Nana*, could and did destroy the lives, fortunes and families of many men. This evil would only be eliminated when the public became truly conscious of the problem.

What angered Zola more than the wild advertising schemes of *Le Voltaire*, were the bigoted reviews and comments on this novel. Most accused him of living a sheltered country life protected from the kind of characters and behaviour he described, thus concluding that he must have made everything up. And yet the critics 'know absolutely nothing about me, have no precise information, instead they collect every story and rumour about me, and then on that they base their reasons and condemn me.'[7] In fact, Zola had documented his work most carefully. He received information from his friends and acquaintances who knew the world of the *demi-mondaine* women. Had he not consulted Flaubert and Maupassant, both well-known roués (later to die of syphilis)? Had he not spoken to Ludovic Halévy about the *filles* of the theatrical world? Had he not gone to see, or had friends inspect for him, various brothels, even down to the food the prostitutes ate and the colour of their underwear? Had he not spent many hours with madams who explained every facet of their calling? The life of Nana was modelled on the lives of several famous Parisian courtesans, especially La Païva (Theresa Lachmann), and a famous actress of the Second Empire, Blanche d'Antigny. All had been documented thoroughly and the novel was firmly based on reality, as was the case with all Zola's books. He had gone to great lengths to obtain accurate descriptions, right down to Nana's death scene, as she lay dying of smallpox in the Grand Hotel.

Those dinners were legendary for their lavishness: green barley soup, reindeers' tongue, mullet *à la Provençale*, truffled guinea fowl, caviar for the lumbering Turgenev, shellfish for Zola, special butter from Normandy for Flaubert, and duckling *à l'étouffade*, which was his favourite dish, ginger for the eccentric Goncourt, bouillabaisse and chicken *au kari* for the others — all washed down with bottle after bottle of vintage wine.[8] The dinners had become a tradition among the self-dubbed 'hissed authors', since they first began in 1874. They usually took place at the restaurant Voicin in the rue Saint-Honoré, though they also met at the Café Riche, Adolphe et Pelé's near the Grand Opera House, and occasionally at Byron's in the place de l'Opéra-Comique.

Alphonse Daudet, a willowy and unkempt figure, hardly seemed at home before the ever-flowing repast, but he rarely missed one of these dinners. Flaubert, who spent more and more time at his house, Le Croisset, a converted eighteenth-century convent situated on the Seine just outside

Rouen, came to his flat overlooking the Parc Monceau every month in order to attend them, except during the summer. He was the grand old man of the party, and when he was not in one of his syphilitic tirades, was as pleasant and engaging as could be. As for the prim Edmond de Goncourt, despite his close friendship with Daudet, he was always rather more reserved and refined, but certainly the biggest gossip.

The five men (Turgenev, Zola, Flaubert, Goncourt and Daudet) were party to these boisterous gatherings because they had all qualified for membership of this select 'club' by having had one of their novels or dramatic works booed or hissed by the public and the critics. Goncourt was here because of his poorly-received *Henriette Maréchal*, Zola for his play, *Thérèse Raquin* (and indeed for just about everything he had written thus far), Flaubert for his play, *Le Candidat*, and Daudet for *L'Arlésienne*. Although no one had ever seen Turgenev's work booed in France, he assured them that it had been in Russia, and in any case, they all liked him too much to have excluded him. Emile de Girardin, the coarse baron of the Parisian press, had had the audacity to claim a place at their table, probably for the play he and Dumas had co-authored years earlier, but the five vetoed that membership. Two unofficial members were permitted to join them on occasion: Charpentier, their publisher, and Maupassant.

On the nights of these monthly gatherings, Alexandrine Zola would not bother to wait up for her husband, who never got home much before two, and sometimes three o'clock in the morning. Perhaps one of the strangest aspects of these meetings of old friends and famous authors (certainly to the modern reader), was that they addressed each other formally as '*vous*'. But all formality ended there and the five became more and more raucous as the hours passed, at times literally throwing out unwanted waiters who had the misfortune to interrupt a splendid session on Naturalism, or a discussion on a recent play by one of the five, or a battle over the merits of Chateaubriand's writing, always a favourite subject of Flaubert, whose *Madame Bovary,* however, was never discussed for fear of a frightful outburst by its author, who could stand no mention of that work. The subjects under discussion ranged far and wide, and even the waiters were occasionally agog at the ease and freedom of talk which often included love, women and sex. After these famous Sunday dinners, Zola often walked Flaubert home, and they would continue to argue heatedly under street lamps.

Those were good days, the very best, as Zola later thought. And yet they were not always cheerful. On one occasion in February 1880 Turgenev gave a special dinner for his friends, as he was planning to return to Russia for several weeks. Four of them were already seated when Zola arrived, leaning heavily on his stout cane and complaining of rheumatism in his hip. Thereafter much of the conversation focused on Zola, and his unhappiness with Laffitte's handling of *Nana* in *Le Voltaire*. Zola claimed that he was forced to do much rewriting, every evening, in fact, and it was killing him, he lamented.[9] The dinner was slightly enlivened by Daudet who had been to the theatre earlier that evening, but the light-hearted dinners of the early days gradually began to grow gloomier, due chiefly to Zola's preoccupation with his health and the subject of death. At this February dinner Turgenev tried to outdo Zola, complaining of a 'constriction of the heart' which had begun several nights previously, and which he somehow associated with a nightmare in which he found himself to be dead. That was the cue for Zola to discuss all sorts of morbid phenomena which made him think he would never complete the remaining eleven volumes of his *Rougon-Macquart* series (a recurrent fear of his). Daudet, unwilling to take a back seat, spoke of his own ill health and his fears of death. Turgenev was in Russia when the men met for the last time as a group at Flaubert's house in Rouen, towards the end of March 1880.

Although Flaubert did not always agree with Zola's writings, he did understand them, and the two remained fast friends; indeed, Zola held him in special respect. The end came without warning on 8 May 1880, when Zola received a terse telgram from Maupassant: 'Flaubert dead.' Zola was staggered, as were Goncourt, Daudet and Turgenev, who received similar telegrams. A few months earlier, Edmond Duranty, an old acquaintance of Zola dating back to his days at Hachette, and a founder of the Naturalist School, had died in poverty and obscurity in the provinces. Then on 17 October Zola's mother, who lived at Médan, suddenly died. Three deaths in one year. At the time of his mother's death he was preparing to write *La Joie de vivre,* but was compelled by this event to drop that subject, and he did not return to it for a couple of years. These three deaths definitely cut Zola off from the past. The psychological implications were complex, but for the time being he simply forced himself to continue to work. He was depressed, of course, but with the exception of dropping *La Joie de vivre* for a while, it did not hinder his work in an obvious way. He worked on three minor novels between 1880 and 1884 — *Pot-bouille, Au bonheur des dames* (To the Happiness of Women) and *La Joie de vivre.* And though he claimed to be quite happy with the results of his work at this time, the three proved to be a temporary low-point in his career, especially coming as they did after the scintillating success of *Nana* in 1880. Although Zola liked *Pot-bouille,* he realized that it was not in the same class as *Nana* or *L'Assommoir,* and he gradually fell into a deeper and deeper state of gloom — indeed the full effect of his mother's death, which had hit him especially hard, was only really felt between 1880 and 1882.

And then one day in August 1882, Zola collapsed. He complained of severe abdominal pains, and his physician ordered him to remain in bed for many weeks, though Zola did gradually begin working again in September on *Au bonheur des dames.* In October he wrote to a friend,

'I am a little better. I have been able to get back to work. Nevertheless I am not at all strong. I fear that something very grave brushed past me . . . I have become such a coward that the prospect of having to finish my book terrifies me.'[10]

1880 was indeed a year of breaks with the past. Lives ended, and Zola finally broke with Laffitte, promising the serial rights for his new novel to *Le Gaulois*. In January 1882 Zola decided to end his career as a journalist which up to now had taken up to fifty per cent of his time (see Chapter 9); he decided instead to dedicate himself more or less to being a full-time novelist. Now, having made a partial break with the past, the real nature of Zola was beginning to appear. *Pot-bouille* had not sold badly in 1882, though certainly not nearly as well as *Nana*. *Au bonheur des dames,* published by Charpentier in 1883, was even less successful than its immediate predecessor, and the continuing sharp decline in Zola's popularity was seen in the extremely disappointing sales of *La Joie de vivre,* which was brought out in February 1884.

Everyone was wondering what had happened to him. Was he burnt out by the age of forty-four? Zola asked himself the same questions throughout this bleak period of self-torment and self-examination. He was lost, floundering and depressed. Edmond de Goncourt, a consistent witness to this long depression, did not know what to make of it. In April 1880 he wrote: 'I dined with Zola today. He is sad, with a sadness which gives to his role as master of the house, something of a sleepwalker.'[11] In fact, Zola was depressed even before the deaths of Flaubert and his mother. Was he worrying that he did not have another *Nana* up his sleeve, that he would never be able to repeat this performance? Was it his unhappy, childless marriage? Goncourt did not understand it. Zola became haggard and lugubrious, suffering palpitations of the heart and expressing the fear that he would not have enough time to accomplish what he had set out to do. Goncourt was baffled. 'Life is truly cleverly arranged in such a manner as to afford happiness to no one. Here is a man whose name is heard everywhere, whose books sell by the hundreds of thousands, who, perhaps of all the authors, has attracted the most attention,' but instead of being pleased, 'he is unhappier, a sorrier figure, and more dejected than the worst outcast'.[12] It is possible, of course, that Zola, unconsciously, wanted to play down his success before Goncourt, whom he probably realized was terribly jealous of him.

In April 1882, Goncourt and others were invited to Zola's flat in the rue de Boulogne, but he had not changed. Goncourt said that he found him 'sad, morose, greatly wishing to leave Paris . . . indeed, to leave life (if one can believe that) . . . I know it is simply the mood of the moment, the way we all feel at times . . .'[13] A few days later over lunch, Zola was still lugubrious and distressed, and he spoke of plots by the French Academy to try to stop publication of his books. But suddenly he said:

Do you want to know a dream I have . . . if I could earn 500,000 francs over the next ten years . . . I would bury myself in a book which I would never have to finish . . . for example, a history of French literature . . . yes, it would be an excuse for me not to have to communicate with the public again, to retire from writing without announcing it . . . I should then be able to rest.[14]

These were, to be sure, most revealing thoughts. He was sad and afraid, knowing that his present work was not up to scratch, and he had not found a satisfactory theme that would restore his reputation as the author of *Nana*.

When Goncourt, the Daudets and the Charpentiers visited Médan in July of the same year, they found a dismal Zola. He was not happy with the novel he was writing, (*Au bonheur des dames*), and he confided to Goncourt: 'Deep down, I know I'll never be able to write another book which will be able to cause a stir the way *L'Assommoir* or *Nana* did.' Goncourt's final comment in his journal that evening was surprisingly perceptive: 'Returning from Médan, I realized that a household can exist without children in a Paris apartment, but not in a house in the country. Nature requires little ones.'[15]

11
A Social Conscience

Despite the fears of Alexandrine, the trek by horseback up the narrow trail leading away from the mountain spa-town of Mont-Dore was not difficult. A couple of weeks after their arrival in the summer of 1884, Zola had tried to arrange for an excursion up to the famous Puy de Sancy. He had been warned against it by some of the local people, including his guide, an old *montagnard* by the colourful name of *Gras Roux* (Fat Red), to whom Zola took a liking. Even though it was only mid-August, the guide argued that the weather was changing rapidly, the season was already too far advanced, especially above 2000 feet, and they would be going well beyond that. Nonetheless Zola tried to set out twice, but each time the foul weather stopped him. He was deeply moved by the imposing mountains and extinct volcanic craters of Monts-Dômes, describing them as a 'lunar landscape'.[1] The waterfalls and raging rivers were splendid; everything about the place appealed to Zola. With rare good humour he wrote: ' . . . for a dyed-in-the-wool naturalist like myself, it is indeed a wildly romantic journey'.[2]

It had taken the Zolas a week to recuperate from the fatigue of the journey from Paris to the mountains, but living in a hotel, albeit at the comfortable Hôtel Chaboury Aîné, was not pleasant for a man used to his study. However, it was an interesting and stimulating change. The day-trips to the Murols and Latour were pleasant, and Zola was enchanted by the greenness of the Vallon de la Scierie. 'Picture the rocky hills of Provence,' he wrote to Paul Alexis, 'but covered with lush grass and the most beautiful trees in the world.'[3] But Sancy, the tallest of the imposing mountain range and the one which Céard had mentioned to him earlier, was on his mind, despite the setbacks to his original plans to conquer it. In the middle of August he had completed reading George Sand's *Jean de la Roche*, and perhaps it was the ending of that book, taking place as it did at the peak of Puy de Sancy, that made him more determined not to miss it.

Theoretically, the Zolas had come to this resort so that Alexandrine might take the waters, and the young Dr Magitot, who was treating her (prescribing so many glasses of water, so many hot baths and showers of the mineral-rich waters), was very friendly. One day he called Zola into his office to look at the phtisis bacillus — which caused consumption — under a microscope. 'Hardly a reassuring sight', Zola wrote, 'knowing full well that the bacillus abounds in these hotels'.[4] If truth were known, this holiday was probably more necessary for Zola, after an exhausting year's work, than for his wife, and he felt refreshed and markedly stronger as a result. His letters to friends became unusually long, full of interest and even good cheer, reflecting his new energy. Zola again seemed to be his old self. Even his wife, whose perennial hypochondria must have been the cause of some annoyance, stopped complaining, finding the rich mineral water cure soothing and efficacious.

It was in the last week of August that they decided to make one last attempt to go up to Sancy before returning to Médan. Dr Magitot accompanied them with his own guide and supplied two horses, both of which seemed in dubious shape, however, and Zola began to worry even before leaving. Neither Zola nor his wife had ever been on a horse before, but he was game, even if it meant many hours in the saddle. Alexandrine began complaining at the very start and maintained a steady incantation from then on, which included a grumble that the saddle was too small for her. Climbing up the mountain, after crossing the Dordogne, was not difficult, even for the uninitiated. Actually reaching the peak they found to be a disappointment, especially after having anticipated what George Sand had described. Their difficulties arose as they began to descend along the hairpin turns of the exceedingly narrow trail, which wound along dramatically sheer cliffs. Zola was worried about his wife's nag getting out of hand, and had an argument with the guide over it. The guide must hold the reins of her horse, Zola insisted. The guide (unfortunately not the good Gras Roux) complained that no one had ever asked him to do that before. But he consented, and for a few hundred metres did hold the reins, dropping them a little later, however, in order to pick flowers. Zola again insisted, but the stubborn *montagnard* simply gave the horse an occasional switch on the rump. Zola feared the horse would now start trotting. The guide continued to gather flowers, stopping occasionally to goad the animal on. The last time he did so Alexandrine's horse bolted forward and she went flying, but with one foot caught in a stirrup. Zola rushed to her side as she lay hanging there, crying hysterically, her head on the path, her foot in the air. It took Zola and Magitot working together to free her twisted foot, but after resting a few minutes the doctor declared her well enough to proceed. By now the mountains were cold as the late afternoon shadows deepened; although they were dressed warmly, they would have to leave quickly if they did not want to be overcome by darkness. Alexandrine resolutely refused to mount the horse again, in spite of her sore ankle, and so they all walked the remaining two hours of the trip down the mountain's winding canyon to their hotel. Madame Zola was in a terrible mood, and Zola was furious with the old guide.

With the exception of the 'wild solitude' of this part of the Auvergne,[5] Zola lost interest in these mountains which had so recently fascinated him. But there was something else on his mind now. He had hardly touched *Germinal* through the month of August. It was high time to get back to that manuscript which he had begun writing in March.

When the police watching Zola's apartment in the rue de Boulogne reported, on 2 April 1884, that the author had left Paris, they were over a month late, for he had left by 23 February. Surveillance of the author had been in effect since September 1873:[6] clearly he was an 'enemy of the people'. The police report indicated that Zola had left for Belgium 'to study the coal-mines for a major novel'.[7] If the detective filing the report was correct about the reason for Zola's departure, the destination was not, for when he, his wife, and Alfred Giard (a member of the extreme left of the Chamber of Deputies) departed from the Gare du Nord, it was for Giard's constituency at Valenciennes, just south of the Belgian border. They sat in their first class compartment talking about the serious situation resulting from the miners' strike in the northern coal-mining towns. The train proceeded via Senlis, Compiègne, Péronne and Cambrai, reaching Valenciennes the afternoon of Saturday, 23 February. It was all settled. They would check into the hotel, where Zola would continue his reading and note-taking, in preparation for Monday morning, when he would begin to carry out his projected series of field trips. He made lists of the things he wanted to accomplish, including visits to mines and mining towns, talks with mine officials and engineers, and plans to accompany Giard when he met the miners in their assembly halls, 'International' centres (communist-inspired clubs), and in their drinking haunts. In January Zola had finally decided to write his 'mining novel', which would tackle pressing social problems. Now he would execute his plans.

When twenty-three scattered groups of workers across France had tried to form a union in 1872, the police immediately intervened, dissolving the group, as they did two years later when a similar union tried to meet in Lyons. A far-reaching law was passed in 1874 making it illegal for women and children to work in the mines. In 1879 a congress met in Marseilles, representing 60,000 workers across the country; socialist spokesman, Jules Guesde, demanded laws ensuring the right of workers to meet and form unions everywhere, and also called for collective ownership of industry. At the very moment Zola was preparing his novel in March 1884, legislation was finally passed permitting unions to form legally.[8]

However, Frenchmen feared the workers and possible rebellion by them, and Jules Ferry had not helped matters when in the previous year he had cried out before the French parliament, 'It is the leftists who threaten us.'[9] Zola was familiar with the fight by the workers for protective legislation, just as he was familiar with the numerous strikes which began to plague the country in the 1860s, increasing in number in the 1870s and 1880s. He could not understand, however, the workers' dislike of sending their own representatives to the Chamber, a feeling which was later summed up by one union leader addressing the General Confederation of Labour: 'To send workers into parliament is to act like a mother who would take her daughters into a house of prostitution.'[10] Zola's parliamentary guide in the north-western mining districts was, fortunately, not that extreme.

Most people opposed the position taken by the workers, and as the provincial newspaper, *Le Progrès de Saône-et-Loire,* said of the strikers at Blanzy and Montceau-les-Mines who had just blown up two church buildings — 'Those individuals are doing everything possible to discredit our republican form of government, limiting themselves to sowing seeds of terror, and not making any specific demands [for changes] . . . '[11] When news broke that an assistant mine director had been killed by miners, Edouard Drumont shouted from the pages of *La France Juive,* 'Victory! Blood has been shed and, contrary to all precedents, it is the blood of the bosses, of the capitalists.'

Zola had gone to north-west France in February 1884 because 12,000 men employed by the Anzin Coal Mines (just west of Valenciennes) had gone on strike. He wanted to document everything for his book, the scenes of which would take place back in the 1860s, during the last years of the reign of Louis Napoleon. The miners of this area were then earning less than 2000 francs a year, and some only half that. The humble miners of those bleak, treeless villages lived in narrow terraced houses built in the shadows of slag heaps near the pithead. Theirs was a hard life and they could not even apply the old French maxim, 'My cup may not runneth over, but it is at least all mine.' No, their wages were poor, their houses were rented from the Anzin Mining Company, the shops were company shops, the streets were company streets, and even the doctors were employed by the company. But even when legislation was passed making it possible to join unions, to develop strike funds and health insurance, French mine and factory workers were cautious. The peasant feared Louis Blanc's socialism and Karl Marx's communism (*Das Kapital* having been translated into French in 1880), for fear that all property would become collective property, and that no one would be allowed a house and land of his own. The mine and factory workers refused to support the organized unions in sufficiently large numbers, which made the closure of entire mines by unorganized miners seem all the more dramatic. By 1890 there were still only 139,000 union members in a country of over four million workers,[12] but their number would soon increase as a result of laws passed in 1881 and 1882 providing free, compulsory primary education for all children between seven and thirteen years of age (certainly the most revolutionary legislation passed in France in the nineteenth century).

The Anzin miners' strike was ideal for Zola's purposes as it permitted him to see the faces, hear the voices, and observe the acts of these desperate human beings who, unprotected by the laws of the land and hard pressed by the harshness of the mine owners, had no choice but to strike when their wages were reduced and they could not keep their families in bread. This would be Zola's industrial, socialist, communist study *par excellence.* Although others had written about miners, for example, Malot's *Sans famille* (The Foundling), Talmeyer's *Grisou* (Fire-damp) and Guyot's *L'Enfer social* (Living Hell), no one had written as Zola was to write.

The strike had begun officially on 21 February (1884); by the twenty-fifth, Zola was at the administration office of the Anzin Company to obtain a pass enabling him to inspect the scene. Henri de Forçade, in charge of the Anzin mines for the Valenciennes region, wrote out a pass on Monday, 25 February: 'Monsieur Emile Zola is authorized to visit the establishments of the Company above and below ground.'[13] And Zola recorded in his 'Notes on Anzin': 'As for the strike, everyone is very calm. At the outset, no misery yet, and they think they will win.'[14] The mood soon changed, however, for these men with no personal savings, and only a modest strike fund, were extremely vulnerable. The Zolas went on daily visits from Valenciennes to the region round Marchiennes and Denain. Zola descended some 1800 feet into the mines and inspected every detail, from pickaxe to the safety chutes of the lifts. He went through the soot-covered villages, the miners' homes, and spent hours talking with the miners, their wives and children, asking questions, then listening intently. The men were not afraid to speak to Zola. At Denain, the centre of union activity, he spoke with Emile Basly, a local leader, and attended the miners' meeting there. When he returned to his hotel room late at night, he sat down to record the day's events. He prepared maps of the mines and the villages, recorded the miners' illnesses, and conversations with company engineers and administrators. He prepared notes about, amongst other things, the strikes, the Anzin Company, socialism, mine engineering and miners' grievances and mores.

Finally, by 8 March, he had what he wanted, and returned to Paris, only too glad to leave the desolation of the northern mines far behind. In Paris he continued to work on the outlines of his theme and the details of each section of the book. But first he had to see more company officials, including Paul Lebret, and the mining engineer, Emile Dormoy. He spoke to socialists in Paris and heard Jules Guesde speak, the same Jules Guesde who would later help him with the technical parts of *La Terre.*[15] As usual, he did a great deal of background reading — this time on miners, the Labour movement, mine engineering and medicine.[16] He went to the Bibliothèque Nationale to look up articles on strikes, consulting most often the *Gazette des Tribunaux* and *Le Temps.* Every movement was an effort for the overweight Zola, but his enthusiasm would not permit him to relent. He was a man dedicated to, and driven by, a cause — the cause of social justice.

By the middle of March most of his documentation was ready. The strike at Anzin continued, and would last a total of fifty-six days, becoming one of the longest strikes in recent French history. By the end of the third week in March Zola was back in Médan, where he would remain (with the exception of his summer holiday at Mont-Dore), until his task was done. With a massive 952 pages of notes prepared he was ready to begin writing the book that was to become his masterpiece.

Only one thing remained for Zola to do, and that was to select a title. He had some difficulty in finding something special for his 'socialist novel'. He considered 'The Underground Fire', 'The Hatching Fire' and 'The Burning Earth', but they did not fit what he wanted to say. He considered 'The Shaking Château', 'The Swing of the Pickaxe' and, more appropriately, 'The Red Harvest', but he soon discarded them and others. Next he thought of 'The Sprouting Seed' and 'Budding Blood', but they were awkward, imprecise and unpoetical. As he later explained to a friend,

> . . . one day, by chance, the word *Germinal* came to my lips [Germinal was the seventh month of the French revolutionary calendar (21 March-19 April)]. At first I did not like it, as it seemed too mystical, too symbolic; but it did represent what I was looking for, a revolutionary April, the flight of a bankrupt society in the springtime. And, little by little, I got used to it, indeed so well, that I was unable to find anything better. If it seems a bit obscure to some readers, it was a real ray of light for me, which illuminated the entire work.[17]

Zola's work went on very well, despite the vast complexity of references and cross-references in his hundreds of notes, and following his summer holiday he returned to his desk at Médan. In letters to his friends he complained that this book was really a great deal of work, this 'damned thing', as he repeatedly called it. But then he always complained like that of every book he ever wrote, so his friends merely smiled, for Zola only said that when he was happily hard at work. He did not think *Germinal* would be a popular book, a big seller, as he told Céard. But that did not disturb him in the least. 'It is one of those books one does for oneself, for one's own conscience.'[18] Finally, on 25 January 1885, he wrote Charpentier, 'My good friend, *Germinal* is finally finished!'[19]

When the book was published in March 1885, it caused a great stir, and though its sales never approached those of *Nana*, it did much better than Zola thought it would. In Clemenceau's newspaper, *La Justice*, Gustave Geoffroy wrote a long laudatory critique, concluding: 'Is this not enough to show in Emile Zola the poet which one usually refuses to acknowledge in the man, the pantheistic poet?'[20] Jules Lemaître, who occasionally criticized Zola in the past, now echoed these sentiments, praising him in *La Revue Politique et Littéraire,* calling him an 'epic poet'. Zola was indeed pleased by this, particularly as his previous works had been so misunderstood.

However, not everyone liked the book. Henry Duhamel criticized it in *Le Figaro* on factual grounds, saying that women did not work down the mines now, but Zola, of course, had set the story towards the end of the Second Empire when women still did work in the mines; Duhamel was simply a sloppy reviewer who had not read the book properly. He also criticized Zola for painting the poor miners as sub-human, living in filth and being more immoral than was true. But in an angry letter to the publisher of *Le Figaro,* Zola wrote that the situation in mining communities was indeed as he had depicted it.

> Do not contradict me out of sheer sentimentality; instead, be so good as to look up the statistics, inform yourself by inspecting the places and situations described, and then you will see if I have lied . . . I am accused of filthy fantasy and of premeditated lies concerning those poor people whose plight has filled my eyes with tears. I can answer every such accusation with a document. Why on earth should I of all people want to slander those wretched souls? I have had only one wish throughout — to show just what our society had made of them, and to raise a cry for pity and justice; France must stop a handful of ambitious politicians from devouring the country, and spend more time interesting itself in the health and welfare of its children, who are the country's real wealth.[21]

Germinal, certainly one of the masterpieces of European literature, has a moral, but its moral is a warning, as the author wrote to an acquaintance at the end of the year:

> *Germinal* is a work of pity, and not a work of revolution. What I wanted to do was to cry out to the fortunate, 'Beware, look underground, see those wretches who labour and suffer. There is perhaps still time . . . but hurry to be just, otherwise, the peril is there for all to see; the earth will open up and engulf our nations in one of the most frightful upheavals in history.'[22]

12
A Plateau

Henry Vizetelly's publishing company had introduced *Uncle Tom's Cabin* by Harriet Beecher Stowe and Edgar Allan Poe's *Tales of the Grotesque and Arabesque* to England, and since then had published works by Gogol, Lermontov, Dostoevsky and Tolstoy, as well as numerous French writers, including Daudet, Malot, Sand, Mérimée, and almost everything produced by Zola's pen. Now, in the spring of 1887, George Moore approached Zola on behalf of Vizetelly enquiring whether he would sell him the English rights to *La Terre*. After various delays an agreement was reached, contracts were signed and exchanged, and Vizetelly, after numerous expurgations, published that novel.

Then, without warning, the National Vigilance Association of London, comprised chiefly of clergymen, attacked the English publisher's 'pornographic literature'. They cited all of Zola's works, as well as Flaubert's *Madame Bovary* and *Salammbô*, Goncourt's *Germinie Lacerteux*, Gautier's *Mlle de Maysin*, Maupassant's *Bel-ami* and *Une Vie*, Daudet's *Sapho* and Paul Bourget's *Crime d'amour*. Curiously enough, in Great Britain at this time Zola was the least well known of all the major contemporary French writers.

Samuel Smith, M.P. for Flintshire, rose before Parliament in May 1888 to denounce in a high pitched voice the 'pernicious literature' then invading Victorian England. ' . . . This House deplores the rapid spread of demoralizing literature in this country, and is of the opinion that the law against obscene publications and indecent pictures and prints should be vigorously enforced and, if necessary, strengthened.' In the ensuing debate, Vizetelly was branded 'the chief culprit in the spread of pernicious literature' and then, discussing Zola by name, Smith said of the author's works that 'nothing more diabolical had ever been written by the pen of man; they are only fit for swine, and those who read them must turn their minds into cesspools.'[1] Henry Matthews, the Home Secretary, not to be outdone, said that modern French literature 'was written with the object of directing attention to the foulest passions of which human nature was capable, and to depict them in the most attractive forms'.[2] How something so foul could be made most attractive is not clear, but Mr Smith's motion was passed, although the government hesitated to institute proceedings, it being their belief that private individuals should do so.

Meanwhile a campaign against pornography raged in the English press. Lord Mount-Temple attacked pornography in a letter to the *Guardian*, then the Church of England's paper, and widened the scope of battle to include Sir Richard Burton's translation of the *Arabian Nights*. The Roman Catholic newspaper, the *Tablet*, published a fresh attack against Zola. A letter in the *Globe* commented that Zola's books 'sapped the foundations of manhood and womanhood', while a Birmingham newspaper said that 'Zola simply wallowed in immorality'.[3] The *Whitehall Review* demanded that Zola's London publisher be prosecuted immediately. Clearly the situation in England was beginning to look ominous.

The pressure built up and a firm of solicitors, Collette & Collette, applied at Bow Street police-court for a summons against the nefarious publisher, Henry Vizetelly, and got it. Three 'obscene' books were named in the summons, all by Zola: *Nana, Pot-bouille* and *La Terre*. Herbert Asquith (later to be Prime Minister), prosecuting for the Crown, referred to Zola's works as 'the three most immoral books ever published'.[4] Messrs. Lewis & Lewis, representing Vizetelly, argued that these books had been carefully expurgated prior to publication, whereas the original (unexpurgated) French versions were circulating and selling freely in England at that very moment. Mr Asquith thought this irrelevant. To support his case, Vizetelly presented equally 'dangerous' extracts from writers whose works were then freely available in England: Shakespeare, Beaumont and Fletcher, Massinger, Ford, Carew, Dryden, Congreve, Prior, Defoe, Swift, Sterne, Fielding, Smollet and Byron. The magistrate declared this a matter for a jury to settle at the Central Criminal Court.

The trial took place at the Old Bailey in October 1888. The Solicitor-General, Sir Edward Clarke, represented the Crown. During the course of the trial it was agreed that all of Zola's books would be withdrawn from circulation in England, and Vizetelly made an undertaking not to publish any more of Zola's works. After numerous delays the case was finally concluded in May of the following year and the sixty-nine-year-old publisher was sentenced to several months in Holloway Prison. Zola was the only writer to have his works outlawed in England in the nineteenth century.

The leaves were almost completely out by the end of the first week of May 1886, as Zola's coach followed the ancient road between Châteaudun and Cloyes, some 160 kilometres south-west of Paris and nearly fifty kilometres west of Orléans. Driving along the well-made road brought to mind the peasants who had been forced to maintain it under the Bourbon kings, and who, during the Revolution, had later been forced by poverty to march along it to Paris. Zola's mind concentrated on the peasants; he had read numerous studies on the subject, including Joseph Bonnemère's work, *Histoire des paysans* (History of the Peasants), and had got the socialist view of the peasant in history from Jules Guesde, the controversial Marxist editor of *Le Cri du Peuple*. Zola had decided some while earlier on an unusual subject for his next work — 'I want to try a kind of poem on the soil'[5] — and it was the rich land of the Beauce, from whence his mother and her forbears had sprung, that he was to study and whose portrait he would paint. His carriage would soon be at Cloyes where he was to meet a farmer who had agreed to act as his guide. Zola and his wife had intended to spend these weeks in May at a local farm, not telling the farmer the real purpose of the visit, but it seems they changed their minds and stayed at a hotel instead.

Before leaving for Cloyes, Zola had spent the entire day at the bustling cattle market at Châteaudun; nothing must escape his eye or nose. The village he would create for this massive, controversial novel, *La Terre*, would lie here in the Beauce, along the river Loir, running through Illiers via Cloyes and Vendôme, and spilling into the larger river Loire. This tome would be his tone poem of the land, and a tribute to his ancestors.

With the completion of *L'Œuvre* in February 1886, Zola was free to dedicate his restless energies to his new task. *L'Œuvre* was typical of his sandwiched-in novels: after every major novel, he had to relax, and as he could not simply stop working, he wrote a less demanding, a less important work, in this case, *L'Œuvre* (that is, following *Germinal*), which sold far fewer copies than his previous half dozen novels. Yet he liked it, even if the public didn't, and Cézanne and Monet complimented him on it as well, and that was all that mattered. Now he was preparing his huge new work, and any work by Zola bearing the title, *The Earth*, had to be huge and startling. What was there in Zola that made him want to startle the world? Perhaps it was that he felt that everyone in the country was complacent and apathetic, and had to be jolted, to start thinking about life, to look round themselves, for was not life startling? Was not mankind amazing?

By mid-June, back at Médan, Zola was ready to begin *La Terre*. He swore that he would not let this book appear in serialized form, as fragmented publication of this kind would ruin the overall effect.[6] But in May of the following year, *La Terre* did indeed begin appearing in Xau's newspaper, *Gil Blas*. His friend had twisted his arm, he claimed; his willpower was not strong enough to oppose him. He had been offered 40,000 francs for the serial rights alone and it would be foolish to throw away that much money — although Zola would not admit to himself that this was the reason for his capitulation. After all, it was argued that those really interested in literature would only read it later as a complete volume when Charpentier published it in November 1887. Had Zola not always admonished his friends never to read his books in a serialized, edited, censored version? (Some of his friends, Goncourt and Mirbeau among them, claimed to adhere to this stricture.)

When *La Terre* came out that November, there was a terrible outcry. The most surprising review, based on the *Gil Blas* publication even before it was completed, came from the outraged Anatole France:

His work is bad and of these unfortunate tomes one might best say that it would have been better if they had never been written. I cannot deny his detestable glory. No one before him has ever created such a heap of filth. That is his monument, the greatness of which no one can contest. Never has a man made such an effort to vilify humanity, to insult every aspect of beauty and love, to deny all that is good and decent.

And then France went on to cast grave aspersions on the name of Zola, from a highly personal, but unrealistic viewpoint . . .

There is in us all, in the humble as well as the great, an instinct for beauty, a desire throughout the world to find that which ornaments and decorates, which give life its charm. M. Zola does not realize this. In man there is an infinite need to love which reflects godliness. M. Zola does not realize this. Desire and humility sometimes combine in precious nuances in the soul. M. Zola does not realize this. Many men want to be just and wise. Some of them only find real joy by renouncing and sacrificing. M. Zola does not realize this. In this world there are some magnificent forms and noble thoughts, as well as pure souls and heroic hearts, but M. Zola does not realize this. Many weaknesses and errors have their own form of beauty . . . Misfortune occurs to make man majestic before man. M. Zola does not realize this. He does not seem to know that it is the decent things in life which grace it, nor that philosophical irony can be both indulgent and gentle. As for common decency, it can inspire only one of two things in humanity: admiration or pity. M. Zola is worthy of our profound pity.[7]

Octave Mirbeau's review of the new book was scarcely kinder, prompting Zola to defend his observations about the peasants and pointing to the extensiveness of his research. 'Will you allow me to be stubborn about my work? Everyone throws out "his" concept of what the peasant is really like. Then why should mine, alone, be false?'[8] Goncourt told Zola that he did not agree with all of *La Terre*, but thought it was, nevertheless, 'painted by the hand of a master'.[9] Huysmans wrote to say that his first impression was 'that of an incontestable grandeur'.[10] Today, of course, it is ranked amongst the five or six great works written by Zola.

One incident concerning *La Terre*, which at first seemed hardly worth noticing, arose soon after its serialization in *Gil Blas*. In the middle of August 1887, an article entitled '*Manifeste des cinq*' (Manifesto of the Five) appeared in *Le Figaro;* it was a vicious, immature attack on Zola's book, on his present work in general, and on his person. (See also Chapter 13.)

Despite Zola's denials to the contrary, he was hurt by the attack, which was signed by five young men named Bonnetain, Rosny, Descaves, Margueritte and Guiches. They were not his 'followers' or friends, though he had met them at Goncourt's and Daudet's houses. It was an unpleasant incident best forgotten, but this was not to be. It now involved two friends, whose friendship had been gradually waning since the deaths of Flaubert in 1880 and Turgenev in 1883, this becoming much more apparent after the publication of the 'Manifesto' article. The five young men were followers and friends of Alphonse Daudet and Edmond de Goncourt, and the rumour soon circulated from *salon* to *salon* that Daudet and Goncourt had known about the attack prior to its publication, and had probably put the young men up to it in the first place. Zola said he did not believe it, and he told Huysmans that he thought young Bonnetain was probably responsible. As for *La Terre*, he said it would stand or fall on its own merits, and was not his affair.

With that, the Zolas packed their trunks and boarded the train for Royan, Charpentier's home, just north of Bordeaux. It was while they were there that the storm began to break, although some events leading up to it had begun before that. In the 1880s Zola had unconsciously isolated himself more and more from his friends, especially Daudet and Goncourt. Jealousy was the primary reason for Goncourt's gradual alienation; Zola's name was on everyone's lips and his books were setting new sales records at a time when Goncourt was being overshadowed. The schism between Daudet and Zola was never that great, some maintained, despite attempts by Goncourt and others to widen the gap. Daudet's son, Lucien, later testified to this, not only claiming 'there was always a real friendship' between his father and Zola, but that Goncourt was jealous of both men. As for Zola's relationship with Goncourt, he insisted that the latter's very presence 'made Zola as nervous as it did Goncourt himself'.[11] Thus the basis for a break predates the 'Manifesto' article of August 1887.

Their friendship was put to the test, however, one evening in April 1886 when Zola and Goncourt both found themselves at Daudet's. Zola indicated his dislike of Edouard Drumont. As a close friend of Drumont, Daudet was angered and disturbed. Writing to Zola a few days later, Daudet said how cruel Zola had been in speaking out against 'this fine lad' (as he called him). 'I am saying all this so that you do not again cause one of your wearisome, neurotic scenes like the one the other evening at my place.'[12] This was pretty strong language and Zola was stung to the quick, replying immediately:

> . . . the post-script of your letter has absolutely amazed me. Am I not allowed to judge Drumont freely, when he, on numerous occasions, has written about me with neither thought nor dignity? He is your friend, and I know it, but am I not also your friend? . . . There is a growing

misunderstanding between us, making it impossible for us to say what we think without wounding each other, and a divergence in both ideas and words which separates us more and more. Your letter has deeply hurt me, for it is yet another proof of the illness which is killing the 'trio'.[13]

This bitter exchange was aggravated the following year when rumour connected the 'Manifesto' with the names of Daudet and Goncourt. Fernand Xau immediately interviewed Zola about the article and this was published in *Gil Blas* on 21 August 1887.

What would be most interesting to know is what has made these young men break out so vehemently against someone whom they do not know at all well. Some have said that perhaps they reflect the views of people whom I hold in high esteem, both in a literary and professional sense, and who profess the same ideas about me. I refuse to believe it . . .

But obviously Zola would not have said this in print if he had not had pretty solid suspicions, especially concerning Goncourt. Interestingly enough, Goncourt, who was in the midst of publishing his celebrated *Journal,* had recorded in that same book on 18 August 1887, his distress at the 'Manifesto', which he cheerfully referred to as 'a literary execution of Zola'. He went on to write (for the whole world to see, of course) ' . . . Daudet knew no more about the 'Manifesto of the Five' than I did about those five who committed their misdeed in the greatest secrecy. At this time when the press is grovelling before Zola, we find it a courageous act,' but he conceded that attacking Zola's physical person was outrageous.[14] The wording of this journal entry is extremely revealing, clearly showing Goncourt's jealousy and hatred of Zola.[15]

When Goncourt later read Zola's rather obvious remarks in *Gil Blas,* he described them as 'Machiavellian and perfidious all under the cloak of bonhomie. Ah, that scurvy, Italianism!' As for answering Zola in the press, 'I do not care to reply, as I find that accusation beneath my dignity.'[16] Although after proclaiming his innocence and that of Daudet, yet again Goncourt concluded, 'what grieves me so greatly also prevents me from shaking hands with you . . . ' But now, as Zola admitted, other factors were involved: ' . . . the harm to our friendship does not stem from this gossip. It results from a so-called rivalry which our enemies are trying to make us think exists.'[17] Obviously their enemies were succeeding, for Goncourt referred to Zola's reply as 'a tortuously affected letter which Daudet called pure funk . . . After that letter I can only write to him: let's embrace each other and let bygones be bygones, idiots!'[18]

Over the next couple of years the infamous five were constantly to be found as welcomed guests in the homes of Goncourt and Daudet, so that Zola found it embarrassing even to attempt a visit. The situation became so acute that Mme Charpentier went to see both Goncourt and Daudet and chided them, saying that if this nonsense did not end forthwith, there would be a complete and final break. Goncourt and Daudet finally gave in and issued an invitation to the Zolas. What is sad about this is that Zola forced such an unnatural resolution of the matter. Why continue to see two men who obviously fostered the greatest ill-will towards him? The press, nevertheless, did not relent, and both Zola and the 'five' were made the butt of many a joke.

Needless to say, the relationships were never again the same. Zola rarely saw Goncourt and Daudet, though surprisingly he and Daudet were able to restore their friendship later (at least formally), when Daudet's health was declining.

Within a fortnight of Zola's belated nomination as a Chevalier to the Legion of Honour in July 1888, Goncourt's long pent-up jealousy lashed out suddenly in an interview he gave to *Le Gaulois*, castigating Zola's acceptance of an inferior award, although he had earlier telegraphed Zola with 'sincere congratulations on those most tardy amends'.[19] That night Goncourt noted in his journal:

> Damnation! I would first be hanged had I been Zola, before accepting the decoration at this late hour. He has not realized that he has lowered himself by becoming a 'Chevalier'. No doubt the literary revolutionary one day will become Commander of the Legion of Honour and Permanent Secretary of the Academy, and will end up writing boringly virtuous books that will be given as prizes to young ladies in boarding schools.[20]

Perhaps it grated on Goncourt's sensibilities that his own membership had been brought about by Zola and Daudet pulling strings. (His application for membership of the French Academy had been refused, and Zola's possible acceptance was a major cause of concern.)

Zola's progress continued rapidly, leaving Goncourt further and further behind. In his pathetic interview to *Le Gaulois*, Goncourt intimated that Zola was breaking with his old friends because he was too good for them. Goncourt's twisted words provoked a quick letter of denial from Zola who asked Goncourt why he condemned him for ambitions which he himself had once nurtured. He also broached the painful subject of the French Academy — painful for Goncourt, that is. 'Rest assured that if ever I present myself for the Academy, I shall do so under circumstances where I shall have to forfeit no measure of my pride or independence . . . '[21] Goncourt's reply was indeed bitter: 'Until the present time, there has been some minor unpleasantness, some reciprocal wrongs perhaps, have separated us a bit, but time and circumstances could have again rebuilt our literary triumvirate, whereas now, I see our situation with real grief as we stand at two opposite poles.'[22]

Although the two men continued to see each other socially now and then, their friendship was shattered beyond repair, as the entries in Goncourt's *Journal* increasingly attest. The final and most bitter blow came when Goncourt informed Zola that he would no longer be acceptable as a judge and member of the projected 'Goncourt Academy'; he was to be replaced by Octave Mirbeau.

The phases of Zola's life were being shed like so many layers of skin. By the end of 1887, he was preparing his notes on the next novel, *Le Rêve* (The Dream). Ostensibly he wrote this book because it was part of the *Rougon-Macquart* series, and to reveal the role of heredity, in this case involving one of the few normal human beings produced by the Rougon and Macquart families. As its title suggests it was also a fantasy. It was about decent people living decent lives, and it seemed difficult for Zola, at least at this stage of his life, to paint a realistic picture of such people. Perhaps wish fulfillment was involved. Zola was unhappy with his wife and was oppressed by a child-less marriage which was proving more and more onerous, indeed almost masochistic. He was looking for a way out, and by sheer coincidence he began writing *Le Rêve* in January 1888. Or was it coincidence that he should write this particular book in that year? He had shifted novels about in the past and could instead have worked on another part of the *Rougon-Macquart* series, but he selected this work and no other. Death had separated him from the past, and by 1887 disputes had cooled several of his remaining friendships. In fact, it all appears to have been some sort of subconscious plan to establish a new life for himself. Disputes with Mirbeau, Daudet and Goncourt followed a break with Cézanne as well by the mid-1880s. Although Zola had not initiated these breaks, he was now willing to take advantage of them. Soon Céard's star was to fall into a more distant place in the constellation, which thus left very few friends: Alexis, Coste, Huysman, Desmoulins, and the Charpentiers and the Bruneaus in particular.

Another reason why Zola insisted upon writing *Le Rêve* now was because he had been dismayed by the intensity of the criticism levelled at *La Terre,* and he must show the world that not every product of his pen was necessarily crude and decadent, unfit for the eyes of young girls. He planned this novel to be a great surprise.[23] Yes, he would again shock the world, this time through an unexpectedly 'decent' book, and that is precisely what his critics were not expecting. (It would also do no harm to help prepare public opinion for the time when he could apply for the French Academy — an ambition that increasingly preoccupied him.)

In May 1888, Alexandrine hired a twenty-year-old girl by the name of Jeanne Rozerot, who had come fresh from Burgundy, to work as a seamstress at Médan. More than halfway through the writing of *Le Rêve,* Zola fell in love for the first time in his life. By the time the novel was completed in August, he was already planning to set up Jeanne Rozerot in her own apartment in Paris (66, rue Saint-Lazare). He, who had remained faithful to his wife all these years, now strayed for good. The energy he had put into numerous friendships would now be transferred to Jeanne Rozerot. Zola had long been weary of society, and often advocated less and less contact with it. He now carried out this policy, for he would never be able to take Jeanne Rozerot into society, not even to the Daudets or Goncourts. Indeed Edmond de Goncourt only learnt about Jeanne from Alexis late in 1889, after the birth of Zola's daughter, Denise (see Chapter 15). Goncourt was not surprised that Zola had grown tired of Alexandrine's coldness and sought a little warmth elsewhere. As for Zola, he felt youthful again, having found new joy and contentment in life, even to the point of asking Céard whether he could learn to ride a horse after a dozen easy lessons, so that he could trot through the Bois de Boulogne. 'Ah! Zola the equestrian, I just cannot see it!' quipped Goncourt.[24]

When Jules Lemaître reviewed *Le Rêve* on 27 October 1888 in *La Revue Bleue,* he called it a real fantasy; the love of Félicien and Angélique was 'unreal', and he charged Zola with the exasperating crime of having written a romantic novel. Although he admitted the charm of the story, Lemaître thought it was a travesty of the real Zola and declared his preference for the frank and harmonious style of *La Terre*. 'This gentleman who has written such beastly things, my dear, makes innocent virgins tremble at the sight of St Agnes . . . Let him leave the virgins out of this!'[25]

Anatole France was not at all happy with the latest novel either, saying in *Le Temps* that it was the work of a hypocrite. 'Cannot he be decent without advertising it?'[26] Little did they know that the old Zola would soon be back with a vengeance.

Billows of black smoke poured from the shining engine of the passenger train, as it stood beneath the vast, soot-covered glass roof of the Gare St-Lazare (the Parisian terminal of the Western Railway). It was an easy walk for Zola from his Paris apartment in the rue de Boulogne to the railway station. On the morning of 15 April 1889, however, he took a brougham, via the rue d'Amsterdam, past the place de Budapest, to the intersection of the rue St-Lazare, where he paid the cabbie and got down, hurrying to the office of the station master where M. Clérault, the Chief Engineer for the Western Railway, was waiting for him. This time, however, it was not a matter of his getting there on time, as Clérault would hold the train, if needs be, for today's unusual guest of the railway. Zola, meticulously dressed, like a good bourgeois, was never one to throw his weight around and make people dance when he snapped his fingers. Leaving the office together, they hurried through the station to the cab of a waiting train where Zola was introduced to the engineer and the stoker. Zola briskly thanked Clérault, and then climbed up into the cab.

When the last of the passengers were safely aboard, the big engine hissed, the whistle shrieked, the throttle was pushed forward and the train clattered out of the station. The heat of the engine hit Zola in the face as he watched intently every move the engineer made. Not unlike Turner, who had himself tied to the mast of a ship during a gale in order to understand more fully the forces of nature before painting his famous sea pictures, Zola was now perched in the heart of the 'beast' about which he planned to write. The train sped through the green countryside of the Seine Valley, chugging past Médan towards Mantes, nearly sixty kilometres away, where Zola would get off. He had already inspected the line from Paris to Dieppe and Le Havre, making several excursions to the coast, and taking floorplans of the railway stations at Malaunay, St-Lazare and Dieppe. He inspected the yards, the loading and switching facilities, nearby factories, various depots, anything that had to do with railway life — all in preparation for his next novel, *La Bête humaine.* Even the murder to be included in the novel was to be documented from the police files. In fact it was based on at least three different murders which had taken place on board French trains in 1860, 1882 and 1886, including the mysterious death of the Prefect of Police of Eure, on the Cherbourg-Paris Express.

Zola returned to Médan with nearly 700 pages of notes and began writing this monumental work in May 1889. It was a revitalized and rejuvenated Zola at work. Having gone on a diet which involved drinking as few liquids as possible, he had lost nearly three stone, and Goncourt declared, 'I would have passed him in the street without recognizing him.' Although now aged forty-nine, Zola had the energy of a man twenty years younger and relished the task he was embarking on. Describing this book he said,

> The originality lies in the fact that the story takes place, from beginning to end, on the Western Railway line between Paris and Le Havre. The continuous rattle of trains is the sound of progress moving towards the twentieth century, and in the midst of it is a terrible and mysterious drama, unknown to everyone — the human beast under the thin veneer of civilization.[27]

Though he made good progress, and the work began to appear in instalments in mid-November in a new weekly paper called *La Vie Populaire,* Zola did not complete the book until 19 January 1890. His critics liked it, for a change, even those who were usually his greatest detractors. Jules Lemaître, writing in *Le Figaro,* called it 'a prehistoric epic under the guise of a contemporary story' expressed with 'a fierce and melancholic majesty'.[28] Anatole France, writing in *Le Temps,* was amazed and called his new creation 'immortal', declaring Zola to be 'the poet of our times'.[29]

13
End of an Era

In many respects the years 1889-92 represent the end of an era for Zola, yet in another sense, the apogee of his career. By 1890 he had certainly given up any serious attempts as a dramatist. Although he had seen his five plays produced by 1889, he was generally not pleased with the results. After this time he made no further attempts in the field of drama, but he did continue to work as librettist to Bruneau in the field of lyric opera.

Zola had become a father for the first time in the autumn of 1889, and his little family was completed two years later with the birth of a son. Thus his life-long wish to become paterfamilias was realized as he approached his fiftieth year. The revived, thinner Zola was indeed a new man.

The years of unrelenting toil and dedication had resulted in a rich harvest, for when the *Rougon-Macquart* series was at last concluded in June 1893, it totalled twenty volumes and some 2,500,000 words. It had been a gigantic undertaking that most authors would never have even contemplated. What is more important, he had achieved precisely what he had set out to do. From a materialistic viewpoint, he was by now a relatively wealthy man. There was little more he could ask for, and with the exception of his plans for future works, there was little more he wanted, and that is a rare event in anyone's life. He was as contented as he would ever be.

In August 1889 he had written to Charpentier saying, 'I want desperately to conclude my *Rougon-Macquart* series as soon as possible. I should like to see it finished by January 1892.'[1] Closing Médan for the season, the Zolas returned to Paris on 10 September 1889, moving into their new (and last) apartment at 21 bis, rue de Bruxelles, where the novelist continued to work *'avec rage'* on *La Bête humaine*, which he intended to have out of the way by Christmas.

Ten days after his return to the capital, Jeanne Rozerot gave birth to their daughter, Denise. Zola was ecstatic — 'I feel as if I were twenty again, capable of tackling any job'[2] — but sadly there were very few friends with whom he could share this delight, for the formidable Alexandrine had made the subject taboo to one and all. She had accepted news of the liaison and then of the pregnancy only after a furious storm which abated somewhat when she had taken this expensive new apartment in the rue de Bruxelles. The accommodation was spacious, consisting of both the ground and first floors, while tenants with their own separate staircase occupied the upper floors.[3] The large dining-room looked on to a garden, an essential that Zola always insisted upon. There were two drawing-rooms and two master bedrooms upstairs, in addition to the author's comfortable study overlooking the street. Later, however, he was to have real problems here with traffic noise, especially during the Dreyfus Affair when the windows of the house were shattered more than once by rocks. The apartment had forced-air central heating, which was not yet common in France, though of course each room also had its own traditional fireplace as well.

With the publication of *La Bête humaine*, Zola immediately began researching his next book, *L'Argent* (Money). 'I don't want to ensconce myself in the countryside without first having collected all my documents.'[4] He was to spend close to four weeks in the Paris Stock Exchange, learning how that unfamiliar world worked. He never bought stocks and shares and did not believe in investing, as he felt that it made a cult of money. He read dozens of books and articles on the subjects of banking, high finance, stocks and socialism, and he took vast quantities of notes on those books.[5] He also took notes on interviews, including an important one with Raphaël-Georges Lévy (of the influential Banque de Paris et des Pays-Bas), as well as collecting miscellaneous material on silver mines, steamship lines and banking projects. Zola's preliminary investigation resulted in the eventual accumulation of 875 pages of documentation, so it is no wonder that *L'Argent* was one of the most difficult and complicated of his books.

Originally he planned to include a section on socialism, as it seemed to rear its head in every subject he tackled. However, he was never able to master the material on that subject, and *L'Argent* contains much less on it than Zola had anticipated. The book has two main themes: the history of the Banque Universelle (based on the Union Générale), and the role of Jews in Parisian finance (see also Chapter 16). In this book '. . . I neither attack nor defend money, I show it as a force which is still necessary today as a factor in civilization and progress . . . '[6] The protagonist is Aristide Saccard, of *La Curée*, who builds up a formidable Catholic banking house, which rises like a meteor, only to fall again just as quickly. He argues that much money has to be available — even if most of it is squandered or its application abused — in order to create the few beneficial things civilization has to offer, such as hospitals, roads, bridges and schools.

Zola began writing the book on 16 June 1890 at Médan where he spent the entire summer, mostly in his study (or at the nearby village of Verneuil where Jeanne and their daughter, Denise, were staying). He was not getting much pleasure from writing about money and the business world, admitting that he found the effort to continue back-breaking. However, by the time he returned to the rue de Bruxelles in mid-October, he had completed two-thirds of the book, all according to plan.

About the only relaxation Zola appeared to find now was in reading, which usually included a novel in the evening before retiring. It was at this time that he read Alphonse Daudet's latest work, *Port-Tarascon*, all at one sitting, then hastened to congratulate that author on yet another successful publication.[7] The postman occasionally brought him some unexpectedly humorous moments, as for example, when the president of the Society Against the Abuse of Tobacco wrote asking Zola whether or not he thought smoking was bad for one's health and also had an unhealthy effect on French literature. Zola replied:

> I have no set opinion on the subject you ask about. Personally, I stopped smoking ten or twelve years ago on the advice of my physician, at a time when I thought I had heart trouble. But to believe that tobacco has an influence over French literature is a bit much; it would really require scientific proof by you. I have seen some great writers who smoke, and their intelligence has not suffered from it. If genius is neurotic, why on earth would you want to heal it? Perfection is such a bore, that I often regret having given up tobacco . . .[8]

Zola and Alexandrine returned to Médan for the Christmas and New Year holidays, as they always did. The traditional Zola house party at this time should indeed have been cheering. But *L'Argent* seemed to cast a long shadow over all the festivities, or as he complained to Daudet: 'My confounded book, which I still have not completed, has nailed me to the table!'[9] It had begun serialization in *Gil Blas* at the end of November and Zola had hoped to complete the manuscript by the first week of January 1891, though he did not do so until the end of the month, and he found this delay maddening.

When *L'Argent* was published in March, it did not sell very well and Zola was not much surprised. The reviews for the most part praised the author's perennial diligence and application. Anatole France found it robust, didactic and encyclopaedic, and although he complained that the style was 'thick and careless', he concluded that 'an extraordinary force animates this heavy machine'.[10]

As President of the Société des Gens de Lettres from 1891 to 1893, Zola had many administrative duties, which included commissioning a statue of Balzac by Rodin. There was some dissent about the method of payment, as Zola vigorously opposed a single private donation. He felt that a work of art purchased by a group of subscribers was a greater tribute to the artist, as it represented the wishes and values of many people, not simply those of an individual.

In the summer of 1891 he asked his friend Frantz Jourdain to offer Auguste Rodin 30,000 francs for the statue of Balzac, the finished product to be delivered by 1 May 1893. However, Rodin's remarkable powers of procrastination resulted in many delays and prompted the Society to commission another statue from Falguière. This was unveiled in the rue Balzac, although Rodin's statue, erected in the place du Palais-Royal, was not completed for another nine years.

Of primary importance to Zola in his role as President was the necessity of establishing a 'literary convention' for the registering of international copyrights between Russia and France. Zola dispatched Elie Kaminsky as the Society's negotiating agent to St Petersburg to secure royalty payments for writers of both countries and to prevent the publication of pirated editions. 'It is hardly necessary for me to repeat my ardent best wishes for your success. It is truly regrettable that such ties of sympathy and integrity don't already exist between our two nations,' concluding that this was indeed 'a fraternal and civilizing task'.[11]

Zola was well suited as representative of the literary society, not simply because of the energy expended, but because of his willingness to encourage younger writers, or even a well-established one who was going through a period of doubt. Nor, for the most part, did he bear literary grudges, even when in some cases he was personally under attack. He was also generous with his own income, especially when it was for a cause in which he believed. For instance, when a few years earlier the small Belgian socialist newspaper, *Le Peuple*, wrote to Zola requesting to publish one of his books, the author replied: 'Take *Germinal* and publish it. I don't want anything from you, since your newspaper is poor and you defend the needy.'[12] Others rarely ever learned of this side of his character, and it would certainly have been hard to imagine Edmond de Goncourt, for example, matching such kindness.

A famous incident involving a sensitive issue concerning Zola's friendship with Paul Margueritte also illustrates the kind of man the author was. Margueritte had been a signatory to the vituperative '*Manifeste des cinq*' published back in August 1887. Among other things the Manifesto had called the *Rougon-Macquart* series an 'absurdity', claiming Zola's genealogical tree to be 'sheer childishness', and it abhorred 'the growing exaggeration of indecency', the 'filthy terminology' in his books, 'his violent preference for obscenity' and considered that he was suffering from a 'disturbance of his equilibrium'. Even though none of the young men responsible for these remarks posed a literary threat to Zola, he had been bitterly hurt, and certain friendships had been irreparably damaged.

Then, upon the publication of *La Débâcle*, in which Zola praises the accomplishments of a division led by General Margueritte, his son, Paul Margueritte, wrote to Zola:

> Let me take advantage of this occasion — I couldn't find a better one —
> to tell you in all honesty of a regret which has been weighing upon me for
> a long time. In associating myself several years ago with that manifesto
> against you I committed an evil act, the importance of which my extreme
> youth prevented me from realizing . . .[13]

In a reply that was modest as well as magnanimous, Zola wrote:

> I am extremely touched, dear M. Margueritte, by your good and noble letter.
> Believe me, it was not expected. But then, that is past history, and I bear
> no grudge. Moreover, you don't owe me any thanks. The glorious death
> of your father leaves him standing upright in history, and it is not simply
> the truthful account of his actions by a novelist that will make him great;
> the actions stand on their own merit. I am no less happy for the circumstances
> which bring us together for it will permit me to shake the hand of a writer
> whom I rate very highly amongst our young novelists.[14]

Zola was equally generous with his peers and their work as well. For
example, he read every book Edmond de Goncourt sent him, and early
in March 1892 congratulated him in glowing terms on the latest volume
of his *Journal* — all this despite the fact that Goncourt had defamed and
ridiculed Zola time and again in his published *Journals*, and pettishly
refused to make him a judge of his literary academy. Zola was similarly
generous with all his friends, as, for instance, with Huysmans, whose recent
book *Certains* (Certain Things), Zola described as 'my great feast over
the past month'.[15] Unlike Goncourt he would not say something critical
with the sole intent of hurting a particular writer.

His graciousness extended even to those unknown to him. In May 1881
Zola received a letter from a group of young men asking him to represent
their district (the fifth *arrondissement* in Paris) in the Chamber of Deputies.
While declaring that he was flattered to be asked, he could not devote
himself to anything part-time, and preferred to carry out his literary
obligations. His letter of regret was both honest and kind.[16]

Zola began to think about the inclusion of a war novel in his *Rougon-
Macquart* series as early as 1869 (a year before the outbreak of the
disastrous Franco-Prussian War), and within a few years was considering
three such volumes: one on the French intervention in Italy on behalf of
the republicans in their struggle for independence from the Hapsburgs;
another on the Franco-Prussian War; and a third on the final stage of that
war, concentrating on the siege of Paris and the Commune of 1871.
Ultimately, he decided to write only one volume, omitting the Italian war,
and concentrating instead on the military campaigns of August and
September 1870, weaving in the Commune at the end.

The book he was to write focused on the causes and events of the battle of Sedan. In his opinion, France was not defeated because of a superior German army, but because of poor French leadership. As usual, Zola was meticulous in his research, later explaining to his Dutch friend, van Santen Kolff, 'I have followed my usual method: walks round the places I'll have to describe in the book; reading all the written documents, which are extraordinarily numerous; finally, long conversations with some of the authors of that drama.'[17]

First he wrote to Alfred Duquet, a historian of that war, asking for a detailed list of all the marches made by the units of the Armée de Châlons, leading up to Sedan. On receipt of this list in April 1892, Zola began his researches in the field, hiring a carriage which he filled with heaps of paper, numerous maps, books and provisions, then setting out for Sedan.

> I visited neither Alsace nor Lorraine. I had wanted to go to Mulhouse and return via Belfort, to follow the same route taken by the 7th Corps during its retreat. My novel opens with that retreat. But I recoiled before the thought of having to ask for a passport [i.e. a German visa] and from the annoying curiosity which my journey would no doubt have aroused [i.e. in territory occupied by Germany].

The title of the work, *La Débâcle*, had been selected a long time in advance. 'It alone states very clearly what my work is about. It isn't only the war, you see, but the downfall of a dynasty and the collapse of an era.'[18]

Considering the wealth of detail and drama centred around Sedan, it is surprising that Zola spent only one week there. Leaving Paris in the middle of April 1891, he went via Vouziers and Chesne, spending one night in each of those places and interviewing peole who had witnessed the war. He reached Sedan on 19 April. During his stay he visited Bouillon and Beaumont, inspecting sites, talking to people, drawing his own maps, and collecting documents. By 25 April he was at Charleville, returning to Paris the next day. He no longer had the patience of his youth to work in the field for weeks at a time, as he had once done for *Germinal*. However, following this visit and his return to Paris, he interviewed dozens of former officers and soldiers of that campaign.

Zola collected more private memoirs, more field maps, read more books and reports, and eventually prepared to sit down and write what was to be his biggest selling novel. Although he had accumulated a daunting surfeit of material — 'I am working violently here to limit this wretched thing,'[19] he told Céard — he was finally able to put his notes aside and begin the text of *La Débâcle* on 18 July.

Several weeks later he wrote to a friend to explain what he hoped to achieve:

First, to tell the truth about the frightful catastrophe which nearly resulted in the death of France. And I can assure you that from the very beginning that did not seem easy, for there are some lamentable factors which our pride has to swallow. But gradually, as I got deeper into that abomination, I realized it was important to tell all . . . I am happy [with the results], and just hope that the readers will take my impartiality into account. While not hiding anything, I did, in fact, want to explain the reasons for our disasters. That seemed to me the noblest and wisest course to follow. I should certainly be content if, in France and Germany, people acknowledge my great effort to tell the full truth. I believe that . . . its honesty will be all the healthier for France.[20]

He went on to explain that the main thrust of the book would be centred round the story of Sedan, including the invasion of the French frontier by German troops, the numerous marches and battles, the inevitable bloodshed, panic and retreats, the relationship of the peasants to the French and German troops, the bourgeoisie in the cities, the foreign occupation of French soil, and the trials of the French under those circumstances. Attempting to cover the entire series of events which took place in 1870 was a huge undertaking, and Zola acknowledged: 'As the saying goes, my eyes are always bigger than my stomach.'[21] He required 'a canvas painted with large brush strokes',[22] as he put it. The book was divided into three general sections. The first would cover the initial defeats of the French Army along the Rhine, after which it fell back to Reims and Sedan. The second section would concentrate entirely on the battle round Sedan. The final part would deal with the German occupation, beginning at Sedan and concluding with the siege of Paris and the Commune.

Zola spent the summer at Médan in order to work on the new manuscript, as well as to keep a close eye on Jeanne Rozerot, who was pregnant again. But in September, after completing the first five chapters of his book, he reluctantly departed with Alexandrine for a holiday in the Pyrenees. The abrupt departure was to spare Alexandrine the humiliation of the imminent birth of Zola's son.

But by January 1892 the 1000-page manuscript was nearly finished: 'I am never happy with a book when I am actually writing it . . . The birth of a book for me is an abominable torture because it can never satisfy my imperious need for universality and totality.'[23] Zola sold the serial rights to *La Vie Populaire*, the first instalment appearing on 21 February 1892. With the conclusion of the serialized version on 21 July, the book was published as a single volume. Although it was Zola's longest book to date, the first 100,000 copies of *La Débâcle* disappeared within days. During his lifetime, 200,000 copies were sold in France alone, making it one of the best-selling works in the French language in the nineteenth century. Zola was delighted: 'The success of *La Débâcle* surpasses all my hopes, and I am as happy as a man could ever be.'[24] Translations appeared simultaneously in Germany, Great Britain, the United States, Portugal, Bohemia, Holland, Denmark, Norway, Sweden and Russia. Everyone read *La Débâcle* — friends, acquaintances, and enemies alike — for it was a subject no Frenchman and few Europeans, could ignore, and having read it, no one could fail to comment on it. Perhaps all the talk would even result in a little thinking.

Gil Blas called this book the 'definitive history of France during the war against Germany'. Gaston Deschamps, writing in *Le Journal des Débats,* referred to it as 'a masterpiece'. Anatole France, reviewing it for *Le Temps,* praised it particularly for understanding what the soldiers felt. Meanwhile, Eugène-Melchior de Vogüé, himself a former soldier, condemned the book from the columns of *La Revue des Deux Mondes*, pronouncing it bad (as he did everything Zola ever published), adding, '*La Débâcle*, in its blood and mud, was bound to be the logical conclusion to the *Rougon-Macquart*.'[25] He was not alone in his condemnation; a former Bavarian officer and a veteran of the 1870–71 campaign wrote a letter to the editor of *Le Figaro*, claiming that Zola had heaped 'mud and ridicule' on the French Army.

Zola's friend Henry Céard wrote congratulating him both as historian and writer.

> I am quite stupefied by the success of your impartiality, by which, disentangling the human and higher truth from the emotional allegations and contradictory witnesses, you were able to speak out without declaiming a catastrophe which remained sad and deeply felt, and to be able to relate the facts resulting from the most incredible military bungling, without making accusations against individuals.[26]

And Huysmans summed it up: 'No one will ever be able to understand better the war of the 1870s, than by seeing it unfold in this immense fresco.'[27]

14
The Universal Republic of Letters

Of Zola's many preoccupations from 1890–93, his application to the French Academy held a predominant position. Created by Cardinal Richelieu in 1635, the Academy was then, as it is now, the most prestigious institution in the country, limited to merely forty members. As in everything Zola did, his perseverance was assiduous when he decided he wanted to join the ranks of the applicants aspiring to gain a seat in the Palais Mazarin, the meeting place of the Academy.

Zola discussed the Academy with numerous people over the years and one of these, Robert Sherard, an early biographer of his, published the following letter he received from Zola on this subject:

> . . . the Academy gives us what men of letters, no less than all other men, desire in this life — that is to say, enjoyment. Our enjoyment as men of letters is to see ourselves famous, to anticipate posterity, to have today the privilege and the pleasure of fame. Life is for enjoyment also. For mere living a man could exist on bread and the simplest dishes of meat; but it is not mere existence that a man desires — it is a certain refinement of life, a certain measure of enjoyment, and so cookery with all its refinements flourishes. And it is with the desire for triumph and enjoyment, and for this reward in my own lifetime, that I am anxious to enter the Academy, but by no means for them alone. My chief reason is to obtain for the Naturalist novel a consecration that it has never yet obtained. I am in a way the literary heir and successor to a number of men of letters who all, for one reason or another, have never crossed the threshold of the Academy. It is their battle as much as my own that I am fighting . . . I shall offer myself again and again so that my suit against the Academy may be fairly tried. I don't want it to be said hereafter that I did not give them every opportunity of admitting me . . . The whole truth is this: the Academy refuses me because of my books.[1]

Gaining a seat in the Academy is a question of filling dead men's shoes. The first one Zola fought for was that of Emile Augier, who died in 1889, but it was also contested by several others, including Fernand Brunetière, Ernest Lavisse, Pierre Loti and Charles de Freycinet (four times prime minister of the country). During the first of seven rounds of voting, Zola received only one vote (that of the faithful François Coppée). De Freycinet won the seat. In 1890 Octave Feuillet died and Zola again entered his name. He knew his chances of success were not good as he had many enemies in the Academy, but he waited for the election results on 21 May 1891, with acute anxiety nonetheless. This time he lost to Pierre Loti, though at least he received eight votes during the first round. Next Zola sought the seat of Marmier, apropos of which Dumas *fils* reportedly said to Edouard Pailleron that Zola would have to win. But Pailleron, himself a member of the Academy and an enemy of Zola, thought not: ' . . . he has introduced debauchery into literature. He is popular, he is rich, he is well paid.'[2] Therefore Zola did not deserve to be elected a member, and sure enough, he lost again. Next year he lost in the contest over the seat vacated by the long-forgotten Mazade, just as he was to lose when he applied for Maxime du Camp's seat, and later that of Taine. Zola was never elected to the French Academy, and was forced to join the ranks of other celebrated losers, such as Molière, Beaumarchais, Balzac and Flaubert.

Hippolyte Taine, perhaps Zola's most consistent foe in the Academy, spoke openly to Sherard of his opposition. He could not fault Zola's manners, temperament, or lifestyle, but he claimed that some of the language in his books disturbed the dignified Academy: 'You must remember that the Academy is at one and the same time a literary institution and a club. Yes, very much a club . . . '[3] Zola simply would not feel at ease there. When Sherard asked Taine why some very famous men had never been elected, he had an answer ready for each and every case. Molière had failed because of the prejudice of his times against actors; Beaumarchais was too Bohemian; Balzac and Flaubert had been excluded, claimed Taine, only because of their untimely deaths. As for Dumas *père,* he was too exuberant — 'a certain equanimity of temperament is an indispensable qualification . . . a certain rapport must be established among the members . . . Look how utterly poor Eugène Sue [a Jew] failed as a member of the Jockey Club. A man may be a great and most admirable genius, and yet not be suited to the membership of a club.'[4] Zola was never considered a suitable choice for the Mazarin Club.

Despite what Taine said, Zola possessed an unusual combination of qualities for a novelist. He was not only very intelligent but extremely diligent, as well as a consistent worker throughout his entire career, and he was not willing to bypass a good subject simply because it required an enormous amount of reading, studying and analysis. *L'Argent* and *La Débâcle* were excellent examples of this single-mindedness which permitted him to tackle unusually difficult tasks. He followed these two monumental novels with *Le Docteur Pascal,* another book that required a crash course in an unfamiliar subject.

The Zolas made their annual return to Médan from Paris on 4 June 1892 with the intention of resting, but this resolution was quickly pushed aside in favour of starting work on the final book of the *Rougon-Macquart* series. Although he was currently involved in rewriting part of the libretto of *L'Attaque du moulin* for Bruneau's opera of the same name, it was *Le Docteur Pascal* which would soon be occupying his thoughts. The theme of the book centred round a subject which fascinated him: heredity. He looked over the old notes he had made of Dr Prosper Lucas's work, *L'Héredité naturelle,* and he contacted Maurice de Fleury, a physician friend who wrote on medical subjects for *Le Figaro,* asking to borrow a French translation of a new biological study of heredity and natural selection written by August Weismann. Also on his reading list was J. Déjerne's *L'Hérédité dans les maladies du système nerveux.* Still another acquaintance, Professor Georges Pouchet, brought Zola up to date on recent theories and concepts on heredity. On psychological problems, he consulted Dr August Motet. Inevitably, Zola had soon accumulated hundreds of pages of notes in addition to those he had previously collected, including many on practical and experimental medicine, for the protagonist of his new work was to be a doctor and scientist.

After settling in at Médan, Zola prepared the 'philosophical outline' of his next work.

> With *Le Docteur Pascal* I should like to sum up the full philosophical significance of the series. I have put into it — despite its black pessimism — a great love of life . . . I have loved life, and I have shown this in spite of all the evil and heart-breaking aspects the series might contain . . . I don't like those pictures and certainly haven't included them in order to be perverse, but rather to show honestly what is involved, in order to be able to say that in spite of everything, life is great and good, since we live it with so much passion.[5]

'I always wanted to end it [the series] with some sort of summing up,' Zola said to Kolff, 'where scientific and philosophical ideas of the whole would be succinctly stated. In short, it is a general conclusion.' Although he added, 'The most painful work for me has been to reread almost all the novels of the series. I cannot reread my own works without becoming deeply sad.'[6] Writing to Kolff again at a later date, Zola explained:

> There is not only nothing of the *idealistic* in it; quite the contrary, as I see it — it is completely *realistic.* The truth is that I'll conclude with the eternal renewal of life, by hope in the future and by mankind's laborious and unrelenting efforts. It seemed to me good to end this terrible *Rougon-Macquart* history by having a last child born, the unknown child, perhaps the Messiah of tomorrow![7]

He completed *Le Docteur Pascal* on the very day he had predicted months earlier, 15 May 1893, which, as he noted, was also his daughter Denise's name day: a fine present for her. Completing the manuscript he prepared two dedications for the book, the official one to his mother and his wife, Alexandrine, and another one, which only Jeanne Rozerot was to read at that time:

> To my beloved Jeanne — to my Clotilde [the heroine of the book], who has given me the royal feast of her youth and who has made me thirty years old once again, by giving me the gift of my Denise and Jacques, the two dear children for whom I have written this book, so that they will learn when reading it one day how much I have adored their mother, how much respectful tenderness they must show to her for the happiness with which she has consoled me during difficult times.

Although Zola himself appeared to be quite pleased with *Le Docteur Pascal*, this concluding work of the *Rougon-Macquart* series proved to be most startling and disconcerting; even Anton Chekhov found it unpleasant and disagreeable. Nor did the plot appear to be convincing. The 'hero', Pascal Rougon, is a conceited, egotistical man who is basically unconcerned with anyone or anything existing outside his house. In his old age he suddenly decides to take his young niece (whom he had raised since infancy) as his common-law wife. She appears blissful at the idea, even though she will outlive him by many years and be left with a child to raise by herself. Perhaps Zola wrote this as a justification for his own position with Jeanne Rozerot. Whatever the reason, it does not ring true, and the final ludicrous note is sounded by the spontaneous combustion and total disintegration of old Macquart, Pascal's uncle. This last tome which was meant to be the philosophical capstone to the *Rougon-Macquart* edifice, left instead a tangle of irresolution and confusion, and more than a hint of the novelist's own inner anguish.

The book was serialized in *La Revue Hebdomadaire* from 18 March–17 June 1893, and was published immediately afterwards by Charpentier in one volume. Zola realized it would never reach the same vast audience as *La Débâcle*, and in his lifetime its sales in France never quite reached the 90,000 mark.

On 9 June Georges Charpentier and Eugène Fasquelle sent out invitations for the celebration dinner they wished to give Zola on the completion of the *Rougon-Macquart*. At noon on 21 June 1893, the Zolas appeared at the Chalet des Iles (Maison Azaïs), on the largest island in the lake of the Bois de Boulogne. This would be Zola's supreme hour, as far as his literary career was concerned.

The police began receiving reports of unusual storm damage that afternoon. The massive grey, threatening clouds began to unleash their torrential rains after the 200 guests had reached the chic island restaurant. It was a deluge, the like of which had not been seen in months, the thunder moving very slowly across the city, deafening those taking part in the festivities. Streets were flooded within minutes, trees were struck by lightning and the temperature gradually rose to 68°F. The freight car of Express Train No. 35, after having left the Gare de l'Est was struck by lightning between Dormans and Troissy. While in Aubervilliers, the roof of the temporary hospital was struck by lightning and caught fire in spite of the downpour, and the fire roared out of control, forcing the evacuation of all the patients.

The Zola celebration was attended by many important and famous people of the day: Raymond Poincaré, then Minister of Public Instruction, Ferdinand Fabre, Edouard Lockroy, Yves Guyot, Hector Malot, Mme Séverine, Arsène Houssaye, Aurélien Scholl, Alfred Bruneau, Fernand Desmoulins and Eugène Fasquelle (who was to succeed Charpentier as Zola's publisher in three years). Illness prevented several of Zola's friends from attending. Maupassant, who had long been suffering, was on his death bed, and indeed was to die on 7 July; Goncourt had been quite ill for months and rarely left his home, while an ailing Daudet, with only three years left, was already receiving daily injections of morphine. However, despite their absence and the terrible, unrelenting storm, Zola was pleased. The great series of twenty volumes which had taken twenty-three years to complete, was finally out of the way and a great success. There were few men in the nineteenth century who could boast of a similar achievement.

As the 200 men and women sat at their tables, Charpentier, Zola's faithful publisher of many years' standing, rose to toast the author, recalling the close ties of friendship uniting the two men. Rising in his turn, Zola replied, emotion choking his words, that what they had come to praise was the principle of hard work, and not the author himself. Others spoke as well: Catulle Mendès praised and thanked Zola on behalf of the poets, as did Edouard Rod, thanking him for the sympathy and help he had frequently given struggling writers. Later, as music filled the room, a French general by the name of Yung approached Zola, and asked him before a large crowd, when the author of *La Débâcle* was going to write *La Victoire*. Zola replied, 'Ah, General. That is something I must leave to you.'

In the summer of 1893 Zola was cheered by an invitation from the Institute of (British) Journalists asking him, in his capacity as President of the Société des Gens de Lettres of France, to speak in London, along with dozens of others that September. At first Zola was very suspicious, for his books had received the worst reviews and sold less well in England than in any other major European country; some titles had even been banned by

Parliament. After receiving the invitation, he wrote immediately to Ernest Vizetelly, his publisher in England, asking about the importance of this congress:

> You know my position in London; my work is still very much questioned there, almost denied. It certainly seems to me that my presence, and the words I might speak, might efface much of the misunderstanding, and that it would be politic to accept in order to influence opinion. But what is your view of the situation?[x]

Vizetelly wrote by return post to assure him that it would indeed be in his best interests to accept. Zola replied that he still felt anxious about the situation: 'I do not wish the English press to promise it will sing my praises, but I should like to be quite certain it will be polite while I am its guest.'[y] He was still hesitant, and asked Vizetelly to sound out others in London about his reception there. After yet another exchange of letters, Zola wrote to Vizetelly on 18 August informing him of his acceptance.

Zola, accompanied by his wife and a dozen French journalists, reached London on 20 September where they were welcomed (in French) at Victoria Station by Sir Edward Lawson (later Lord Burnham). Zola and the others each replied briefly and then drove to the Savoy Hotel. Included among the French contingent were Céard, Duret, Magnard, Scholl, Robbe and Xau. The congress was held in Lincoln's Inn Hall where, a couple of days later, Zola read a paper in French on 'Anonymity in the Press'. Zola's main theme was to plead strongly for signed articles in the fields of literary and dramatic criticism. But then, on the subject of those journalists who did not sign their own work, Zola argued that they ought to share the income earned by their employers. 'Do you have pensions for your retired journalists? After they have devoted their anonymous labour to the common task, year after year, is the bread of their old age assured them?' Zola asked, both startling and pleasing the English audience.

The itinerary of Zola's short London sojourn was crowded. He attended a dinner given by the Institute of Journalists at the Crystal Palace, a reception at the Imperial Institute, and another given by the Lord Mayor at Guildhall. Numerous theatres were thrown open to the French guests, a luncheon was given at Taplow, a warm reception was held in Zola's honour at the Press Club, and still another at the Athenaeum Club (where he was made an honourary member — a mark of esteem never accorded him by any French club). The trip concluded with a splendid dinner very much to Zola's liking at the Authors' Club, where he was the special guest of honour. After thanking his English hosts for their kindness and generosity, Zola said he hoped that they had found him 'perhaps less black than report painted him', which was greeted with laughter and applause, and he concluded, ' . . . at the close of every banquet it is right to propose a toast, so I drink now to the novelists of England and France, to the good fellowship of all authors in one universal republic of letters.'[10]

By now Zola had indeed been wined, dined, fêted and fawned over, but it was not over yet. He went on numerous tours of the London area, including one directed by George Moore along the Thames to Greenwich, others to the National Gallery, the British Museum Library (the organization of which Zola praised highly), the French Hospital, the French Club, numerous almshouses, Westminster Abbey (which he thought was Catholic), and ending in a friendly luncheon given him by his new London publisher, Andrew Chatto.

The Zolas returned home to the rue de Bruxelles delighted by their surprisingly pleasant and interesting visit to London, but also thoroughly exhausted. Zola was later disappointed, however, that some strong criticisms, or more accurately, denunciations, were made in England following his departure, especially by the Anglican Church. The then Bishop of Worcester declared: 'Zola has spent his life corrupting the morals and souls not only of thousands of his fellow-countrymen and especially of the young, but also by the translation of his works, thousands and hundreds of thousands of souls elsewhere.'[11] The Bishop of Truro and the headmaster of Harrow School echoed these sentiments. It would take something of vast magnitude to change their minds about 'the most lewd writer in the world' (as G.W. Story of the *New York Times* called him) — indeed, it would take a Dreyfus Affair.

15
Young Love Once More

What happens to a man who, at the age of forty-eight, decides to risk everything he has spent a quarter of a century building up? Were it simply a case of leaving one's profession for another, it would be quite easily understood, but compromising one's wife (in a Catholic country), jeopardizing his and her position, just as they are finding themselves ensconced in well-earned security, comfort and respectable middle age — that is something else. Why was Zola's decision to take a mistress so shocking, not to the French public, but to his old friends who knew him well? Unlike many of his fellow writers, he had been dedicated to one woman for many years, and unlike Dumas or Hugo, he had never behaved like a playboy. If the public had a sensational view of Zola from what appeared to them to be indecent novels, his close friends had always considered him a model of propriety. He took his profession as a writer very seriously, and had distinctly 'bourgeois' leanings, for when he was not working, he was at home with his wife and mother. He did not flirt with women. He lived the life of a dedicated zealot. What then caused him to deceive his wife for the first time after eighteen years of marriage?

It sounds very dramatic and to some, very romantic, that a fat, middle-aged man suddenly fell in love, trimmed a few inches off his famous paunch, made a lovely domestic his mistress and ultimately fathered two children by her. As true as these facts are, one must dig very deeply to see what brought about such a sad and complex situation. Although Zola and Alexandrine were never wildly in love with each other (for that was a luxury those two, hardened by their own grim experiences with reality, could not afford), they were at least devoted to each other, and in many respects wanted the same things of life. But Zola, an only child, wanted a house filled with children and Alexandrine could not (or would not) provide offspring. (The theme of family and childhood is, of course, constantly recurring throughout Zola's works.)

Frustrations had soon made themselves felt, and apparently it was not long before the novelty of creating their own home wore off and gave way to sheer anguish. Zola's uncertain income, which fluctuated enormously right up to 1881, must have contributed considerably to the tension. We do not know whether Alexandrine offered support or criticism of his endeavours, but we do know that Zola was not an easy man to live with when it came to principles and ideals, areas in which he refused to compromise. He began to suffer from insomnia, and when he could sleep, he was plagued by nightmares. His wife's genuine maladies, including bronchitis and allergies, later developed into hypochondria, and Zola too became preoccupied with his health. Neither seemed to find love and fulfilment within the marriage, although it no doubt provided a certain stability and orderliness to their lives. Their disagreements gradually worsened, and Zola came to dread the terrible nightly scenes, never knowing quite what to expect. The answer to this domestic strife was for him to leave his wife, or to find the right woman with whom he could live in quiet harmony and have children. But the couple remained together, year after bitter year, and every night remained a source of constant unpleasantness. As a result, Zola was stalked by depression and fear of death. But Zola did not betray his wife's confidence in him before 1888. He never had affairs, never carried out flirtations, even at a time when such behaviour was considered normal in France. Life was too serious for such nonsense, thought Zola, and he was too scrupulous to lower himself to actions which could contradict the very values of his existence.

Zola was and always had been a tortured soul. To be sure, by 1888 he had proved himself successful as both journalist and novelist, becoming immensely rich in the process. But his marriage had proven barren, and ever since the death of his mother and Flaubert, years before, Zola appears to have felt an ever-growing loneliness. He could create love and companionship with pen and paper, but he could not find it in reality. Alexandrine was a faithful and a diligent wife, but she appears to have been as insensitive to her husband's emotional problems as he was to hers. They could not communicate their needs and wishes to each other. Although Alexandrine corresponded frequently with her cousins, the Labordes, about personal and household matters, Zola could not write intimately to his friends, except indirectly through talk about literature or complaints about his health, the latter becoming more and more frequent over the years.

However, there is yet another aspect to be considered in assessing Zola's actions. By the age of forty-eight, he had already achieved substantial success with *L'Assommoir, Nana,* and *Germinal* behind him. He not only had the remaining titles of the *Rougon-Macquart* series in view, but also plans for works well beyond that point. To a certain extent the future seemed quite secure, with the challenge for mere existence and survival simply an unpleasant memory of a grim past. He and his friends (and their children) were growing older and he was probably depressed by the fact that he had fewer years left ahead of him than behind him. What then was life for? Was it to become relatively meaningless at the age of forty-eight? Was it all to become a downhill affair for the remainder of his days? Old age would soon be upon him with nothing to show for it but books. There was, of course, one answer, although Zola probably did not calculate it so coldly: romance and children. He could be rejuvenated, with a young wife and babies in the nursery. He could fight off death and oblivion through the formula he espoused ten years later in his novel *Fécondité* — the renewal of life. That is what he had been missing and the hope he could now cling to.

When Madame Zola hired a new house domestic from Rouvres-sous-Meilly in Bourgogne, in May 1888, she little guessed what changes would be wrought. Within a few months Jeanne Rozerot, a carpenter's daughter, became Zola's mistress. It is difficult to imagine a man as timid, formal and awkward as Zola, making advances to an equally timid young woman, whom he barely knew. At first he appears not to have meant it to have been anything more than a passing affair, perhaps even an act of defiance — although nothing has been established, as Zola covered his tracks carefully and confided in no one during the period of courtship. But Jeanne's lovely face and innocent eyes appear to have been too much for him. He could not bear to give her up, and perhaps guilt already played a role in this. In the first of several irrevocable steps, he leased a flat for the twenty-year-old Jeanne Sophie Adèle at 66, rue Saint Lazare, near his Paris home.[1] But this was insane: his wife would soon discover his secret, as would his friends (from whom he had thus far carefully concealed entirely this part of his life). What was he to do? Abandon Jeanne Rozerot who had given herself to him in all sincerity, thinking that he was equally sincere in his love for her? She had, of course, left the household without disclosing the reason for doing so to Madame Zola. She had no other income and was now fully dependent upon Zola in a strange city. On the other hand, Zola had deceived his wife, he who had always prided himself on his integrity. This was just the beginning of an untenable situation which he was never to resolve.

There were solutions of course. If Zola truly loved Jeanne, they could have lived together openly and unashamedly, with or without divorce, as other more Bohemian characters had done. However, it is probably fair to say that he never loved deeply enough to make such a commitment. If he had been deeply in love with Jeanne, would he have continued to sleep in the same bedroom with Alexandrine for the rest of his days, regardless of the responsibilities he might have felt towards her? For a man as emotional and unsure of himself as Zola, that would have been impossible. In a professional capacity Zola did not think twice about throwing down the gauntlet to the reading public of France, but he did not have the courage to decide between the two women in his life. The result was an unhealthy balance: he could not break with, or give himself entirely to either woman.

The situation became more complicated in 1889 when Jeanne announced that she was pregnant. He was absolutely ecstatic at the thought of becoming a father at long last, but at the same time he felt despair mingled with guilt, two emotions that were to plague him ever after. He *must* make a decision. The lives of two decent women depended upon it. The rest of his days would be spent in convincing himself that he had decided correctly regarding his personal life, but this was sheer delusion on his part because he had merely postponed making any decision at all.

And, indeed a few years later Zola appears to have regretted his failure to insist upon a divorce:

> I am for the couple whose love renders their union indissoluble. I fully support the man and woman who love each other and who have become parents, who love each other forever, till death. For this is real truth, real beauty, real happiness. But I am also for absolute freedom in love, and if divorce becomes necessary, then it should take place without any hindrance, by mutual consent and even by the wish of just one party if needs be.[2]

Unfortunately he did not apply these words of wisdom to his own case.

On 20 September 1889, Zola's first child, Denise, was born in the flat in the rue Saint Lazare, but her birth was one of the best kept secrets in France for the next few years, and when gradually some of Zola's closest friends learnt about it, they did not know how to cope with the situation. Even Alfred Bruneau, who was to become one of Zola's most devoted friends, never alluded to Jeanne and the children in any of his surviving correspondence.[3] This is all the more surprising in that Bruneau himself was a devoted family man. Paul Alexis, however, not only accepted the idea of Jeanne, Jacques and Denise, but moved into a neighbouring house in the country, and his two girls grew up with Zola's children, so that they were practically one family. (According to Albert Laborde, a cousin of Alexandrine, only Henry Céard and Paul Alexis had been informed before 1891 about Zola's second family.)[4] The pressure on Zola must have been intense, but he was apparently prepared to live with it. As the news of his fresh complications reached other friends, some of them disappeared from the scene (Céard and Huysmans), while others remained staunchly by Zola's side, especially the Charpentiers, Alexis and his wife, Eugène Fasquelle, and the Bruneaus.

Some older friends found the situation particularly delicate as they were close to Alexandrine. This is especially true of Henry Céard. Although he had been drifting away from Zola's literary group for several years prior to this, he resented the awkwardness of the situation he found himself in, but he later took advantage of it for his own needs. Alexandrine demanded of Céard and other friends that they take sides, which left them in a horrible predicament. She had a powerful personality and never relented as far as her role in Zola's life was concerned, holding on with a blind obstinacy which defied all logic, leaving old friends very bewildered; her scenes with him were apparently quite horrendous. The break with Céard came in June 1893, after he failed to attend the dinner given by Zola's publisher to celebrate the completion of the *Rougon-Macquart* series. As a close friend of long standing, Céard knew Alexandrine's cousins, the Labordes, and, odd as it seems, it was to them that he explained his reasons for not attending the festivities:

Take into consideration what dangers would have resulted from my presence. As an old friend of the family, and in the name of seventeen years' close friendship, I would have been expected to say a few words. My silence would have been most conspicuous. What I would have said, regardless of my precautions could have led possibly to a serious incident. I would have had to give the poor woman [Alexandrine] her due [in Zola's success], and my very compliments would have caused wounds and sadness. She was extremely upset by a newspaper article of which she must have spoken to you, which, moreover, seemed to me to be unnecessarily aggressive and cruel to the point of being odious. She reproached me for not standing by her and protecting her. I feared a scandal would have resulted, however. Even with the best intentions in the world, I might have caused a real scandal. Therefore I decided to remain at home.[5]

When Alexandrine was finally informed of her husband's liaison with Jeanne Rozerot, by an anonymous letter possibly written as late as November 1891 (and sent by Céard?)[6], she was at first staggered and then furious. Furniture literally flew through the air followed by a hail of imprecations, and the rooms of their house in Paris became chambers of hell, where maids scurried for safety but Zola remained, entrapped by himself. Facts about what precisely occurred are rare. It is known that Alexandrine sought out her husband's correspondence at Jeanne Rozerot's and destroyed it. There was talk of separation or divorce, but — if the scraps of information available are correct — *Zola* would not have it.[7] (Perhaps he feared that it would have shown him in the wrong by appearing to abandon his wife, or was this because somehow he felt sorry and responsible for her?) The cooling down process took many, many months, indeed years, emphasizing all the more vividly how wrong he was not to have made a clean break with Alexandrine. Zola remained with her for the rest of his life, visiting Jeanne and Denise (and later Jacques, born on 25 September 1891), as often as possible. This was, at least on the surface, most cowardly behaviour, and if only for the sake of the children, he should have left Alexandrine. The irony of the situation hinges on this monumental writer of prose, a rational figure, an idealist and crusader, being caught up in painful perplexities as well as in moments of confusing beauty, as a result of his controversial irresolution. During his lifetime his biographers, Robert Sherard and Ernest Vizetelly, tried to ignore the very existence of Jeanne and the children, and even the French press tended to play this down until the time of the Dreyfus Affair, when Jeanne Rozerot and their children were harrassed by reporters, who even broke into their house. Failing to resolve once and for all the issue regarding the two women in his life was to prove the most serious and long-lasting mistake of his existence.

The extent of Zola's torture was reflected in nearly every letter to Jeanne and the children, as for example that of 29 July 1893, written at a time when they were on separate holidays:

. . . I had hoped to bring some happiness to your youth and not to make it necessary for you to live like a recluse; I should have been so happy to be young with you, to have grown young again with your youth and, instead of that, it is I who have caused you to age, who sadden you constantly . . . It is quite true, the worst part about being kept away from the seaside now has been not being able to be the dear old Papa with my sweet children. I should have been so happy to have carried my darling little girl in my arms, and to have shown Jacques how to make a sandcastle . . . [8]

Unfortunately, the situation was as painful and unsatisfactory when they were all in Paris:

I am not happy. This separation, this double life that I am forced to live ends by making me despair. But I beg of you to be kind to me and not to want me beside you when things are not going as I should have wanted them to do. I had dreamt of making everyone around me happy, but I see quite clearly now that this is impossible, and I am the first to be affected. [9]

The unrelenting pain affected all parties. The children inevitably asked why they rarely saw their father and why he did not live under the same roof with them like other fathers. The letters reflecting the anguish of Jeanne Rozerot and Alexandrine Zola have either been destroyed or secreted away. Madame Zola apparently discussed her marital woes with her cousins, but Albert Laborde has carefully edited the few letters he has produced, suppressing all others, and consequently there is no public record reflecting the true depth of Alexandrine's feelings.

Ultimately, Alexandrine came to grips with the situation, at least superficially. She admitted the existence of Jeanne and the two children, but did her utmost to keep the children from their father. She, Alexandrine, was Madame Zola and no other woman would usurp her place, regardless of the humiliation she suffered and the anger she felt. She knew that Zola wanted to adopt the children and legally give his name to them, but by French law he could not do so till the eldest child reached the age of fifteen and Zola died before that could be done. Alexandrine promised Jeanne that she would carry out Zola's wishes in those respects, but of course she never did adopt them, although she finally arranged for them legally to take their father's name. Alexandrine did meet the children occasionally when their father took them for walks in the Tuileries or along the Champs Elysées, but she never went beyond that. She remained a most stubborn and bitter woman, although outwardly pretending to befriend Zola's young children, and after his death she cut off almost all funds and property from the estate which could have eased their financial plight in the years following.

This chapter of Zola's life simultaneously brought him his greatest contentment as well as his greatest grief. His ideal of hearth and home was to elude him forever, though his intentions were perfectly clear, as when he wrote to Jeanne:

> I want you and my sweet little ones to be able to share this [his glory and fame]. One day all the world must recognize them as my children and thus everything happening here [in London where he was being honoured by the British press] will also be for the three of you. I want them to be able to share their father's name. [10]

16
Anti-Semite Evolué

Zola's anti-Semitism, something most biographers have tried to conceal, ignore or play down for many decades, was a real and important factor in his life which cannot be overlooked. Zola's works reflect his antipathy towards Jews, and though he was later considered the hero of the Jews of France, that came only towards the end of his career, and even then perhaps, he was not so much a spokesman for the Jews, as for principles.

The evolution of Zola's anti-Semitism can best be seen in his published writings. In 1874, at the age of thirty-four, he published a play entitled *Les Héritiers Rabourdin*, concerned with the avarice of the heirs apparent to Rabourdin's estate. The one Jewish character in the play, a secondary figure called Isaac, appears as a stereotyped money-lender. In fact, Isaac also sells antiques, but both his furniture sales and money-lending bring him to the doorsteps of the Rabourdin home as the Devil incarnate. Zola spends little time describing him and does not emphasize his role, painting a far gloomier picture of Rabourdin's relatives and their unsavoury schemes to obtain money. This one was one of the first times Zola mentioned Jews, and between 1874 and 1890 Jewish characters all but disappeared from his works.

In 1891 Zola published his novel *L'Argent*, which had two themes: the constant fight for superiority between Jew and Christian in the Paris stock market, and the creation of one of the most famous Catholic banking houses in modern French history (based in reality on the Union Générale). This, the most openly and viciously anti-Semitic work Zola ever wrote, was published when he was fifty-one. In it he describes the world of the stock market, banking and speculation as being controlled by international Jewry. (This is all the more ironic because it is the very kind of attack that he later set out to combat.) The distortion perpetrated by Zola in *L'Argent* is surprising and disturbing. He had never made a secret of his admiration of Balzac, and Balzac's hatred of Jews is revealed throughout *La Comédie humaine*. But in *L'Argent*, a novel reaching a considerable reading public, Zola makes Balzac look like an amateur. To be sure, some of this is modified in that it is seen through the eyes of Saccard, an openly anti-Semitic character, but nonetheless the scenes described reflect the author's views.

As a young man Zola had not often come into contact with Jews, and probably only came to know a few in the world of the arts. In fact, it would be fair to say that he hardly knew any Jewish families well prior to the Dreyfus case. Most of the Jews he did know were writers, publishers, journalists or theatre people. For example, he knew Sarah Bernhardt fairly well, and even wrote some plays for her (at her request) but she never performed in them, and perhaps this left a residual anger with Zola (see Chapter 8). And naturally Zola's collaboration with Busnach had not helped matters. The only Jews portrayed in his written works (until after the Dreyfus Affair) are money-lenders and speculators (with the exception of Sigismund in *L'Argent*).

In *L'Argent* Zola gets to descriptions of Jews almost immediately, once again dealing exclusively in stereotypes that stress the negative.

> Pillerault was very tall and very thin, with awkward gestures and a nose as flat as a sword's blade, and a face as bony as that of a knight errant who appeared to know well how to play a reckless game . . . He was of the exuberant nature one would expect of a stock-market 'bull', always ready for victory; whilst Moser, to the contrary, short, with yellowish skin and ravaged by a liver problem, constantly complained about all sorts of possible pitfalls. As for Salmon, a very handsome man, about to turn fifty, sporting a superb jet black beard, he passed for an extraordinarily strong man. He never spoke or responded without a smile, a smile whose meaning was never clear.

As often as not, Zola's Jewish characters are made to appear very un-French, unassimilated, and the more important they are, the more Germanic their names. Schlosser is an unethical speculator, Busch is a real schemer, and Gundermann is 'the banker king, master of the stock market and the world, a man of sixty, with an enormous bald head and a thick nose'. He does not even drink what normal Frenchmen drink, preferring milk to wine.

Physical descriptions were always important in Zola's works and they could be used in the most deadly manner. Indeed, whenever there is a large, bustling, unhealthy-looking crowd of speculators, Zola describes it as *'toute une juiverie'* (a pack of Jews), likening the individuals to dried up vultures with hooked noses, emitting guttural cries as if preparing to devour their prey. Indeed about the only 'kind' description of a Jew is that of Busch's younger brother, Sigismund: 'He was of unusual intelligence, this Sigismund, having studied in German universities, and being able to speak German, English and Russian, as well as his mother tongue, French. He had known Karl Marx in Cologne in 1849, and had become his favourite editor of the *New Rhine Gazette*.' Although he had nothing to do with speculation, Sigismund was yet another stereotyped

Jew: he was unusually brilliant and a superb linguist, but he was in poor health because Jews — even educated ones — always lived in squalid conditions and had no interest in cleanliness or fresh air. But at the same time he lived in a higher world, hoping for the day when a major redistribution of the world's wealth would take place. In short, he is not only an idealist, but a communist and revolutionary as well. How could he win? Most Victorian Frenchmen, including Zola, had little admiration for communism and feared revolution. As incidental scenes to all this, Zola describes intense Jewish life amid the squalid tenements located behind the stock market. There the entire family, frequently obnoxious people, work as a tightly-knit unit for one purpose only — filthy lucre.

Such views, published in a best-selling novel of the day, most certainly did nothing to halt the growing anti-Semitism in France after the creation of the Third Republic. One really gets to the heart of Zola's negative views of Jews in the Catholic Saccard's feelings and descriptions of Gundermann (based on James de Rothschild):

> Ah! the Jew! He had against the Jew the ancient grudge against that race, found especially in the south of France. He, in his mind, accused that race of the usual things, that despised race which no longer has a country, or a prince, which lives like a parasite amongst the various nations pretending to recognize their laws, but in reality obeying only its God of theft, blood and anger — and its mission given to them by God, of ferocious conquest, was being fulfilled everywhere, establishing itself in every country — like the spider in the middle of the web — in order to stalk its prey, to drain everyone's blood, to fatten itself at the expense of others. Do you ever see a Jew working on his hands and knees? Are there any Jewish peasants, or Jewish labourers? No, work dishonours them, and their religion almost forbids it, exalting only the exploitation of the work of others. Ah, the rabble! Saccard seemed filled with rage, while at the same time he admired that race, envied their prodigious financial faculties, that innate science for numbers, that natural ease with which they undertook the most complicated operations, that flair and luck which assured them success in every venture they undertook. At this game of theft, thought Saccard, Christians don't stand a chance, they always fail, whereas take a Jew who can't even read, throw him into some shady deal, and he will extricate himself and will even end up with all the profit. That is the gift of the race, its very reason for existing in the various countries which are made and unmade. And he predicted with certainty the ultimate conquest of everyone by the Jews, when they will have accumulated the fortune of the entire world, which would not be long in happening, as every day they were allowed to extend their operations freely, and one could already see in Paris a Gundermann sitting on a throne more solid and more respected than that of the Emperor.

It is disturbing to think that such an intelligent man as Zola, who was succeeding admirably in his career by dint of talent and hard work, should harbour and broadcast such bigoted thoughts.

If 1891 marks the peak of Zola's anti-Semitism, it also marks the beginning of great change within himself. Some of this change must be attributed to the fact that by the autumn of that year he was happier than he had ever been, with the birth of his second child, Jacques. (Interestingly, one of the bright spots in his description of French Jews, was the closeness, warmth and love he found in their families.) It is not altogether clear what set off this change which would lead a few years hence to his inextricable involvement in the Dreyfus case.

Zola's view of French Jews now began to alter considerably and he became involved in a major re-examination of his values. This startling modification was first seen in an article entitled, *'Pour les Juifs'* (On behalf of the Jews), which appeared in 1896. Even now it is hard to believe that the Zola who published *L'Argent* in 1891 could have modified his views so drastically within a five-year period. Indeed, he begins this article as if he had never written *L'Argent*:

> For several years, I have seen — with increasing surprise and disgust — the campaign which has been carried out against the Jews of France. It seems a monstrous thing to me, beyond common sense, truth and justice, something stupid and blind, which could lead us back to the Dark Ages. What is more it could lead to the worst of abominations, religious persecution, resulting in bloodshed in all countries.[1]

What is so very strange about this new, vastly altered approach to what Zola called 'the Jewish question', is that at this stage he still did not know of Dreyfus's innocence. What brought about this volte-face? Unfortunately there is no written evidence pointing to the factors involving his change from abuser to defender. It may be argued that Zola was never completely anti-Semitic, that even in *L'Argent* one can find phrases which reflect his own doubt as to what he was saying. While it must be acknowledged that he publicly modified his views and attempted to put a halt to abuses against the Jews, it is still possible to detect some reservation in his statements. Zola probably never really liked Jews personally — though he later came to admire some of those who sacrificed all in order to save Dreyfus — but he defended them now because his 'French brain' told him that anti-Semitism was the work of third-rate minds. His reasoning told him that anti-Semitism was fallacious and evil. His principles told him that anti-Semitism was unacceptable, and Zola was above all a man of principles.

First of all, what is it that the Jews are being put on trial for? What is it that they are being reproached with? Some people, even some of my friends, say that they cannot stand them, that they cannot even shake hands with them without feeling a shiver of repugnance . . . I don't ask whether this repugnance is rooted in the ancient anger of the Christian for the Jews who crucified his God,[2] a secular atavism of scorn and vengeance . . . The effort of civilizations is to erase this savage need to throw ourselves upon someone else who is not exactly like us. Throughout the centuries, the history of peoples is simply a lesson in mutual toleration. [They are accused of] being a nation within a nation, of having their own private religious caste, and being thus beyond national borders, a sort of international sect, without a real country, capable one day, if they triumphed, of controlling the world.[3] But above all they are a practical and well-informed race; they bring with their blood a need for lucre, a love of money, a prodigious ability for business . . .

But why is this so, Zola asked? He put it down 'to 1800 years of imbecilic persecution', which had restricted Jews to living in certain areas, thus ensuring the survival of their culture and traditions, and the development of skills that would one day overcome the brute force of persecution.

And the result is that now terrified of this accumulated labour . . . you think of nothing better than to return to the year 1000 to the persecutions of yore, to preach another holy war with rage in your hearts . . . Really, you are intelligent fellows, and you have there a brilliant social concept. With 5 million Jews among more than 200 million Catholics you tremble, you call the gendarmes, you bring about a terrible reign of terror . . . That's what I call courage! Persecution, is that what you really want? If there are still Jews [in the world], it is your fault. They would have disappeared long ago, they would have been assimilated if they had not been forced to be on the defensive. The day will come when the Jew will be merely a man like the rest of us, he will be our brother. Embrace the Jews, absorb them and blend them with us. We will be enriched by their qualities, for they do have some. Let's put an end to race warfare by mixing the races.[4]

Zola felt that anti-Semitism was often used as a political weapon, sometimes arising during times of economic difficulty. He apparently felt that it was not a fundamental characteristic of French people, but 'simply the passion of some muddled brains, in which beats a sectarian and cloudy Catholicism . . . '[5] However, he did not exclude those who might use anti-Semitism to get publicity and gain notoriety.

The recent rebirth of Jew-baiting appalled Zola, but as he admitted, 'there is a handful of lunatics, imbeciles or slick operators, who cry out to us each morning: "Let's kill the Jews, let's gobble them up, massacre them, exterminate them, burn them at the stake!"'[6] Zola roundly condemned this, presenting instead his own solution: 'Let us disarm our hatred, love one another in our cities, love beyond national frontiers, labour to achieve finally one single happy family of mankind.'[7] The only sour note (to his Jewish readers) was in his tactless conclusion: 'Let Jesus therefore tell his exasperated faithful that he had pardoned the Jews and that they too are human beings!'[8]

The extraordinary difference between his novel *L'Argent* and his article, *'Pour les Juifs'* is hard to explain. If today *L'Argent* appears as a testimonial to anti-Semitism, Zola probably did not consider or intend it as such. Perhaps his aim was to show the Jews (as well as the Christians) of France that their way of life was wrong. Money-lending and speculation were bad for the individual and the well-being of the country. The life of working-class Jews in filthy tenements was debasing. Jews holding themselves aloof from Christian society were thereby harming and restricting their own lives, as well as defeating the progress of the nation. This is perhaps the most charitable interpretation one can make of the picture of French Jewry as portrayed by Zola in *L'Argent*. It was one of the rare times when he failed to paint the picture he had set out to do, and his open distrust and dislike of Jews only added to the prejudice of his times.

In *'Pour les Juifs'* Zola appears in a modified guise, calling for common sense and world toleration to prevail. But his dislike of Jews was not concealed, and the only 'Jewish traits' he discussed are certainly negative and one-sided. While warning the French to be wary of those calling for the destruction of the Jews, the answer he proffers is little better. He declares that the solution is for Jews to cease being Jews, to be fully assimilated so that ultimately there will be no differences between the various groups within society. (Throughout his article it is interesting to note that he always refers to the French Christians as 'us', and to the Jews as 'them'.)

Zola's open and whole-hearted involvement in the Dreyfus case marked the time when, in revolt against the barbarism of his fellow Christians, he had to take an irrevocable step to alter the wrong committed in the name of Church and Flag. (See Chapters 17 and 18.) In the final analysis he was always a man of principles. His principles altered his final writings as well, for his last books, outlined or completed, were to deal with his beliefs in hard work, truth and justice. The last novel he was to complete, *Vérité* (Truth), was published posthumously in 1903 and dealt with a Jewish school teacher wrongly accused of the death of a student. If France would not acknowledge the full error of its ways from the Dreyfus Affair, Zola would force a lesson upon it through his book which would be on the shelf for all to read in later generations.

The unfinished series of novels, *Les Quatre Evangiles* (The Four Apostles) were inspired by Zola's humanitarian ideals. *Vérité* was the third of the series, and little is known of what he wanted in his final, unwritten novel, *Justice,* but apparently it involved Zionism and perhaps the return of all the Jews of the Diaspora to a renewed city of Jerusalem. Needless to say, such a book would have been open to more than one interpretation. And the concept of Zionism as the 'final solution' for the Jewish population of the world, would reflect new doubts by Zola about his earlier assimilationist ideas.

Thus, the evolution of Zola's attitudes towards Jews was extraordinary. Brought up in a world where Jews were despised, especially in the south of France during his own early years, he did not fully overcome this part of his heritage until a few years before his death. That he faced and struggled with this problem for so long was remarkable. Had he never been anti-Semitic, his role in the Dreyfus Affair would have appeared decent and heroic. But in the light of his own previous, outspoken anti-Semitism, his later stance in the Dreyfus case is striking, and perhaps leaves man with hope for the future. And in this context the final words of Marc Froment, a character in *Vérité,* come to mind: 'Children, children don't make a god of me . . . I am merely a conscientious worker who has done his day's task.'

17
Zola vs the Vatican

Zola was delighted to conclude the *Rougon-Macquart* series, and had been looking forward to doing so for many years. He was now anxious to get to work on a new series which he was to entitle *Les Trois villes* (The Three Cities), to be comprised of three volumes: *Lourdes, Rome* and *Paris*. The hero of these volumes was a young, idealistic priest by the name of Pierre Froment. The Froment name now introduced by the author to his reading public would feature not only in this series, but in his final one, *Les Quatre Evangiles*, as well. For the first time in his works (with the exception of Dr Pascal Rougon), Zola was to have a steady stream of heroes, all playing major roles in the development of his concepts, and all bearing the name of Froment.

The three cities of Lourdes, Rome and Paris equated the concepts of faith, hope, and charity for Zola. In the first novel, *Lourdes*, Abbé Pierre Froment, a young intellectual involved in social work, goes to Lourdes to regain his faith in the Church, only to have it dashed to pieces. Lourdes, a new shrine of miracles, had gained world prominence during the reign of Emperor Napoleon III as a result of the alleged visions of a young girl, Bernadette. The grotto at Lourdes with which she was associated quickly became a shrine to Bernadette because of the special healing powers attributed to the spring which flowed from the walls of that grotto.

All his life Zola had been the enemy of established religion and had never made any attempt to conceal this. Religion was more than a philosophical issue at this time, however, for it was à la mode to be anti-religious and anti-Vatican in French republican and socialist circles, especially towards the close of the nineteenth century; for once Zola was not alone, but a man with considerable public support. The only difference was that he put down in black and white what most others would only think. His criticisms were searching, deep and disturbing, and in most instances, supported by facts. He was the enemy of medieval ideas and always the foe of deception, and in this instance felt that the Catholic Church was deceiving terminally ill persons who were coming to Lourdes with expectations (encouraged by the Church) of being healed after bathing in the miraculous waters of the grotto. It was, he claimed, one huge hoax intentionally perpetrated by the Church. Why was it that no one would speak out and tell the people the truth? He would do so, but at the same time he would reveal other major criticisms of the Church, including its use of miracles and superstition to hold its followers in thrall, or to attract converts.

Fortunately, when Zola began his preliminary work on *Lourdes* in August 1892, he recorded every step of his preparations in a special diary which was only published for the first time in 1958, entitled *Voyage à Lourdes* (Voyage to Lourdes). He was to prepare a similar one later for his research on *Rome*.

The Zolas took the Pyrenees Express from Paris to Lourdes (electing not to take the crowded pilgrim train), arriving at 8.30 a.m. on Friday, 19 August 1892. He would remain there carrying out his research until 1 September. That very morning he set to work following his usual rigorous, well-organized approach. First, he enquired about the administration of the grotto and arranged to meet with the Church officials involved. He then studied the hospitals (the Church controlled two, the town of Lourdes, one), and medical supervision. He noted how the tours were conducted at the grotto; he studied the healing baths, the church services, the sales of grotto water and souvenirs. Zola interviewed, whenever possible, those who had known Bernadette, or at least those who had known someone who had known her. He met with numerous merchants, hoteliers and municipal officials to learn their views of the grotto (and the latter were to throw a party for Zola before he left). Nearly everyone involved was helpful to the inquisitive author who was seen everywhere, pen and notepad in hand. Occasionally he travelled to nearby towns when it was necessary; no inconvenience was too great if it would help him arrive at the truth.

His findings were as dismal as he had probably expected they would be. The key to the Lourdes shrine itself was Bernadette. He studied her family background and found no history of nervous disorders, but he did believe that inculcation of past ideas and superstition were factors resulting in Bernadette's 'hallucinations', as Zola called them, and he found a physician in Lourdes, a Dr Balencie, who supported these views. (Interestingly, Zola heard talk in the same community of at least two different 'witches' then living in Lourdes.) Today, Bernadette, like Joan of Arc, would probably be considered schizoid.

But was healing really the aim of the *'pères de l'Immaculée Conception'*? Zola thought they were chiefly good businessmen who had even succeeded in setting up *succursales* (branch offices) in New York and Rome. The fathers received a rebate on the railway fare profits; special pilgrims' trains left Paris daily. The hotels often handled up to 30,000 people, and yet the town itself had only a population of 7000 in 1892. Commercial stands were set up on Church property along the entrance to the grotto, where one could buy anything from a bottle of holy water, to cheap souvenirs of Bernadette and the grotto, including medallions, wallets, snuff boxes, paper-weights, bracelets, candles, and even pipes. If one considers simply the sale of candles, say one for each of the 30,000 pilgrims, the profit becomes formidable. Bernadette was obviously not only good business for the Church, but the only real business of the town itself.

Church officials had set up a couple of 'hospitals' in which the incurably ill were crammed, with dozens of beds per room. Each pilgrim paid for this, of course, and that provided another source of revenue for the fathers. But medicines were not administered in these hospitals, and the doctors on call were not permitted to treat those who were ill; they merely served as clerks to make an official record of each person's illness, and to list any healing which resulted from the grotto baths and prayer — but even this was not done in a systematic manner.

In some respects the town suffered from the grotto trade, and a large number of prostitutes were to be seen everywhere, day and night. Many townsmen had strong words to say about the administration of the shrine, from jealousy over the volume of business transacted by the priests, to the large amount of land owned by the Church (which was exempt from taxation).

On Thursday, 1 September, Zola and his wife boarded the train for a fleeting visit to Genoa via Marseilles and Monaco. The novelist's notebooks were filled with thousands of facts, comments, descriptions and interviews.[1] He had been most successful and now it was all there for the time when he would be ready to begin his book the following year.

Upon returning to Paris, Zola resumed work on the last novel of the *Rougon-Macquart* series, *Le Docteur Pascal,* and only started actually writing *Lourdes* in the winter of 1893, completing it in 1894. It first appeared in serial form in *Gil Blas,* and according to Ernest Vizetelly, Zola's English biographer and translator, Zola was paid 50,000 francs for this alone.[2]

When Charpentier published *Lourdes* on 15 August 1894,[3] it caused an immediate furore, and on 21 September its author learnt it had been placed on the Vatican's *Index Librorum Prohibitorum* (a list of books Roman Catholics are forbidden to read). Zola was denounced by every right-wing, orthodox publication as a depraved man set on destroying law, order, society and civilization. During his own lifetime, *Lourdes* was a best-seller, with sales approaching 150,000 copies by 1902, and it remained far more successful in that sense than *Rome* and *Paris,* which were also later placed on the Vatican's Index — a relic from the sixteenth century that the reading public largely chose to ignore.

By the autumn of 1894 Zola was preparing for his first trip to Rome, where he was to carry out the research for his projected novel of the same name. In mid-October, before leaving Médan, he indicated to Vizetelly his interest in seeing Pope Leo XIII,[4] although he must have realized that that was merely wishful thinking for an author with several books on the Vatican's Index. He apparently made no attempt to arrange such a meeting when actually in Rome.

The Zolas arrived by train very early on 31 October, to begin their thirty-six day sojourn in Rome. Throughout that stay Zola recorded his activities in great detail in a 400-page diary similar to the one he had used in Lourdes.[5] As usual he had a long and intensive schedule prepared. He knew more or less what background material he needed, and immediately went about his task the very morning he stepped from the train. He had studied his Baedeker very closely before leaving Médan and now went nowhere without it. He walked the streets of Rome according to priority of subject matter. He wanted to see the ruins of the ancient city, as well as learning about the modern influences in Roman society, particularly the royal family and the Roman aristocracy. He also wanted to meet Church and state officials. He spent a considerable amount of time studying the administrative mechanisms within the Church, such as how the *Index Librorum Prohibitorum* functioned.

The very day of his arrival he was received by the French Ambassador to Italy, M. Albert Billot, and he was given full co-operation and assistance by everybody but the Vatican staff. He met the French community; he was introduced to Roman aristocracy (some pro-Vatican, some pro-royalist), municipal officials, and national ministers of such departments as Finance and Post and Telegraph. Everywhere he went with his familiar notebook, constantly observing, his wife frequently accompanying him. He made numerous studies of the Forum and the Palatine Hill, of the via Giulia, of St Peter's, of Frascati, of church services and ceremonies (beginning with the All Saints' Day ceremony in St Peter's on 1 November). He observed everything, from the type and number of men and women present, to the architectural details of the buildings, and the designs, types and quantity of marble used. He went to many museums, studied the paintings (especially those of Raphael, Michelangelo and Botticelli), the artefacts, the grottos and catacombs; nothing was too great or too small to escape his attention. He noted the smells, the colours, the shapes, the politics and, of course, the mores of modern Rome, which in the end left him depressed and with rather a poor opinion of the Romans.

He was surprised to find that the subject of 'poisonings' among those involved in Church politics was more current than he had expected (some high officials had certain inner-circle opponents poisoned in order to eliminate them), and he alludes to this towards the end of *Rome*.[6] He was also genuinely amazed to find that there was no real bourgeoisie: the aristocracy, for the most part, furnished the men of the professions, and beneath them there were only the bureaucrats, and finally the peasantry. Zola was surprised to find the working classes at such a low, uninformed level — almost feudal. He came to Rome with a negative view of the Vatican and the clergy, and this was exacerbated. His opinion of the Roman aristocracy was also revised downwards; they were, for the most part, useless and decadent, and indeed 'dying'.[7] They appeared to have no aims to improve the new Italian State or society. (Giuseppi Tomasi di Lampedusa's view of the aristocracy, as seen in *Il Leopardo* (The Leopard), paralleled Zola's.) Rome was in an appalling state, Zola thought, from every possible viewpoint — economic, health, commercial, educational and political — and almost no one cared, since almost nothing was being done, least of all by the Church, according to Signor Bonghi, President of the Roman Press Association. This total apathy shocked Zola deeply. He had expected a considerable amount of it, but nonetheless, he had found more than he had bargained for. This was reflected in arts and letters as well, for how often in the nineteenth century did one hear of famous Roman artists? Nor had he quite realized how isolated Rome was from the rest of Italy. As a Frenchman, he expected the capital to be a national hub, much as Paris was of France, but Rome was little more than the headquarters of a Church which he felt to be decadent, feudally atavistic and totally incongruous in the modern world, and of course the seat of the Italian royal family.

He received full co-operation from nearly everyone, though he was somewhat hindered by his own total ignorance of the Italian language. The Roman press welcomed him as one of their own (both as journalist and republican). He was a declared foe of the Vatican, as were most Roman newspapermen, including Attilio Luzzatto, Director of *La Tribuna*, and it was Luzzatto who was particularly helpful on political questions.

M. Hébert, former Director of the Académie de France à Rome, and a well-known painter in his own right, acted as Zola's guide for the next several weeks, giving historical and artistic explanations of the important buildings and works of art. The Zolas were also received socially by the Héberts on several occasions. Other expatriate Frenchmen who helped Zola included Henri Darcours, Director of *La Correspondance de Rome*, and, perhaps surprisingly, M. Lefebvre de Behaine, the French Ambassador to the Vatican and a cousin of Edmond de Goncourt. Unlike the author of *Lourdes*, the ambassador was a devout Catholic. Of all the Italians he met, only Prince Odescalchi seemed to appeal to Zola. Odescalchi, who was keenly interested in art, was considered rather a renegade in Roman circles, for he looked sympathetically upon socialism and considered himself a republican.

Towards the end of the stay, King Umberto I received Zola at the Quirinal, and two days later he was present at the opening of parliament. Although he enjoyed the ceremony, which the King and Queen attended, he dismissively recorded in his notebook that none of it would be of any use for his research.

The Zolas left Rome on 5 December, returning to France via Florence, Venice, Brescia (where they met a cousin, Carlo Zola, an appeals court judge), and Milan, reaching Paris early on 16 December. Zola returned to his desk eager to begin his new book. He had now been writing professionally for more than thirty years and had yet to lose any of his zeal for work. He was to spend all of 1895 writing *Rome,* and by February of the following year he was correcting page proofs.

Rome is the story of Abbé Pierre Froment who, after returning from his disastrous sojourn in Lourdes and spending many years working in Paris slums, turns to Rome as his last hope, despite the fact that he has lost his faith in the Church. He goes to Rome to defend a book he has written about a new Christianity, but the book is assigned to the Index and the Pope persuades Froment to renounce it as well. The priest returns to Paris, broken and without hope.

When *Rome* was published in the spring of 1896, the power of the Roman Catholic Church ensured that the press reviews were blistering. Zola's outspoken views could not have made them otherwise. In his opinion, religion was wrong and outmoded. He claimed that the Catholic Church was no longer the centre of European life, and furthermore that superstition played an important part in the Church's hold over the Roman Catholics of the world. Zola also claimed the Church was so upset because he had removed all the mysteries of the workings of Lourdes and was doing the same for Rome, including the exposure of manipulations by Church officials. The Catholic Church had been the only major Western religion to restrict, intentionally, the amount of knowledge made available to its followers by such moves as declaring new ideas to be heretical, or suppressing books and opinions. This practice had been severely criticized by honest and scholarly men ever since its inception, and Zola now joined their ranks.

In *Paris,* which Zola began in the last days of spring, 1896, Pierre Froment again appears, unhappy with the way in which the Church is dealing with the woes of mankind, and feeling the need for radical change. Standing in Sacré Coeur Cathedral, in Montmartre, Pierre tells Abbé Louis of his intention to leave the Church: 'For 1800 years now Christianity has been impeding mankind's march towards truth and justice. This march will only be able to continue when Christianity is abolished . . . and is no longer seen as the absolute and definitive moral-religious code.'[8]

On leaving the Church, Pierre concludes that truth and knowledge as supplied by science, are the only saviours, the only real answers to man's woes. When he later marries and becomes a father, he declares that children are 'the future harvest of truth and justice'.[9] This indeed was Zola's testament of beliefs.

He worked on *Paris* throughout the last half of 1896 and during the first several months of the next year. It was one of the most personal novels he ever wrote, and he considered it one of the most important. *Paris* began appearing in serial form in September 1897 in *Le Journal* (the paper of his old friend, Fernand Xau). He managed to finish correcting page proofs of the complete novel by the end of January 1898, as he was simultaneously preparing for his trial. The book went on sale in March of that year. It was really a study of the calamities that had befallen Paris by the 1890s, including political, financial and social cataclysms. Zola was only unhappy with one aspect of this book: he found his own ideas about a better future too nebulous, but at least it served as an indication of where the future lay.

As expected, the political right wing attacked the book, particularly the de-Christianization of Pierre Froment. More surprisingly, the socialists were disappointed with the work as they had hoped he would paint a more favourable picture of their goals. It must be remembered, however, that Zola was not a socialist, although he did understand and sympathize with some of the aims of Jacobin socialism. Nonetheless, the influential socialist leader in the Chamber of Deputies, Jean Jaurès, found *Paris* to be a positive work, 'a hardy protest against the powers of lies and servitude'.

Zola's chief concern at this time, however, was not socialism, but Roman Catholicism. In *Les Trois villes* he denounced the Church unequivocally, as he was to do in the last novel he completed before his death, *Vérité*. But he did not limit his attacks to fiction. In 1895 and 1896 he wrote three articles (which were to appear later in an edited volume entitled *Nouvelle Campagne* (New Campaign), which accurately summed up his views on the Catholic Church.

The first article, *L'Opportunisme de Léon XIII* (Leo XIII's Opportunism), appeared in *Le Figaro* at the beginning of December 1895. In this piece Zola complained that the Catholic Church put God in a back seat and made the Pope a dictator for life. Furthermore, he felt that the present Pope, Leo XIII, was a poor administrator, for he was two-faced, agreeing with all sides in order to gain wider support. In fact, the Pope was only too acutely aware of the dangers the Church faced in the 1890s, hence his equivocal attitude. According to Zola, the Church had become so hidebound in its traditions and practices that it would eventually founder and collapse rather than rethink and change.

Zola's next piece, *'Rome, a-t-elle jamais été Chrétienne?'* (Has Rome Ever Been Christian?), also dates from 1895.[10] In it he suggested that Rome was Catholic rather than Christian. For him, 'paganism' was winning over a Church and Rome that were medieval and moribund: 'By removing itself from the modern world, it is gradually escaping the living world;

it is interested in neither the science nor the industry of the present-day world . . . [Rome] has always lived off others, and today seems to be dying . . . Catholicism is dying with it . . .'[11]

In his final piece, *'La Science et le Catholicisme'* (Science and Catholicism), published in 1896,[12] Zola deals with basic Church dogma:

> It is said that religion is eternal, but, in fact, science is also eternal, and more so. Then a misunderstanding develops because one confuses the word 'religion' with 'Catholicism'. I certainly want religion, the religious feeling, to be eternal, and I believe it will be. But it does not necessarily follow that Catholicism must be eternal, for Catholicism is only a religious form, and it has not always existed, for other religious forms preceded it and still others may follow . . . As I see it, Catholicism is condemned to disappear as science develops, because science has already destroyed its dogmas and it will continue to do so . . . No doubt faith will always exist . . . but dogmas will be reduced to symbols, religion will each day be stripped of more of its grossest superstitions, its miracles, its affirmations which are contrary to the laws of nature, and it will instead take refuge more and more in morality, in the idea of an unknown and superior power, in a deism disengaged from all mythology . . .

Once more Zola advocated faith and trust in the young to push towards the truth of the future, claiming that science offered the greatest hope for educated and healthy minds.

But even before Zola recorded the final lines of this article in the autumn of 1897, he was becoming involved in events which were to change his life and nearly shatter it: the Dreyfus Affair.

TOP LEFT Zola at 30 (*National Portrait Gallery*); TOP RIGHT Alexandrine; BELOW Jacques, Jeanne, Denise and paterfamilias at Verneuil-sur-Seine (*Zola Research Programme, University of Toronto*)

TOP LEFT Old comrades: Zola and Paul Alexis (*Zola Research Programme, University of Toronto*); TOP RIGHT Médan (*ET Archive*); BELOW Zola and Georges Charpentier, his publisher, with their wives and, in the foreground, Fernand Desmoulin, in the garden at Médan (*Zola Research Programme, University of Toronto*)

TOP LEFT Zola, *homme de lettres* (*Mansell Collection*); BELOW LEFT William Busnach, playwright and gambler; TOP RIGHT Jules and Edmond de Goncourt; SECOND FROM TOP, RIGHT Henry Céard, who was caught up in Zola's marital problems; BELOW RIGHT Composer and friend Alfred Bruneau (*all Bibliothèque Nationale, Paris*)

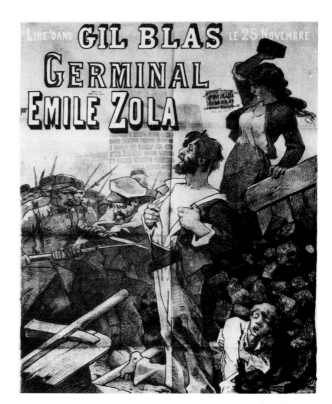

Germinal appears in serial form in *Gil Blas* in November 1885 (*ET Archive*)

The poster for *L'Assommoir* at the Ambigu Theatre in 1879 (*Musée Carnavalet, Paris; Collection Céard, photography Jean-Louis Charonet*)

TOP The first page of *Germinal* (*ET Archive/Bibliothèque Nationale, Paris*); BELOW Emile and Alexandrine; an unhappy marriage (*Zola Research Programme, University of Toronto*)

Le Petit Journal

SUPPLÉMENT ILLUSTRÉ

Huit pages : CINQ centimes

ABONNEMENTS

DIMANCHE 31 JUILLET 1898

Numéro 4

LE PROCÈS ZOLA A VERSAILLES
Départ de Zola

TOP LEFT Zola knocking at the door of the Académie Française (*Cliché Musées de la Ville de Paris — SPADEM 1987*); TOP RIGHT Zola as St George; BELOW The novelist's funeral, 5 October 1902; (l. to r.) Duret, Bruneau, Hermant and Charpentier (*both Mansell Collection*)

18
A Courageous Coward

France was still reeling from the shock of the assassination of Sadi Carnot, President of the French Republic, in June 1894, so the discovery of six bits of paper in a wastepaper basket that September, albeit discovered by a French spy in the German Embassy, seemed hardly startling in comparison.

Upon assembling the pieces, French Army intelligence officer Major Hubert Henry found them to contain a list of classified documents about the latest French field artillery. The list had apparently been sent by a French Army officer to the German military attaché, Colonel Maximilian von Schwartzkoppen. Bearing neither personal names nor title, the document was thereafter referred to simply as the *'bordereau'*. The traitor who had written it had to be found. The suspicions of the seven officers manning the Military Intelligence Service of the Second Bureau, under the command of Major Jean Conrad Sandherr, settled upon a man on the General Staff whom no one liked, a thirty-four-year-old artillery captain from Alsace called Alfred Dreyfus. He was rich, he was aloof, he was intelligent and he was Jewish — indeed he was the first Jewish officer ever to serve on the General Staff of the French Army. Major Henry leaked this news to Edouard Drumont who quickly published the story in his anti-Semitic paper, *La Libre Parole,* announcing to Paris that treason had been committed and that Dreyfus, 'the Jew', was no doubt the man.

Lawyer Edgar Demange attempted to defend Captain Dreyfus before the court martial which assembled on 19 December 1894. Demange, a Catholic and highly respected lawyer, was then at the pinnacle of his career, but despite his recognized abilities, he could not cope with the unknown. The *bordereau* itself was produced in court, but evidence of Dreyfus's involvement was entirely non-existent. Indeed there was not enough to convict him. Not only was the reputation of the Army at stake, however, but the careers of officers who had stated that Dreyfus was guilty. Working behind the scenes, War Minister General Mercier — with the full cooperation of the Army Chief of Staff, General de Boisdeffre, and his deputy chief, General Gonse, as well as Major du Paty de Clam — expected, insisted upon, a conviction. Major Henry, now in a desperate situation, forged the first of several documents which were submitted so secretly to the members of the court-martial board, that neither Captain Dreyfus nor his counsel knew of their existence. It was these forgeries that clinched the case for the Army, although they constituted a violation of both military and constitutional law.

Among the documents forged and presented by Major Henry to the board in December 1894 was one signed, 'Alexandrine', purportedly written by Colonel Schwartzkoppen to the Italian military attaché, Alessandro Panizzardi, in which Dreyfus was allegedly mentioned. Germany and Italy, along with Austria, constituted the members of the anti-French Triple Alliance. (Germany still occupied the two French provinces of Alsace and Lorraine, seized during the Franco-Prussian War of 1870-71.)

In spite of protesting his innocence and refusing to do 'the honourable thing' by committing suicide, a bewildered Dreyfus was found guilty of treason and sentenced to life imprisonment. On the morning of 5 January 1895 he was stripped of his commission before a military parade in the courtyard of the Ecole Militaire in Paris and then dispatched to Devil's Island off the sweltering coast of French Guiana in South America.

Although Mathieu Dreyfus, the industrialist brother of the convicted man, believed in his innocence and worked for his rehabilitation from the very beginning, it was not until Lieutenant-Colonel Picquart became head of Army Intelligence in July 1895 that momentous changes began to take place. Ironically Picquart was a fellow Alsatian, and had even instructed Dreyfus at the Ecole de la Guerre, but added to this was the fact that he had also appeared at the court martial on behalf of the prosecution and had represented War Minister General Mercier at the Ecole Militaire on 5 January when Dreyfus had been stripped of his commission.

When, after the exile of Dreyfus, more French military documents continued to reach the German Embassy, Colonel Picquart scrupulously pursued the matter. In the course of his investigation he came to realize that Dreyfus had been convicted on the basis of forged documents and between then and the autumn of 1896 more evidence was to emerge, including the *'petit bleu'* telegram (from the German military attaché to Major Esterhazy), and another forged letter by Major Henry, subsequently known as 'the forged Henry', in which Dreyfus was named.

Appalled by what he had learnt, including the name of the real author of the *bordereau*, Major Esterhazy (the son of a general), Picquart informed his superiors, who immediately had him transferred to a war-zone in Tunisia. He was replaced as head of Army Intelligence by Lieutenant-Colonel Hubert Henry — the forger himself. Fortunately, even before leaving his post in Army Intelligence, Picquart had consulted his old classmate and fellow Alsatian, Louis Leblois, now a practising lawyer in Paris, and shown him various documents. Thus it was Maître Leblois who pursued the matter in Colonel Picquart's absence. Key people, including

Alsatian Senator Scheurer-Kestner, were informed, some of whom appealed to the French government to recall Dreyfus and begin a new trial — all in vain. It was at this juncture that Zola, with absolutely no personal involvement in the case, was persuaded of the miscarriage of justice and himself entered the fray.

Zola neither claimed, nor wished for, the keys to an ivory tower. Although disputes and clashes upset him greatly, life was a struggle and it had always been so. Indeed, he would have it no other way, and so claimed the privilege and honour of participating in that struggle. He defended his principles which he realized would result frequently in an inevitable amount of criticism and opposition. In his youth he had fought for the new painters and writers, and then after completing the *Rougon-Macquart* series in 1893, he began his highly controversial series on the Roman Catholic Church and religion in general.

Thus Zola was not an out and out coward. Despite the unpleasantness, anxiety and depression he might experience, he would certainly attack when principle was involved. To be sure, when he had attacked the Church, at least he had the support of a large number of 'republicans', and therefore was far from being alone. And of course until he began to assume an active role in the Dreyfus Affair, he had always expected resistance and counter-attacks, but at a certain level only. From the moment he took this latest role upon himself, however, he began to realize that this was very different. Most of the French press would crucify anyone who dared attack the Army, as he well knew from his own experience after the publication of *La Débâcle*. But this novel had merely criticized the Army for incompetence. Now he had before him in his Paris study, his *'Lettre à M. Félix Faure, Président de la République'*, which Ernest Vaughan, one of the publishers of the new Parisian daily newspaper, *L'Aurore,* wanted to entitle *'J'accuse'*. If Zola published this document, filled with unheard of accusations against the Army — anti-Semitism, criminal activities on an impressive scale — and with similar charges against well known national figures, he was also beginning to realize how far-reaching the consequences might be. He would face imprisonment and possibly a heavy fine; the sales of his books (his main source of income, as he had no investments) would suffer appreciably; friends of many years' standing would no longer speak to him; and perhaps worst of all, the press, and even some of the better tabloids would delve into his private life as they had never done before. He had spent too many years as a journalist not to know how every aspect of his personal life would be brought into sharp focus, not to mention the boundless possibilities of sheer invention when it was not simply grossly distorted by daily papers across the land. It was one thing for him to suffer threats, slander and abuse, but should Alexandrine, Jeanne and the children be exposed to it too? If he wanted to avoid this, he simply had to throw the letter into the fireplace and write to Georges Clemenceau (also with an interest in *L'Aurore*) and Vaughan, informing them that he would not jeopardize the sanctity and sanity of his private life for the sake of the article — after all, he had written so many already in defence of Dreyfus. But he could not deceive himself. There came a time when one had to take a stand, or no longer be able to respect oneself. And this was not simply another article; indeed, it was like no other.

After completing his latest novel, *Paris,* at the end of August 1897, Zola had more free time to himself, just at a moment when much intense activity was taking place involving the Dreyfus Affair. By October, while preparing to return to Paris for the winter, he was drawn into the case. As Senator Scheurer-Kestner was gathering new information, Marcel Prévost, a well-known novelist, approached Zola, informing him of the situation and of the growing momentum. He then put Zola in touch with Colonel Picquart's lawyer and old friend, Maître Leblois, who in turn arranged for a meeting with Senator Scheurer-Kestner. What really convinced Zola of the innocence of Dreyfus was the declaration by a banker called José de Castro, that he recognized the handwriting of the *bordereau* as that of one of his clients, Major Esterhazy. There could be no mistake about it, he insisted. And of course Colonel Picquart had been claiming Esterhazy's guilt for over a year now.

Then in November, Fernand de Rodays, publisher of *Le Figaro,* met Zola by chance and asked whether he might be interested in writing something for his paper on the Dreyfus case. Zola prepared a series of articles, the first of which, entitled *'M. Scheurer-Kestner',* appeared on 25 November, and praised the senator for his interest and involvement in the Affair. The article was low-key by Zola's standards, not intended to rouse the world, but it ended in a statement of great personal significance to Zola, for it would become his motto — echoed by his followers — throughout the Affair: 'Truth is on the march and nothing will stop it.'[1]

The publisher of *Le Figaro* received some criticism from his readers when the article appeared, but nothing out of the ordinary. Then on 1 December Zola's second article, *'Le Syndicat'* (The Syndicate), appeared, in which he scoffed at the naïveté of the French people for believing in such fairy-tales as an international Jewish syndicate. On the other hand, a syndicate should be created — not a Jewish syndicate, but one of courageous Frenchmen willing to work for justice. Rodays received more complaints about this article and numerous subscriptions were cancelled, but Zola was also sent a few complimentary letters, including one from the Chief Rabbi of France, Zadoc Kahn, who referred to the articles as 'strong, courageous and French'.[2] The novelist had some difficulty in persuading Rodays to publish the third article, *'Le Procès verbal'* (The Proceedings), but it finally appeared on 5 December.

By now Zola was becoming more exasperated and his language less cautious. In *'Le Procès verbal'* he attacked the gutter press for writing with a complete disregard for truth, caring only about sales. Then he attacked anti-Semitism, accusing it of being 'the guilty party' and a real problem in French society. 'To return to the Wars of Religion and the religious persecutions of yore, to want whole races exterminated, is such nonsense in our modern times that even to attempt it seems stupid.'[3] Finally he exhorted the French people to display 'justice and humanity'. Although the article could hardly be described as inflammatory, so many critical letters reached Rodays' desk that he felt constrained to cancel Zola's remaining articles.

Because of the passions aroused and the intensity of opposition he now encountered, Zola felt more determined than ever to proceed, and published his next article in pamphlet form at his own expense. Entitled *'Lettre à la jeunesse'* (Letter to the Country's Youth), it was an emotional appeal to the students of France: 'Youth of the country, be humane, be generous. Even if you think we may be wrong, support us when we tell you that an innocent man is undergong terrible suffering and that we are exasperated and heart-sick as a result . . . We are marching towards humanity, towards truth, towards justice!' It almost sounded like a litany.

This pamphlet was followed by another on 6 January 1898, entitled *'Lettre à la France'* (Letter to France), a France which he addressed in the informal *'tu'*:

. . . France, is that you there, being taken in by a most obvious lie, joining the mob of criminals against some honest people, panicking under the stupid pretext that the Army is being insulted — that there are plots afoot to sell you out to the enemy? . . . Today anti-Semitism is a tactic . . . to lead [people] back to the [Catholic] altars. What a triumph, if a religious war could be unleashed!

France must come to her senses, restore justice and self-respect, put an end to the mockery of justice in the military courts, stop their secret sessions and the withholding of important documents. What folly to think that one can prevent history from being written. It will be written, and those responsible will be duly named and recorded, no matter how small their role.

So concluded the last article before he began preparing his *'Lettre à M. Félix Faure'*. Many friends, acquaintances and even strangers, hailed each of the preceding articles, and after reading the *'Lettre à la France'*, Armand Charpentier, the novelist, told Zola that he found it 'fine, eloquent and courageous'.[4]

The Dreyfus case had become bogged down: the government, the Army and the Church had dug in their heels, and Dreyfus was dying a slow, painful death on a wretched tropical rock for another man's crime. It would take more than harassment to make the French government backtrack now and permit a revision of the Affair, which is what Zola and his friends were aiming for. A mere article, even one by a well-known literary figure, apparently had little effect, and even when Senator Scheurer-Kestner himself had gone to the heads of government to reveal the truth, and taken the unprecedented step of publishing his views in the Parisian daily, *Le Temps*, it was to no avail.

No, it would take a jolt of unusual magnitude to shock the government into action. Zola felt that his 'Letter' to the President of the Republic would indeed bring about the desired results, but why should he bother for the sake of a Jew, innocent or not? He had never liked Jews, as his novels demonstrated. And yet there was more at stake than just one man — *principles* were involved — justice, truth and national integrity. In many respects Zola did not wish to act, and indeed it would have been easier to end the whole thing before it got completely out of hand. If he denied his principles, however, he could no longer respect himself; it would make a mockery of everything he had ever stood for. No, it must be done, so he slipped the manuscript into a large brown envelope and sent it to Georges Clemenceau and Ernest Vaughan at the offices of *L'Aurore*.

When *'J'accuse'* appeared in the streets of Paris on 13 January 1898, it caused an immediate sensation that even Zola and Vaughan had not foreseen. Over 300,000 copies were sold before the morning was out — a record probably unmatched by any Parisian paper. Thousands of copies were burnt by army sympathizers, but no one could stifle its message now: the gauntlet had been thrown down to President Faure. A court martial had exonerated the guilty Major Esterhazy a couple of days before — 'the supreme affront to all truth, to all justice,' wrote Zola.[5] The real culprit behind this miscarriage of justice, Zola now claimed, was Lieutenant-Colonel du Paty de Clam who had been backed by many men, including Colonel Sandherr (then Director of Army Intelligence), General Mercier (Minister of War when Dreyfus was sentenced), General de Boisdeffre, with his Vatican support, and General Gonse. General Billot, the new War Minister, arrived fresh on the scene and could have altered the wrong done to Dreyfus and the French nation, but he chose to add to the massive cover-up. Zola concluded by accusing Lieutenant-Colonel du Paty de Clam of having been the 'diabolical contriver of the judicial error . . . of having then defended his baneful work for the past three years by the most preposterous and culpable machinations'.[6] He accused General Mercier of acting as an accomplice. He accused General Billot of having stifled the truth, of having suppressed the documents which he knew would prove the innocence of Dreyfus, and thereby committing an outrage against humanity and justice. He accused Generals de Boisdeffre and Gonse of having acted as accomplices, and General de Pellieux and Major Ravary 'of having carried out a cunning inquiry . . . of the most monstrous partiality'. The three handwriting experts called in by the Army — Belhomme, Varinard and Couard — who saw the lying and fraudulent documents for what they were, but who concealed their true findings, were also accused in their turn. Zola then accused the War Office of having carried out an abominable campaign in *L'Eclair* and *L'Echo de Paris* in order to sway public opinion and to cover its tracks. Finally, Zola accused the first court martial of having broken the law by condemning Dreyfus on a piece of evidence withheld from him and his counsel, and he accused the second court martial of having covered up this illegality on orders, and of committing another crime by knowingly acquitting the guilty Esterhazy.

As Zola had not been given access to the documents of the case, some of his assertions and conclusions were not entirely correct. For instance, he did not mention Major Henry and his criminal role, nor did he realize that he was exaggerating the part played by Colonel du Paty de Clam. As brilliant as his intuition and analysis were in an extraordinarily complicated affair, Zola had no way of knowing how responsible General Mercier was, and clearly underestimated his central role. Yet the essence of what he wrote was perfectly true, and it was to open many eyes.

If this long and unique incantation was dramatic and even repetitious, it was the perfect tool for drawing attention to the government cover-up in the Dreyfus case, and it was Zola who now single-handedly changed the case from 'an affair' to 'The Affair'.

In one fell blow Zola had stung the public, the government, the Army and the Church. Prime Minister Méline deplored these 'abominable attacks' by Zola, while Count Albert de Mun, the champion of the Army and the Church, descried '*J'accuse*' as 'a miserable outrage against the heads of the Army'. After reading the article, Maurice Barrès, a prominent nationalist and author, and a member of the Academy, concluded, 'this man is no Frenchman'. On the other hand, François Coppée represented those few who dutifully supported the Army, but insisted on maintaining friendly ties with Zola. 'The friendship of your champion of yesterday in the Academy could not do otherwise, but as you see, it remains quite intact, as does my high and profound esteem for your talent and your accomplishments as a novelist.'[7]

Zola had made his decision and his life would never again be the same. He was marked for greatness and history would not forget him, nor would his fellow countrymen. And as Georges Charpentier wrote shortly afterwards, 'What glory for you in the future! But what nastiness and humiliation for the present.'[8]

On 20 January Zola was formally served with the papers by the Assize Court of the Seine charging him with defamation. Of the 2000 lines in '*J'accuse*', General Billot, Méline's War Minster, had limited himself to contesting just one of the numerous charges made by Zola, namely the illegal conduct of the second court martial in covering up the use of secret documents 'on orders', and in knowingly acquitting a guilty man. Zola was disappointed with the content of the papers; General Billot's legal experts were unable to answer the rest of the charges so they had simply ignored them.

> The said passages containing the accusation of such a nature as to bear upon the honour and esteem of the first Court Martial of the Military Government of Paris which met on the 10 and 11 January 1898, and relative to its functions, thus to have defamed it publicly and as a result of its function . . . the infractions prescribed and punishable by Articles 23, 29, 30, 31, 35, 42, 43, 45, 47, and 52 of the Law of 29 July 1881, [and by Articles] 59 and 60 of the Penal Code.[9]

Upon receiving his copy of this assignation, Zola's new lawyer, Maître Fernand Labori, warned him, 'from the legal viewpoint it contains some consequences about which I must talk to you as soon as possible . . .'[10]

On Sunday 23 January 1898, following High Mass in the cathedrals and churches of France and sermons against Zola, a rash of police reports began to reach the desk of President Félix Faure in the Elysée Palace. From Angers to Avignon, from Nantes to Marseilles, from Rouen to Lyons, in Bordeaux, Besançon, Grenoble, Moulins and Orléans, students were demonstrating in large numbers (in quiet Toulouse, 400, in little Perpignan, the local prefect of police reported 500 students, and in Caen, 1500), running through the streets and frantically chanting: 'Down with the Jews! Down with Zola! Down with Scheurer!' In Choisy-le-Roi, Zola's effigy was burnt in the place Rouget-de-Lisie, as almost the entire population looked on and joined in the same cries that were heard across the nation that day: 'Death to Dreyfus! Down with Zola! Death to the Jews! Death to the traitors!' followed occasionally by the singing of the *Marseillaise*. The police looked on, refraining from any serious interference. It was the same everywhere, as the well-rehearsed (and in many instances, well-paid) 'students' chanted their hatred before Jewish shops and homes. President Faure did not like his Jewish countrymen any more than the rabble in the streets did, and thus even when the demonstrators were detained by the police, they paid no fine in most cases, or perhaps a nominal one franc. Still, this sort of thing could not continue. For it was a bit too obvious, hundreds of students, thousands of students, repeating well-prepared phrases on the same day, at the same time throughout the country. It would cause more harm than good, and thus the Minister of the Interior (who was the titular head of the nation's police) was instructed by Prime Minister Méline to make a semblance of cracking down on street demonstrations. But of course it was really Zola's fault; if he had not written '*J'accuse*', none of this would have been happening.

The cold wind swept up the Seine, sending snow flurries swirling through the grey January sky, across the massive stone quays and against the now dark, lugubrious walls of the Bourbon Palace. Inside, the vast Chamber seemed darker than usual, though every lamp and gas jet had been lit. The session was well attended as Deputies fought for their turn to address or harangue their colleagues; it seemed no one could remain silent or neutral on this issue. At last a distinguished looking, if somewhat portly, gentleman with a full grey beard was recognized, and he climbed the stairs to the tribune. Standing there for a moment, he gazed slowly round at the members of parliament sitting before him in their places in the Hemicycle — the legislators of the land. Like Zola, he had been hard to convince. Lucien Herr and other friends from the Ecole Normale had spoken to him about the matter and finally he too had recognized the innocence of Dreyfus and the machinations perpetrated in order to shield the guilty and their accomplices. Jaurès began to speak, slowly but firmly, with great resonance, and for a moment, one would have thought oneself in a university lecture hall and not the Chamber of Deputies, as the former professor of philosophy addressed the assembly:

I invite the Government to explain its handling of the legal actions against M. Zola, the abuses concerning secret documents and the closed-door hearings which have enshrouded the trials of ex-Captain Dreyfus and Major Esterhazy. How could the Prime Minister claim that the honour of the generals was above the decisions of the courts?[11]

When Prime Minister Méline rose and interjected, 'The Government has applied the law . . . ', he was greeted by applause.

Jaurès continued: 'Put an end to restricted or closed hearings. The country must finally know the whole truth.' A small amount of applause came from the socialist groups on the left in an otherwise silent Chamber, as Jaurès returned to his seat.

On the other side of the Seine demonstrators again roamed the streets, and after burning a stack of pro-Zola newspapers, wandered up the boulevard de Sébastopol, their numbers swelling to include students, paid agitators, a few bored and curious onlookers, and some who had drunk a little more absinthe than they could handle. Reaching number 36, they stopped before a small cloth merchant's shop and apartment, 'Salomon, Schill, Dreyfus et Cie', and the mob began chanting 'Down with Zola! Down with the Jews!' The Montrouge line Gare-de-l'Est tram drove past as the mob moved in round the building. Some of the passengers on the tram shouted back at the demonstrators, 'Long live Zola!' As the horses drew up the demonstrators turned and charged at the tram. A noisy scuffle broke out and suddenly revolver shots rang through the crisp January air, shattering a window of the shop. More people joined the demonstrators (later estimated by the police to have reached about 500 in number). Then a large number of police appeared, subduing the fracas temporarily. They half-heartedly pursued a few demonstrators who fled up the rue de Turbigo, and then proceeded to the place de la République, reaching the boulevard Voltaire, still shouting, 'Down with Zola!' Jostling and shouting they reached another shop, number 208, with the name 'Bernheim' above the window. They began shouting, 'Down with the Jews, Down with Zola!' Someone suddenly started throwing rocks at the upstairs windows where the Bernheims were having dinner. Windows were broken and one person at table was struck by a rock. Although the police finally caught up with the mob and managed to subdue it, only about ten of the 500 demonstrators were arrested and taken down to the eleventh *arrondissement* headquarters where they were later released because the Jewish families wished to maintain a low profile and declined to press charges.

Zola was very disappointed in the amount of support he received, and was especially dismayed by the strong opposition of the students, in whom he had put so much faith. Not to be outdone by their elders, Henri Rochefort, Paul Déroulède, Edouard Drumont, Albert de Mun and Maurice Barrès, students around the country drew up their own letters, petitions and resolutions, of which the following is typical:

> The law students of the University of Lille, having met in a general assembly, wishing to end any misunderstanding and in order to affirm unequivocally their true feelings in the Dreyfus affair, strongly protest against the vilifications addressed by M. Zola to the French Army and to its chiefs.
>
> United in heart, regardless of what is said, with their comrades in all French universities, they energetically demonstrate their disapproval of this anti-French campaign, and, confident in the destiny of their country, they bring glory to themselves by joining all patriotic French youth by calling out, 'Long live France! Long live the Army!'
>
> This item on the agenda has been unanimously adopted by 1005 votes with two abstentions.[12]

Government and municipal officials also attacked Zola almost incessantly, a typical letter being the following from the mayors of Limonest (Rhône):

> Sir,
> You have had the impudence to address us with the mutterings of your disturbed mind. Please note what we think of you and of your work.
>
> You speak to us on behalf of humanity, truth and justice. But under this guise, we are not deceived as to your real self. Whether he is called Iscariot, Bazaine, Dreyfus or Zola, every Judas is a traitor.

The injuries you have hurled at the Army, however, can neither intimidate it, nor lower the flag. This flag which has carried the glory of France to the four corners of the earth, laughs at those worms who crawl on their bellies.

In spite of your hypocritical language, France will have in the future, as in the past, triumphant days of glory, truth and justice.

With our most scornful regards . . . [13]

The hate campaign against Zola was shamelessly fuelled by Henri Rochefort, whose writings in the newspaper *L'Intransigeant* earned him the title of 'King of the Gutter Press'. He commanded huge support among the French people, and had many foreign admirers of his anti-Semitic articles, including sixteen students from the Gymnasium of Moscow, who sent him the following encouragement: 'Kindly accept the assurances of our perfect and profound consideration relative to your energetic struggle against the hideous campaign of the Jews and the acolytes of Dreyfus, against the glorious French Army.' [14]

Although the vast majority of letters and petitions sent to, or concerning, Zola were unfavourable, some were supportive, and even the wife of Captain Dreyfus received one signed by 1958 women of Christiana, pledging their support: 'The Norwegian women, who have been following your struggle with deep sympathy, send you their most ardent wishes, from the depths of their hearts, that truth and justice win out.' [15]

Zola also received encouragement from eighty writers and artists from Finland who sent 'the expression of our admiration and sympathy for the illustrious master, whose moral courage and character equal his talents'. [16] Such unexpected kindess from such unexpected places surely lightened Zola's heart. Meanwhile at home, Anatole France (hardly an admirer of Zola's literary works), organized a writers' petition to the government calling for a review of the Dreyfus case. [17] Later, two other petitions reached the government supporting Zola and Dreyfus, one signed by Claude Monet, Jules Renard, Frederick Houssaye and Emile Durkheim, the other prepared by, among others, two famous Paris publishers, Armand Collin and Max Leclerc. [18] Still other petitions were signed by various university professors in Paris, and sent despite the threats of their students. Zola also received a letter commending him on his courageous work, signed by his friends Fernand Desmoulin, Catulle Mendès, Edouard Rod, Léon Dierx and others. [19] Although Zola was not a socialist, he received welcome support from the Federation of Belgian Workers who congratulated him on his courageous protest for citizens' rights.

But the enemies of citizens' rights were especially persistent in France, and a good example of this was seen in the meeting organized by one Boucher-Cadart, in the mayor's office of the town of Ile-Saint-Denise. As the local papers later described it, 'The patriots of the region met there in order to protest against the schemings of the defenders of Dreyfus. Posters were put up everywhere, bearing in large letters: "Patriots, rally round the flag! . . . Our motto is: Down with Zola! Down with the Dreyfus syndicate! No more German Jews! Long live the Army! Long live France! Long live the Republic!" "[20]

Behind the scenes Zola worked intensively with his lawyer, Fernand Labori. A steady stream of urgent telegrams, letters and hand-delivered notes (to avoid perusal by the police), flowed between the rue de Bruxelles and Labori's office at 12, rue de Bourgogne. Not infrequently Zola would be summoned for consultation with just a couple of hours' notice. Over the next year or so, during which time the two men worked closely together, they still addressed each other as *'vous'*, despite a growing friendship, which allowed Labori to progress from *'Mon cher monsieur Zola'* to *'Mon cher illustre et grand ami'*. At the first of their conferences, late in January 1898, the two men discussed strategy and how to bring the Dreyfus Affair into the open. At meeting after meeting Labori prepared Zola and tried to contact witnesses and take statements which the lawyer considered to be highly important.

During an interview in the first week of February with the influential Parisian daily newspaper, *Le Matin*, Zola was asked what he thought about his forthcoming trial. 'I await it with tranquillity. I hope we will end in shedding light on the Dreyfus trial . . . That is all I desire . . . '[21] When questioned about possible witnesses, Zola stated:

> That is an unimportant question. If there are witnesses, we shall act with them, if there aren't any, we shall carry on without them. More important are the pleas entered by Maître Labori, my defence lawyer, and by M. Clemenceau, acting on behalf of the managing editor of *L'Aurore*, and the personal explanation which I plan to deliver to the jury myself. These elements will suffice, I hope, to enlighten public opinion in the affair of ex-Captain Dreyfus . . . an extremely lucid affair . . . of childish simplicity.

When later speaking to a reporter of *Le Temps*, however, he addressed himself to other aspects of the forthcoming trial, seemingly oblivious of the threats to him and his cause which seethed throughout France.

> Some think I'll be acquitted because civilian law courts cannot condemn a citizen for having shown his profound respect for the law by the violent indignation he has felt resulting from the outrage committed against the law by a court martial. I have no opinion. Whatever the decision by the jury, I'll abide by it. My conscience is clear, for it alone has dictated my conduct, and I place that verdict above all others.

But I shall defend myself because this defence is necesary for the revelation of the truth.

I have no ties with the Dreyfus family. I have never seen M. Mathieu Dreyfus and I have never met Madame Dreyfus. The unfortunate wife of the condemned man of Devil's Island has sought several times to see me, no doubt to express her gratitude for the help I have given her husband's cause. She even went to Maître Labori's office at a time when she knew I was there . . . I refused any meeting in order to keep complete freedom of action. I have the right to proclaim my independence before the court and point out clearly to it that the sole motive guiding me was my conviction that a judicial error had been made [in the court martial] and that the obstinacy of those involved not wishing to right the wrong was resulting in the greatest dangers to our individual freedom just as it is to our public freedoms.

But there is something other than the violations of the law in the first court martial of 1894. There remains the certainty of the innocence of Dreyfus. As far as I am concerned, his innocence is as clear as the sun in the sky. That too I shall attempt to demonstrate to my judges . . . I have absolute confidence in our ultimate success.[22]

At 10.45 a.m. on 7 February, Zola climbed into the hired carriage waiting for him and proceeded to the most ancient part of Paris, the Ile de la Cité, and the Palace of Justice.

19
'There is No Zola Case!'

Even Victor Hugo could not have hoped to have been tried in a more historic building than the Palais de Justice, with its massive thirteenth-century foundations sunk deep into the Ile de la Cité, the ancient seat of warrior kings and the heart of Paris.

'*"J'accuse"* is a monument worthy of taking its place in the memory of mankind alongside the *Declaration of the Rights of Man and Citizen*,' reminisced Jean France,[1] who as a young police official witnessed many of the crucial events in Paris in 1898. At the time of the trial, however, which began on 7 February 1898, that view was distinctly in the minority, as most Parisian newspapers and 'patriots' called for Zola's head, and Jules Guérin's street gangs (members of his Anti-Semitic League), would have been more than happy to oblige. But the anger and hysteria of civilians was as nothing compared with the outrages which the French judiciary, politicians and army officers were prepared to perpetrate even within the walls of the Palais de Justice itself.

The Prime Minister had led the way, denouncing Zola and his 'abominable attacks', just as he had done with Dreyfus in December: 'There is no Dreyfus Affair!' From the morning of 13 January, immediately upon the appearance of '*J'accuse*', the Chamber of Deputies quickly became a cockpit of intrigue and acrimony, and Zola's name was on everyone's lips. The Count de Mun called the article a 'bloody outrage'. Prime Minister Jules Méline, addressing the Hemicycle of legislators on the twenty-second, continued the battle on behalf of his government. 'You [Zola] do not have the right to cause army chiefs to be scorned. It is by just such means that we prepare fresh editions of *La Débâcle* . . . Why do we not pursue the entire article? Because the honour of our army generals does not require the approval of a jury; it is above any suspicion.'[2] The phrase, 'above the law', would be invoked by army officers time and again throughout the trial.

'Those who prepare the future débâcles,' riposted Jean Jaurès, 'are not those who point out these errors, but those who commit them! . . . Do you know what we are suffering from? What we are all dying from? Ever since this affair began, we have all been dying from half-measures, enforced silence, equivocations, lies and cowardice.'[3]

A scornful Count de Bernis leapt to his feet: 'You are the Jewish syndicate's spokesman!'

Jaurès turned to him: 'Monsieur de Bernis, you are a scoundrel and a coward!'[4] The Chamber roared as Bernis rushed over to Jaurès and struck him; the stage was well prepared for the fiasco to follow.

Zola was always national news, but when threatened by the mighty French Army and possible imprisonment, it was an event of international importance, and journalists from a dozen countries vied with their French colleagues to obtain interviews and photographs of the *dramatis personae*. On the steps and crowding the three doors of the main entrance, smart soldiers in blue and braid, with shining silver scabbards, rubbed elbows with bevies of black-robed lawyers and elegant ladies who had enough influence to find a place here for what promised to be the event of *tout Paris*. As for the personalities who were to appear on these steps in February, there had never been anything quite like it: past, present and future presidents of the republic, prime ministers, foreign ministers, ministers of justice, war ministers, senators, deputies, members of the French Academy, celebrated professors and authors, a curious variety of army officers, among them Casimir-Perier, Loubet, Méline, Dupuy, Brisson, Delcassé, Trarieux, Thévenet, Freycinet, Hanotaux, Cavaignac, Waldeck-Rousseau, Scheurer-Kestner, Mirbeau, France, Barrès, Generals Boisdeffre, Gonse, Mercier and Billot, Colonels Henry, Picquart and du Paty de Clam and no end of rabble rousers, including Edouard Drumont, Paul Déroulède (who was to attempt to overthrow the government a year later), Jules Guérin, and, of course, Henri Rochefort, the 'gutter-press king'. The more illustrious names alone filled entire pages of the long police reports.

'The Zola Affair', as *Le Figaro* now insisted upon calling it, and the passions it aroused, were no mere isolated incidents; they were the tip of an ugly iceberg, representing the conflict between the Establishment and the forces challenging it. Through the manipulation and connivance of Judge Delegorgue and the Attorney-General, Edmond van Cassel, the government attempted to strangle the case by limiting the criminal complaint against Zola to just fifteen lines of *'J'accuse'*, and prohibiting the defence counsel from discussing the Dreyfus case ('the thing judged'), and much of the Esterhazy case as well. This made it impossible to call most of the nearly 100 witnesses whose names they had submitted. Zola's lawyer, Labori, and his colleagues were also forbidden to ask critical questions of the State's witnesses — many they were not permitted to question at all — and the judge granted himself the unique right to interrupt Labori's witnesses before cross-examination began, contrary to accepted courtroom procedure, and was party to the suppression of secret documents. There had been some pretty shameful farces in nineteenth-century French legal history, but the combined courtroom illegalities carried out by the Ministry of Justice and the French Army throughout the Dreyfus Affair and the Zola trial astounded the world and brought scorn upon France for years to come.

The bustling crowds in the corridors, the Salle des Pas Perdus and the steps and courtyard of the Palais de Justice reflected the exhilaration of the times, while inadequate police control over the comings and goings of the lawyers, judges, witnesses, soldiers, politicians and the curious only added to the confusion and the problem of security. Zola, his family and friends received obscene letters and numerous threats every day. Stones smashed the windows of his home in the rue de Bruxelles, the crowds at the Palais de Justice frequently jostled him, forcing his friends to surround him on journeys to and from the courtroom — all this, despite the fact that an extra 220 police were on duty to provide security. At best the Prefecture of Police was disorganized, at worst perhaps deliberately lax. One day, for instance, a loud, isolated Zola supporter, responding to hooligans, was chased down the boulevard du Palais, captured, beaten and about to be thrown into the Seine when the police finally came to his rescue. Another day Louis Leblois, Colonel Picquart's lawyer, who was working closely with Labori, was deliberately shoved down the sweeping stone steps of the main staircase in the Palais, though fortunately he was able to save himself by grabbing hold of the balustrade. The enemies of Zola and his supporters felt secure and brazen enough to try anything, even within the Palais de Justice. On another occasion, as Zola, Labori and Bruneau were crossing the courtyard, Prince Henri d'Orléans shouted his congratulations to Major Esterhazy who was also leaving at that moment. The ecstatic crowd carried Esterhazy off in triumph, as shouts of 'Down with Zola! Death to the Jews! Long live the Army!' rang out — but remained unchallenged by the police stationed outside. To avoid unruly mobs, Zola was forced to leave by a side exit on more than one occasion. After having once been struck by shattered glass in his carriage, he tried to take less obvious routes between his home and the court. Then one morning the carriage with just Zola and Fasquelle inside was approaching the embankment when a band of men, perhaps Guérin's followers, suddenly appeared out of nowhere, rushing towards them, stopping the horse, trying to push the carriage in the direction of the river. The police intervened just in time to prevent the vehicle from plunging into the rain-swollen waters of the Seine. The death threats Zola received were real enough, and so were these 'patriots', many of whom were paid five francs a day for their devotion to the cause.

The need for a bodyguard was, therefore, real and urgent. Alfred Bruneau and Fernand Desmoulin, armed with a pistol, took charge, dropping other commitments in order to stand by their friend. After the attack near the Seine, the authorities asked to be informed daily of Zola's movements to and from the court. 'Desmoulin and I took alternate turns in notifying the police first thing every morning . . . ' Bruneau related. Some protection was then provided. 'Two carriages waited in front of the house, where we, Zola and us, got into one of them, the police into the other, their job being to keep the crowds at a distance and to repulse any surprise attacks . . . '[6]

Zola's choice of chief counsel turned out to be a wise one. Fernand Labori, a tall, handsome and affable man with a distinguished blond beard, whom Eugène Fasquelle introduced to Zola that January, was nearly twenty years younger than the novelist, but had already established a national reputation for himself defending Auguste Vaillant, an anarchist who had thrown a bomb into the Chamber of Deputies. The political right wing could not help but be wary of an opponent who was both a brilliant scholar and a remarkable orator. Labori agreed to defend Zola on condition that he would receive no payment for his services; the only fees would be for the junior lawyers involved, Hilde and Monira, and of course the usual court fees. Labori was idealistic and dynamic, unintimidated by anyone or anything, and thus a man after Zola's own heart.

Despite the bitterly cold February weather and the frequent days of rain through the trial, the courtroom was apparently stiflingly hot. It was so crowded that many lawyers who came as observers were forced to sit cross-legged on the floor. Zola sat with Perrenx, managing editor of L'Aurore, who had also been charged with defamation, facing the three judges in brilliant scarlet gowns: MM. Lault, Bousquet and in the centre, the presiding judge, the short, plump M. Delegorgue. To either side of them sat the jury. Several feet to the right sat the public prosecutor, Attorney-General Edmond van Cassel[7] and his assistants. The constant drone of dozens of excited voices filled the room and Judge Delegorgue was to have considerable trouble in maintaining order throughout the fifteen days of the trial. Nor was there any lack of activity at Zola's table where notes were exchanged and a steady stream of *petits-bleus* continued to arrive all day, forming an impressive stack several inches high.

Under French law Zola stood not only accused, but guilty, the onus falling upon him to prove his innocence to the jury of twelve men who were selected without incident the first day, and who included three small merchants, a roof-builder, a copper worker, a clerk, a landlord, a tanner, a seed salesman, a metal worker, a market-gardener and a cloth merchant. No member of the professions or educated classes was represented among them, and to facilitate possible intimidation, their names and addresses were published in the Parisian press.

In his complaint of defamation against Zola, War Minister General Billot stated, 'Chiefs and subordinates are above such outrages; the opinion of Parliament, the country and the Army has already placed them beyond reach of attack.'[8] These were not just idle words, nor were they limited to soldiers alone. In his opening address to the court, the Attorney-General, van Cassel, warned (and Delegorgue was shortly to decree) that discussion of the Dreyfus case and grounds for its possible appeal were not relative to the present case and could not be discussed under any circumstances. The name 'Dreyfus' was forbidden. The jury, van Cassel continued, had only one responsibility: to decide whether or not the January 1898 court-martial board of Major Esterhazy had acquitted him 'on orders'. Van Cassel grimly concluded that no new or unknown documents had been introduced here to establish the innocence of Dreyfus, but he totally ignored the possibility of any secret documents pertaining either to Dreyfus or Esterhazy.

Labori's reply was brief. 'I am not much astonished, Gentlemen, at the difficulties which Monsieur Zola meets in this affair, and I expect that this incident, which is the first, will not be the last.'' He argued that the cases of Dreyfus and Esterhazy could not be separated, as they were essentially one and the same. Both Dreyfus and Esterhazy had been prosecuted for the same crime of treason and the crucial document at both trials had been the same *bordereau* (listing the documents sold to the Germans). But in fact Esterhazy had been acquitted: 'The question remains unresolved and we are here to deal with it . . . Either we are to be prevented from offering any proof, and in that case shall just have to wait and see; or, on the contrary, we are to be permitted to examine the situation of ex-Captain Dreyfus as well as that of Major Esterhazy . . . [for] it would hardly be possible for us to prove the guilt of Major Esterhazy and his acquittal in obedience to orders, if at the same time we did not have the right to prove the innocence of ex-Captain Dreyfus.' The challenge had been made, both sides had drawn their swords, the battle was about to begin.

Critical to Labori's defence and exoneration of his client was the testimony of nearly 100 witnesses. Both Delegorgue and van Cassel realized this and were quick to put a spoke in that wheel. General Billot was not authorized to answer the summons, the Keeper of Seals informed Delegorgue. Former President of the Republic, Casimir-Perier, replied in writing: 'I am unable to enlighten justice . . . constitutional responsibilities would impose silence upon me.' Lieutenant-Colonel du Paty de Clam (one of the perpetrators of the Esterhazy cover-up), declined the honour of appearing: 'I am bound by professional secrecy'. Mademoiselle Blanche de Comminges sent a doctor's certificate excusing her. Captain Lebrun Renault informed the court, 'I am bound to silence by my professional duty.' Major Ravary declared, 'My presence at the trial would be absolutely useless. I therefore abstain from appearing.' General Mercier (one of the masterminds of the conspiracy), informed the judge that he had received an authorization from General Billot not to appear. Major Esterhazy's arrogant refusal came in the form of a brief letter:'It is plain . . . that in this trial the object of M. Zola is . . . to reverse by revolutionary method the decree of acquittal rendered in my favour

[11 January 1898] . . . I consider that I am not obliged to respond to M. Zola's summons.' General de Boisdeffre's excuse followed: 'I could furnish no useful information.'

An infuriated Labori at last leapt to his feet, his arms shooting out of the broad sleeves of his black gown: 'All these witnesses seem to imagine that they constitute a caste apart, and that it is permissible for them to rise above the law, above justice itself, and personally appoint themselves judges as to whether or not they are useful witnesses in a trial! . . . we insist and we protest!'

It was to no avail it seemed, and when Mme Dreyfus was called to appear, Judge Delegorgue would not permit her to speak. Zola, who had been leaning with his hands and chin on his silver-headed walking stick suddenly lost his composure and got to his feet.

I demand to be allowed the same rights accorded to thieves and murderers. They can defend themselves, summon and question witnesses, but every day I am insulted in the street; they break my carriage windows, they drag my name through the mud, and the gutter press treat me like a crook. I have the right to prove my good faith, my integrity and my honour.

'Do you know Article 52 of the Law of 1881?' the judge asked.

'I don't know the law and right now I don't want to know it. Instead I appeal to the integrity of the jurors. I make them judges of the situation in which I am placed, and I entrust myself to them.'

Labori next tried to reintroduce the Dreyfus case. 'M. Zola has made two assertions. He has asserted that the court martial of 1894 convicted in the person of ex-Captain Dreyfus, an innocent man, by illegal methods.

'He is not prosecuted for that,' retorted Delegorgue, reiterating that Lucie Dreyfus would not be heard.

'Will you permit me then, Monsieur le Président,' continued Labori, 'to ask in our common interest, what practical means you see by which we may ascertain the truth?'

'That does not concern me!' snapped the judge.

When Zola next spoke it was to complain of the legal process that confined the case to just fifteen lines of 'J'accuse', ' . . . these things I declare unworthy of justice . . . I do not place myself above the law, but I am above hypocritical methods!' 'Bravo!' shouted Labori, clapping his hands.

Later that day Labori's witness, Louis Leblois, was making his initial statement when Judge Delegorgue interrupted him. Labori immediately protested at this violation of courtroom procedure.

'Permit me, Maître,' the judge responded sarcastically, 'I suppose that the court is entitled to question witnesses.'

'It is not entitled to interrupt M. Leblois.'

'I did not interrupt M. Leblois, I simply asked him for indications on a point . . . '

'I do not pretend to discuss with you the duties of an assize court judge,' responded Labori. 'You know them better than I do . . . the Code of Criminal Examination authorizes witnesses to give their testimony without interruption and to be questioned after their deposition is finished.'

After both Leblois and Senator Scheurer-Kestner had completed their testimonies in which they explained how they had been informed of illegalities in the Dreyfus case, including various previously unpublished documents, former President Casimir-Perier was called to the stand, despite his previous refusal to do so. Although he stated that duty prevented him from telling the whole truth, he was nonetheless, sworn in, but almost invariably whenever Labori questioned him, the judge intervened: 'The question cannot be asked.'

'Was M. Casimir-Perier aware that at a certain moment a secret document was laid before the court martial in the Dreyfus case, outside the proceedings of the trial and without the knowledge of the accused?' Labori persisted.

'The question cannot be asked,' Delegorgue repeated.

Zola was on his feet again. 'Is it understood, then, that no attention is to be paid to the word "illegality" contained in the complaint? Then why was it included in the first place?' (In *'J'accuse'* he had referred to the 'illegality' carried out by the 1894 court martial.)

'On that point the court has rendered a decree,' said the judge. 'There can be no testimony regarding the thing previously judged.'

'We offer no testimony regarding the authority of the thing judged,' Labori added.

'It is the same thing,' Delegorgue insisted.

'No, no,' protested Labori.

'You maintain that in the Dreyfus case there was an illegality?' asked the judge.

'Yes,' asserted Labori.

'Then it is the same thing,' replied the judge. 'It is useless to insist.'

'But the Esterhazy case is also a thing judged,' Zola interjected.

'Not at all,' Delgorgue replied.

'Then there are differences in the thing judged?' asked Zola.

'You cannot ask that question,' declared Delegorgue.

The session was adjourned shortly after this exchange.

When court reconvened on the third day of the trial the presiding judge asked if the testimony he had refused to hear from Mme Dreyfus concerned Zola's good faith in the Dreyfus case, or in the Esterhazy case.

'I really do not understand,' replied Labori. 'M. Zola has committed an act which is considered criminal. We maintain, however, that it was an act of good faith and we ask the witness what she thinks of M. Zola's good faith. As to the Dreyfus case and that of Esterhazy, they are connected only indirectly with the Zola case.'

Judge Delegorgue's next remarks went down in the history books: 'There is no Zola case!' he snapped.

When, at this stage, Albert Clemenceau noticed that several of the witnesses were actually in the courtroom listening to the proceedings (contrary to French courtroom practice), he pointed this out to the judge.

'The trial is not in progress!' shouted Delegorgue.

A disdainful, protesting General Boisdeffre finally took the stand that day and Labori questioned him about the Esterhazy case, including a mysterious 'veiled lady'. Boisdeffre tripped himself up time and again, claiming at one moment, for example, that he had only heard of the veiled lady because he had read about her in the newspapers, then moments later, perjuring himself by saying, 'We did all we could to find out who the veiled lady was, but we discovered nothing.'

Nor was the testimony given later by General Mercier much more intelligent. When asked, for instance, how two newspapers *La Libre Parole* and *L'Eclair* had come to know secret information about the arrest of Captain Dreyfus, the General claimed he did not know, but ' . . . since you ask my opinion, though it is not based on any proof, I believe that the information given the newspapers could have come from the Dreyfus family.' He was unable to explain why the Dreyfus family could possibly have wanted to advertise their personal tragedy, particularly in two well-known anti-Semitic papers. He assured the court, 'I had the most crushing proof of the guilt of Dreyfus in my hands, but that proof was of such a nature that to have divulged it [to the public] would inevitably have led to war . . . ' It was learned subsequently that the so-called 'crushing proof' was comprised of forged documents which he was at least partially responsible for creating and using. Leaving the stand the grey-haired conspirator added one more closing lie: 'On my honour as a soldier, Dreyfus was a traitor who was justly and legally condemned.'

By 10 February the hubbub round the Palais de Justice was worse than ever, and considerable amounts of money were seen changing hands for a good place in the queue leading to the courtroom. At that day's session Delegorgue and Labori began with a furious squabble over the judge's persistent refusal to allow certain questions to be asked. 'You ask questions that violate the decree which we have rendered,' repeated the heated presiding judge, to which an irritated Labori retorted, 'I shall ask all the questions I think useful to my needs, whatever your opinion of them may be.' It was not the best way to humour the court, but the lawyer had no illusions about that.

Against his will, and in spite of his earlier refusal to appear, du Paty de Clam was called to the stand to testify, his resentment reflected in his grimly locked jaw and the heavy tread of his boots as he marched across the floor, stopping to give a stiff military salute to the judges, and turning sharply, another to the jury. He remained rigidly at attention, and shortly thereafter was excused by the judge. Clicking his heels he marched off, as muffled laughter rose from the spectators. Labori burst out: 'Never before have I seen an Assize Court like this!' If the judges could not trust secrets to be kept, then the trial should be conducted behind locked doors.

When General de Pellieux testified, little did anyone realize how badly the questioning by Albert Clemenceau would damage the State. Pellieux had been appointed by the Army to take charge of the investigation surrounding Major Esterhazy, and now in the course of his interrogation, the garrulous General revealed that he had searched Colonel Picquart's apartment (illegally, as it turned out, because Picquart was not present, as the law required), but had not searched Esterhazy's.

'How did it happen to occur to General de Pellieux to search the premises of a witness, but not those of the accused?' the lawyer asked.

'I did not have Major Esterhazy's premises searched because I was a judicial officer of police and did not deem it necessary.' After all, Esterhazy was only accused of treason. When Pellieux then admitted the existence of a secret document which had been used in the trial, a furious Colonel Henry was heard to say, 'It's crazy what Pellieux's doing,' and this brought sniggers from the audience.

With the completion of Pellieux's testimony, General de Boisdeffre took the stand, confirming every word Pellieux had said, adding, 'You are the jury, you are the Nation. If the Nation has no confidence in the army chiefs, in those charged with our national defence, they are ready to step down to leave this weighty task to others.' Applause and cheers filled the room. When Labori tried to cross-examine him, the judge declared the incident closed.

Supporting Ludovic Trarieux's earlier testimony, M. Thévenet, also a former Minister of Justice, stepped into the witness stand and commented on the use of a 'secret document'.

'It is said that neither Dreyfus nor his counsel was made aware of a secret document . . . It is, in my opinion, not just one question involved in this trial, but the capital question of this entire discussion.' The officers concerned could have answered simply 'yes' or 'no', whether or not a secret document had been involved in the case — but the Generals chose to remain silent.

> I say, gentlemen, that here we touch upon a question which is not simply a point of law, but of much higher principle — that of the freedom to defend oneself, the imprescriptible right which every accused man has of knowing on what evidence he is accused. Is it true that the first court martial considered documents which were not made known to Captain Dreyfus and his lawyer?

Unfortunately, the question elicited no reply. The long-awaited appearance of a youthful looking Colonel Picquart drew considerable attention the next day, as he related how he first discovered the similarity in the handwriting of the *bordereau* with that of Major Esterhazy in 1896. Not being a handwriting expert, however, Picquart took specimens of Esterhazy's writing and submitted them to two experts, M. Bertillon and Major du Paty de Clam. 'As soon as I showed M. Bertillon the photograph he said, "It is the handwriting of the *bordereau*." I said to him, "Do not be in a hurry. Take this specimen and examine it at your leisure." He replied, "No, it makes no difference. That is the handwriting of the *bordereau*".' Bertillon asked Picquart where he got it, the colonel replying that he could not divulge that information but that it was written after the *bordereau* had been produced. ' "Then the Jews have had someone practising for a year to get the writing of the *bordereau*," Bertillon said, "and they have succeeded perfectly, that is plain." ' The audience in the courtroom buzzed with excitement.

The second person to whom he showed a sample of Esterhazy's handwriting was Colonel du Paty de Clam, who was then a major. After a few minutes' study he declared it to be the handwriting of M. Mathieu Dreyfus. Picquart then explained that as a result of his findings he was suddenly ordered off the case as the chief investigating officer and told to leave immediately for Tunis. 'I suspected that conspiracies were afoot.'

Labori's final questions to Colonel Picquart focused on the charge of treason made against Esterhazy. When asked if the arrest of Major Esterhazy was almost vital in order to arrive at the truth, Colonel Picquart replied that he had thought so, but his superiors had thought otherwise.

'But, without arresting an officer,' asked Labori 'is it not possible to watch him so that he can have no chance of doing still more reprehensible things and of concealing his tracks?'

'Certainly,' replied Picquart, 'there was already enough against Esterhazy to send him to a fortress.' (As a result of this testimony, three days after the conclusion of the trial, Colonel Picquart was arraigned summarily by his superiors, charged with violating the interests of the Army and dismissed from the service with no further claim to his pension.)

Colonel Henry's appearance the following day, Saturday, caused a minor sensation when he contradicted his own testimony and that of an official report prepared by Major Ravary. Leblois faced him squarely: 'Either Colonel Henry is not telling the truth, or else the truth is not told in Major Ravary's report.'

'I will not permit you to call my words into question. I will not permit it,' Henry stammered.

'Variations as to facts, variations as to dates,' continued Leblois. 'It is very difficult for a witness with the best intentions in the world to follow his adversaries over ground so shifting.'

After Colonel Picquart had established Henry's various contradictions and prevarications, Henry retorted: 'I formally maintain my assertion, and I say again: Colonel Picquart has lied.' A courtroom of shocked army officers whispered among themselves, and Picquart, anger in his eyes, raised his arm to slap Henry, but regained control of himself at the last minute. An officer never called a fellow officer a liar, and certainly never in public. Whether Henry was in their camp or not, it could only harm their case against Zola. (Following the trial, Picquart challenged Henry to a duel for this remark, and wounded him in the arm.)

Jean Jaurès, who was to lose his seat in the Chamber of Deputies in the spring elections as a result of his support of Dreyfus and Zola, now addressed the court:

> I come to this bar to declare, not only the complete good faith of M. Zola, but the high moral and social value of his act. I consider that the conduct of the Esterhazy trial which I attended justifies M. Zola's most vehement indignation. It also justifies the anxieties of those who, profoundly respectful of national honour, do not wish the military power to rise above all supervision and law.

A couple of days later, when Paul Meyer, a member of the French Institute, a Professor of the Collège de France, and a Director of the Ecole des Chartes, with a national reputation as a handwriting expert, was called to the stand, Labori asked that he now be confronted with the original three handwriting experts in the Esterhazy Case. The judge forbade this.

'They are bound by professional secrecy,' declared Delegorgue.

'But, Monsieur le Président, I beg of you,' pleaded Labori.

'No, no, they were right.'

'I insist . . . ' said Labori.

'No, I have said no!'

'But I have to ask a question.'

'You shall not ask it.'

'I insist, Monsieur le Président.'

'I say that you shall not ask it.'

'Oh, Monsieur le Président, it is an interesting one!'

'It is useless to shout so loudly,' replied the judge.

'I shout because I need to make myself heard.'

'You cannot ask that question.'

'You say that, but I say I wish to ask it,' persisted Labori.

'Well, I say that it is an understood thing. The Court must keep out of the debate anything that would uselessly prolong it. I say that this is useless, and it is my right to say so.'

'But you do not even know the question!' said Labori in exasperation. However, the judge could not stop Professor Meyer, and then later, Professors Auguste Molinier and Célerier, from testifying that the *bordereau* was indeed in Esterhazy's handwriting.

When Labori later attempted to introduce a motion about General de Pellieux's critical pronouncements in court concerning Dreyfus, the judge complained that, 'According to Article 311 of the Examination Code, I tell you that you must explain yourself with moderation.'

Labori retorted, 'Will you tell me, Monsieur le Président, what expression has fallen from my lips that was lacking in moderation?'

'Everything you say!' declared Delegorgue.

But Labori, not one to be easily intimidated, replied: 'Pardon me. I refuse to accept your warning unless you make it more precise.'

'I repeat that this incident has now taken up ten minutes,' said the judge. 'Prepare your motion.'

'If you ask me to be moderate,' persisted Labori, 'and ask me in terms that resemble a warning or a censure, and if you do not tell me *why* you inflict this censure upon me . . . '

'Will you speak in support of your motion?'

'But, Monsieur le Président, do you hold to what you just said?'

'I owe you no explanation,' said Delegorgue, his hands shaking, as he denied the lawyer's request and motion.

Labori now insisted that Colonel Picquart be recalled in order to confront Pellieux.

'He will come when he is free,' the judge replied.

'Yes,' snapped Labori, 'at five o'clock this afternoon when the hearing is over!' Shortly after this the session was adjourned till the following day.

On the tenth day of the trial, 17 February, Labori again asked for information about the secret documents, requesting that General Pellieux explain himself, and that the documents themselves be produced. However, it was Gonse who took the stand next. He confirmed the testimony of General de Pellieux but declined to make the documents public. When Boisdeffre appeared to testify the next day, he also confirmed all that Pellieux has said, concluding quickly that he could say nothing more. 'You may withdraw, General,' said the judge. 'Bring in the next witness.'

Labori leapt to his feet saying, 'Excuse me, *I* have some questions to ask.'

'You do not have the floor,' said Delegorgue. 'The incident is closed.'

'Excuse me, Monsieur le Président.'

'You do not have the floor,' the judge repeated angrily, and turning to the clerk demanded, 'Bring in Major Esterhazy.'

Labori ignored this and repeated, 'I have some questions to ask the witness!'

'This was an incident outside the trial,' maintained the judge. 'You do not have the floor.'

'Monsieur le Président, I ask for the floor.'

'I do not give it to you.'

While this exchange was going on, Esterhazy was completing a letter to his nephew — 'This Zola case was a big mistake . . .'

Labori and Delegorgue clashed half a dozen times a day, and the lawyer exhausted himself physically and emotionally, in confronting the massive cover-up which descended from the Elysée to the Palais de Justice.

> The debate has now gone far beyond the issue of the condemned man on Devil's Island, who concerns us not because of his suffering . . . but because he suffers as a result of a violation of the law, and a verdict rendered in the name of the people, in the name of the country . . . It is justice, freedom and law that are now at stake . . .

Later, when Esterhazy was brought back to the stand and Labori questioned him, the major replied, 'I shall not answer these questions.' A frustrated Labori insisted that the judge require Esterhazy to answer him, to which Delegorgue responded, 'Oh, come now.'

Albert Clemenceau then interjected, 'How is it that one cannot speak of justice in a courtroom.'

Delegorgue replied, '. . . there is something above that — the honour and safety of the country.'

When the judge then prohibited Labori from questioning Pellieux, the lawyer said, 'Really, I ask myself if it would not be better to quit the court-room than allow myself to be gagged and bound in a strait-jacket like this.' The judge then noted that Zola's lawyer was not saying 'serious things'.

'Monsieur le Président, you abuse the right that your lofty position gives you. You have no right to insult me.'

'No,' said Delegorgue sharply.

'You have injured me . . .' continued Labori. 'I really don't know what kinds of friends of justice this court is composed of, but I can tell you this: I ask questions, the value of which only I know, and you forbid those questions, you forbid their answers. Therefore I protest when you say, "You are not saying serious things." I simply cannot accept that!'

A new tension was in the air as the summing up finally began on Monday, 21 February. Attorney-General Edmond van Cassel, who had rarely said a word during the trial, now addressed the jury, reiterating Zola's charges in *'J'accuse'*, and asking for irrefutable proof of those charges. He mentioned the support of 'international experts' and Bernard Lazare, the author of *Anti-Semitisme, son histoire et ses causes* (Anti-Semitism, Its History and Causes). 'They are surrounded by too much Jewish money and too much mystery . . .' he said in reference to the handwriting experts whom Labori had questioned. 'Dreyfus [a Jew],' he contended, 'belongs to a rich and powerful family . . . Alfred Dreyfus alone was in a position to procure the documents concerning national defence which are enumerated in the *bordereau.*' As for Esterhazy's acquittal, it was 'regular, deliberate and legal', he insisted. He blamed Zola's revolutionary views for breeding the violence currently demonstrated in the streets (conveniently ignoring the fact that most of the violence was directed *against* Zola).

> For the sake of his personal vanity he has imposed upon you these twelve sessions that have made the heart of the country bleed. The Dreyfusards have not hesitated to attack the Staff to compromise national defence. Their outrages have overwhelmed the silent and obedient Army in which every Frenchman sees the image of his country. They have insulted it outrageously . . . No more unpatriotic campaign could have been conceived . . . No, it is not true that a court martial has rendered a verdict in obedience to orders. It is not true that seven officers have been found to obey anything other than their own free and honest conscience. You must condemn those who have outraged them, gentlemen of the jury. France awaits your verdict with confidence.

Zola had been waiting many weeks for the moment when he could speak to the public face to face. By French law he was permitted to address the court and jury a final time and now at last, unhindered by the presiding judge, he could tell France what he had meant in *'J'accuse'*. Always a diffident public speaker in the past, his passion now overcame his natural reticence.

He argued that on 22 January Prime Minister Méline had addressed the Chamber of Deputies informing them that Dreyfus was guilty, that the Army was national honour personified, and furthermore, that anyone who dared to contradict this simply was not a patriotic citizen. Méline insisted that Esterhazy was rightfully acquitted in the first trial and that he, as Prime Minister, had great confidence in the twelve citizens in whose hands he entrusted the defence of the Army. If Zola contradicted this then he was no patriot. That a prime minister or head of state of any country should pass judgment on someone before he had stood trial was unheard of. He was making a mockery of the law. M. Méline, Zola claimed, had endeavoured to make the jury convict him out of the respect for the Army.

> Before the conscience of all honest people, I denounce this act by a public official to put pressure on the judicial system of the country. These are abominable political practices, dishonourable to a free nation. I stand before you of my own free will. I alone have decided that an obscure and monstrous matter should be brought before your jurisdiction, and I alone take full responsibility, having chosen you, the highest and most direct emanation of French justice, that France at last may know all and decide. My act has no other object, and my person is nothing; I have sacrificed it, satisfied to have placed in your hands not only the honour of the Army but the threatened honour of the entire nation.

Zola regretted his naïveté in expecting the court to be fully informed of the facts. Certain officers had remained above justice, afraid of the judgement that a fair jury would hand down to them, and defence witnesses had been terrorized in the hope of preventing Zola from proving his case. The Army was more dishonoured at sheltering the likes of Esterhazy than at Zola's challenge to their system. Then he passed on to the issue of his allegedly insulting the Army.

If certain individuals in the War Office have compromised the Army by their conduct, is it an insult to the entire Army to say so? Is it not, rather, the work of a good citizen to free the Army from all compromise, to sound the alarm in order that the misdeeds which have forced us into this fight, may not be repeated and lead us to new defeats? However, I do not defend myself. I leave to history the judgement of my act, which was a necesary one. But I declare that they dishonour the Army when they allow the gendarmes to embrace Major Esterhazy . . . I declare that this valiant Army is insulted daily by the rogues who, pretending to defend it, sully it with their base complicity, dragging in the mud everything good and great France still stands for. I declare it is they who dishonour this great national Army when they mingle with the cry of 'Long live the Army!' the cry of 'Death to the Jews!' and 'Long live Esterhazy!' It is shameful, and yet only your [the jury's] effort to arrive at truth and justice can cleanse that.

Judicial errors had been made, he continued, but the mistakes would only be compounded if the jury convicted him.

The question now is whether France is still the France that gave us the 'Rights of Man', and liberty to the world; whether it can now give it justice as well . . . Dreyfus is innocent! I swear it. I stake my life upon it . . . I may be condemned, but some day France will thank me for having helped to save her honour.

By the time that van Cassel had completed his summation and Labori rose to address the jury, the spectators were shouting and waving their fists: 'Enough! Enough! Down with Labori!' But despite this interruption and crude attempt at intimidation, Judge Delegorgue made no attempt to silence them or to restore order. However, Labori was finally heard above the din, and told the jury: 'You are higher than the Army, higher than the judicial power. You are the justice of the people, which only the verdict of history will judge. If you have the courage, declare Zola guilty of having struggled against all hatreds on behalf of law, liberty and justice.'

A clearly shaken Labori rejoined his colleagues as the jury retired for their deliberation. The trial had lasted an exhausting fifteen days, and the testimony would later fill two entire volumes, exclusive of thousands of pages of notes, documents and evidence.

Madame Séverine, an eyewitness, described the courtroom scene at this time. 'Passions rose as invectives filled the air. In the thickening yellow gaslight of the congested room officers in uniform stood on benches, shaking their fists in the air, shouting imprecations.'

To everyone's amazement the jury deliberated for only thirty-five minutes. As the twelve men filed back in, an apprehensive silence filled the room. Monsieur Dutrieux, the foreman, gave the verdict: both Zola and Perrenx were found guilty by a majority vote. (The majority vote, it was later learned, was 7-5.) Cries of jubilation deafened the room. 'Long live the Army! Long live France! Down with the insulters! Down with the Jews! Death to Zola!' The three judges sat impassively for a moment, making no attempt to bring order to the courtroom. 'These people are cannibals!' Zola said, as his weeping wife threw her arms round him.

The judges then withdrew to decide upon the sentence, returning a mere five minutes later. It was 7.35 p.m. M. Perrenx received a four-month prison term and a fine of 3000 francs. Zola, in addition to the same fine, was given the maximum penalty — one year's imprisonment. The trial was over . . . for the time being. The army officers in the court roared with delight. Outside the crowds were boisterous, hysterical, and some were singing *La Marseillaise*. Mme Zola and Georges Clemenceau left through the main entrance of the Palais de Justice, while Zola, Labori and their friends took a side exit leading to their waiting carriages. There were fewer than twenty bystanders there, but curiously enough, for the first time since the beginning of the trial, there were no taunts, just a single, 'Long live Zola!'

Monsieur Blanc, the Prefect of Police, had taken extraordinary security measures involving thousands of police patrolling the bridges across the Seine, the boulevard Sébastopol, the boulevard Saint-Michel, Saint-Germain, the Opéra, the grands boulevards, the Hôtel de Ville, the Assemblée Nationale and of course the Luxembourg Palace, to name just a few of the more prominent positions, while some 400 more police were being held in reserve. As an added precaution 975 mounted troops were distributed through all twenty *arrondissements* of the city, while cuirassiers de la Garde patrolled the streets and squares of the Ile de la Cité, the Tuileries, the Conservatoire des Arts et Métiers, the Ministry of the Marine, and the Château d'Eau.

The monarchists and the Army were celebrating vigorously in the Jockey Club and salons without restraint, the most spectacular victory celebration by far, however, was that held by 700 'royalists' in the hall of the Société d'Horticulture, in the rue de Grenelle. There had been nothing like it since the days of Napoleon III. Zola and Alexandrine left their friends that evening around 11.45 p.m. and returned to the rue de Bruxelles, where they found the street swept clean of all pedestrians and vehicles, with police stationed every five feet and hidden reserves round the corner on side streets.

As Jean France, a witness to the day's events noted, 'I had the feeling that we had barely escaped a revolution.'[10] Years later, Prime Minister Georges Clemenceau remarked, 'If Zola had been acquitted that day, none of us would have left there alive.'

20
Flight

Following his condemnation by the Assize Court in Paris on 23 February, Zola's life was so busy as to leave scarcely a moment for thought. He had been correcting proofs of his latest novel, *Paris,* right up till the time of his first trial, and when it was published on 1 March, he was able to devote himself entirely to his battle with the French Republic.

Fernand Labori immediately submitted his case to the Court of Appeals, which met on 2 April and quashed the sentence of the first court, as the original proceedings against Zola should have been initiated not by the Minister of War, but by the court martial which Zola was accused of libelling. It was a technicality, of course, but Labori was fighting for time. Less than a week later the court martial board agreed to serve as plaintiff in a new trial, at the same time recommending that the Grand Chancellor of the Legion of Honour strike Zola's name from the Legion's records. (This eventually took place at a ceremony on 26 July.) On 11 April Zola received a fresh summons, this time to appear before the Versailles Assize Court on 23 May. Maître Labori immediately requested a change of venue, on the grounds that Zola should be tried in Paris where *'J'accuse'* had been published (and where a more sympathetic jury could be found), but the Court of Appeals rejected this while at the same postponing the trial till 18 July.

When Prime Minister Jules Méline's government fell, Zola and his friends hoped that the new Prime Minister, Henri Brisson (generally considered to be more sympathetic to Dreyfus) would order a re-trial for the ex-army captain. Instead, on 10 July the three handwriting experts named by Zola in his *'J'accuse'* article, MM. Belhomme, Varinaud and Couard, won their defamation case and Zola was sentenced to two months' imprisonment and ordered to pay a 2000-franc fine and a total of 15,000 francs in damages to the three experts, a sum which Labori considered excessive.[1] In any event they appealed against that decision as well. Brisson's new government was indeed a disappointment to Dreyfus and Zola, for although on 12 July Esterhazy (the real author of the *bordereau*) and his mistress, Marguerite Pays, were arrested (charged with forgery, the use of forged documents, and complicity), so was Lieutenant-Colonel Picquart, accused of having revealed classified documents relating to the nation's security to unauthorized parties. Zola called the arrest of Picquart 'yet another ignominy'.[2] As it turned out Esterhazy was soon released and later fled to England (much to the relief of the French government and Army), while Picquart was to remain in the prison of Mont Valérien the rest of the year and a good part of the next. Under no illusions, Zola admitted, 'the future seems full of uncertainty. I no longer know where we're going — we'll simply have to wait and see.'[3]

But the novelist, too angered (by recent events and the receipt of more death threats) to take his own advice, returned to his desk at Médan and wrote a long, bitter attack against Brisson. It was one of the most dramatic, moving and honest criticisms by a private citizen of any prime minister in French history, though it was not rushed off in the heat of the moment. Zola wrote to Fernand Labori on 12 July — one week before his next trial — informing him that Vaughan was personally bringing the proofs of the article to the lawyer for his opinion.[4] 'I'd be lowering myself if I didn't intervene now. But I want your approval, for so far as I'm concerned you are the sole master of this affair, and whatever you decide I'll abide by.'[5]

'*Monsieur Brisson*', as the article was entitled, appeared on the front page of *L'Aurore* on Saturday 16 July. Zola began by reiterating some of his accusations in the Dreyfus Affair, referring to Colonel Henry's forgery as 'that monumental mystification', then chiding Brisson for his failure to recall Dreyfus for a fresh trial, while having the audacity to arrest another innocent man, Colonel Picquart. Brisson's actions were unconscionable: 'You are poisoning the nation with lies,' Zola insisted, calling him 'a compromised man' who had lost his 'political honour'. Zola had lost his respect for a Prime Minister who 'let justice be murdered before his very eyes'. Brisson was the assassin who had 'killed an ideal, and that is a crime for which you will be punished . . . These are times,' lamented Zola, 'when souls cry out in anguish.' He reminded Brisson of the travesties of justice and morality perpetrated against him and his colleagues during his February trial. 'Every abuse, every [physical] threat was permitted, yet not a single person was arrested.' And now, in two days' time another trial was to take place in Versailles, while the police continued to ignore those threats. 'Monsieur Brisson,' Zola concluded, 'you [as Prime Minister and Minister of the Interior] are personally responsible for public order . . . if we are murdered on Monday [18 July], it is you who will be the murderer.' Paris was stunned.

It was a bright day and the sky a clear blue on 18 July as Zola and his artist friend, Fernand Desmoulin, set out from the rue de Bruxelles via L'Etoile for the residence of Georges Charpentier at 3, avenue du Bois de Boulogne. Despite the early morning's warmth (it was just past eight o'clock), Zola shuddered and looked distractedly from the corner of the cab.[6] He had a right to be preoccupied and Desmoulin knew better than to disturb him, today of all days. Labori had said it all the night before at his home during their final strategy session: he must be prepared for any eventuality, and more realistically, for an unfavourable outcome to today's trial. Back in January former Prime Minister Jules Méline had made it perfectly clear to the Chamber of Deputies where his sympathies lay: with Esterhazy, the Army, and established order. The jury would be wise to heed his view of the situation he had intimated. Zola had defied him, however, through his 'revolutionary' attempt to challenge both the Army and that very order.

Charpentier, who, following the death of his son three years earlier, had retired to his seaside home in Royan, near Bordeaux, had now returned to Paris in mid-summer for one purpose: the trial. Everyone wished Zola well as he climbed into his livery-stable brougham at 9.45 a.m. Desmoulin ordered the driver to take the most direct route through the Bois de Boulogne and Sèvres, and they reached Versailles by 11.20. The new Prime Minister had indeed taken Zola's article to heart, for the most extraordinary precautions had been taken by the prefect of police. Not only were policemen on bicycles waiting at the city's outskirts to escort the celebrated author, but there were others stationed every fifty feet along the entire length of the avenue de Paris leading to the Assize Court. There were few curious bystanders watching his approach however.

In the courtroom Zola appeared with fellow-plaintiff, M. Perrenx, managing editor of *L'Aurore*. The proceedings proved to be as negative as Zola had expected. Later, in a consultation room in the courthouse, Labori and Clemenceau advised him to leave the country so that the court would be unable to serve him with the final papers, for although the trial was not yet over, the outcome was a foregone conclusion. Imprisonment would render him unable to speak freely in person or in writing on behalf of Captain Dreyfus or himself, although he could well become a martyr, and lodge another appeal in due course. On the other hand, he could flee.

Zola was torn between the alternatives. All his friends, however, felt nothing could be achieved by spending a year in jail. Why accept that verdict when it had been deliberately shaped and encouraged through illegal and outrageous court procedures, denying the admission of elementary evidence, forbidding questioning and the calling of critical witnesses? The French judicial system had made a mockery of itself and everything it represented before the eyes of all intelligent and just Europeans.

The prefect of police of Versailles, M. Mouqin, even aided in what was to become the escape by permitting them to slip out quietly and getting their brougham for them. Zola and Labori drove away from the Assize Court before sentence was pronounced: they were defaulting the case. The papers would be served at his home later, probably the next day. Mounted police had to use force to restrain the by now large and boisterous crowds along the main thoroughfare of Versailles. Soon they were passing through silent woods and Zola took out some bread for Labori and himself, which Charpentier's daughter, Jane, had packed that morning. Labori and Zola spoke little and when they did only one subject was discussed — whether Zola should leave the country, and if so, how. Zola reluctantly came round to the idea of exile as their journey took them through Saint Cloud and the Bois de Boulogne, back to Charpentier's house.

When Clemenceau and Desmoulin arrived later, a final meeting was held and it was decided that Zola would take the nine o'clock boat-train for London that evening. Desmoulin was sent to inform Alexandrine and to bring her back to Charpentier's. Zola also had to notify Jeanne and the children, but he could not see them. There had been no preparation whatsoever for flight and when Alexandrine arrived she brought only what she could conceal in a folded newspaper, for a suitcase would have attracted attention, the Zola residence being under more intensive police surveillance than usual. They all drove in a closed fiacre to the Gare du Nord. To avoid attracting attention, Charpentier went in first and bought a one-way ticket for Zola. Alexandrine, Desmoulin and Charpentier then accompanied him to an empty compartment at the front of the train. They left him as the whistle sounded, announcing the train's imminent departure. For the first time since he entered the Dreyfus Affair on 13 January, Zola was completely alone. He turned down the lamp and sat back in the darkness, with only the rhythmic clatter of the wheels and an occasional shriek of the whistle breaking the silence, as the locomotive sped north-westerly through the thickening night towards the coast and the Channel. The full impact of the previous six months and that day's proceedings in Versailles now struck him. This was just the beginning of the solitude that would be his companion for the better part of the next year. French justice was dead and, as a result, he was forced to flee while the guilty parties were not only free, but were toasted as national heroes. The situation could have been taken from one of his novels; it was grotesque.

Dinner had been served at Charpentier's earlier, but Zola had been too upset to eat very much; now suddenly, as the train approached Amiens he grew very hungry. At the station he stepped out into the shadows to buy some bread and chicken from a vendor, only to return just as quickly to his curtained carriage.

At Calais he boarded the ferry at 1.30 a.m. and soon he was no longer on French soil — a terrifying fact in itself for a man whose life and works had centred round one subject: France. Though there was no moon, it was a clear night. He stood at the railing, watching the lights of Calais twinkle and then disappear. 'I must admit,' he later recorded, 'tears filled my eyes, and never had my poor being felt such anguish . . . I have already suffered a great deal in my life, but never had I undergone such a crisis as this.'[7]

The train from Dover arrived at Victoria Station, London, just after 8 a.m. on 19 July. By now it was raining heavily — a gloomy beginning for a very dejected foreigner who could speak no English and whose only possessions were a nightshirt wrapped in a newspaper, and a few hundred francs in his pocket. Clemenceau had recommended the Grosvenor Hotel, and Zola, standing at the entrance of the dingy station, hailed a cab. The cabbie tried to explain to the bewildered gentleman that he was just a hundred yards from it, but Zola did not understand. The cabbie gave up and drove the exhausted man the short distance, Zola only then realizing what the driver had been trying to tell him. He entered the hotel to change his currency and gave the night porter a shilling for the cabbie, the usual fare for short journeys. As Zola had no luggage, the hotel clerk required a deposit of one sovereign, and he was given an undesirable room at the very top of the hotel, set aside for suspicious and apparently indigent travellers.

That Tuesday, 19 July, so eventful for Zola, was equally so for Ernest Vizetelly, who upon returning from London to his suburban home just before seven o'clock, was handed a letter by his wife:

> My dear confrère,
> Tell nobody in the world, and particularly no newspaper, that I'm in London. And oblige me by coming to see me tomorrow, Wednesday, at eleven o'clock, at the Grosvenor Hotel. Ask for M. Pascal. And above all, absolute silence, for the most serious interests are at stake.
> Cordially,
> Emile Zola[8]

Vizetelly, formerly Zola's publisher, and now his English translator and friend of many years' standing, had already read about the outcome of the trial and realized what was involved.

Waiting for the arrival of Vizetelly, Zola spent the first part of the morning walking along Pall Mall, to St James's Park, and then back to some shops near Buckingham Palace where he bought some underclothes, socks and shirts. From now on his chief concern was to find a safe hiding place where French detectives could not track him down and serve him with the papers, and he made sure that those round him acted with equal caution. Upon his arrival, Vizetelly warmly embraced Zola, who had just been joined by Fernand Desmoulin. The main question, of course, was where Zola should go now. Desmoulin suggested Hastings or Brighton as a place of refuge, but both coastal areas would be too crowded at this time of year and Zola feared he would be quickly recognized, for he was nearly as well known in England as in France, and his picture could be seen even in bookshops across London. To add to their difficulties, Zola obstinately refused to part with his clothes, which were distinctly French in style. His white French billycock hat made him extremely conspicuous, as did his gold pince-nez and his light grey, French-cut suit, with the rosette of the Legion of Honour. Zola remained adamant about this, however, for quite some time; to him hiding was anathema. He did agree not to use his own name, but the alternatives were not always good. For instance, he signed in at the Grosvenor as M. Pascal, but of course he was well known to all of Europe as the author of the recent best-seller, *Le Docteur Pascal*. Obviously, it was not easy for Vizetelly to hide such an unwilling ward.

When they took a walk to St James's Park that afternoon, the novelist was recognized by two ladies speaking French, and although they continued on their way Zola became more and more anxious. Perhaps his clothes *were* a bit too conspicuous. After all it would only take one accurate newspaper article to upset all his plans. Thereafter great care was taken to scrutinize the daily papers to ascertain whether his whereabouts were known. Papers from France and England speculated on Belgium, Holland and Norway. Strangely enough most thought him to be in Norway, staying with Bjoernstjerne Bjoernson, the celebrated Norwegian playwright. At least one French paper reported definitely seeing him in eastern France with his wife, cycling to the Swiss border.

The main priority, after finding a safe place to stay, would be to obtain legal advice to learn whether or not the court papers could be served by French police in England, and whether England could or would extradite him. At this juncture Zola thought optimistically that it would be a matter of a few weeks before he could return to France, and that he would be back by the end of October at the very latest. The solicitor recommended by Fernand Labori, Mr Fletcher Moulton, QC, was unfortunately in Cornwall canvassing for a seat in the House of Commons. Too anxious to await that lawyer's return, he decided instead to consult Vizetelly's solicitor, Mr F.W. Wareham. They met for the first time in a smoking-room of the Grosvenor Hotel. Wareham quickly assured Zola that he could not be extradited for his alleged offence, as it did not come within the terms of the Extradition Act. Furthermore, there was no way through diplomatic channels by which a French criminal libel judgement could be served in England. In fact, the only real danger was if a French process-server (with witnesses) could literally place the judgement in Zola's hands, and then attest to it. Only under such circumstances would Zola have to return to France and go to prison. However, Wareham was uncertain whether French law allowed process to be served on a subject out of the jurisdiction, so he urged that Maître Labori be contacted for clarification. Zola was more comforted by this news than he had anticipated.

In order to avoid possible discovery before the legal position was clear, Wareham invited Zola down to Wimbledon to stay with him for the time being, and the anxious author gratefully accepted. He packed his few belongings, and went back down to the lobby. Vizetelly hailed a hansom cab, calling for Charing Cross Station. As they drove along Buckingham Palace Road, Vizetelly tapped the cab-roof with his walking stick. 'Did I tell you Charing Cross just now, driver? Ah! Well, I made a mistake. I meant Waterloo.'[9] Vizetelly took this somewhat melodramatic precaution in the event anyone had heard him give the destination at the hotel. The days of hiding were about to begin.

It took a few days for a means of communication to be established between France and England, and it was only on 23 July that Labori received Zola's first letter from his place of exile (he was now staying near Vizetelly), explaining what Francis Wareham had told him a few days earlier and then asking his advice. Labori replied to 'Mon bien cher Monsieur Beauchamp', confirming what Wareham had said: 'It seems quite true that French agents have no authority to act on foreign territory, and that foreign [police] agents will refuse to act for them.'[10] Zola could not be touched. 'But,' he warned, 'it is always possible that someone will try to serve the papers anyway . . . the only danger left to be cautious about might come from letters or from persons wishing to join you there. To be more precise, Mme Beauchamp is most certainly under surveillance.'[11]

Labori then discussed the various actions French law could take. When Zola returned to France, the courts would have to hear him. 'You will *have* to return [one day]; it's as simple as that, and your return, even if it means going to prison, will be *a triumph* . . . within three months the matter will have taken giant steps forward . . . '[12] No wonder Zola assumed he could return by the end of October. As for the court's fine, Labori agreed that the sale of Zola's furniture must be avoided if at all possible and that he would arrange for a third party to buy it for 8000 francs which he felt — incorrectly as it turned out — would cover the amount set by the court. All Zola had to do was name the person he wanted to carry out this transaction. Labori closed by giving him an address in Paris to which to send future correspondence (M. Paquin, 61, avenue du Bois de Boulogne, then changed to 3, rue de la Paix), reminding him, 'Don't sign them [with your real name] and don't put your address on the letters.'[13] Later he was instructed to enclose his letter in three envelopes, the first two addressed to M. Pacquin, the third to Labori.

> Now don't worry about a thing. In spite of the frightful difficulties at the moment, I feel more optimistic than ever. The Picquart and Esterhazy Affairs are going to shed some light, and I am convinced that if you do indeed have to go to prison — and I really don't believe that will be the case — it would be for a very short period.

It closed with a touching expression of friendship and loyalty to his 'good and great friend'.[14] From the language of this letter and of those to follow it can be seen how Zola inspired real devotion and admiration from those round him.

Zola's legal affairs were not his only concern at this time. He was anxious to start writing again, if only to cover his various legal bills, and he was also anxious about Jeanne and the children. Especially trying, however, was the matter involving a right-wing journalist by the name of Judet who had published three defamatory articles in *Le Petit Journal* against François Zola (the novelist's father). Much to Zola's surprise, the Judet affair was going to uncover another Army conspiracy and was to preoccupy Zola much of the time between now and 1900 (see Chapter 25).

Elaborate precautions continued to keep Zola's whereabouts hidden from the French authorities. Vizetelly had assumed responsibility for Zola's safety in England because he saw him more often than anyone else did, and it was he who posted his correspondence and brought him letters and newspapers from France. Reports in two London papers, the *Daily Chronicle* and the *Morning Leader,* stated that the celebrated French author had been seen in the Grosvenor Hotel in London. Vizetelly, on Zola's instructions, informed the press association that the information was incorrect, and this stopped most enquiries for a while. Vizetelly was then called up for jury service and his acceptance persuaded reporters that Zola could not be in England, as Vizetelly would surely not have agreed to spend a week away from his friend — precisely what Vizetelly wanted everyone to think. Still, the threat of discovery was ever present.

Incidents continued to occur, causing Vizetelly considerable anxiety. Madame Zola remained under constant police surveillance at her home in the rue de Bruxelles and all her incoming and outgoing mail was intercepted first by the *Cabinet Noir* of the Paris Prefecture. For this reason neither Zola's wife nor his closest friends were informed of his various addresses in England. Indeed only one person in Paris knew of his precise whereabouts, and that was Dr Larat, a cousin of Desmoulin. All letters to England, including those from Zola's wife, were brought to him, and he then forwarded them. Zola's letters were sent by Vizetelly, who also addressed the envelopes in order to throw off the French authorities who knew the novelist's handwriting only too well.

Vizetelly was quite well known in London literary circles. As the only authorized English translator of Zola's works, most London bookshops carried many of his translations, and newspapers frequently sought interviews with him concerning Zola, but naturally he refused them all. He was growing increasingly jittery, and was particularly startled on one occasion when he dropped in at Wareham's Bishopsgate Street office to be told that 'a singular-looking little Frenchman' had earlier presented one of Maître Labori's visiting cards, requesting an interview with Zola. Such a meeting was out of the question, of course, especially as he was a total stranger to Vizetelly, but the man claimed to have a letter from Labori to Zola. Vizetelly and Wareham arranged to meet this man at the Salisbury Hotel in Fleet Street. Vizetelly described this stranger as 'most unprepossessing'. 'He was very short, with a huge head and a remarkable shock of coal-black hair.'[15] He claimed to be a diamond-broker, and that in his capacity as a regular traveller he had agreed to help Labori. After a couple of days' negotiating, the stranger finally agreed to hand over the letter to Wareham and Vizetelly and it was opened in his presence. It was indeed from Labori, and once again their worst fears proved groundless.

A few days later, Vizetelly was returning home on a train from Waterloo and was followed into his compartment by five men, two of whom he recognized as the proprietor of the Raynes Park Hotel (situated half a mile from his house) and his son. The two other men were speaking in French. Vizetelly became extremely anxious, particularly when he heard them discussing whether to get out at Wimbledon or Raynes Park. He had an important message from Zola to deliver to Wareham that evening, and he certainly did not want to lead these men to his office.

When the train pulled in at Wimbledon, Vizetelly got up to leave, and so did the Frenchmen. Vizetelly quickly left the compartment and rushed out of the station. He practically ran the entire way to Wareham's Wimbledon office. But when he turned round he saw the two Frenchmen and the Englishman and his son coming directly towards him. Beginning to panic, Vizetelly crossed the street, and to his great relief the four continued straight on. Still fearing the worst, however, Vizetelly retraced his steps towards the railway station and entered the saloon bar of the South-Western Hotel. There, to compound the already fraught situation, he came across a foreign gentleman whom he knew. He had spoken to Vizetelly on other occasions about the Dreyfus case and this evening he approached him with a smile, asking if it was true that M. Zola had been seen in Wimbledon. As Vizetelly was about to reply, the door opened and the two Frenchmen appeared, their English friends directly behind them. 'I was virtually caught like a rat in a trap,' Vizetelly later recorded. 'I was the more startled, too, when my foreign acquaintance (about whom I really knew very little) abruptly quitted me to accost the newcomers.' Vizetelly, leaving his drink untouched, rushed out and dashed back to Wareham's office, where he seized the knocker in a frenzy and made a terrific racket. The door suddenly opened and Everson, Wareham's managing clerk, appeared looking amazed. Vizetelly sat down on the stairs to catch his breath and related what had just transpired, concluding that Wareham must be warned, and Zola must move immediately.

The clerk listened quietly, and asked what these Frenchmen looked like. Much to Vizetelly's relief and surprise, Everson was familiar with them as they had been in Wimbledon for about nine months and were musicians, not detectives.

21
Exile

For France the years 1898 and 1899 stand out as among the most unpleasant and divisive since the Hundred Years' War. The nation was stunned by Zola's astonishing accusations in January 1898 and subsequent months brought fresh disclosures to a proud yet pessimistic people who revelled in their colourful history. Every schoolboy studied Montaigne, and suddenly it was possible to feel a kinship with the uncertainty of his times. Zola, Dreyfus, dishonourable army personnel, corrupt and opportunistic politicians, the assassination of President Carnot, the public beating of President Loubet (see Chapter 24), the amazing blunder of Fashoda,[1] the renewed threat of war, this time with England, and the ever-present threat from Germany — everything served to undermine the established order. Of these, the Dreyfus Affair and the Fashoda Incident became the two most singular and unrelenting subjects. Both erupted in 1898, sending tremors through the Paris 'establishment' as no Krupp cannon could ever do, so that the fall of two French governments (those of Jules Méline and Henri Brisson) seemed almost incidental. Would there be war? Would there be yet another revolution, or a *coup d'état*? How many shock waves could a nation withstand before it began to crumble and disintegrate? How much corruption, fraud, political egotism, selfishness and self-deception? The country was divided against itself and threatened to collapse in a state of anarchy if this continued. France was at a crossroads, and few realized that this crossroads was, in fact, the razor's edge. Zola was one of those tortured few.

Unlike Otto von Bismarck, Zola could not live out of a suitcase. He disliked travelling intensely, even under the best of circumstances and claimed to be 'a most sedentary soul, almost insanely so, only really at ease under my own roof'.[2] Now he was a wanted man, not even a traveller, separated from his two families, his friends and the only world he knew or understood. Determined to make the best of his enforced exile, he decided to put down roots, regardless of how temporary they might be. Vizetelly, Desmoulin and Zola searched hard for a suitable abode and twice they took short leases on houses — 'Penn' and 'Summerfield'. Both had their drawbacks; he disliked rooms which did not communicate with one another, making it always necessary to return to a central hall, but on the other hand that remarkable 'institution', the English garden, was a marvel and joy to the lonely and somewhat disorientated man of letters.

He rented 'Penn' for the better part of August, and then moved into 'Summerfield' in the nearby village of Addlestone, Surrey, until mid-October. The move was awkward, as it took place after Jeanne Rozerot and the children, now aged eight and five, arrived for a long visit in the second week of August. But at least Zola was together with his second family, whom he had so missed.

More awkward than moving from one house to another was arranging for the visit of his family in the first place. His legal wife, Alexandrine, wanted to visit him at that time, and it was only thanks to the diplomacy of his old friend, Fernand Desmoulin, that a solution was found. Desmoulin's delicate task of seeing both ladies to work out a mutually convenient schedule had been completely successful, despite Madame Zola's original insistence on seeing her husband forthwith. Her ill-concealed hatred of Jeanne made her all the more intent on being Zola's first visitor. By the end of July these 'negotiations' had left Zola feeling confused and unable to cope with the problems of his love triangle. If only he had been more decisive in the early years and chosen one of the two women. Zola, the man who challenged the whole of France, shrank, however, from making a choice between his wife and Jeanne. By the end of the first week of August, Alexandrine finally informed her husband that she would yield to Jeanne and the children. Zola told Desmoulin, 'I am going to have my children [here], but you can't imagine how badly I feel about my wife. Have you told her everything, and above all that it is not my aim to cause her pain, and that I can't be happy here knowing she is unhappy?'[3] What tortured Zola was the fact that he could not make either woman happy until the marital situation was clarified by separation and divorce, and though Alexandrine might have agreed to divorce years before, he would not or could not take the necessary step. The ambivalent situation had always been a problem, but now, following his involvement in the Dreyfus Affair, it was sorely aggravated, as unscrupulous French journalists were constantly watching every movement of Jeanne, the children, and Alexandrine. Zola brooded and read with great anguish the scurrilous articles in the Parisian press about Jeanne, such as one entitled, *'M. Zola retrouvé'*, which appeared in *Le Petit Journal* towards the end of July.[4]

Jeanne and the two seasick youngsters arrived on 11 August as scheduled and Zola was delighted. He was a devoted, if somewhat strict, father, and an equally devoted husband — in his own way — to both women. It was hot throughout August, allowing the children to play in the large, splendid garden at 'Summerfield', and they all took daily walks together through the countryside and the villages of Beulah Spa, Chertsey, Cobham and Byfleet, which Zola found so tranquil and lovely. Occasionally too, Jeanne and Zola would take bicycle excursions. Soon the strange little Frenchman with a grey beard had become a familiar sight and was often seen about the countryside with his camera. Zola never used his real name in England and at 'Summerfield' he was known as Emile Beauchamp. He tried to appear less French in dress, in spite of his strong disapproval of hiding like a common criminal. The billycock hat was replaced by an English straw hat, and the red rosette of the Legion of Honour was removed. But buying new articles of clothing presented real problems as he had no mastery of the English language.

One day when no recent French papers were available, Vizetelly brought a couple of English newspapers and Zola, dictionary in hand, sat down to decipher the mysteries of the language. It was then that he decided to profit from his sojourn in England by asking Vizetelly and a French friend for help. He soon received a book of English grammar, a conversational manual, a set of Nelson's 'Royal Readers' for children, and a copy of the *Vicar of Wakefield* in French and English. He first learned to count in English and then a few words (though his spoken English was always extremely limited). He became interested enough to enquire about some English names — of villages, rivers and even the names of houses, which were used instead of numbers. He enjoyed writing to friends in France, translating and explaining some of the house names, such as 'Summerfield' (*champ d'été*).

Everywhere his curiosity was aroused, and he was constantly observing and questioning. During the summer Vizetelly's fifteen-year-old daughter, Violette (who was bilingual, having a French mother), kept house for Zola and also acted as interpreter when her father was not there. Much of her time was taken up with the ceaseless energies of Zola's mind.

Zola was startled by the splendid weather he encountered in England, as in true French fashion he had expected a damp, cold climate. He and his family happily spent most of their days at home. Having completed a short story, *'Angeline'*, in the first week of August, he continued to work on his new novel, *Fécondité*, every morning, followed by an after-lunch siesta. He was a typical Victorian, firmly believing in the work ethic. Every afternoon Denise and Jacques had to spend a couple of hours on their homework, and Zola was shocked at his daughter's spelling which simply would not do for the offspring of one of France's foremost *'hommes de lettres'*. But he loved his children dearly and much of his time over the ensuing weeks was centred round them.

England was a source of great interest for Zola, and he became a close observer of the minutiae of daily life. For example, he was intrigued to find bicycles in great general use, not simply for pleasure, as in France, but for running errands and shopping as well. He had never liked to see French women on bicycles, wearing riding skirts; French women were generally plump and did not carry themselves as well as their English counterparts: 'The English women are most elegant in skirts, very gracious on their bicycles, and sit straight on the seat, draped in long folds.'[5] Everywhere he went be found footpaths littered with women's hairgrips, and he became fascinated by the subject and even considered the possibility of an essay on this phenomenon. English sports were a source of wonder to Zola, and 'the game played on the grass — cricket, I believe — continues to stupify me . . . '[6]

While taking his daily walks and bicycle rides, he observed the countryside with great pleasure and interest, especially the amazing greenness of the land, the splendid old oaks, even crows, and the miles of mature holly hedges, so thick that even 'a skinny cat could not pass through them'.[7] English architecture in many cases was not so admirable, however, and back in 1893, when he had visited the National Gallery he thought it to be a 'wretched' affair. What England needed was a Louvre. On the subject of houses, he especially disliked the 'guillotine' (sash) windows, which he referred to as 'prison windows which can never be opened completely, and from which one cannot easily lean, like our free windows in France'.[8] Also on the subject of houses, he found a lack of variety, and he was disturbed by the terraces built for the working classes which looked ugly, squalid and demoralizing. The countryside villages were different, however. 'These little English towns are most pleasant, perfectly clean, cheerful and of simple lines. I don't know where this country hides the houses of its poor; they aren't to be seen.'[9]

When Zola later left his rented house for a suite of rooms in the Queen's Hotel, Upper Norwood, near Crystal Palace, he was able to observe the detached, middle-class villas opposite and was amazed by the lack of life. He rarely saw a soul moving about — how unlike France, a land of constant activity — and thus when a wedding reception was held at his hotel, he would unabashedly lean out of the window and enjoy watching the splendid carriages and the beautifully dressed people.

Zola had always been very fond of pets and missed not having his little dog, Pinpin, with him. When he was informed late in September that the little dog, '*mon pauvre Pin*', had died of a broken heart during his absence, there followed 'days of sadness that I spent in my little sitting-room, before the first coal fires [of Autumn]'.[10]

Food, of course, would inevitably be a subject of interest to a Frenchman, and Zola found English food and cooking abominable. 'Never any salt in anything,' the author complained.[11] He thought apple pudding was a terrible concoction, but occasionally he would try a plum tart (though here too he thought the English ruined the dish by serving it hot instead of cold). 'The large slices of roast beef are good, [but] the cutlets and steaks served rare and bathed in water [i.e. gravy] are inedible . . . And the bread, good Lord, this half-baked English bread, all crumbs, is more like a sponge.'[12] After he was introduced to the mysteries of the fishmonger's shop he consumed haddock, kippers, bloaters and smoked fish, though his English cook could not understand how anyone could serve haddock or kippers for dinner instead of breakfast. He liked a good joint of meat, but could not have that for every meal. On balance, however, he considered English food a small price to pay for freedom: 'By living on a diet of roast beef, ham, eggs and salad, I live quite well.'[13] Nonetheless, the English kitchen was no place for a Frenchman, and as Zola himself put it, 'One day all the people of the world might reconcile all their differences, but never will they become reconciled on the subject of cooking.'[14]

Most excursions made by Zola and his family were limited to nearby villages, as fear of the French authorities restricted their movements. On one of these occasions he bought two very large purple porcelain cats which he kept near his bed, and which represented to him English artistic tastes. Occasionally he went to Virginia Water, where he would stroll round the small lake. In September, when Georges Charpentier visited him and his family, they spent a few days at Eton and Windsor, the latter especially impressing Zola and his children. Denise was always to retain happy memories of that visit — the great herds of royal deer, the massive stone walls and spacious grounds of the castle, St George's Chapel, the Albert Memorial Chapel with its monuments to dead royalty, the State Apartments — how splendid it all was. There was so much of interest this fifty-eight-year-old father wanted to show his bright, young children, but which was forbidden to a wanted man.

On 10 October he accompanied Jeanne and the children to London, and a few days later saw them off at Victoria Station. If his lawyer's optimistic prognosis had come about, Zola would have been leaving with them, but as it was, Labori wrote shortly before Jeanne's departure recommending Zola to have a little more patience.[15]

In the middle of October, a much resigned Zola, using the new alias of Mr J. Richard, moved into the Queen's Hotel, where he was to spend the remainder of his time in exile. The hotel was very expensive and rather unusual, in that it consisted of a series of private pavilions connected with the larger main building. Each pavilion had a separate private entrance and staircase, thus obviating the use of a central lobby, and as the guests had private dining rooms, the central dining room could be avoided as well, which was ideal for Zola.

He changed suites a couple of times during his stay there. His original apartment on the ground floor overlooked the exensive gardens, but later, after the leaves had fallen, he found the view bleak and depressing and moved instead to a smaller suite on the second floor. He had two sitting-rooms commanding views of both the garden and the quiet road which ran past the hotel grounds. One of the sitting-rooms became his study. The hotel was frequented by an upper-middle class and aristocratic clientèle (whose numbers had included Emperor Frederick), and thus was a quiet and discreet place for a man in Zola's circumstances. He never tired of praising the English for their discretion.

Though his last suite of rooms was smaller, it was also warmer in every sense. The rather large sitting-room became his study. Its walls were covered in a flowery, pastel wallpaper, though devoid of paintings or pictures. Some small blue vases on the mantlepiece were reflected in a large gilt-framed mirror. Several chairs stood to either side of the fireplace, against the opposite wall was a sofa, while along another wall stood a small sideboard. There were several tables in the room, all of which were fully utilized. One in the centre of room served as a dining-table, though it could barely accommodate four people. Next to Zola's reading chair, the armchair near the fireplace, stood a small gypsy table which usually held the latest newspapers and the book he was in the course of reading. Vizetelly lent him Stendhal's *La Chartreuse de Parme* (Charterhouse of Parma), and then *Le Rouge et le noir* (The Red and the Black), both of which he had read decades earlier, but which so fascinated him that he anticipated writing an essay on them. He thought the *Chartreuse de Parme* 'a most extraordinary book', and his interest was intensified because of the similarity between his situation and that of Fabrice in the story. Later he read Balzac's *L'Envers de l'histoire contemporaine* (The Underside of Contemporary History), which he found 'a little revolting' and 'against all my social and literary concepts . . .'[16]

Another sturdy table held his office supplies, including piles of paper, scales for weighing letters, pens, pencils and envelopes. A larger table standing before another window held the rest of his books. Zola chose a small mahogany table on which to do his writing. It was only three feet long and two feet deep, holding a small inkstand, paper-weights, a piece of old newspaper which Zola used as a blotter, and of course his single pen with its 'j' nib and heavy ivory handle. This writing table stood before the central window, overlooking the road and houses opposite. Paraffin lamps were used for lighting purposes until electricity was installed towards the end of his stay.

There was never anything of the temperamental artist in Zola's actions or working habits. Once he began a new book, every day was a work day. At his specific request, he received few visits, except from friends and business associates: Desmoulin came on several occasions, Eugène Fasquelle and his wife five or six times, his English publisher, Andrew Chatto (of Chatto and Windus), his American publisher, George Brett (of Macmillan & Co.), Charpentier, Yves Guyot (publisher of *Le Siècle*), George Moore, the novelist, Georges Clemenceau (in the guise of 'Admiral Maxse')[17] and Labori once each, and Vizetelly several times a week. Surprisingly he seemed to have no close friends among the English writers of the day and rarely mentioned English literature, with the exception of Shakespeare.

He read the newspapers and post after breakfast and was generally at work by ten o'clock, continuing without a break until about one o'clock when he would stop for lunch and a siesta. If the weather permitted, he would take a long stroll through the hotel grounds, very often with Vizetelly (who took care not to disturb him in the morning).

It was in England that he began the first of a new series of books, *Les Quatre Evangiles* which was to include *Fécondité*, *Travail* (Labour), *Vérité* (Truth) and *Justice*. *Fécondité* was begun at 'Penn' on 4 August, eleven months after the completion of his previous novel, *Paris*. Zola liked strong themes, and accordingly always wrote a series of interrelated books; he needed the length and variety involved to develop his ideas. It has been said that the author's finest works were contained in the *Rougon-Macquart* series which had been completed with the publication of *Le Docteur Pascal* in 1893. Critics were not as happy with the ensuing trilogy, *Les Trois villes*, which was completed towards the end of 1897, just as Zola was about to enter the arena on behalf of Dreyfus. Fruitfulness, labour, truth and justice were more than mere titles of books for their author — they were the four cardinal principles of life and, indeed, civilization, replacing the faith, hope and charity he had explored in *Les Trois villes*, but which he felt the Catholic Church had not lived up to.

Discussing his work with Vizetelly one day, Zola explained:

> My novels have always been written with a higher aim than merely to amuse . . . I have chosen it [the novel] as the form in which to present my views on the social, scientific and psychological problems that occupy the minds of thinking men. I might have chosen another form . . . [but] today it [the novel] contains, or may be made to contain, everything — and that is why I am a novelist. I believe I have certain contributions to make on certain subjects, and I have chosen the novel as the best means of communicating these contributions to the world.[18]

Fécondité was the only novel Zola wrote from beginning to end outside France, and it was in many respects a critical sociological survey of the French people. Why was France so decadent and her leaders so puny — mentally, morally and physically? Most of the answers led back to two subjects: population and family. The intellectuals and leaders in France, for instance, usually did not have large families — perhaps two children as a general rule — and yet the national birth rate was declining when compared with the rest of Europe. Zola interpreted this decline as an indicator of national weakness. (He scoffed at the notion of over-population, believing that the land would always provide enough food for everyone.)

The middle and upper classes took very little interest in the children they did have. Unwanted children could be disposed of during pregnancy through abortion at one of the many quack abortion clinics to be found throughout Paris. Or an illegitimate child could be taken off one's hands by paying someone to do so. But the children of the household also suffered, for they were often brought up by nurses. Zola held that depriving a child of its mother's milk was a crime, believing it to be the only proper nourishment for a child's physical and mental well-being. Not to have a large family was criminal; to have no children was worse — it was a tragedy for the couple and society. Children were literally wealth and power in his eyes. It was the duty of man to procreate and labour hard in life, thus contributing to the health of society. In life, truth and justice (terms Zola repeated many times), must not merely be dogmas, but everyday realities. If France was suffering as a result of numerous scandals — the fall of the Union Générale Bank, the Panama Affair, the Grévy-Wilson affair, involving the forced resignation of President Grévy, the strange death of President Faure, Déroulède, anarchists, and the Dreyfus Affair — it was because there were not enough Mathieus and Mariannes (the hero and heroine of *Fécondité*) in the country.

A main weakness of *Fécondité* was Zola's pontificating — the repetition of the necessity of fruitfulness and hard work, and of the beauty of motherhood. But the book also had it strengths: richly detailed (almost Dickensian) descriptions of family gatherings, and masterly handling of tragedy.

When Alexandrine came to visit her husband later in October, Zola's life was much as it would have been at Médan. It was a quiet existence, but was it always tranquil and reasonably happy? And how did Alexandrine feel about the subject of her husband's current work when she herself had proved barren? The ideal tranquillity Zola described in the Froment home in *Fécondité* was never a reality in his Médan household. And now his wife suffered 'from the English climate'. She had bronchitis and colds almost continually till December when she finally returned to Paris.

Throughout his life Zola could become easily bored and restless, like many creative people, and now he chafed to return to France. In letter after letter to his wife, Charpentier, Desmoulin, Fasquelle, Labori, Mirbeau and others, his pending return was a recurrent theme. He felt all the more restless when he saw Jeanne and the children return in mid-October — indeed he became very dejected. When October proved to be a premature date for his own departure, he aimed for December, which in turn became April, then May and finally June. The deciding factor would be the result of the court inquiry into Lucie Dreyfus's request for the revision of her husband's case. When the results were announced, Zola would return.

22

'Soldiers of the Revolution'

While in England much of Zola's time and thought centred on one subject; the Dreyfus Affair. He spent many hours writing to his friends in France, and just about every letter had something to say on the Affair. In contrast these same letters rarely mentioned anything about the new novel he was then writing (*Fécondité*), which was rather surprising as this was to be the first of a new series to which he planned to devote the next few years. Under normal circumstances he would undoubtedly have been more preoccupied with his artistic production, but he was haunted by the Dreyfus case and how it had shattered the privacy and peace of his personal life.

Zola had been so despondent when he first arrived in England that he refused to read a newspaper for a fortnight or so. 'At that moment I lost faith; I believed it to be the end of France,' and he spoke of 'the gradual state of despair I fell into, the absolute pessimism'.[1] Eventually he allowed Vizetelly to supply him with several English papers as well as with *Le Siècle* and *L'Aurore,* but his mood remained erratic. At times he wrote to friends trying to cheer them up, assuring them that truth and justice were bound to win, though it might take many years. At other times he fell into a despondency — everything was wrong. France was corrupt and society was disintegrating, while the Paul Déroulèdes rabble-rousers and the clerical-military coalition were succeeding in fomenting a right-wing revolution, such as was seen in 1830 and 1851. Octave Mirbeau's article in *L'Aurore* that August only gave credence to such fears.[2]

Within the first two months of his exile Zola was astounded and depressed to hear of certain developments in the Dreyfus Affair. Colonel Picquart was arrested on 13 July, charged with divulging secret army documents about national defence to Maître Leblois (for which he would be brought to trial the following March), while a month later Major Esterhazy was released by another court. 'We'll all be dead by the time it [truth] wins out . . . I am still trembling with disgust and anger. I am simply enraged, even within the great calm of my solitude.'[3]

Colonel Picquart was transferred to the Mont Valérien prison-fortress, an abomination in Zola's eyes: 'Oh, how deeply concerned I am about Picquart. He is a hero . . . tell him that not a day goes by when I don't think of him,' Zola wrote.[4] Labori replied, insisting that 'the Picquart and Esterhazy cases are going to shed light [on all this], of that I am deeply convinced'.[5] But Zola considered the condemnation of Picquart as 'the supreme crime, the crime to make honest people revolt at long last'.[6] By December 1898 some other French writers were beginning to take up the colonel's cause, even demanding that courts martial be abolished altogether. Zola was delighted. 'Who would have even thought us, in our ivory towers, capable of that, we so disdainful of everyday affairs and of having to join in any kind of a fight. We are definitely going to end by becoming soldiers of the revolution.'[7]

Back in August 1898, even before all the documentation was drawn up on Colonel Henry and Major du Paty de Clam, Zola felt that from a circumstantial viewpoint alone, they had to be the real culprits behind the rigging of the Dreyfus Affair. 'When Esterhazy and his mistress are behind bars, du Paty de Clam will be compromised and found to be an accomplice . . . ' wrote Zola, and when that happened he would be able to return to France, 'even if nothing new has come up and they strangle us at Versailles . . . '[8] He was fed up with justice in French courts under the Third Republic. 'There is Esterhazy, whitewashed by a civilian court, just as he was by the military. Like you, I am hoping for something unknown to intervene in our behalf.'[9] 'In the evening,' he wrote to Mirbeau, 'when night falls, it seems like the end of the world.'[10]

Meanwhile, even on holiday at Samois, Fernand Labori was kept busy seven days a week, driving himself relentlessly 'because of the crazy existence I have been leading ever since your departure'. He scarcely had time to write Zola, and when he did manage to do so, it was usually late on a Sunday evening and in the early hours of Monday.[11]

On 31 August Zola received a bolt out of the blue in the form of a telegram from France: 'Be prepared for a great success.' Nothing more, no word of explanation, just the signature of a friend. As there was nothing in the newspapers to clarify this, both Vizetelly and Zola were mystified. Zola, who was not very well at the time, paced up and down in the sitting-room, letting his fertile imagination run riot, trying to guess just what the message could allude to.

It was only with the arrival of the London papers the next morning that he learnt what the telegram referred to, as he listened intently as Violette Vizetelly translated for him. Colonel Henry had been arrested and had confessed to his part in the Dreyfus case. The article was followed by a brief news item: 'Colonel Henry has been found dead in his cell at Mont Valérien.' Zola was as surprised as anyone, and almost delirious. Henry had admitted forging the very document that General de Pellieux had introduced during Zola's first trial as proof of Dreyfus's guilt. Later Cavaignac had brought forward the same document in the Chamber of Deputies where he too, had vouched for its authenticity. Picquart, of course, had consistently claimed it was a forgery, a claim that had landed him in a military prison. Zola was ecstatic and felt that the evil house of cards would now come tumbling down and he would soon be able to return to his homeland. 'At last I believe we are on our way to victory,' he wrote to Labori. But they still had hurdles to clear; the battle would only be won 'when the innocence of D . . . is recognized and he is set free'.[12] And he warned that they would have to be especially wary now, for he had no doubts that the *bandits gabonnés,* literally 'braided crooks', in other words the army top brass, would stop at nothing to save face.[13]

Colonel Henry's admission and subsequent suicide had struck the Army a severe and unexpected blow that set off a chain of events. The day that Henry committed suicide, General Boisdeffre resigned his commission and General de Pellieux followed suit. Three days later Godefroy Cavaignac, still chafing from the searing attacks by Jean Jaurès in his series of articles in *La Petite République* that August, resigned as Henri Brisson's War Minister, to be replaced by General Zurlinden. The following day Esterhazy fled to England, and a fortnight later Zurlinden resigned from the Brisson Cabinet. A little more than a month later Zurlinden's successor, General Chanoine, stepped down from the same post. And then in London on 25 September Esterhazy admitted that it was he, not Dreyfus, who was the real author of the *bordereau* of 1894 which had been sold to the Germans.

This stunning series of events was followed by an announcement from the Paris Court of Appeals that it would consider Lucie Dreyfus's request for a review of her husband's case. On 29 October that same court announced the launching of a full-scale inquiry. (The same day the Legion of Honour announced that Major Esterhazy's name had been struck from its roster.) Labori praised Zola. 'I consider the latest decision by the Court of Appeals as one of the most important and significant results that we have obtained yet. The moral effect is enormous. It assures victory . . . It's your work; without you nothing would have happened.'[14] Zola was generous and frank in his reply:

> You are far more responsible for the good results. You are as victorious as I; my triumph is yours as well, for it is you who made of my protest what it eventually became: a resounding inquiry, such an eloquent cry, that has since increased the thirst for truth throughout the world . . . Dreyfus will be acquitted and my only fear remains the possible new infamy that could be brought about by another court martial if full light is not shed on the case.[15]

Back in July Zola had been found guilty of libelling the three handwriting experts employed by the Army to testify to the authenticity of the forged documents. He had been fined 17,000 francs (including a court fine and damages), and sentenced to two months in jail, but on 10 August the Court of Appeals reduced the prison term to one month, while increasing the damages against him to 40,000 francs. Zola wrote to Labori immediately.

I quite understand that this is the result of our having defaulted and that the amount will be halved when we appear. But I should like to know if . . . we must deposit the money with the court right now. If this is the case, please see Vaughan [publisher of *L'Aurore*] and tell him that he must certainly contribute to this amount. *L'Aurore* has a financial interest in this entire affair [Zola had not accepted payment for any of his articles on the Dreyfus case], and it is quite impossible that I be left solely responsible. Vaughan has written to me saying that he is very hard up; so am I. The situation should be explained to our friends. Work out an arrangement that will relieve me . . . [and] please inform me on this matter. I would also appreciate your opinion on the entire present state of affairs, and what you think about the near future.[16]

As Zola's correspondence with Vaughan always seemed to be quite friendly, it is not entirely clear why Zola doubted that Vaughan would support him — but his instinct turned out to be right.

In the second week of October the courts ordered the auctioning of Zola's furniture from his Paris home in the rue de Bruxelles. This promised to be another Parisian spectacle, but it was pre-empted by Zola's friends. Vaughan obstinately refused to help the author out, but Eugène Fasquelle, who had succeeded Charpentier as his publisher, purchased one of Zola's tables for the full amount demanded by the court — 32,000 francs.

Zola was deeply touched and grateful, for his own expenses were increasing. And, of course, he had to support two households and pay for his children's education. Zola's financial responsibilities were a source of real anxiety. Although until 1897 his annual income was quite high (155,000-200,000 francs), Vizetelly suggests this amount was reduced by nearly two-thirds in 1898, as a result of his involvement in the Dreyfus Affair and the subsequent unfavourable publicity, which caused a drastic slump in the sales of his books. His annual income never regained its former level during his lifetime, and he had no savings or investments to fall back on. He had to work.

However, Zola did not feel isolated in his crusade for truth in the Dreyfus affair; he belonged to a team which included Lucie and Mathieu Dreyfus, Labori, Vaughan, Perrenx, Clemenceau, Joseph Reinach, Charpentier, Fasquelle and many others. In November and December of the same year, Joseph Reinach, one-time lieutenant of Gambetta, Director of the newspaper *La République Française* and member of the Chamber of Deputies, wrote two articles for *Le Siècle* about Colonel Henry and Esterhazy, charging that Henry had been an accomplice in committing treason. The result was that Henry's widow promptly sued Reinach and won. And to think that the 'republicans' had criticized the corruption of Napoleon III's Second Empire.

Reinach had always worked hard for what he considered to be the right cause, but Zola was suspicious of his motives and merely considered him an opportunist. Less than a year later, however, Zola realized his estimation of Reinach had been utterly incorrect, and in April 1899 he wrote a rare letter apologizing to Reinach for his former unfounded suspicions:

> If you have been thinking of me when writing your articles for *Le Siècle*, I can tell you that in my solitude here I read them with a growing passion and admiration. One of my first visits [upon returning] to Paris will be to confess to you my wrongs, the unjust opinion I had of you, the mule-headed ignorance I maintained of your courage and talent. You have been admirable throughout this entire monstrous affair.[17]

Labori and Zola had long been attempting to help Picquart, but the powers that be — 'that band of cowards led by a pack of knaves', as Labori called them — had put obstacles in the way at every juncture.[18] Then in the first week of March 1899, the Court of Appeals announced that Colonel Picquart's case would be heard at long last, in June, before the Paris Court of Appeals. In the meantime he was transferred to the Cherche-Midi Prison in Paris. To Zola's immense satisfaction, most of the charges brought against Colonel Picquart were dropped for lack of corroborating evidence and he was released.

By the beginning of April 1899, following a brief visit by Fernand Labori and his wife,[19] Zola was quite beside himself. *Fécondité* had been coming along nicely, thanks to the almost total solitude in which he found himself, and he anticipated completing that novel by May or June. But he could no longer bear his enforced exile. Time after time he had postponed his return, but now would endure no more, and despite the opposition of all his friends, Zola bombarded them with letters, pleading for their support. On two earlier occasions Labori had entreated Zola to be patient, latterly suggesting that he move to a warmer place, such as Genoa.[20] But when Labori discussed the probability of a court order being issued in April for the return of Dreyfus from Devil's Island, and the equal likelihood of Zola's return, the author grew very restive.[21] He now made his most determined and persuasive attempt to convince the lawyer once and for all that now indeed was the time for him to return:

> I am surprised by the great anxiety of my friends about my desire to return to France. I still don't know what the Court is going to decide about Picquart [in June] . . . But a Criminal Chamber . . . against him has already decided that the aspects related to the Dreyfus affair could not be judged until the Court [of Appeals] has completed its investigation. And it seems to me that this is enough to elucidate my own case.
>
> It is obvious that my trial is related to the Dreyfus Affair . . . It is known that Esterhazy wrote the *bordereau* . . . [even though] a court martial

decided that he did not. If the Court [of Appeals] finds, to the contrary, that he did write it, isn't that in itself a decisive argument that I cannot be judged before the results of the Court's findings are known? That would be contrary to all common sense and all justice.

It is understandable that the military courts pursue Picquart because they want vengeance. But why should the civil courts go after me in an equally vengeful manner? I am not trying to escape them, when I merely ask that light be shed, before I in turn am judged . . . While the Court is carrying out its investigation, we can open our own at Versailles, where we can call all the same witnesses before the jury of the Seine-et-Oise, as are called in Paris . . . forcing the generals to appear and swear under oath, publicly. Whatever happens we still have recourse to the Court of Appeals, which can prove them wrong yet again . . . At times I wonder whether my immediate return to France wouldn't be an excellent tactic, to show them that we are no longer afraid and to force them to withdraw. An article is all ready for publication in L'Aurore, which would explain why and how I am returning.

Finally, if my return is judged to be impossible by my friends, at least let them give me the reasons for such alarm, that I might understand them. I shall only remain where I am if they demonstrate to me that by returning I would compromise the cause.[22]

But even as Zola was writing this document Fernand Labori came down with severe influenza, and for a time his doctors feared for his life. Zola was extremely worried and wrote emotional letters to Labori's wife, sharing her anxieties. Thankfully Labori pulled through, but it was a draining eight-week struggle.

Ever suspicious of the tactics and thinking of their opponents, Zola and Labori had long considered the possibility of the government offering a general amnesty in order to ensure silence, and put an end to all the trials and investigations concerning the Dreyfus case. In some dismay Zola wrote to Labori: 'I should be most unhappy about an amnesty that would allow me to be acquitted. Would it be possible to refuse such an amnesty and to ask for a trial all the same? And if I cannot refuse it, what will the immediate consequences be? You must tell me what I should do.'[23]

Throughout the long flow of correspondence between Zola and Labori, the novelist is clearly a sceptic and pessimist, warning Labori to guard against optimisim and prepare for a long and difficult battle. Zola's anticipation of an amnesty by the French government was soon to become a reality (in December 1900). The politicians and many army generals had much to conceal, and President Félix Faure was ensuring that though prime ministers would come and go, only a man of conservative stamp opposed to revision would be appointed to that post.

The unexpected death of President Faure on 16 February 1899 sent a shock wave rumbling through France once again, for it was alleged that Faure had died under mysterious circumstances, and the attempt by the palace guard to hush things up ensured yet another scandal. Indeed it was only learned decades later that he had died in bed with a lovely young woman, the wife of a colleague and well-known national figure. The scandal did not surprise Zola, who had never liked Faure, and he was looking forward to a new face in the Elysée Palace. On 18 February, when Emile Loubet was selected as his successor, Zola grew more optimistic. Before the announcement of Faure's death earlier that month, Zola had written to his old friend, Octave Mirbeau:

> Labori, it seems, is always full of confidence concerning the final results, regardless of the courts involved. He feels that only a *coup de force* could prevent the establishment of the truth. I must tell you that, for my part, I am haunted by the darkest foreboding. Those crooks cannot have done what they did without their having the firm intention of carrying out the worst infamy. They would all try anything, even the supreme murder, to kill justice. If my reasoning would still like to hope for the best, a voice within tells me that this is sheer naïveté, but that everything is possible if a logical equity would restore the country's health and strength. I therefore expect a catastrophe, though I can't say what is going to engulf us next.[24]

Zola's black mood worsened as he contemplated the bleak picture he had painted, and when he heard that the courts had gone against Reinach he was moved to declare, 'I am so sad I could die.'[25]

'The election of Loubet is an excellent step, I believe. Are we now going to have a chance to finish with this awful nightmare?'[26] Zola asked Eugène Fasquelle a few days later. In that same letter, he talked of beginning negotiations with Vaughan for the serialization of *Fécondité* in *L'Aurore*. He informed Fasquelle that he could not hand over his latest novel till the end of May. 'See Vaughan as soon as possible and speak to him about this. I believe that the financial terrain is quite solid. Therefore take your precautions. Keep to the figure I gave you and it will be accepted.'[27]

Though it is not known what sum Zola eventually received for serialization from Vaughan (Vizetelly thought he received only half the usual fee)[28], the negotiations were quickly concluded, as Zola signed and returned both copies of the contract on 9 March. When it came to money, Zola distrusted most newspaper publishers, but as his works were selling so badly, he found himself in a weakened bargaining position.

By 25 March most of the loose ends had been sorted out and Zola asked his publisher to give his copy of the contract to Alexandrine for safe keeping.[29] 'I have some new chapters [just written] and some corrected proofs for you. But hoping that it is possible, I'll bring all that myself.'[30] In an optimistic vein he wrote: 'It seems to me that our affairs are now going better and better. Until recently I was cautious about my illusions; I didn't want to declare myself satisfied. We must recognize, however, that every day another step is taken towards establishing the truth. And I have ended by letting myself become most hopeful.'[31] *Fécondité*, which was completed on 27 May, was published as a single volume in London and Paris in October 1899.

Zola was growing increasingly restless in England, especially after a brief second visit by Jeanne and their two children at Easter-time in early April. It was following this visit that he wrote to Labori, pleading to be allowed to return to France.

Towards the end of May Zola received a letter from Labori — the first he had written since his close brush with death: 'I have been up for two days now. Next week I shall leave for the countryside, no doubt having had the great joy of seeing you again before then . . . [for] Fasquelle and our friends have told me that your return has been definitely decided.'[32] He added that the publication of the Ballot-Beaupré Report on Dreyfus had made Zola's return possible. 'There is your victory, you must be proud and happy; it's all due to you.'[33]

The Court of Appeals was to announce its decision concerning its review of the Dreyfus case on Saturday, 3 June 1899. 'I have had quite enough; nothing in the world could keep me here one hour longer. They could threaten me with arrest at the frontier for all I care.'[34] Before leaving England Zola wrote to Vaughan asking that his article, *'Justice'*, which he had prepared in April, be published in *L'Aurore* on Monday, 5 June.

> But you must arrange to keep its publication secret from everyone but our friends, of course . . . if you must put up posters advertising it, only do so during the night of Sunday-Monday. I should like to draw your attention to the variation insert concerning Picquart, which I feel must accompany the article. If Picquart is not freed on Sunday . . . the article must be published as it stands. But if Picquart is free, omit the last fifteen lines on page sixteen and the first five lines of page seventeen . . . [35]

Zola was returning to France now regardless of the consequences, but he harboured no illusions about the homecoming he would receive from the majority of his fellow countrymen. 'I can ask myself, now that I am more or less sure that truth will out, if the country will ever thank those who have saved it from its shame.'[36] Pointing to monarchical and military atavism, chauvinism and defeatism as the causes of the country's malaise, he lamented the people's continuing unawareness, even after he and others had sacrificed so much to give France its ideal of justice and humanity. 'Instead they continue to go about parading the French flag as of yore, and hence the future is closed to them . . . We must wait for history to judge us, when all of the present social and political conditions will have disappeared.'[37]

On 3 June the Court of Appeals met and announced its long overdue decision. It annulled the court decision of 1894 condemning Captain Dreyfus, and now ordered his return for a new court martial to be held at Rennes. Following this announcement, Zola received a 'coded' telegram: 'Cheque postponed', which meant that Dreyfus was to have a new trial. Beside himself with joy, Zola prepared to leave, and Eugène Fasquelle and his wife came especially to England to accompany him on his return journey. Although Labori agreed that the decision by the Court of Appeals was significant, he was still anxious about Zola returning to France too precipitously.

> I can understand as well as anyone at what point your interminable exile, which has so constantly weighed upon you, should indeed become intolerable in the end. But at the same time it would be less than courageous on my part if, just out of respect for your legitimate desire to return, I did not tell you exactly what I thought.[38]

Then, after explaining his own reservations about Zola's return now, he acknowledged that he was a minority of one, and he gave his blessing as well.

Zola left the Queen's Hotel on Sunday afternoon, 4 June, travelling with the Fasquelles from Crystal Palace station to Charing Cross and then to Victoria Station. There they were joined by Wareham and Vizetelly and his wife. Following a merry, if hasty dinner with his friends at the railway station, Zola commented, 'It seems to me more than ever, that I am living in a dream,' and gave one of his rare laughs. For the first time in nearly a year he could relax. He bade farewell to his friends and to the England that had been his home and refuge for just under eleven months; he hoped to return, he said, for a visit following the Paris Exhibition of 1900.

Zola and the Fasquelles travelled all night by boat-train, via Dover and Calais, reaching the Saint-Lazare Station in Paris just after five o'clock in the morning on Monday, 5 June. A few hours later his article, *'Justice'* (which contained many of the views expressed in his letters over the past year), appeared in *L'Aurore*.[39] He was back in France; he had come full circle. Seven days later Henri Brisson's government fell.

23

The Zola-Bruneau Collaboration

As Zola entered the fourth decade of his life in the early 1880s, leaving behind the financial and literary uncertainties of his youth, he entered a period of personal crisis, triggered by the deaths of two people who meant a great deal to him — his mother and Flaubert — culminating in a nervous breakdown of sorts. His middle forties found him on a curious indefinable plateau, a sort of emotional no man's land, where he managed to hold his own by continuing in a perfunctory, if not always smooth, manner. This period of transition drew to a close, however, as he approached his forty-eighth year. A new, reinvigorated Zola emerged, full of boundless hope and energy. He was now eagerly anticipating the close of his *Rougon-Macquart* series, as he wanted to move in new directions; in fact, he was already considering a trilogy on religious and social issues which he was to entitle *Les Trois villes*. In 1888 he also met Jeanne Rozerot, who was to be his mistress for life and the mother of his children. Finally, in that same year a talented musician and composer was introduced to him, a young man who was to become a very special friend and for whom he was to work in a totally new art form, as librettist. That man was Alfred Bruneau.

It is said that Zola had rarely been to the opera before 1888, and he publicly announced his dislike of all opera in a series of articles he had written in *Le Bien Public* between 1876 and 1878.[1] While tolerant of opera's use of fantasy, he strongly objected to the unrealistic portrayal of the characters.

In March 1888, when Frantz Jourdain introduced Bruneau to Zola, Bruneau was thirty-one years old — seventeen years younger than the author. Although, like his father before him, Bruneau was an accomplished musician (he had won top honours as a cellist at the Paris Conservatoire), it was as a composer, indeed as an avant-garde composer in lyric opera, that he wished to establish himself. Having studied harmony under Savard and composition under Massenet, his first project (an opera called *Kérim*), had failed after its third public performance. At the time of meeting Zola, Bruneau was working as a proofreader for the prestigious Hartman Company (Massenet's publisher), and thus he approached the great man rather diffidently. He had come to ask if he would permit him to compose an opera based on his early novel, *La Faute de l'abbé Mouret*. Zola informed him that Massenet had obtained the musical rights to that work years before. Questioning Massenet about this, Bruneau quickly learnt that his former teacher had not yet begun work on that text, but would not relinquish it in his favour. Accordingly, Bruneau wrote to Zola informing him of this.

On 31 March 1888, Bruneau received a note from Zola asking him to call, and to his surprise Zola offered him a book he was still writing but would not complete for several months — *Le Rêve*. Bruneau was delighted, but informed him of his disastrous first attempt at opera, *Kérim;* needless to say, Bruneau was rather startled to be told that Zola had himself seen and liked the production. So began the long, mutually fulfilling relationship between the two men.

Bruneau quickly became devoted to Zola and remained so even decades after Zola's death. This relationship has generally been ignored by Zola's biographers, yet it was of the greatest importance to both men. Although Zola always treated Bruneau as an equal, Bruneau looked up to his colleague, much as son might look up to his father. In his letters (after 1895) Bruneau addressed Zola as 'Dear great master and friend'. Although they always used the *'vous'* form of address, they became so close that by 1899, when Zola introduced Alfred Dreyfus and his wife to the Bruneaus, he referred to them as his 'family'.

Bruneau, who, with his pince-nez and beard looked remarkably like Zola himself (and indeed was frequently mistaken for him), was a very quiet, retiring family man; his wife, daughter and music were his entire world. Despite his devotion to Zola, his puritanical background (which in some ways Zola so admired) would not, it seems, permit him to come into contact with Jeanne Rozerot, Denise and Jacques, and consequently Bruneau never once mentioned them in the couple of hundred letters he addressed to Zola between 1888 and 1902.[2] The result of this friendship, which matured over the years, was a relationship which became for Zola perhaps second only to that of Jeanne and his children.

The Zola-Bruneau collaboration was amazingly productive in the field of the new opera which, considering that Zola's fictional works continued to appear at a regular pace, and that he was later deeply involved in the Dreyfus case, was a considerable achievement.

During Zola's lifetime Bruneau based two of his operas on works published by Zola, the libretti for which were prepared by Louis Gallet, with Zola's help. In addition, Zola wrote six more libretti — *Messidor, Ouragan, L'Enfant-roi, Lazare, Violaine la chevelue* and *Sylvanire, ou Paris en amour* — of which he lived to see only the first two produced. Following Zola's death, Bruneau prepared three additional operas based on works by Zola: *Naïs Micoulin, La Faute de l'abbé Mouret* and *Les Quatre journées*.

The first two operas of the Bruneau-Zola collaboration were based on *Le Rêve* and the short story called *L'Attaque du moulin*. The libretti for these two works were prepared by Louis Gallet, 'the great librettist of the hour', as Bruneau described him, having worked with Saint-Saëns, Bizet and Massenet.[3] Apparently the decision to ask Gallet to do this was jointly made by Bruneau and Zola, and it was to prove a wise and profitable move. Gallet, in fact, worked full-time as a hospital administrator (being Director of the Hôpital Lariboisière), but over the years he had also established a substantial reputation for himself both as librettist and journalist. Inevitably Gallet's hospital commitments often hindered his writing. Meetings with Bruneau were 'interrupted constantly, either by the vehement entry of the finance officer . . . or by the sudden arrival of several surgeons'.[4] Thus a difficult task was compounded by an unlikely set of circumstances.

Interspersed with Bruneau's progress reports to Zola — Gallet 'hasn't done a thing and thus I am stopped . . . '[5] — were enthusiastic and sincere avowals of admiration. Working with Zola, Bruneau declared, 'is and will remain the greatest joy of my artistic life; it has become dear and precious to me above all others'.[6] After receiving Zola's corrections to Gallet's draft, Bruneau wrote, 'What fine lessons on the theatre you have given me there! I can't tell you how touched and grateful I am for all that you are doing for me.'[7] In fact Zola's past experience with the theatre was now yielding unexpected dividends.

Finally, by May 1890 agreement had been reached to stage *Le Rêve* with Léon Carvalho, at the Opéra-Comique, with Mme Simonnet playing the role of Angélique, Mme Deschamps-Jéhin as Hubertine, and Engel as Félicien, its première set for 18 June 1891. But if Bruneau benefited from Zola's career as a playwright, Zola for his part was eagerly soaking up these new experiences. For example, he wrote, 'My dear Bruneau, I have nothing to do tomorrow and I shall no doubt go to the Opéra-Comique; it is simply the case of a man's curiosity . . . I'll find a quiet spot in the rear, so as not to disturb you.'[8] A fortnight later the première was held and Bruneau recorded his impressions:

That evening, following the performance and our visits to congratulate the artists and after seeing Carvalho [the theatre manager], and gaining his approval to cut the last, badly done, scene, we went to a restaurant for dinner. While eating . . . Zola had an idea which delighted us all — to go out at day-break to get the latest issue of *Le Figaro* from the printer's, to read Vitu's review. And with the sun rising . . . we ambled through the deserted streets to the intersection with the rue Drouot. Men were just beginning to carry out the bundles from the building. We rushed over and grabbed our coveted prey.

We expected to be attacked unmercifully. But Auguste Vitu's review surpassed our worst expectations. With the neighbourhood ringing with our laughter, we finally returned to our homes, happy and exhausted.[9]

Henry Bauer was one reviewer who spoke glowingly of the new production in *L'Echo de Paris*. *Le Rêve* was launched, despite Auguste Vitu. It ran till 30 June when the theatre's annual season officially closed,[10] and then toured the capitals of Europe with resounding success.

So pleased was Carvalho with the box-office receipts that he arranged for *Le Rêve* to be the first production when the theatre reopened in the autumn. He also asked Bruneau and Zola for another work, to which they agreed, without indicating the subject — but that was good enough for Carvalho.

Work on their new opus, *L'Attaque du moulin* (taken from a short story in *Soirées du Médan*), began in the summer of 1891. As it was to be written in blank verse (like *Le Rêve*), which Zola did not feel up to, he and Bruneau decided to continue their collaboration with Gallet. It was agreed that Gallet would prepare an act, send it to Bruneau, who would read it, make a copy for himself, and then forward it to Zola. Zola would then comment on it, making whatever alterations he chose, returning the corrected manuscript to Gallet. It would then go to Bruneau once again, and he would begin to compose the music for it.

Work on the new opera went fairly smoothly. Zola spent much more time on it, and made a considerable number of detailed modifications. Although his name is not to be found printed on the music as a co-librettist, Zola was an important contributor to the final product and Bruneau has published several of Zola's letters to him showing how the author approached this work:

> For the stanzas on the knife, I felt it necessary to break the rhythm and introduce some prose, to make it seem more realistic. Brevity and vigour seemed to be what were needed. On the other hand, I enlarged the tone almost to lyricism for the farewell scene in the forest. That's what you wanted, wasn't it? Tell me frankly if you wanted something else. My only aim is to please you with my commonplace doggerel.[11]

As early as May 1892, Parisian newspapers, notably *L'Evénement* and *L'Echo de Paris* were speculating about *L'Attaque du moulin*.[12] Although Bruneau noted that Gallet was greatly disturbed by the general style of his music,[13] 'I am working hard, and happily so', he reported early in August, 'thanks to the strong encouragement I have received from you.'[14]

In 1893 Fernand Xau of *Le Journal* asked Zola to prepare an article for his paper in which he would develop his ideas on the operatic theatre and the roles of the librettist and composer. This was timed to appear just before the première of *L'Attaque du moulin,* thus providing excellent publicity, as well as an interesting subject for Zola. He began by stressing the importance of 'the right poem': a good plot with flesh and blood characters. Zola then dismissed the issue as to whose task was easier, that of the librettist or the composer.

In fact, nothing takes less time and is easier to prepare than a poem. In three weeks a skilful manufacturer should be able to do that quite nicely, if he doesn't worry too much about the quality of the verse. But then consider the tremendous task of the musician: a score requires many months, sometimes even years, of work and that does not even include the orchestration — altogether more than 1000 pages of music to write. According to theatre tradition, the librettist receives the same box-office receipts as the composer, which seems to me quite unjust.[15]

His suggested solution to this inequity was that the composer should write his own libretto. He said he had discussed this with Bruneau, who had disagreed with him, but Zola felt this was simply modesty. (In fact, Bruneau did prepare his own libretti following Zola's death.) In conclusion Zola wrote: 'The idea of two fathers for this child who should have only one heart and one head greatly disturbs me.'[16]

L'Attaque du moulin opened at the Opéra-Comique on 23 November 1893 and proved to be another success. The two men agreed to continue their collaboration, both feeling pleased with their mutual efforts, but they decided to abandon blank verse in favour of prose, something which Zola now strongly advocated.[17]

That Bruneau was a highly talented composer, no one could deny, but at the same time it was perfectly clear that Zola's influence had helped advance Bruneau's career. Louis Gallet, for example, had only agreed to work with Bruneau after he had been offered *Le Rêve* and gained a commitment from Zola. In Paris there were only two theatres capable of staging operatic productions, which naturally restricted Bruneau's ability to earn a living as a composer, but Zola's name opened doors throughout Europe, and he was also able to put Bruneau in the way of some extra work — in journalism.

For Bruneau it began in September 1892, while he was holidaying with his wife and daughter at Sables d'Olonne in the Vendée. He wrote to Zola that he was leaving for Paris because he had received a telegram from Jules Guérin informing him that Victor Wilder of *Gil Blas* had died a few days previously, and that a successor was under consideration.[18] Guérin said that they were interested in having him replace the deceased, and could he come to their offices to see them? On arrival Bruneau was informed that the editors had not yet made up their minds and that other candidates were also under consideration. Without asking directly for Zola's intercession, he received it; Zola sent a telegram to *Gil Blas* supporting Bruneau's nomination. 'How can I thank you for everything you have done for me?' Bruneau wrote to Zola. 'If anything can tilt the balance in my favour, it will be your dispatch.'[19] But when the editors still hesitated to make a decision, Zola sent another telegram to Guérin: 'Take Bruneau', to which they replied, 'Shall take Bruneau if [you] give [us] *Lourdes.'*[20] No doubt Guérin had been holding out for this all the while. Zola did agree to sell the serial rights of *Lourdes* to *Gil Blas* and Bruneau began what was to prove an impressive career as a Parisian music critic.

This was not the end of the story, however, for within a year or so *Gil Blas*, once a most influential newspaper, began to decline and Bruneau decided it would be necessary to leave. The right opportunity occurred in June 1895, when Charles Darcours, the music critic for *Le Figaro*, died. Negotiations were again long and complex, further complicated by Fernand Xau of *Le Journal* asking both Zola and Bruneau to join his staff. *Le Figaro* at that time was owned by Francis Magnard and was under two managing editors, Fernand de Rodays and Antonin Périvier, men of totally different temperaments and political outlooks. Bruneau was invited to the offices of *Le Figaro* and interviewed by Périvier, always a difficult individual. He indicated that he was hesitant about Bruneau because of his avant-garde music. Bruneau discussed his credentials, pointing out his strong classical education at the Conservatoire and his recent article on *Djelma*, which was playing at the Opéra.[21] But, of course, this was all a pretext on the editors' part, for what they wanted was a commitment from Zola. Finally Périvier came into the open, saying he would hire Bruneau on condition that Zola also agreed to write a weekly column. This was a double humiliation for the young composer, as it implied he could not stand on his own merits, and would involve yet again the intervention of his prestigious friend. Zola saw it differently, however, considering it simply a practical means of helping a young man up the ladder. Generous contracts were drawn up for both of them and Bruneau then resigned from *Gil Blas* on about 1 September 1895.[22] The composer was to prove a great asset to *Le Figaro* where he remained for the next seven years.

The first entirely Zola-Bruneau production was the opera *Messidor,* and Bruneau was in possession of Zola's libretto by the end of 1893.[23] Each act of this new work was to represent one of the four seasons, concluding with the feasting of love and labour in the spring. Bruneau did not complete *Messidor* until September 1896, and it was first performed on 19 February 1897, at the Académie Nationale de Musique, transferring afterwards to the Opéra, with Mlle Berthet starring as Hélène, Alvarez as Guillaume, Delmas as Mathias, Renaud as the shepherd, and Noté as Gaspard. This work was somewhat unorthodox in that it also had ballet scenes. As it turned out, Bruneau and Zola were unhappy with both the ballet and Gailhard's and Bertrand's production in general.[24]

'I have thought about the décor of the ballet,' wrote Zola 'and I am really worried about it. It is definitely not right. A shoddy décor often kills an act, and then is cut at the last moment. I should gladly put myself out now in order to avoid a real worry later.'[25]

A more pleasing production was later staged in Munich, however, where it was splendidly conducted by Richard Strauss — a man Bruneau greatly admired.

Messidor had gone to the Opéra, and not to Carvalho's Opéra-Comique, as a result of a falling out between Bruneau and Carvalho in 1894,[26] but meeting again by chance three years later, the two men decided to make it up. Not long afterwards a contract was signed for a fresh production of *L'Attaque du moulin,* scheduled for December 1897. Several months later an all-star cast was assembled and everything was ready for its opening night, when Carvalho suddenly died. Des Chapelles replaced Carvalho, but for some reason Bruneau felt it inappropriate to continue under these circumstances. What would no doubt have been the best production ever of this work was now withdrawn.[27]

Bruneau received Zola's draft of his new opera, *Ouragan* (Hurricane), on 10 November 1896,[28] but everything came to a sudden halt fourteen months later with Zola's participation in the Dreyfus Affair. Though Bruneau had completed his scoring and orchestration by May 1899, the première did not take place till 29 April 1901.[29] Most of their correspondence during the intervening years was exclusively concerned with the trials of Dreyfus and Zola. Zola's sudden decision to flee the country prompted Bruneau to write:

> I was stupefied last night to read that you had left — left without my being able to clasp you in my arms and to say goodbye. I had to spend the entire day at a meeting, which prevented me from being with you [at Versailles], though my thoughts were with you, and after an adjournment I rushed over to the offices of *Le Figaro* to get the latest news.[30]

Zola's part in the Dreyfus Affair also affected Bruneau directly. When *Messidor* was performed at Nantes during Zola's trial, there was such a disturbance that the cavalry was called in to quell the riot, and Bruneau was asked to withdraw the opera. 'Therefore it was decided quite purely and simply not to produce our works there ever again,' he later commented, 'and it was the same for a fairly long time in a large number of French cities.'[31] Even in Brussels, where all previous operatic works of the two men had been extremely popular, the effect of Zola's trial was to close the opera after two days.[32] For the next couple of years, Bruneau's income was severely cut back and it was only thanks to his job at *Le Figaro* that he was able to make ends meet.

Zola wrote often to Bruneau from England, expressing gratitude for his friendship and pleasant anticipation of hearing the first three acts of *Ouragan* immediately upon his return. However, he also warned of possible government action later:

You must not deceive yourself that any theatre receiving a government subsidy will produce our works; they will do so only if we are victorious. That is yet another of the good reasons I have for hoping so ardently for victory. It would be too painful for me to know that by losing I had dragged you down with me.[33]

'Even if we win,' he wrote in January 1899, 'I am worried about the future. It will take a long time before people will pardon us for having been right about Dreyfus.'[34] However, he drew strength from Bruneau's continuing support and friendship, clearly illustrated in the following letter from Bruneau:

Every day the three of us have been thinking of you, wherever you are, awaiting the time when we will be reunited, when we can take up our lives by your side, where we left off, where we found happiness, and which will finally mark an end to the unceasing abominations which have been creating so much confusion for so many months. Immediately upon your return we will put our new apartment in special order so that it will be most comfortable when you come, and it will be a great joy for me to be able to play my [first] three acts [of *Ouragan*]. I don't know what will happen once my score is completed, but I do know that I have put my whole heart into it, all the anguish and humanity resulting from this frightful drama, of which I have been a part while composing this work, and all the indignation I have felt, all my pride in being your friend, all my tenderness, all my admiration for you . . . [35]

Unlike some who claimed to be close to Zola at this time, Bruneau was a real friend who admired him both for his literary genius as well as for his personal traits.

By 12 October 1898, Bruneau could report some progress on *Ouragan,* despite the usual problems associated with moving into a new flat.

As for me, I've worked quite well. I have only about ten more pages to write before finishing my third act which I'll complete once the carpet-layers have left, giving us a chance to catch our breath. I believe it will be lively and vigorous . . . The fourth, which is shorter than the others, will go quickly and I should certainly have finished the composition and orchestration within a year's time.[36]

In mid-March 1899, Bruneau informed Zola:

Did you know that Empress Eugénie [the widow of Napoleon III] was passionately with us [in the Dreyfus case]? [Gaston] Calmette, who lunched with her a few days ago, related to me her deep admiration of you, her absolute conviction based on various public evidence as well as what she learned in England where it is all documented.[37]

And then he proceeded to tell him of his work on the opera:

> As soon as you return, I'll be able to play my entire score for you. I have
> only the last scene of the work left to compose. Therefore I am quite sure
> to be ready and that presentation will bring me a great deal of joy. I'll begin
> work on the orchestration forthwith, which I hope will advance quickly.[38]

In early May Bruneau's wife, writing on behalf of the composer, who
was recuperating from an illness, informed Zola: 'My husband has worked
well. He has just finished composing *Ouragan*.'[39]

The story of *Ouragan* centres round the inhabitants of a village on the
island of Goël. It deals with their lives as fishermen, their stormy personal
relationships (complicated by three women loving the same man), the
inevitable jealousy, and death. Finally, the hero (Richard) and the young
heroine (Lulu) sail away from Goël, leaving behind forever their sad
memories.

Ouragan was to be staged by Albert Carré at the Opéra-Comique and
it opened to public acclaim on 29 April 1901, with Bourbon as Richard,
Maréchal as Landry, Dufranne as Gervai, Marie Delna as Marianne, Jeanne
Raunay as Jeanine, and Julia Guiraudon as Lulu.

In an interview with *Le Figaro* Zola described *Ouragan* as,

> . . . a very simple, very compact, very great work, where unleashed human
> powers come into conflict, pushed to the state of paroxysm. It is the hurricane
> of our passions which, all of a sudden, and without reason, blow across
> our blue sky, amidst the ordinary happenings of our daily existence, causing
> chaos and destruction, leaving us devastated and bleeding before our lives
> can start again.[40]

The following year, commenting on a presentation of *Ouragan* and the
reaction of the audience, Bruneau wrote to Zola,

> It sounded just as I had intended it, and I am most pleased, for I felt, more
> than at any other time, that it strongly expressed my warm feelings and
> admiration for you. It was obvious to everyone and I am proud. Thank you
> for allowing me to sing about your faithful friendship, for having given
> me such a magnificent libretto and for comforting me with the fine joys
> of affection and work.[41]

After one performance, Bruneau told Zola that he heard cries of, 'Vive
Zola!'[42]

Every performance was an extraordinary success, and the receipts
proved it, but neither Bruneau nor Zola thought of stopping and resting
on their laurels. In August 1899, news of the attempt on Labori's life (see

Chapter 24), and the general tenor of the Rennes proceedings, left Zola feeling greatly depressed and hardly in the mood to write lyric opera. Bruneau, of course, understood this and was unfailingly patient.

> When calm returns to us, you can write a fine libretto for me from which I promise myself much joy. The only music I have in my scores is that which you inspire, and it is quite certain that if I had not known you, I should never have made music, at least not in the true sense of the word as I know it.[43]

Zola wanted each opera to differ from the preceding one, just as his novels did, and the next project was *L'Enfant-roi* (The Child-king). The story involves a baker (François) and his wife (Madeleine). François is desolate that they are childless, but later discovers that his wife has a sixteen-year-old son (Georget), whom she had as a result of a liaison with a cousin years before her marriage. There is a stormy scene between the couple, but the opera closes happily with François accepting Georget in their household.

Zola probably handed the manuscript of this new text to Bruneau early in 1900, and it progressed so well that by September 1901 the composer could report to Zola that he had already completed scoring the second act: 'Never has a score given me so much happiness to write.'[44] Zola and Bruneau corresponded throughout the composition of *L'Enfant-roi* and discussed possible future projects with enthusiasm. Zola was considering three storylines, but eventually opted for *Sylvanire*.

Bruneau's last letter to Zola before his death, was written on 16 September 1902, and in it the composer announced the completion of their latest joint-work:

> Madame Zola's nice letter, which my wife just received, tells us that you have already written one act of *Sylvanire* . . . How delighted I am to think that I'll be able to see the entire poem when I return to Paris . . . I have completed the orchestration of *L'Enfant-roi* . . . Once again it seems that preparing a work has never given me such sheer joy.[45]

Zola replied nine days later and Bruneau received the letter on the day of Zola's death, just a few hours before receiving word of the tragedy:

> You should be really happy, for there you have another work completed; I am counting on it very much . . .
> *Sylvanire*, or *Paris en amour*, a title which I prefer for several reason, is coming along. I am happy with the results so far. But when I work for you, you know my scruples. As soon as you're here, we will read the text, and you will tell me frankly what you think of it. I fear the tenor's part

is the most difficult. There is a lot of movement and even lightness, and a great deal of variety, and it is very poignant towards the end. But it resembles no other work; it is all new as a lyrical drama, and I am terrified to think what Gailhard will say.[46]

Bruneau was absolutely shattered by the news of Zola's death. He was devoted to his 'dear great master and friend', yet the closeness of their relationship has apparently never before been fully known or appreciated.

After Zola's death, I had the horrible impression that I should never again be able to work and that I had lost the courage and faith to do it. Daily he showed me the importance of those two key virtues without which the true artist, who must combat obstacles from his youth to old age, would have to remain silent and withdraw from the world.[47]

Madame Zola gave Bruneau the completed manuscript of *Sylvanire, ou Paris en Amour* following the funeral. It was indeed almost revolutionary in its audacity, the story taking place in an opera itself, and including the use of operatic ballet. Bruneau showed the text to Pedro Gailhard, director of the Paris Opéra, and 'warm discussions' ensued, but in the end Gailhard turned it down. Thirty years later Bruneau noted,'I experienced then one of the most bitter moments of my life.'[48] With that rejection behind him, Bruneau set to work on another libretto, *Lazare* (Lazarus), which Zola had written in 1894, but upon its completion Bruneau met with another rebuff. As for *L'Enfant-roi*, it was not produced by Carré at the Opéra-Comique until 3 March 1905.[49]

24

'What Must Civilized Nations Think of Us?'

On 16 February 1899, President Félix Faure, who had so obstinately defied justice and 'defended' the French Army in the Dreyfus Affair, died and was replaced by Emile Loubet, who was considered a more reasonable man. When Prime Minister Dupuy's government collapsed on 12 June, to be replaced ten days later by that of René Waldeck-Rousseau, the Dreyfusards' cause grew even more hopeful,[1] especially as Dupuy's government had announced on 3 June that Dreyfus would be recalled to France for a new trial at Rennes. So outraged was the Catholic nationalist, Baron de Christiani, at this development, that on the following day he caned President Loubet before a large crowd at the Auteuil racecourse. When Dreyfus was told on 5 June that the verdict of his 1894 court martial had been quashed, and that the cruiser *Sfax* had been dispatched to the South Atlantic to bring him home, he wrote: 'I was immensely, indescribably happy . . . Happiness followed by inexpressible anguish, as the dawn of justice was finally about to rise before me. After the court's decree, I believed that all was going to be over at last, that it was a mere formality.'[2]

After a long, uncomfortable sea voyage, Dreyfus was told on the night of 30 June that he was to be transferred from the *Sfax* to a civilian steamer. Gale-force winds whipped the seas that evening, making it almost impossible for Dreyfus to lower himself into the small boat which was to ferry him to the steamer. He was ordered to leap down, which he did, gashing his legs on the gunwale as he landed. Weakened by the cold weather and the deep wound, a fever set in, and he was ill for several days afterwards. Although French newspapers stated that he was expected to disembark at Brest on 1 July, he actually landed at Port Haliguen on the rugged peninsula of Quiberon, where, in 1791, the Republican Army of the Revolutionary government had massacred a large number of émigrés. It did not bode well for Dreyfus.

After dinner that same evening, Henry Céard, who spent each summer at this small port, heard that some fishermen claimed to have seen the *Sfax* off the coast of Quiberon and that Dreyfus was to be landed there, not at Brest. 'The entire population, about 150 people, went at once to the pier,' noted Céard.

One hour, two hours went by; the *Sfax* did not appear. At nine o'clock [p.m.] a closed calèche, drawn by two white horses, arrived at the port. Monsieur Viguié, Director of the Sûreté Générale [police] climbed down.

At the same time a company of the 116th Regiment of the Line came from the village, having just arrived from the fort at Penthièvre, together with many gendarmes. They cleared the quayside and all traffic was forbidden in the immediate neighbourhood.

The weather was frightful. It was windy and stormy, there was a heavy downpour, and the soldiers shuffled uncomfortably as the night grew still darker. Eleven o'clock struck, then midnight. All we could hear was the whining of the wind, but no light appeared at sea. By now even the most intrepid of inhabitants had left. Only the troops remained. At 1.45 a.m. a lifeboat appeared. The oarsmen landed and surrounded Dreyfus. By the light of a lantern. I could see him, wearing a raincoat and a soft travelling hat. He left the boat and, accompanied by two gendarmes, walked slowly, as if exhausted, up the ramp and to the carriage, where he was met by Monsieur Viguié.[3]

Another source decribed him as 'anaemic, skeletal-looking in appearance'.[4] 'He climbed up,' Céard continued, 'the troops surrounded the carriage, and it moved slowly towards the Quiberon railway station, one kilometre away from Port Haliguen. A special train will now take Captain Dreyfus to Rennes.'

Despite the maturity of his years and his experience in public life, Zola was feeling the strain. Dreyfus had returned, his trial set for 8 August, to be held in the old lycée at Rennes, in Brittany; but Zola had other preoccupations as well. When would his appeal be heard, and when would he come to trial? Month after month he waited, only to be met with postponement. He also wanted to bring to trial the three handwriting experts — Belhomme, Couard and Varinard. The three had lied under oath about the handwriting of the 1894 *bordereau,* declaring it to be the work of Dreyfus, although Esterhazy had since admitted, and was to admit again, in French and English newspapers, that he had written the *bordereau.* Zola was a worried man, and his anxiety was compounded by a series of defamatory articles about his father written by Ernest Judet. As if this were not enough to keep Zola occupied, he was working on his new novel, *Travail,* as well as on the libretto for a new Bruneau opera. The growing turmoil within the country can hardly have helped his concentration.

Jean Jaurès, the prominent socialist leader, had taken up where Zola had left off on 10 August 1898, by publishing a series of articles in *La Petite République* entitled *Les Preuves* (The Proofs). These explained how the Army had based its case against Dreyfus on forged documents and perpetrated a substantial cover-up. On 13 August, Captain Cuignet was asked to investigate the case by War Minister, Godefroy Cavaignac. Cuignet informed him that there was indeed a forged document (known thereafter as the 'Henry forgery'). This was one month after Colonel Picquart's arrest. On 30 August Colonel Henry admitted his forgeries, and General Boisdeffre, who had known about the cover-up all the time, resigned. The following day Henry committed suicide in his cell at the Mont Valérien Fortress. The way was cleared for a complete revision of the Dreyfus case, and Mme Dreyfus formally applied for a new trial.

Zola was full of optimism on his return to France in June 1899, and his reappearance, and that of Dreyfus, attracted considerable attention. On 18 July the nationalists were thunderstruck when an interview with Esterhazy appeared in *Le Matin* in which he stated that *he*, and not Dreyfus, was the author of the infamous *bordereau*.

It would be hard to imagine a more dramatic opening to the new Dreyfus court martial in Rennes on 8 August. On the sixth day of the trial, Dreyfus's principal lawyer, Labori, was shot in the back at close range just outside the lycée where the trial was being held. The nationalists had struck again. His assailant, seen clearly by several onlookers (including police on duty outside the building), was never apprehended. Although Labori, a remarkably resilient man, was able to return to the improvized courtroom on 22 August, he was not well enough to take an active part, and was too weak to deliver his own final summation. But as he told Zola, 'In spite of everything that has happened, I can't believe that they would commit the infamy of condemning him again.'[5]

The army officers conducting the Rennes court martial announced their verdict on 9 September: Dreyfus was found 'guilty of communicating with the enemy under extenuating circumstances', reached by a decision of five to two, and he was condemned to another ten years in prison. The cover-up this time seemed incredible even to the most obtuse politicians. Who was worse, President Emile Loubet, Prime Minister Brisson, or the top army generals? How could the nation's elected representatives allow this to occur?

Zola, beside himself with rage, gave vent to his feelings in an article in *L'Aurore* entitled *'Le Cinquième acte'* (The Fifth Act).

> I am thunderstruck. And it is no longer anger, the wish for vengeance, the need to cry out about the crime, to demand the appropriate punishment for it in the name of truth and justice; it is, rather, amazement, sheer terror in a man who sees the impossible happen, rivers suddenly flowing backwards up to their sources, the earth trembling beneath the sun. And what I am crying out about is the distress of our generous and noble France, it is the fear of the abyss towards which she is now heading.[6]

Everyone thought that the Rennes trial would be the fifth and final act of 'the terrible tragedy through which we have been living for nearly two years.' If Rennes was not to be the end, however, asked Zola, what will be? How much more will the country have to endure?

> As I wrote in my Letter to the President of the Republic [*'J'accuse'*] after the scandalous acquittal of Esterhazy, it is impossible that one court martial would undo the work of a previous one. That is contrary to discipline . . . the decision which lacks the courage to pronounce a clear 'no' or 'yes', is stark proof that military justice is incapable of being just, since it is not independent, since it refused to accept valid evidence, which in turn meant again condemning an innocent man, rather than jeopardize its own infallibility . . .
>
> What must civilized nations think of us . . . ? The whole world is convinced of the innocence of Dreyfus. If some distant people had any lingering doubts, the blinding blow of the Rennes trial will have clarified everything . . . What frightens me is that this defeat of French honour seems irreparable, for who would overturn the verdicts of three courts martial, where would we find the heroism necessary to confess to the error, in order to be able to go forward again, our heads held high? Where is the government with enough courage and concern for the public welfare? Where are the legislative chambers which will finally understand? Who will act before the inevitable final collapse of our society?[7]

Upon reading this article, Labori, convalescing from his gunshot wound, responded, 'We have just read *L'Aurore*. Bravo, bravo, encore bravo!'[8] Privately, of course, Zola had long had an idea of what the government would do to end the Dreyfus Affair once and for all. 'Everything seems to be moving in the direction of a pardon for the poor man and towards a general amnesty . . . '[9] He was right once again, and on 19 September President Loubet signed a pardon for Captain Dreyfus. Later, on 14 December 1900, he signed a general amnesty for *everyone* connected with the Dreyfus case (see Chapter 25). Zola, for one, was against pardoning Dreyfus; there was no justice in being pardoned for a crime he hadn't committed. And as for a general amnesty, that simply meant the real criminals — du Paty de Clam, Gonse, Boisdeffre, Billot, Esterhazy, Mercier and others — would never have to face prosecution and imprisonment.

Zola returned to his desk to pen another article for *L'Aurore,* this one entitled, *'Lettre à Madame Dreyfus'* (Letter to Madame Dreyfus):

> They are returning the innocent man, the martyr, the husband and father to his wife, son and daughter, and my first thoughts are for the family reunited at long last, despite the humiliating sadness, the revolt which continues to cause such anguish in the souls of decent people . . . how sad it is, however, that the government of a great country has resigned itself . . . to be merciful, when it could have been just . . . [we] are going

to continue the struggle, to fight as hard for justice tomorrow as we did today. We must have the innocent man completely exonerated, not so much for his sake, he who is covered with glory, rather, to exonerate and rehabilitate France, who will otherwise surely die from this excessive iniquity.[10]

Zola's interest in the Dreyfus Affair was to continue unabated, and whenever he saw an opportunity to fight, he did so, with the tenacity and determination of a bulldog. On 29 May 1900 another article of his, *'Lettre au Sénat'* (Letter to the Senate), appeared in *L'Aurore,* in which he asked why his own case, stemming from the *'J'accuse'* article, had been postponed ever since his return to France. What did the government fear? Of course the Senate was then considering a general amnesty to whitewash the affair, and Zola reiterated what he had said when testifying before a Senate Committee. He protested against the proposed amnesty law as 'a virtual denial of justice, and from the viewpoint of our national honour, a permanent stain.'[11] It would deny him the trial he wanted and flout the law by meting out the same justice to honest men and scoundrels alike. He concluded by saying:

I am simply writing this letter for the great honour of having written it. I am doing my duty, but I doubt if you are doing yours. If your relinquishment of law has been a judicial crime, your amnesty law is going to be civic treason, the abandonment of the Republic to its enemies.[12]

With the signing of the Amnesty Law on 14 December 1900, Zola, Dreyfus and all those on their side were effectively checked. Thus it was that Zola wrote the last important newspaper article of his career, another open letter, this time addressed to President Loubet:

It will soon be three years ago that I addressed a letter to your predecessor, M. Félix Faure, to which he paid no heed, unfortunately for his good name. Now he is dead and our memory of him is obscured by the monstrous iniquity which I disclosed to him, and to which he became an accomplice, by using the power of his office to cover it up.

Now you are in his place, and we have . . . the final denial of justice — this 'villainous amnesty' . . . Rest assured, a page of your own life is now going to be stained; it is your magistrature which now runs the risk . . . of being tainted by that indelible stain . . . The Affair cannot be concluded as long as France does not know what wrong has been committed . . . but the mission I set out to accomplish is finished. I did the best I could, as honestly as I could, and now I'm going home quietly. Only I should like to add that my eyes and ears are still going to remain wide open . . . And I am still waiting.[13]

25
Another Conspiracy

At the end of April 1898, a right-wing Parisian newspaper, *La Patrie*, published a seemingly innocuous editorial commenting on the Dreyfus case:

> People are asking what General de Boisdeffre is waiting for, why he does not simply crush his opponents (enemies of both the Army and France) with one fell blow. All he has to do is disclose one of the numerous pieces of evidence which the General Staff possesses establishing the guilt of Dreyfus, or at least to publish some of the dossiers on a few of the most notorious apologists of the traitor, or on someone related to them (dossiers in the possession of the Army Intelligence Service, or in the War Archives).[1]

The editorial was aimed at Zola in particular, but even if he had bothered to read this paragraph, he would no doubt have dismissed it as yet another pathetic gesture, the boast of several dossiers sounding like the usual meaningless threats from the right which had been inundating France ever since the publication of *'J'accuse'*. But Zola did not know that a conspiracy was afoot and steps already taken to mount a fresh attack to discredit him and the Dreyfus cause by the same officers already prominent in the Affair — Colonel Henry, General Gonse and General Billot — and that the civilian courts were fully prepared to cooperate with them.

It all began officially on 23 May 1898, when a journalist named Ernest Judet published an article in *Le Petit Journal* accusing François Zola (the author's father, who had died fifty-one years earlier) of being a thief, allegedly having embezzled regimental funds while he was an officer in the French Foreign Legion in 1832. Zola was shocked, when on 25 May Judet published a second article in which he quoted conversations with one General de Loverdo, repeating the accusations against Zola's father. He replied three days later in an article in *L'Aurore* entitled *'Mon Père'* (My Father), vowing to defend his father's memory.

> Since I possess a pen, and as forty years of labour have given me the power to speak to everyone and to be heard, and since the future is mine, well then, Father, rest in peace in your grave where my mother has gone to join you. Your son is on guard and he will defend your memory.[2]

Later Zola explained what steps he took:

> I wrote to General Billot, Minister for War . . . asking him to give me my
> father's dossier, as criminal proceedings [against Judet] had just begun.
> When M. Cavaignac succeeded him as minister in July, I then wrote to
> him, asking the same thing. Both refused me, claiming that 'the dossiers
> of officers are secret dossiers, kept solely for administrative use'.[3]

Then, on the very day of Zola's trial at Versailles, 18 July, Judet published
his third article on François Zola, this time quoting from two alleged letters
by Colonel Combe, François Zola's commanding officer. On 29 July Labori
wrote that he was convinced 'the Combe letters about your father are
forgeries', and that he now wanted to institute proceedings based on this
revelation.[4]

Judet was brought to trial for defamation on 3 August, found guilty
regarding the first two articles of 23 and 25 May and ordered to pay Zola
5000 francs in damages. Having received Zola's approval, Labori followed
this up the same day by filing criminal charges against Judet concerning
the two fraudulent Combe letters. Opting to press these charges in the
criminal courts rather than the civil courts meant that Zola would receive
lower damages, but he was not interested in money — he wanted
justice.[5]

In order to substantiate their claim of forgery, Labori and Zola had
to study François Zola's army file, to compare the letters published with
the originals. But the War Minister refused to comply. After great
persistence by Zola, General Zurlinden released the material, however,
to M. Flory, the judge examining the Judet case, whereupon it was found
that one of the Combe letters was missing along with other documents.
It transpired that the first Combe letter referred to by Judet existed only
in his imagination, while the disappearance of the other documents remained
a mystery.

On 28 September Labori wrote to Zola from 'Les Marguerites', his
country house in Samois, agreeing to his request for two handwriting experts
to be brought in to study the 'Combe letters'.[6] 'The truth of the matter
is,' he added two days later, 'I don't think we can expect much in the
way of results at the present,'[7] though if Judet entered a counter-suit
against Zola — which was to be expected — he felt it would strengthen
their demand to see François Zola's official army file. But a week later
Labori had to report: 'The judge refused to let me see his file.'[8]
Disappointing as this news was, it simply confirmed yet again their well-
founded suspicions that the Army did indeed have something to hide.

When the court convened on 11 January 1899, Judge Flory dismissed
the forgery charges against Judet. He stated that the documents he saw
looked authentic, and Judet's counter-charge of 'calumnious denunciation'

was upheld. 'I was condemned by default,' Zola wrote, 'and ordered to pay [Judet] 500 francs in damages.'[9] Zola defaulted because he was still in England at this time, though he eventually paid the amount he owed, unlike Judet who never paid the 5000 francs from the first trial.

On 9 December 1899, Zola wrote to the War Minister, General de Galliffet, once again asking to see his father's file, and that an investigation be opened to ascertain how Judet and his newspaper had been given access to it when his own son had not. Galliffet's reply to Zola was the usual one — that his father's file could not be shown to a civilian, whatever the relationship. A second letter from the War Minister proved more helpful. In it he informed Zola that the Deputy-Chief of the Archives Office, M. Hennet, clearly recalled having handed the file to an officer, now deceased. And that officer was none other than Colonel Henry.

On the same day, 16 December, Zola wrote to the Prime Minister, M. Waldeck-Rousseau, to bring all these facts to his attention, and asked him to submit this case to his Cabinet. 'It seemed impossible that the son of a man injured and defamed should not have access to this file which had already passed through suspect hands and which had been displayed in the newspapers in the most abominable manner.'[10]

Four days later René Waldeck-Rousseau informed him that he would be allowed access to his father's army file, and on 3 January 1900, Zola, Jacques Dhur (a friend), and Fernand Labori went to the Office of Administrative Archives at the War Ministry, where they were received by the bureau chief, M. Raveret, and his deputy, M. Hennet. Although Hennet was a bit fuzzy in his account of the history of François Zola's file, the facts gradually emerged. It turned out that when Henry's agent came to sign for the file in March 1898, he did not sign for it in the special register which existed for just that purpose. Instead he merely signed a separate receipt, which was later given back to him when the file was returned to the archives, thereby removing any written trace of that transaction. As this procedure violated army regulations, and Colonel Henry obviously did not have the authority to do this, Zola made further enquiries and discovered that it was Henry's superior officer, General Gonse, who had sent the original request for the file and asked for the irregular signing out procedure. Zola was also curious as to why M. Hennet had gone to all the trouble of putting the François Zola material into a new file, giving it a special number (it had had none before), and preparing a table of contents for it. Hennet admitted that he was requested to do all this by General Gonse.[11]

When Zola opened his father's file for the first time on 3 January, it was sealed and had been since its return on 8 June 1898. As had been noted by Judge Flory, it contained only one letter attributed to Colonel Combe, the other having 'disappeared'. Eight other missing pieces listed on the table of contents had not been returned by Henry. Why had Hennet not noted that at the time? It was all very strange. If Zola's father had indeed been guilty of theft, where were the legal documents regarding the charges, the official interrogation and his defence? Henry or Gonse would not have tampered with them. There was only one document in that file at present concerning the charge against François Zola, and that was the Combe letter. 'The paper seemed old, perhaps a bit too old,' said Zola. 'The ink also seemed old. But the document contained neither an official letterhead, nor the [Army] seal . . . '[12] Furthermore, lines were added to the letter, letters were added to words, and Combe had misspelt his own name in some places! Zola, Dhur and Labori had found more than they bargained for; their foes had been very clumsy. The letter was a forgery, obvious even to their untrained eyes.

Zola wrote again to the War Minister, telling him of his discoveries and requesting three more things of him:

> First, I asked him to carry out a search, for it seemed impossible to me that a judicial file on the case did not exist which would explain the confusion as well as the gaps in the administrative dossier. Then I also asked him to look through the files of the engineering department, to look for the fortification project with its blueprints, which my father had submitted to the Minister for War in 1831. Finally, I asked that two separate handwriting experts be brought in to study the Combe letter — he to appoint one expert and I to choose another — and to have the study take place there, based on a comparative study of other copies of Combe's handwriting which the bureau of archives could supply.[13]

General de Galliffet's *chef de cabinet,* General Davignon, replied on 9 January saying that Zola's requests had been carried out and that another dossier concerning François Zola had been discovered in the Department of Legal Affairs and Military Justice. Zola was asked to meet with the War Minister on Saturday, 13 January. For once the Army was working quickly, efficiently and on overtime.

That Saturday Zola met General de Galliffet in his office and was introduced to the Director of the Department of Legal Affairs and Military Justice, who was also the Inspector General, M. Cretin (State Counsellor, attached to the Ministry for War). Zola found the army officials most cooperative, and was impressed by the intelligence and integrity of M. Cretin who put the newly-found dossier at his disposal.

It was an old folder, without number or table of contents, and in which Zola found only one pertinent, but most important, document: a letter dated 17 September 1832, from the Duke de Rovigo, Commander of the French Occupation Forces in Algeria. According to de Rovigo, the entire investigation concerning François Zola began when it was found that he was missing. A thorough investigation was carried out and it was even thought that he might have drowned (intentionally or otherwise), but then a woman's name came into the picture, a Madame Fischer, the wife of a former legionnaire sergeant. François Zola, who was still a bachelor, was apparently very fond of her, and when further enquiries were carried out, it was found that Sergeant Fischer and his wife were about to set sail for France. They were brought from their ship and questioned by the military authorities, and in the meantime 4000 francs were discovered in their trunks. They claimed it was their money, though they later confessed that 1500 francs belonged to François Zola. (Had Zola disappeared in order to find that money?) During the subsequent investigation it was learned that certain regimental funds, for which Lieutenant Zola had been responsible — but to which the sergeant had access — were missing. The Fischers were imprisoned and Lieutenant Zola wrote to the authorities stating that if he were given immunity from prosecution he would step forward and make good any deficiency. The *Conseil d'administration* of the Foreign Legion agreed to his request. De Rovigo later wrote to his superior officer in France, the War Minister:

> M. Zola was only suspected of poor administration. There was no judicial complaint against him . . . He certainly did nothing contrary to the law. I did not exercise my legal authority since there was no legal complaint lodged against him. As regards the enquiries of the *Conseil d'administration* of the Foreign Legion, they have been completely satisfied and the matter dismissed. How could it now lodge a complaint and by what right could I sign an order against the best interests of a man who has fulfilled his duty?[14]

This was the perfect evidence to establish the real facts of the case. In addition, these facts differed from those in the alleged Combe letters, further substantiating Zola's claim about forgery. (For example, the alleged Combe letter stated that charges had been brought against François Zola. No charge-sheet was ever found in Zola's personnel file or judicial file and then de Rovigo himself stated most plainly that no charges had been brought against him.) In reality Colonel Combe was the presiding officer of the *Conseil d'administration* mentioned by de Rovigo, and had only taken up this post in Algiers well after the first part of the Zola enquiry had already been completed, and after the date on the forged letter.

When Zola and Labori wanted to make their findings absolutely conclusive by collecting genuine samples of Colonel Combe's handwriting and having two handwriting experts study the forged letter, General de Galliffet refused most adamantly.

As for General de Loverdo and his allegations (quoted by Judet in his article), he was again interviewed by a reporter who asked how he could possibly have claimed first-hand knowledge when, in 1832 he was only thirteen years old. Loverdo now made an astonishing volte-face and claimed that his father had tried to help François Zola. However, no reference to Loverdo's father was ever discovered. Whoever was responsible for this whole scurrilous episode — Loverdo, Henry or *Le Petit Journal* — the end result was the same, and Zola was determined to undo the damage.

When Zola went back to study the original dossier in the War Archives, he noticed two lines pencilled in on the table of contents: 'There exists no dossier at the Office of Military Justice. We have been assured of it.'[15] Initially both Raveret and Hennet had assured Zola personally that there was none. Later, of course, he discovered this was not so. Without informing Raveret of his discovery Zola went back to see him at the War Archives and asked him about the additional two lines.

'There is a notation in pencil here,' said Zola, 'which does not appear to be in M. Hennet's writing. Who wrote it?'

'Why, I did,' replied Raveret.

'Ah! And you are quite sure that there is no other dossier at the Office of Military Justice?' asked Zola.

'Oh, absolutely sure, sir. I was told specifically.'

'But who told you?'

'General Billot himself,' declared Raveret.

Zola had obviously stumbled upon a hornet's nest, for Billot had been War Minister under Méline's government at the time Zola had published *'J'accuse'*, and when Zola's court case had been dealt with in such a blatantly illegal fashion. The François Zola file had been seen by Henry, under General Gonse's orders, between March and 8 June, while Billot was still War Minister, and now Zola discovered that Billot had personally lied to Raveret by claiming that François Zola's judicial file did not exist. 'All this leads us to the most disquieting suppositions,'[16] Zola commented, understating the enormous significance of his latest discovery. To be perfectly certain of his facts Zola then asked Inspector-General Cretin if he had had any difficulty in finding François Zola's judicial file containing the de Rovigo letter. 'Oh, good Lord, no!'[17] replied Cretin.

Zola's conclusions were staggering but well-founded. It was the War Minister himself, General Billot, who had had François Zola's old file placed in a new one, given a special reference number and a table of contents, in cooperation, of course, with General Gonse and Colonel Henry. What had at first appeared to be a simple case of defamation by an inconsequential journalist, was now proving to be a national scandal of monstrous proportions — indeed another Army conspiracy.

The file containing François Zola's fortification plans and blueprints could not be found, but they no longer seemed of any immediate importance. Zola tried to analyse what had happened in 1832: 'A woman [Mme Fischer] was certainly involved. Only, what was her exact role? Did my father give her the money she was carrying?'[18] Or had François Zola disappeared in order to retrieve his missing money? Or had he simply gone in pursuit of his mistress? Looking at the matter from a different angle, Zola reflected that times were terrible in Algeria in 1832. Murder, pillage and corruption were widespread, so who would notice an unimportant lieutenant in charge of supplies, whose books were not in order? Maybe senior officers were too preoccupied in saving their own skins? The answer was never found, but the malicious resurrection of the episode had done considerable harm.

> In the Dreyfus Affair, in order to keep an innocent man on Devil's Island and to save the real criminal from the executioner and the forgers from prison, they [the Army] made themselves guilty of a good many crimes, but the one they committed with the purpose of shaming me by dishonouring the memory of my father was certainly the most vile, the dirtiest and most cowardly of all.'[19]

As for François Zola, would he have remained in Algiers maintaining a civil engineering office between 1833 and 1838 if he had been guilty? Would he have gone on to design the famous Zola Canal at Aix, and make fortification plans which he discussed with King Louis-Philippe and his Minister, Thiers? Would the town of Aix have named a boulevard in his memory after his death?

Despite the new evidence he had, Zola was thwarted in his legal proceedings against Judet. The civilian authorities delayed and postponed as much as they could, while the Army and the courts would not allow him to introduce his startling new proof that the Combe letter was a forgery.

Finally, Zola's greatest fear was realized. On 14 December 1900 the French Government declared a national amnesty covering everyone and every aspect of the Dreyfus Affair (including the Judet defamation). Zola was beside himself. Everyone was exonerated, not only Dreyfus and himself, but all the villains as well. What would he do now? Zola mulled over the avenues open to him. He could no longer pursue the matter in the criminal courts, but through the civil courts he could attempt to have the two fines of 30,000 francs and 7500 francs restored to him. Could he force Judet to pay his 5000 francs? The alternative course would be simply to drop the whole thing, once and for all, though of course no one could stop him from writing a novel about the whole dreadful affair.

After many weeks of reflection Zola made his decision which he published in an open letter to Fernand Labori in *L'Aurore* on 8 March 1901. He was going to end his role as it had begun, with pen in hand. Condemning the amnesty law, he began:

> We have been fighting for truth and justice, defending our sacred cause . . . and then they sully and destroy it in our hands . . . Very well then, my friend. I have thought it over and prefer to abandon everything.

I don't want to be an accomplice to this by accepting their amnesty. I don't want to see our affair, so noble and devoid of personal interest, wind up as a base question of money . . . In the Judet matter I have been awarded damages of 5000 francs in a criminal court, based on principles that satisfy me. If I sued M. Judet, it was because of circumstances over which I had no control. I have no faith in French social justice, and in any event, I would certainly not confide my honour nor my father's to it. The defence of my colleagues and myself, in questions of conscience, was quite simply something I had to do, and that sufficed.[20]

26

'I Have No Intention of Trying to Amuse People'

'Oh! this crisis has really done me some good!' exclaimed Zola to Jean Jaurès during his visit to England in April 1899. 'It certainly put things in perspective for me, and at the same time revealed many deep-seated problems plaguing our society which I had not even known existed. I am going to do everything in my power to free men.' But what is the best means of achieving what is best for mankind?

> The time has passed when it was enough to dream and predict. We must know. We must state the precise methods by which we are going to organize and liberate.
>
> As for me, I'm reading and looking, not in order to think up a new system to add to all the others, but rather to extract from socialist works that which best agrees with my values of activity, health, prosperity and joy.
>
> A friend has lent me [works by] Fourier and I am amazed by what I find in them. I don't know yet what the outcome of my research will be, but I do know that I want to pay tribute to work and to force those men who now profane it and who sully its motives, to respect it at long last . . . [1]

Although correctly quoted by Jaurès, these words paint an inaccurate picture of Zola, seeming to indicate that his awareness of the ills of modern society in general, and of the working classes in particular, developed only after his trial. This was far from the truth. It seems that he rarely accepted any aspect of life without thinking about it in depth and reacting to it in print. Most of his articles and novels reflect this, and *Germinal* was an especially good (early) example.

Germinal was a study of the working classes and their quality of life. Zola's research for this book plunged him into the grim existence of industrial workers, which led him to the coal pits at Anzin and opened his eyes to the desperate circumstances of the striking miners. It was not by chance that he considered calling this novel *Moisson rouge* (Red Harvest) rather than *Germinal*. His observations on industrial life made him ill at ease with his own social milieu, and he saw his book as an attempt 'to cry out to the fortunate people of this world, to those who are the masters:

"Beware, look underground, see those wretches who labour and suffer".'.² Zola intended *Germinal* to be two things — a description of the intolerable conditions in which human beings forced other human beings to exist in order to create the wealth for their own private pleasures, and a warning that man must become aware of these tragic conditions and correct the injustice before it was too late. In an attempt to come up with some real answers to these problems, Zola began to write a sequel called *Travail*, for as he put it, 'The time has passed when it simply sufficed to dream and predict. We must know.'³

The central character in *Travail* is Luc Froment (one of the four sons of Pierre and Marie Froment, first met in the novel, *Paris*). The story takes place in two industrial sites: L'Abîme (based upon the real town of Beauclair) and La Crêcherie, both towns having large steel mills and foundries. Luc, an engineer by profession, goes to La Crêcherie at the behest of its owner and his old friend, Jordan, to help him out on a temporary basis. But Luc remains permanently, ultimately transforming both La Crêcherie and L'Abîme, as well as the attitudes and commitment of all the people there. The owners of the steel works are convinced to hand over much of their wealth to the workers in a profit-sharing scheme, and an almost Utopian community is founded, where men can work at whatever they please, for as long as they please; where they share in the profits and live in pleasant, modern cottages; where education, theatres and medical facilities are available to all. Here men live a communal, fraternal life and, as a result, distrust and crime disappear altogether. Science not only creates a superior quality of life for the workers (providing them with better machines which are easier to work, electrical power and lighting), but also replaces religion; it is not needed when men can live comfortably and with dignity in clean houses, with good wages and proper food. The local church in Beauclair is eventually abandoned, even by the diocese itself, and the Abbé Marle dies a symbolic death when the neglected church finally collapses on him. Neither priest nor church is replaced. The novel that began by describing the harsh realities of industrial life becomes a platform for Zola's ideals. His message was not only that men could live differently and better, but that this could be achieved without violence and without revolution. Through the cooperation of capital and labour, men of good will and foresight could work together to create a better world.

More of a sermon than a novel, *Travail* was to attract much criticism — something which Zola anticipated. However, he held strongly to his great plan for the future, the only possible future, according to him. He believed that work makes life worthwhile and beautiful. Without work men become idle and empty, aimless and useless. The wealthy, who reap the benefit of their workers' labour are depicted as leeches and destroyers of society.

Although Zola had been branded a socialist in 1885 upon completing *Germinal*, it was not until the turn of the century that he was indeed partially converted to socialism. In *Travail* he attacks capitalism and the business middlemen who each rake off a profit and consequently push up prices. Surely it would be better to rid society of shop owners, business men and industrialists, and have a socialist society made up of workers sharing profits in cooperative ventures? There is enough wealth in society, he argued, if only it were reapportioned.

As far as Zola was concerned, *Travail* was probably his most important work to date. It eminently displayed his feeling that life was a serious, often tragic, matter, but it would not do to give up hope. Giving in to pessimism and weakness leads to corruption, as seen in the Second Empire and the Third Republic. If evil and sloth are not fought, society becomes evil and slothful and selfishness and decay set in. In short, man must be willing to fight for what he believes is right.

Zola began writing *Travail*, the second volume of *Les Quatre Evangiles*, on 15 March 1900. His background reading was prodigious, including books on industrial problems, as well as works on and by anarchists and socialists.[4] The more he read, particularly of Fourier, the more amazed he was. Here was a world — the whole concept of socialism — of which he had been largely unaware. He borrowed, rejected, sifted and modified, coming up with a mixture of socialism and his own individual ideas. In his search for realism, he wanted to visit a steel works and see men working before gigantic flames pouring molten metal. Eugène Fasquelle introduced Zola to a M. Ménard-Dorian, owner of the large Unieux steel works in the Loire Valley,[5] who invited him to his house and mill to study his operations. Zola accepted with alacrity and, notebook in hand, was soon talking to the workers and investigating every aspect of their lives — visiting their homes, touring the mills and even making maps of the buildings. After spending several days at the mill, Zola returned home to read up on industrial engineering, particularly the use of electricity, which he had seen applied so successfully at Unieux. He interviewed specialists in this field and studied the heavy electrical and industrial machinery then on display at the Exposition in Paris. Finally, he made at least one visit to an experimental socialist community. By the end he had accumulated over 500 pages of notes plus another 440 pages of plans for the text. The finished manuscript ultimately totalled a hefty 988 pages.

Travail set out to show a selfless and vital new society: 'The intensity of life in the anarchic commune — that's the picture I must paint. The happiness of the individual, in the midst of general happiness.'[6] He advocated limiting national government to the barest minimum (though he does not say how), and throughout his novel there is neither need nor mention of politicians and government. He seemed to envisage small, New England-style town meetings as the ideal government. Private property would be replaced by communal property; capitalists would be re-educated by participating in new communal projects and would gradually disappear altogether, as they were won over to the new order. Here Zola was fuzzy on the issue of collectivism. The (ideal) 'City', i.e. the *'phalanstère'*, to use Fourier's term, created by Luc Froment in *Travail,* was the result of the voluntary association of capital, knowledge and talent (much like an Israeli kibbutz), but at the same time, in theory, Zola appears to have rejected the concept of collectivism. His City seemed closer in spirit to the *'familistère'* created at Guise in 1859 by Godin, where the community, made up of less than 2000 people, was the living model of the 'City of the Future'. However, he was dissatisfied with Guise, finding that it lacked solitude and liberty. This disturbed him greatly, and he noted that it was, 'A question to be resolved',[7] though he failed to do so. It became clear to him that living closely together, as working men, created problems that could lead to 'a mortally uniform, regimented and structured society'[8] — something he feared as much as rapacious capitalism. 'I must maintain, in this work, progress and freedom, all the cherished ideas from Greece, Rome, the Renaissance and the French Revolution. There seems to be a movement towards the levelling of conditions and of intelligence, but that is not what I want.'[9] What was Zola seeking? He referred to it as 'a purified form of anarchy'.[10]

Zola's ideal City posed more questions then it answered. For instance, how would it relate to the rest of the country, both financially and politically? What would happen to existing industrial cities with mixed economies and many non-industrial workers? What about national defence? How could one prevent a 'levelling' of society and a change in the quality of education to suit all needs? What would happen to the intelligentsia of these new cities? Zola had stumbled on a hornet's nest; he did not intend to 'create a new system', but simply to adapt something from 'socialist models' which 'agrees with life as I see it, with my love of activity, and contribute to health, prosperity and joy'.[11]

Zola worked on the huge manuscript of *Travail* from March 1900 till 6 February 1901. Serialization began in *L'Aurore* in the first week of December 1900, and the complete book was published in May 1901. Its reception was curious. The socialists immediately claimed Zola as one of their own, and held banquets in his honour, though he rarely attended any.

> It is not I who am important, nor is it even my work; what you are celebrating is the effort to further justice and the fight for human happiness, and in that, I am with you all . . . Our hopes are high, the future is still in the realm of dreams. But, as of today, it is certain that future society is to be found in the reorganization of labour, and that this reorganization alone

will result in the just division of wealth . . . the City of Peace is the final achievement. In our bitter and troubled times, the workers' associations being created are the embryo of that future City . . . every day we travel a little further towards the brotherhood of man, which is currently made so much fun of. Let the critics laugh, evolution is unrelenting; solidarity is simply the wish of good people, it is also a force of nature . . . it will become more and more effective and will end by grouping all humanity into one and the same family.[12]

In 1901 France was seething with discontent, so it was not surprising that Zola's latest book should attract many letters from people asking for his support. It is to his credit that he always remained accessible to them. One such instance concerned Laurent Tailhade, a journalist who had been sentenced to a year's imprisonment following a virulent article he had written about the forthcoming visit to France by the Russian Emperor, Nicolas II. Several people wrote to Zola concerning Tailhade, including M. Le Grandais, the publisher of a small paper called *Libertaire*.

You wish to offer me the place of honour at your protest meeting against the iniquitous condemnation of my *confrère* and friend, Laurent Tailhade. I accept it and thank you, for I am with you in the name of men of letters who are under attack, in the name of truth and justice, which have been violated once again. There is no crime in having one's own opinion, and the freedom to write it should be absolute. Moreover, it is childish to believe that it can be stopped . . . I see his call to violence simply as the exasperated cry of universal misery, for it is not killers to whom he will give courage, but to apostles and heroes.[13]

When a group of students decided to stage a protest on the anniversary of Louis Napoleon's *coup d'état,* they nominated Zola as guest of honour. Although he declined to attend, he happily accepted the honour.

Though not there physically, I shall be with you all the same, at least in thought, with all my faith in a future of freedom and justice. To protest once again against the *coup d'état* of 2 December is to protest again against any future *coup d'état*. And that, of course, is your own desire — to state your hatred of any army that would prepare itself against its own people . . . And all honest citizens must be with you in this.[14]

How times had changed, and Zola was delighted to have groups of French students with him at long last.

Literary critics, on the other hand, were somewhat bemused by *Travail,* and though it provoked some discussion among them, it was politicians, more often than not, who took up the subject. Those on the right obviously disagreed with this new spokesman of the left, and some critics claimed that Zola was not writing literature but espousing a political cause. There were a few who admired the work, in part or whole. Maurice Le Blond, the future husband of Denise Zola, wrote, ' . . . it is a lyrical prophesy, a parable magnified into a *chanson de geste,* it is the poetry of an apostleship, it is a formidable sermon, the great socialist sermon . . . '[15] Marcel Théaux commented, 'How I admire his robust and courageous faith, his stubborn and frenetic optimism . . . !'[16] For most of the critics, however, Zola was either an enigma or a threat to society; naturally, socialist spokesman Jean Jaurès disagreed with them, 'What an admirable work! It has an epic grandeur . . . '[17] — this from a man who was for many years one of Zola's staunchest foes.

Ernest Vizetelly wrote from London that *Travail* ' . . . has been regarded less as a work of fiction than as a combination of sermon and pamphlet to which the [English] reviewers and the public did not seem to take very kindly.'[18] Zola replied:

> I have never consulted public taste, and I am too old nowadays to modify my work in order to please it. I am writing these books with a certain purpose before me — a purpose in which the question of form is of secondary importance. I have no intention of trying to amuse people or thrill them with excitement. I am merely placing certain problems before them, and suggesting certain solutions, showing what I hold to be wrong and what I think would be right.[19]

But writing a novel of this nature was not the only publishing controversy in his life at this time, as the Stuttgart Affair was to reveal.

When Georges Charpentier, acting on behalf of Zola, signed over the German rights to *La Débâcle* on 28 January 1892, little did the author realize that sixteen years later the results of that very contract would be debated vehemently on the floor of the National Assembly in an attempt by ultra-nationalists to discredit him.

The subject arose in March 1908, when the French Minister of the Interior, Gaston Doumergue, introduced legislation to move the remains of Zola from Montmartre Cemetery to the Panthéon, at a cost of 35,000 francs. The anti-Dreyfus faction, led by Rochefort, Drumont and Déroulède, denounced these plans in nationalist and Catholic newspapers and organized protests in Paris. Jean Jaurès rose before the National Assembly on 19 March, defending the government's bill. Maurice Barrès then went to the podium to register his negative vote, describing an attempt to glorify Zola as the glorification of a traitor, that it was not right to praise the author of *La Débâcle,* a book denigrating France at a time of national humiliation (a reference to the defeat of France in the Franco-Prussian

War, 1870-71). Barrès went on to discuss the cover of the instalments of the book appearing in Germany in 1900.

'I wish it were in my power to show this Chamber, with the aid of a projector, the cover of the German edition of *La Débâcle,*' said Barrès. 'It has been sold in separate instalments to an extraordinarily large number of German readers. The work has appeared in twenty-five instalments, each of them showing a German soldier throwing down a French flag-bearer, rolling him in the mud and about to bayonet him.'

'That could have happened,' interposed M. Allemane.

'It was not Zola's fault that we were defeated at Sedan,' added M. Gerault-Richard.

'If we hadn't been ruled by Napoleon III, Zola could not have written *La Débâcle,*' declared M. Levraud.

'In an Assembly where there are so many vigorous dialectitians, it is always possible to take any side of an argument,' replied Barrès. 'Nevertheless, it is impossible that you don't find it most deplorable that a powerful writer of great renown allows himself to produce this, and with this type of publicity [the cover]'.

'One can't prevent translations,' said M. Allemane.

'I'll be only too pleased to hand a copy of this instalment [of *La Débâcle*] to whoever wishes to respond to me at the podium,' challenged Barrès. 'It would not, of course, be difficult for my opponent to be more eloquent than I, nor would it be difficult for him to find arguments with which to oppose what I said before, because naturally I am in one camp and you are in another, and both camps have powerful arms. But there isn't one among you who wouldn't be terribly embarrassed, distressingly embarrassed, to have to justify this harmful and most unfortunate exploitation of our fatherland.'[20]

Despite Barrès' eloquence, and the protests of the nationalists, the debate was soon concluded in favour of moving Zola's remains to the Panthéon. Barrès was wrong, however, in stating that every instalment bore the cover drawing described, for only the first six did. Why? More than a mere quibbling over figures is involved in this, for the difference between six and twenty-five involves a story which M. Barrès was either unaware of, or wished to suppress.

The Stuttgart Affair, as we may call it, began in March 1900, when Zola was informed that the first instalment of a new German edition of *La Débâcle* had appeared throughout the German Empire, and that it had just been denounced by Drumont in *La Libre Parole* because of its cover — a colour drawing — indeed the very one Barrès later discussed in the Chamber of Deputies. Zola obtained a copy of the German edition and wrote at once to Herr M.A. Loewenstein of the German publishers, Deutsche Verlags-Anstalt, in Stuttgart, stating that he was

. . . most disagreeably surprised to learn of the colour print on the cover. I cannot accept this drawing, which I find offensive, and I must ask you formally to have it removed from every instalment . . . I appeal to your courtesy, to make you understand how painful and unacceptable such a drawing is. A publisher who purchases the translation rights of a novel does not purchase the right to illustrate that novel without first showing the [proposed] drawings to the author, especially when those pictures contradict the very spirit of the book. You must be fully aware that I could never have authorized the publication of such a cover. I repeat that it wounds me most deeply, and that I think you will withdraw it without forcing me to break off relations with you, and without having to take necessary measures against you.[21]

Zola, of course, had enough legal worries in March 1900, and the last thing he wanted to do was get embroiled in something else. He went on to express the hope that any new illustrations would not have 'an unfortunate and aggressive character against France. I ask you in advance to suppress all those which I would be forced to call upon you to remove. In this there is a simple question of tact.' He then asked for a prompt decision by them.

Herr Loewenstein replied within a week, apparently genuinely amazed at Zola's viewpoint.

We feel it is not necessary to tell you, *cher maître*, that we infinitely regret learning that you were dismayed by this drawing. Had we known what an offensive effect it would have on you we certainly should not have accepted it ourselves; but as the German victory over France in the war of 1870-71 conforms to the historical facts, we felt that this drawing would help the sale of the illustrated edition, and by doing so would further popularize your excellent work in Germany. The very success of this edition shows that we were not mistaken. Please take into consideration, *cher maître*, that this edition is destined for German people only. It is not meant, however, to be aggressive to France in any way.[22]

As for the illustrations, Loewenstein insisted that none was of an offensive nature. 'We even hope to sell the plates of our illustrations to your French publisher, for an illustrated French edition.' Expressing the belief that Zola would change his opinion of the cover, he nonetheless offered to commission a new one: 'Although . . . a change of cover would cause us considerable trouble and be most costly for us, we are, however, ready to consent to your request and to suppress the drawing in all further instalments which have not yet gone to the printers.' This meant that if Zola so wished, a new cover would be drawn for the seventh instalment and used on all subsequent instalments, subject to Zola's approval. 'You see, *cher maître*, that in order to please you, we are doing all we can, under the circumstances.' The director of the firm also enquired when Zola would be able to send him the first chapters of his forthcoming novel, *Travail*.

Zola replied the very day he received Loewenstein's letter, insisting that the cover drawing be replaced with a new one:

> I must repeat that the engraving in question goes against the general meaning of this novel. You tell me that your edition is destined solely for Germany. I do not doubt it, and that is what aggravates the offensive character about which I am complaining, for there are people in France who delight to say the drawing has met with my approval and would accuse me of celebrating with you the crushing of our Army . . . Common sense must make you realize that it is absolutely impossible for me to accept such a situation.[23]

Zola also wanted to protect himself from further legal complications, as well as from further accusations by the anti-Semitic and nationalist press in France. Thus he demanded that Loewenstein formally agree to submit every drawing for his prior approval, and that he supply written confirmation of certain facts:

> . . . that the drawing published had not been shown to me previously, that I did not even know you were preparing an illustrated edition of *La Débâcle*, and that upon my request, as soon as I had been informed of it, you agreed to suppress the colour drawing of the cover, and to replace it with another. Finally, add that you have promised to publish no drawings in this text that will be offensive to France.[24]

And then dangling a carrot on the end of the stick, Zola concluded, 'As soon as this matter is straightened out, I shall give you the information you have requested about my forthcoming novel.'[25]

Zola received a letter of abject apology from Loewenstein and an associate, E. Mayer. They greatly regretted that he had been insulted as a result of their cover and reiterated that they had never intended any offence to France. Zola was then given the written statement he had requested, and a new cover drawing was submitted for his approval.

Zola wished to put an end to this correspondence as soon as possible, but unfortunately he was unhappy with the new illustration:

> It is impossible for me to accept the new drawing. It is the same idea, the consecration of the victory of Germany . . . As I see it, Germany was but the fatal accident [for France], and her triumph was only due to the internal illness of which we were gradually dying [i.e. the rule of France by Napoleon III]. Your [drawing] of a huge, victorious German, next to a small broken Napoleonic shield is contradictory to me; in fact, it is the

opposite of what I am saying, France being the scapegoat, and Germany having only an accidental importance . . . please renounce this symbol which no Frenchman would ever accept.[26]

The directors of the German publishers were obviously unhappy with Zola's reply, and waited for one of their absent colleagues to return at the end of April before answering the thorny Frenchman in Paris. Finally, Loewenstein replied, enclosing two new illustrations and hoping that Zola would agree to one of them.[27] Loewenstein liked the one with a large figure of Mars, expressing the opinion that it would surely be acceptable to every Frenchman. The alternative illustration showed a French grenadier (Rochas) lifting a glass of wine in one hand while pulling a servant girl out of a tavern with the other.

Zola replied, reluctantly, almost apologetically that the figure of Mars did not bother him — 'it is the German coat of arms, held by Mars, which does. For it is still the same symbol, the idea that my *Débâcle* was written in order to celebrate the defeat of France by Germany, which is absolutely false.' Opting for the alternative illustration, he wrote: 'Hopefully, France will not mind if your cover reminds them that she had formerly conquered the world, celebrating this with wine and women.'[28]

So ended a sensitive issue at a time when the Dreyfus Affair was still very much alive and kicking. Zola never published this correspondence with the Stuttgart publishers, and, of course, was not present in 1908 when Barrès chose to attack him. However, he never underestimated the ruthlessness of the right-wing Catholic opposition, and his foresight in demanding that the German publishers provide written exoneration for him ensured that history would ultimately get the facts straight.

27
The Test of Friendship

When Henry Céard, a young government employee and aspiring author, first visited Zola's apartment in the rue St Georges in April 1876, there was little to indicate that this was to mark the beginning of a close, seventeen-year friendship.

As it turned out, the two men had much in common. Both took writing very seriously and were staunch supporters of the 'naturalist' school, both greatly admired Flaubert, and both were to share many of the same friends for years to come. Céard and Maupassant were perhaps the most cultured and intelligent of the five young men who regularly composed the Médan set (Huysmans, Hennique and Alexis being the others). Both Zola and Céard had strong creative powers, but whereas Zola worked daily on his writing, Céard 'dissipated his in secondary activities'.[1] Céard was clever, very intense and a superb raconteur, but unlike Zola, never seemed to find his niche. He had spent a few years as a medical student, then as a bureaucrat at the War Ministry, ultimately becoming Deputy Director of the Carnavalet Library, but he was also a drama and literary critic, a short-story writer, playwright and novelist. The uncanny self-confidence that Zola possessed, Céard lacked completely.

Unlike Alexis and some of the others, Céard never became a blind disciple of Zola. He honestly admired much of his work and, in many respects, the man himself, but he was too intelligent, too honest and too independent to become any man's sycophant (unlike Alexis), and Zola respected him all the more for these very qualities. It was only natural then that two such men, who saw or wrote to each other frequently, should become close friends. Indeed, Céard and Alexis were the first — and for quite a while the only — of Zola's colleagues to meet Jeanne Rozerot and to become friends of their children. When the friendship soured — over Jeanne and Alexandrine, then permanently ended during the Dreyfus Affair — their former intimacy made the rift all the more painful and sad.

Although Zola and Céard always addressed each other as *'vous'*, their correspondence indicates a growing intimacy. In 1876 Céard's letters began 'Monsieur' becoming 'Mon cher Monsieur' by 1877, and giving way to 'Mon cher Zola' by the following year.

And yet there was an undisguised impertinence, even disdain, on the part of Céard — just as there was with Maupassant and even Daudet — and it is hard to imagine why Zola apparently chose to ignore it. An early example of this attitude dates from the summer of 1877 when Zola was on holiday at Estaque and Céard, still a very new friend, wrote to him: 'I know a fine woman who went to the seaside at Trouville one day, who only got her feet wet. Are you like that?'[2] This could be interpreted as gentle teasing, but in fact it formed a pattern over the years of a more serious nature. Some of Zola's friends, especially Maupassant, knew they could abuse him with impunity because he wanted their friendship and would gloss over such behaviour.

Zola frequently went out of his way to help young authors, which in Céard's case included introducing him and his work not only to Parisian journalists, editors, publishers and theatre directors, but to some editors in Russia as well. These latter contacts resulted in the publication of several articles by Céard, and two books — a novella, *La Saignée*, and a novel, *Mal éclos*. Indeed, Céard earned much of his early income as a writer from contacts made through Zola.[3] Nor was he loath to ask Zola for advice: 'As for the position of political correspondent they want to fill, do you think I could really offer myself, showing them what I've done for *Les Droits de l'Homme* and *Le Radical*?' By all means, Zola replied, 'you should apply for the post . . . the more positions you can obtain, the better.'[4] Later, when Céard informed Zola that a Russian journal was charging him for the cost of translation, Zola was outraged and told him that this was simply taking advantage of his youth.[5]

Zola also gave him badly-needed encouragement in his creative writings. 'I have a terrible feeling they will find me too mediocre, and that your credit there will be compromised as a result,' he confessed concerning works he had submitted to a Russian editor.[6] When Hennique and Céard abandoned their play, *L'Abbé Faujas* (based on *La Conquête de Plassans*), Zola kept after Céard in particular to take it up again and rewrite it. When Zola was later unable to attend the opening — and as it turned out, the sole performance — of a play Céard and Charles Grandmougin had written, he wrote apologizing for his absence: 'I should have liked to be there to applaud most warmly your *Pierrot Spadassin* . . . ' but his regret was tempered by 'the hope that you will be able to have your play produced [in the future] at an important theatre.'[7] He was always there to encourage his friends and colleagues, for he well knew what it felt like to be alone and discouraged.

At this stage Céard not only admired and praised Zola's works, but occasionally applauded his courage as well. At a time when Zola knew that his name was to appear in the New Year's honours list as an appointee to the Legion of Honour, he deliberately wrote highly critical remarks in his column *'Les Romanciers contemporains'* (Contemporary Novelists), about two well-known and highly influential writers, Jules Claretie and Louis Ulbach. (Over the years both men had repeatedly criticized Zola's works, Claretie having said of the play *L'Assommoir* '. . . everything M. Zola touches, turns to mud . . . An odour of bestiality emanates from all his works.'[8] Louis Ulbach unfailingly described Zola's works as obscene — 'Always this same wretched word!'[9] complained Zola.) The result of Zola's critical remarks was that his name was suddenly withdrawn, and it was not until July 1888 that he was finally appointed to the Legion of Honour. 'Bravo!' responded Céard with youthful exuberance, 'I admire how serenely you exasperate that crowd.'[10] But as Zola later assured Claretie ' . . . although they may have been impassioned, the severity of my criticisms [of your works] has never been due to any personal animosity.'[11]

On more than one occasion Zola was indebted to Céard for helping with the research on some of his novels and plays, and for running a myriad of personal errands — anything from obtaining heraldry information for the decoration of his billiards room at Médan, to ordering several tons of coal in Dieppe. He even attended plays for him when he was unable to do so, taking notes upon which Zola could later base his reviews in Laffitte's *Voltaire.*[12]

A gentleman with a solid classical education, Céard has been described as one who had a 'most lucid mind, and whose critiques revealed real perception'.[13] Attending the première of Jules Claretie's *Beau Solignac,* Céard described the reception of all five acts as *'glaciale',*[14] which Zola quoted in his review. Céard's accurate review of another Claretie play, *Les Mirabeau,* again echoed in Zola's subsequent critique, was not much kinder.[15] Although this period of semi-ghost writing probably did not last more than a couple of years, it clearly helped Zola who continually over-committed himself. Zola and Céard had similar tastes in, and expectations of, the theatre, and Zola knew he could rely upon the notes Céard provided, although it is not clear if Zola ever paid him for this work, either in money or kind. Céard offered his services — 'Please, I insist, let me help you, *sans scrupules . . .* '[16] — and Zola accepted them. The inevitable happened on 22 November 1879: Zola was unable to attend either of two plays being performed that night. Yet again Céard saved the day: 'I asked Hennique to go to the Ambigu and he will send you his own notes; I went to the Vaudeville, and here are mine.'[17]

Among the books he helped research for Zola were *Pot-bouille* and *La Débâcle.* However some of Céard's most helpful contributions were made in *Nana.* In one instance he corrected an error in dialogue, but he was particularly useful in explaining medical matters.[18] When Zola needed a clinical description of smallpox and the course of the disease as it might have applied to Nana, Céard was able to recommend and explain various medical texts, and he also found excellent photographs of smallpox victims, exclaiming, 'You simply cannot imagine how vividly these scientific photographs reveal the horror of the thing![19] Then Zola asked him to send 'an exact scientific and very detailed decription of a death masque of a female victim of smallpox, and at the same time, a description of a room in the Grand Hotel'.[20] Céard obliged him as best he could and included notes on prostitution as well.[21] 'I have found some acquaintances who are going to open the Grand Hotel for me,' he was able to report. 'I should have your notes ready by the end of the week.'[22] In short, Zola could never have written some of his books as quickly or as accurately as he did, without a considerable amount of time-consuming help from some very generous friends, and he was most grateful for their assistance.

The disintegration of the friendship between Zola and Céard probably had deep roots. Did Céard feel that Zola was 'using' him? Was he envious of his success? His own writings were hardly in the same league as Zola's, and his comparatively low government salary sometimes made him peevishly declare that anyone earning less than 40,000 francs a year could not even afford an annual holiday. Meanwhile, sales of Zola's books literally soared, breaking all sorts of records and assuring their author of acclaim and solid financial security. While the two writers certainly respected each other, Céard sometimes had fits of deep depression and said things he later regretted. Ironically, the real break occurred in 1893, at the time of the celebration dinner to honour Zola's completion of the *Rougon-Macquart* series.

Who could possibly have anticipated the full fury of events as little as a month before that famous dinner of 21 June? Outwardly everything was normal, even tranquil. There was a feeling of timelessness in the air, such as one experiences on a warm, uneventful summer's day in the country. Céard had just arranged with Zola to rent a house for Jeanne and the children in the neighbouring village of Cheverchemont, a stone's throw from Médan, and again on Zola's orders, bought a horse. In his usual meticulous way, Céard gave detailed information about feeding and exercising the horse:

> Two kilos of hay and five kilos of straw daily. Hay, twice a day, morning
> and evening. The straw at noon. Ordinarily, when she does not get a lot
> of exercise, six litres of oats daily, two at each meal . . . lack of exercise
> will stiffen the forelegs. The best thing would be to put her out in the open,
> in the field in front of the house.[23]

Apart from domestic arrangements, they continued to talk about literature and the theatre as they always did, and Zola provided the usual theatre tickets throughout the season.

And yet beneath the surface all was not well, the emotional shock waves growing with seismic intensity. Those terrible scenes caused by Alexandrine over Jeanne and the children on almost a daily basis, sometimes within earshot of the servants, drove Zola to despair. He would spend many a sleepless night up in his study, while during the day he sometimes fled the house to give her time in which to calm down. In the past when her anger did not abate, Zola had sent an urgent plea to Céard: 'My wife is going crazy. Can you come right over to the rue St Lazare and do what has to be done?'[24] Bad as it had been, the scenes grew worse as the time approached for Charpentier's dinner, and Céard was called upon as intermediary time and again. 'My dear friend, in the name of my deep affection for you, and that which you have for me, come to Médan and give me a few moments of your time . . . '[25]

For some emotionally disturbed people, key events in one's life precipitate terrible crises, and apparently the forthcoming dinner to honour her husband was just such an event for Alexandrine. On 5 June she arrived unexpectedly at Céard's apartment in Paris. She was in tears. 'She says she can't put up with it any more and definitely speaks of a separation,'[26] he informed Zola. Warning that this could only lead to a 'noisy trial', he tried to soothe the hysterical woman. 'Beyond any question of great friendship involved and the possible means of reaching a reconciliation, I thought it best to seek out someone would serve as a more effective intermediary from both the judicial and humane point of view . . . '[27] Clearly Céard was put in a most unenviable situation, and still he tried to save the marriage.

That Zola saw fit to bring in a good friend and let him take the brunt of Alexandrine's anger, rather than settling his own problems, was certainly not to his credit. Nevertheless, the question remains: why did Zola not agree to a separation and later a divorce? Apparently, with the celebratory dinner just a few days away, he felt the time was not appropriate. Rather than grasp the nettle, he would do anything to calm things down, and he consulted a lawyer by the name of Jacquemaire, just as Céard had suggested. After days of hysteria and further acrimony, negotiations resulted in a reconciliation of sorts, just before the couple were due to appear together, arm in arm, at the dinner. However, the reconciliation was achieved at the cost of the friendship. The crisis of 5 June was the last straw for a tormented Céard, and he flatly refused to attend that dinner and all others. Zola and Céard rarely saw or communicated with each other again after 1893, and this division was further deepened in 1898 when the two men took opposing sides over the Dreyfus Affair.

Over the years Zola was to lose many of his friends, chiefly through death, but others, such as Edouard Rod, dropped by the wayside during the Dreyfus Affair. The few remaining old acquaintances — men whom he could call by their first name — thus became all the more important to him. Paul Alexis was probably as close a friend as Zola would permit himself to have. (Céard and Bruneau, also good friends, were to play different roles in his life.) Alexis — *'mon vieil ami'* — stood by Zola throughout the darkest hours when the storm broke concerning Jeanne Rozerot and, later, the children. His wife befriended Jeanne and his children grew up with Denise and Jacques. (Thereafter he was forced to address all his correspondence to Zola in care of Jeanne Rozerot's home.) And yet despite this intimacy, even becoming Jacques's godfather, his relationship with Jeanne remained on a semi-formal basis; he always addressed her as 'Madame'. Zola did not see Alexis very often, apart from during the summer, for Alexis retained strong ties with his family in Aix, as well as with his three brothers.

It is clear, however, that the Alexis friendship became an increasing burden to Zola, especially during the last years of his life. When Zola was deeply involved in the Dreyfus case and the many subsequent lawsuits, Alexis seemed to be quite insensitive to all the demands on Zola's time and pestered him relentlessly about quite trivial matters. Being both indecisive and poorly organized, Alexis sought Zola's opinion on virtually everything — yet if Zola was annoyed, he rarely showed it. It was almost as if he were dealing with a tiresome child, but a child he loved and whose feelings he did not wish to hurt. Another extenuating factor at this time was the serious illness plaguing Alexis's household, which resulted in the untimely death of his wife. Further complicating their friendship was Alexis's vanity and frustration; he yearned for greatness and recognition as an *homme de lettres,* but his abilities warranted neither. Even the correspondence he maintained with Jeanne Rozerot was tinged with self-interest, arising mainly from his need to consult Zola, or to ask another favour of him. Towards the end, it seemed that Alexis only kept up the friendship with Zola so that he could use him to achieve his own ends. Zola, on the other hand, remained a true and steadfast friend, but he was undoubtedly hurt by Alexis's insensitivity.

Alexis had little imagination and even less ability as a writer, succeeding on rare occasions only by hanging on to Zola's shirt-tails. In fact, had it not been for Zola, it is doubtful that Alexis would ever have had access to Parisian newspapers, publishers and theatres. He often had to cajole Alexis into writing and when he did finally write something, it was too often a poor imitation of something Zola had already produced. Zola was one of the first to support naturalism and realism openly, and Alexis clung doggedly to that school, even after Zola had admitted that there might be other different, equally valid views of literature. The attempts that Alexis made to imitate Zola, both in novels and plays, proved to be pathetic and painful.

While Alexis walked in Zola's shadow, he did not scruple to ask favours more and more often. In 1892, for example, Alexis asked him to see the Minister of the Interior (Loubet) to obtain a *sous-préfecture* for one of his brothers. Zola replied that he did not know Loubet (the future President of the Republic) personally, but he would try. His request for an interview with the Minister was not granted, which put Zola in an exceedingly embarrassing position, for as a personal rule he never asked favours of anyone. But Alexis persisted and Zola tried again, despite his embarrassment, while explaining to his old friend that he was not nearly as influential as he seemed to think.

> You are living in a dream world, my good friend, when you think that an ordinary writer like myself can obtain the nomination of a *sous-préfet* in five minutes flat . . . Several people have already asked me to intercede on their behalf with the Legion of Honour, which I agreed to try, knowing very well what my chances of success were, and naturally I failed. Rest assured the nominations of *sous-préfets* are reserved to repay old political favours . . . [28]

As he had expected, Zola was again unsuccessful. Undeterred, Alexis wrote again at a later date asking him to see another government minister to obtain a different post for another brother. Patient to the last, Zola did so, but the results were negative.[29]

At the beginning of 1896, Alexis was writing a play entitled *Vallobra* and was keen to get some favourable publicity: 'I should like to ask you . . . for a New Year's gift. That is to say, a big favour . . . If one of your forthcoming articles in *Le Figaro* should happen to be entitled 'Vallobra' . . . my fortune as a dramatic author would be made, thanks to you.' This was pretty heavy-handed by anyone's standards. Alexis then asked him to read the manuscript of his play, a reasonable enough request, but followed by remarks of astonishing audacity. 'I don't wish to seem to outline the plan of your article, but I dare to hope to provide you with the material from which to prepare one, a fine one. None of your readers would be surprised to find you dedicating an article to your old faithful friend, a person known today as "the last of the Naturalists" '. In conclusion, as if he had not already gone well beyond the bounds of both friendship and decency, he referred to a well-known actor and director: 'If he reads about *Vallobra* in an article by you in *Le Figaro,* he will certainly produce it. It is a question of life and death for . . . the godfather of your son.'[30]

Zola, who was inundated with work and kept no secretary to help him, had already planned his series of articles for *Le Figaro* (1895-96). When he told Alexis that he could not read the play for the moment, and that he was unable to include it in his present series. Alexis was extremely upset:

> My ardent supplication has reached deaf ears; depression remains my consolation . . . I expected something different from our friendship dating

back twenty-five years, by recognizing the value of my *œuvre* . . . I was
naive enough to hope that *Vallobra* would bring about a miracle in you.
But you weren't even willing to try; that is what I find so humiliating and
sad. As for the other reasons you give for your refusal, you won't mind
if I say I hardly find them convincing.[31] *Vallobra* thus far has been
rejected by Carré, Claretie and . . . Zola![32]

Though Alexis continued to dwell upon this play in future correspondence,
it was never produced.

Letters from Alexis via Jeanne were rarely something to which Zola
looked forward. During the later years, and with increasing frequency,
they contained such phrases as, 'I should very much like to see Emile and
ask his advice as soon as possible . . . '[33] He displayed neither tact nor
consideration, inviting Zola to look over an article he had written for
Clemenceau when his trial for defamation was just days away. And in
1900, when Zola was still heavily involved in the Dreyfus case and the
Judet Affair, not to mention his own writing, Alexis wrote asking for further
advice about *Vallobra,* which he had rewritten as a novel and which a
reluctant Eugène Fasquelle had agreed to publish: 'Should it be published
on 15 October, or do you think the end of January [1901] would be
preferable? That is the big question . . . what do you advise me to do?'[34]

In his attempts to achieve even greater fame and fortune, Alexis did
not hesitate to ask Zola to have him made an officer of the Legion of Honour
— a ludicrous request as Zola had himself been expelled from it years
before.[35] But perhaps Alexis's greatest wish was to be named as one of
the ten members of the newly-composed Goncourt Academy (to be
established upon the death of Edmond de Goncourt). Alexis began this
campaign in 1896 and would continue until his death.

During the last night of the vigil for Goncourt, with Hennique, Mirbeau
and Geoffroy, I learnt that when the eight meet to complete the Goncourt
Academy, they intend to offer you one of the two remaining seats.[36]
Well then, regardless of what you decide for yourself, I ask the following
in the name of our old friendship: first, should you accept, impose as
a sort of condition on them that I should be elected the tenth member;
second, should you refuse it, please ask them to give me the place they
were offering you.

It was much to the credit of the long forbearing Zola that he did not rebuke
Alexis for this astonishing request. But the letter continued:

Would you advise me to go and see [Alphonse] Daudet at the right moment,
and what should I say to him? Would it be preferable for you to speak to
him yourself, taking advantage of his warm feelings for you? I make no

attempt to conceal from you . . . that the question of my being made a member of the Goncourt Institute is a most serious one.[37]

Zola went along with Alexis's entreaties, trying to put forward his name, but fresh messages continued to flow from his pen. 'No need, my old friend, to remind you of your three promises: first, to inform me of the dates and the time when it will be critical for me to arrive [in Paris]; second, to see Daudet as soon as possible; third, to see Huysmans.' He signed this letter, 'Your future Academician'.[38] Three weeks later Alexis wrote to Zola reminding him that he must see Daudet.[39] A week afterwards he repeated his entreaties to see Hennique, Huysmans and Daudet.[40] These messages, sent to Jeanne's apartment, where forwarded by special messenger.

Finally the day came in April 1900 when the long-awaited elections for the Goncourt Academy were held. Twelve days later Alexis wrote to Zola.

Since my execution on Saturday, 7 April, I have been living in a tomb . . . I haven't seen a soul and no one has written to me. Neither Huysmans — my old comrade of nearly a quarter of a century, nor Hennique — the Jesuit, the traitor, nor Geoffroy — who had promised me to do all that was necessary. My sole consolation (and it is a sad one), is that in order to deprive me of that seat, it took the work of a traitor and a crazy man (the only friends I have addressed as '*tu*') and the blind cowardice of the others.[41]

Zola's reply has not survived.

From this time forward, Alexis was plagued by bad luck and sorrow. His eldest daughter, Paule, who had barely survived scarlet fever several years earlier, now came down with typhoid, which she was also to survive, but only after months of convalescence. Alexis's wife, Marie, while nursing Paule, contracted the same illness and died at the end of May 1900. Marthe, the younger daughter, was sent to stay with Jeanne Rozerot for a while. Zola, who corresponded regularly with Alexis throughout the two illnesses, wrote him a touching letter of condolence:

My dear old friend, it is now five o'clock. I have been upset all afternoon. I must tell you that. However, I know you have your father with you and that relieves me a bit. I am waiting to learn the day and time of the funeral. If you need me prior to that, send me a note. Ah, my poor friend, your Calvary has been indeed a hard one. You have been struck down so harshly that I simply can't believe it. At such a time there is no possible real consolation. Don't forget about your two dear little girls, however, who are really going to need you now. You must not give up, for we are all here to help you and give you courage.

I embrace you most tenderly, you and your dear children.[42]

Paul Alexis died at his home in Levallois-Perret (where his wife had died), on 28 July 1901. Writing to a colleague a week later, Zola said, 'It is a great loss for me; he was yet another whom I had known from former times, and who has now disappeared. Little by little I have been left the sole survivor of our literary group.'[43]

28

The Truth

Just as the Dreyfus Affair was a watershed in the history of modern France, so too was it in the life of Zola, though he was not to live long enough to see it properly concluded in July 1906, when Dreyfus was fully exonerated. At first, Zola had thought the Dreyfus case to be simply a judicial error; then he saw it as a problem of anti-Semitism, and finally as a conspiracy by military officers and high-ranking politicians (and probably influential Church officials as well), to frame an innocent man.

The Catholic Church had taken a very active, and none-too-secretive part in attempting to shift the guilt from Esterhazy — the Catholic — to Dreyfus, the Jew. Its intervention was seen most dramatically in Drumont's blatantly anti-Jewish fulminations in *La Libre Parole,* and those of the official Assumptionist newspaper, *La Croix.*[1] (Thus, for example, it was not uncommon for this Church organ to refer to 'Jewish tyranny', and, 'the Jewish peril', which was 'destroying Christian society' and 'subjugating Christian people'.)

Although the Army generally had little interest in religious affairs, it was supported by the Church, whose influence reached far beyond Metropolitan France to the colonies. The Jesuits, a usually independent and highly discreet religious order with vast international links and financial resources, were apparently a potent force in the Dreyfus Affair. Good detective though he was, Zola made little headway in documenting actions by the Jesuits; they covered their tracks very well indeed.

Official ties between Church and State were not severed till December 1905. In the meantime, France was both a republic and a Catholic country. Although republican politicians protested their independence of, even opposition to, Church interests in the Chamber of Deputies, in reality they were often tied to those very interests. (Even Jaurès, staunch opponent of the Church, had his daughter baptized and given a convent education.) The complex relationship between Church and State was rendered even more complex in the Third Republic by the role of the Jew in this society. A republican deputy of 1898-99 depended on his constituents to keep him in office, and these same constituents were prey to the ignorance and superstitions carefully cultivated by the Church. Zola clearly demonstrated this by examining the role of local religious orders, such as the Capucins and Ignorantines, and noting how effectively they manipulated and controlled local education at both primary and secondary school levels.[2] With the vast majority of school children attending institutions run by Catholic religious orders, the Church could count upon substantial support throughout the country — a support clearly reflected in the parliamentary elections of May 1898, when those espousing the Dreyfus cause were resoundingly defeated (for example, Jean Jaurès and Joseph Reinach, and later Fernand Labori in the 1902 elections, the latter not being elected until 1906), while outspoken right-wingers, such as Paul Déroulède, won decisive victories.

Zola later admitted to Jaurès how the case had really opened his eyes. As a journalist he had attacked the subject in the press, but he soon realized that he could not achieve much by simply telling the truth and setting down the facts for all to see. After giving it some thought, therefore, he decided to bequeath his country a permanent literary legacy based on the Dreyfus Affair under the title of *Vérité* — the third volume of his series, *Les Quatre Evangiles*. In this novel he would reveal the complexities of the issues and unravel the web of intrigue, setting the action in a small town called Maillebois. He would introduce anti-Semitism to this story, describe the various factors leading to it and show how Church and State conspired to keep it alive. Ignorance was the key factor, Zola felt, and what better way of emphasizing this than by building his novel round it?

Vérité was to prove a much longer work than its author had originally anticipated, exceeding 1100 manuscript pages. He began writing it on 27 July 1901. In his preliminary notes he wrote:

> . . . if human progress is so slow, it is simply because most people don't know. Education is the basis of knowledge and the means of learning the truth, which is what universal happiness is all about. The most recent example of this is the Dreyfus Affair. If France was not with us [during the Affair], it is because she did not know, in fact, she could not know, nourished as she was not only on lies, but by a state of mind that did not permit her to reason things out logically . . . Thus she was quite incapable of [rendering] justice . . .[3]

Following his usual approach, Zola began researching this novel months before he started writing it. He needed information on public education, as well as on the teaching orders responsible for the Church schools. He wrote to friends such as Eugène Fournière, editor of *La Revue Socialiste,* and collected articles from French periodicals on the Jesuits, public education, the relationship between municipal officials and the Church, and the secret administrative files held by State educational authorities about their teachers. Lhermite, an editor of *L'Aurore,* put Zola in touch with a state school teacher from Courtenay (Loiret) by the name of Dauvé, who had suffered grievously at the hands of his superiors after expressing strong republican sentiments at an annual Bastille Day celebration. (Church officials had put pressure on Dauvé's superiors, and they in turn transferred him from his present school to a much less desirable one, resulting in a drastic reduction in salary as well — at a time when teachers earned between 900 and 2000 francs per annum.) Dauvé was living in such squalid conditions that his one-year-old child had recently died as a result of inadequate food, heating and medical care.[4] Dauvé carefully explained all to an attentive Zola, who overlooked no fact or avenue of research which might prove pertinent.

Vérité was to prove as devastating a revelation of corruption in French society under the Third Republic — a corruption resulting from power and fear in religious, educational and political circles — as the *Rougon-Macquart* series had done earlier for the Empire of Napoleon III. Zola's later works display an increasing socio-moral purpose, but his literary and creative powers were undiminished.

Vérité begins with the story of a young, orphaned student (a baptized Jew). He is killed after being sexually attacked and his body is found in the dormitory of a school run by Ignorantine Fathers. The boy's Jewish uncle, Simon, head of the state primary school in Maillebois, is accused of the crime, though there is no evidence to point in his direction. Marc Froment (brother of Luc, in *Travail*), is a state school teacher in a neighbouring town and a friend of Simon and his brother, David (a former army officer). Together they attempt to uncover the truth about the real culprit, an Ignorantine monk by the name of Gorgias.

The story unfolds, revealing how those who might help the accused — parents of schoolchildren, shopkeepers, even a wealthy Jew — refuse to be drawn into the Affair. The story shows just how rabid anti-Semitism was at this time, and how it divided families, including Marc Froment's. (His wife, a lapsed Catholic, turns against him, as apparently Alexandrine had opposed Zola during much of the Dreyfus Affair.) Writing autobiographically, Zola admits that Marc 'hardly liked Jews, through some sort of atavistic scorn and loathing which, despite his open-mindedness, he had never been troubled to question . . . ' But Marc, as a good friend of Simon, overcomes his own anti-Semitism to help. Two trials ensue, and as in the case of Dreyfus, two condemnations. Later in the book Marc Froment, the idealist, comes to a sad realization:

> Man's development does not advance by leaps and bounds, nor by dramatic gestures. It was folly to believe that justice would be acclaimed by millions of people, to think that the innocent party would be returned from prison in the midst of a great national holiday, making the entire country a nation of brothers. Every step of progress, the smallest and most legitimate one, has had to be achieved by centuries of struggle. Every step forward taken

by mankind has required torrents of blood and tears, hundreds of victims sacrificing themselves for the happiness of future generations.

And then Marc looks back upon the part he has played in the Affair:

But he no longer regretted not having been able to achieve something admirable in this prodigious Simon Affair, a lesson which could have taught the people, with one dramatic gesture. No doubt no such instance, at once so complete and decisive, could ever take place: the complicity of all the powers, of all the oppressors, striving together to crush one poor man, one innocent man, whose very innocence jeopardized the pact of human exploitation previously agreed upon by the powers of this world; the patent and clear-cut crime of the priest, the soldier, the judge and the government official, all working together in yet one more attempt to deceive the people, the most extraordinary assortment of infamies thus caught open-handed with their lies and murders, would have left only one thing for them to do — to sink into an ocean of mire. Finally the division of the country into two camps, on the one hand, the former authoritarian society, decrepit and condemned, and on the other, the young society of the future, already set free and moving towards the greatest truth, justice and peace. If Simon's innocence were to be recognized, it would mean that the reactionary past would have to be obliterated at one blow, if even the most humble person were to see the joyous future appearing in all its glory. In no period of history could the revolutionary blade have cut so deeply into the old worm-eaten social edifice. A gigantic and irresistible impetus could have carried the nation towards the future City. In a few months the Simon Affair could have done more for the emancipation of the people and for the reign of justice than a hundred years of political squabbles.

Zola concludes with Marc returning to his school, 'to the only work which he could count on to achieve his goal — the instruction of poor and humble folk in the truth, the truth engendered by knowledge which alone can ultimately make a people capable of justice.' However, over the years, Marc and David gather new evidence pointing directly to the real guilty party, Father Gorgias, and ultimately Simon is returned from his tropical penal colony.

Zola worked on this novel throughout the winter of 1901-02 at his Paris home, returning in June to Médan, writing like a driven man until August, even managing to correct the first batch of galley proofs. His relief was enormous.

I have finally finished this frightful *Vérité* which has required such a great deal of me over the past year. The novel is at least as long as *Fécondité* and contains such a variety of characters and such an intertwining of facts, that never before has a book required such sheer discipline on my part. I have emerged in quite good spirits, but my head really needs a good rest![5]

On 10 July Zola completed his arrangement with Ernest Vaughan for the serialization of the novel in *L'Aurore,* and agreed that the first instalment should appear on 10 September. At about the same time he completed negotiations for its foreign serial translations. Eugène Fasquelle published *Vérité* as a single volume in mid-February 1903, but Zola, alas, was not to see that day.

Zola's importance to world literature (demonstrated by being twice nominated for a Nobel Prize), could not be easily ignored by his critics, yet that is precisely what happened in the case of a large number of periodicals representing the 'patriotic' right. Indeed, their uniform silence almost suggests a mutually-agreed policy regarding *Vérité.* Zola's final work was unusual for the number of periodicals which did not review or even mention it: *La Revue Critique de la Littérature, La Quinzaine, La Revue Bleue, La Revue Blanche, La Revue de Paris,* and the mouthpiece of the establishment, *La Revue des Deux Mondes.* Of the reviews that were written, many were negative, and some even cruel: 'These are the last 750 pages of a powerful writer who died at least three to six books too late . . . '[6] This reviewer was also irritated by Zola's moral line and his 'splutterings' about virtue and justice. He preferred literature to amuse, a view frequently espoused in French circles, which greatly distressed Zola.

Gaston Deschamps' comments, appearing in *Le Temps,* took a much more invidious approach, reminding readers that Zola shared 'responsibility for the civil unrest [in France during the Dreyfus Affair] of which the most eloquent pages of this new novel bring a troubling echo . . . '[7] Zola, no doubt, would have expected just this sort of response from a man who had criticized him so consistently and so unjustly in the past. Deschamps criticized the book for being anti-clerical, and for creating unrealistic characters and events, thereby intentionally distorting the truth. Simon's enemies could surely not have been as cruel and simple-minded as Zola depicted them. And as for the opportunism of the public prosecutor, various republican officials and senior members of the teaching hierarchy who refused all help to Simon or Marc, that was really beyond the pale. Deschamps concluded: 'To tell the truth, Emile Zola seems in a great hurry to have agnosticism introduced into our schools, an agnosticism from which even M. Combes[8] would have recoiled.'[9]

It was apparently the religious question which most vexed the critic of the *Athenaeum,* a London periodical, but he also found Ernest Vizetelly's preface and notes to be 'of a highly controversial nature':

Zola, in the text, while nominally attacking Rome, is in fact, at war not only with the beliefs and observances peculiar to the principal branch of the Western Church, but also some of the fundamental dogmas of Christianity maintained in all countries, even by Evangelical Protestants. Putting aside what is controversial, we find the translation reads pleasantly.[10]

Eugène Fournière, reviewing the novel in *La Revue Socialiste,* a journal once strongly anti-Semitic, began by discussing the author:

> Having lived through the tragic history of these past few years, Emile Zola wrote about it, and then he died. As if our human deeds, even and perhaps especially those of a genius, were regulated by some sort of implacable and mysterious symbolism, he was allowed to complete the work of truth, but not that of justice [the title of the last, unfinished volume of the series].[11]

After four pages of analysis for his socialist readers in which he emphasized that ignorance was the chief sin of the world, Fournière concluded:

> Each of Zola's works — especially the last one — was an act towards the emancipation of mankind, revealing to us the urgent task: everyone must learn. Democracy exists and no citizen has any obstacle other than his own ignorance, between what it is his right to do and what he actually does. In order to overcome that obstacle, we invite you to read this supreme book by the great man who has disappeared from our midst. Keep your appointment at the breach, or rather, at the workshop, with him whose tool has fallen from his hands.[12]

Georges Pellisier's review of *Vérité* appeared in *La Revue,* finally doing justice to Zola's magnificent last novel.

> *Vérité,* like *Travail,* is a work of faith, enthusiasm, divination, the work of a seer . . . After having been constrained to paint the baseness and turpitude of human life, Zola prophesies and magnifies. In the past he was accused of revelling in obscenities and of speculating on scandal. Nothing was more unjust. By placing the evils directly before us, Zola felt that he was acquitting himself of a duty: his pessimism revealed to him the worst aspects of human nature, and his 'naturalism' demanded that he expose them. But even then, when he is cynical, he is ever pure and the brutal candour with which he paints vice can only inspire our disgust of it. Moral even in his books which dealt with immorality, his innate idealism freed itself gradually from the theories of art which had been constraining it . . . *Les Quatre Evangiles* revealed Zola as a glorifier of labour, the missionary of progress, the apostle of all the virtues by which our nation is gradually freeing itself from error and evil.[13]

29

A Political Assassination?

The stables, outbuildings, copses, fields and the house overlooking the
Seine at Médan would have been an ideal place for children to live and
romp, but without them, the country retreat never really became a home
— as even Edmond de Goncourt had noticed. Unable to have Jeanne
Rozerot and the children with him on the estate at Médan, Zola did the
next best thing. Every summer he rented a house for them, first in
Cheverchemont, then in the village of Verneuil-sur-Seine, where he could
watch the children play through the long, copper telescope placed on the
balcony of his study. The year of self-imposed exile had embittered Zola
in some respects, and he particularly regretted the separation from Jeanne
and the children, but at least he could try to make up for it now. His
daughter, Denise, later recalled:

> When he finally came to an understanding with his wife, he could divide
> his days between her and us, and he came over every day after lunch.
> Nothing could have prevented him from coming, neither bad weather, nor
> insuperable heat, not even a physical ailment. It was enough for him to
> know that we awaited him impatiently.[1]

Denise had many vivid recollections of those summer days: 'My earliest
memory of my father is of him climbing up the long sunny hill leading
to Cheverchemont, holding his big grey and green umbrella . . .'[2]
Bicycle excursions were very much a part of those memories. 'There, at
Verneuil, from the summer of 1899 onwards, how many splendid bicycle
outings we went on through the woods. When we did not set out
immediately on such an expedition, we stayed in the garden.' There in
the extensive walled-in garden, surrounded by flowers, they would have
English tea under the shady plane trees, or play boules or croquet with
Paul Alexis and his family. 'My father enjoyed his hobby of photography
with the same passion he undertook everything. As a result we now have
vivid memories of those days.'[3]

Jacques, like his father, was very interested in the sciences. Botany
particularly fascinated him, and he was often seen collecting and identifying
specimens, thanks to a book Zola had just bought him. 'My father practised

botany with us, for he finally got me interested as well. We also knew an old gravel quarry where we could find fossils. Zola spoke constantly about work . . . he was greatly preoccupied with our education, and saw to it that our homework was not forgotten during our holidays.'[4]

Unlike many of his Victorian contemporaries, Zola was an indulgent father and 'he never punished us', noted Denise.

> Once, however, in England, he became angry with my brother who was a bit wayward when it came to eating unauthorized snacks . . . But how we were spoilt! We couldn't express a wish for anything without it being produced. At Christmas, on New Year's Day, on all the birthdays, little gifts fell from his pockets. Zola liked to cheer up the house and brought armfuls of flowers all year round, stopping to buy them from one of the women in front of the St-Lazare railway station, and those women were always expecting him. Once in a while, he would buy the whole cart of flowers from one of them, and they would be stupefied and delighted as they filled his carriage. On New Year's day he sent us sweets which were hidden in the drawer of a small piece of Chinese furniture, or in an enormous incense-burner, or in a copper boot, or in some other knick-knack he was sending my mother. And there was a splendid variety of sweets, in all sorts of little boxes and wrappings accompanied by little sayings which filled us with delight.[5]

Zola's devotion to Jeanne, Denise and Jacques was evident to everyone. 'Zola surrounded us with the poetry of his dreams, providing us with all the tenderness of a united family, and with the love of his heroes from *Fécondité*, Mathieu and Marianne.' As for Jeanne, 'She provided Zola with the gentleness he needed, with her lovely smile, her fair eyes, splendid youth and admiring love, welcoming him to a warm hearth, safe from the outside world.' And unlike Alexandrine, she was 'always cheerful'.[6] Despite the joy they found in being together, Zola sadly acknowledged, 'I am not at all happy. This separation, this double life which I am forced to live, ends by making me despair . . . I dreamt of making everyone round me happy, but I can see that is impossible.' When apart, Jeanne 'accepted the "secluded life" and received only very close friends'.[7]

In light of Zola's written and spoken views about religion in general and Catholicism in particular, it may seem surprising that he had his children baptized and confirmed. The baptisms were apparently at the request of Jeanne Rozerot, and Zola conceded, having fathered the two children out of wedlock, though it seems unlikely that he would have agreed had the circumstances been different. 'But above all he felt that the lack of religion would be an obstacle in my life,' explained Denise later, 'as I then had no name and no inheritance.'[8] Paradoxically, Zola enjoyed teaching Denise her catechism, and did so for more than a year.

Once back in Paris their schedules became more rigid and demanding, but Jeanne and the children never lived far from Zola, and he made it a point to see them often. In fact, he personally enrolled Denise in school in 1895, and Jacques at the Lycée Condorcet in 1897.[9]

On Thursday afternoons Zola would come over to collect the children for a walk. 'It was no longer a question of concealing this [from Alexandrine] as he came to see us openly, and Mme Emile-Zola expressed the wish to see and get to know us,' Denise later explained. Alexandrine would occasionally ask to have the children walk with her, sometimes in the Tuileries, or up the Champs-Elysées or in the gardens of the Palais-Royal. 'We were a little afraid of "the lady", as we called her . . . but our father was there and we felt reassured.' Though 'the lady' always brought them presents, the promenades were constrained. 'These meetings always seemed a bit unreal, as our mother was always absent and her name was never mentioned, and furthermore, we were never given the slightest advance warning when they were to take place.'[10] Fortunately for the children, those unannounced meetings were infrequent.

Zola took Jeanne and the children to their first opera on 19 February 1897, at the Académie Nationale de Musique, to the first performance of Alfred Bruneau's *Messidor* for which Zola had written the libretto.[11] When their father had to join the composer to take a bow, it was the first time the children realized that he was indeed a famous man.

Denise wrote that her mother 'lived unknown in Zola's shadow, but she remains in the story of his life as the comfort of his last years . . . '[12] Although there were many times, certainly on all official occasions, when Jeanne could not be at Zola's side, they did begin to appear together in public more and more frequently. 'During the winter of 1901-02, my father went out with us more often. Every year in October Mme Emile-Zola went to take her cure at Salsomaggiore [Italy] . . . And we children awaited those October days impatiently, for our father would then see us more often than usual. The entire afternoon, dinner, the whole evening — all was reserved then for my mother and us.'[13] The four of them would sit snugly before the fire, just like any other Parisian family, forgetting for the moment that Alexandrine would soon return from Italy and their bliss would be destroyed. After dinner Zola would sit back in his large blue armchair and read the newspaper, then the children would appear 'and usually he would gather us up on his lap, Jacques and me, and tell us stories'.[14]

Zola wanted them to know his Paris and he took them on endless excursions, including several to theatres, to see Carpeaux's *La Danse*, Rude's *La Marseillaise*, and Goujon's *Fontaine des innocents*, explaining everything to the children. 'It was wonderful to listen to him, he would get so excited that he was often carried away by his own enthusiasm.'[15] Zola also took them to see Sarah Bernhardt in *L'Aiglon*, and on another evening to see Gustave Charpentier's *Louise* 'which he wanted us to applaud as a musical masterpiece, one in harmony with his own perceptions of what an opera should be'.[16]

On other occasions he would take Jeanne and the children for walks along the quays of the Seine. 'Stopping often along the embankment, Zola would point out some sailors and explain their work.'[17] But what they really enjoyed were the walks to the lakes of the Bois de Boulogne where he would take photos of the children feeding the black swan. During some of these excursions he would mention various dramas he would like to write, but of those he listed, he only lived to complete the first two.[18] At other times, when the children were at school, he and Jeanne would go off on long walks, arm in arm. 'Ah! the happiness of those years between my mother and father in the tenderness of their union, their union so confident and faithful.'[19]

When researching his novel, *Paris,* Zola was accompanied by Jeanne and the children. 'I fully believe,' his daughter commented, 'that we must have climbed up every monument in the city, including the towers of Notre-Dame Cathedral and the Trocadéro. In the lift carrying us to the top of the Trocadéro, he told us how ill at ease he felt being locked in a compartment sealed off by four walls without an opening.'[20] That did not deter them, however, from going on to Sacré Cœur.

'Sometimes the four of us went to dine at some large restaurant in Paris. In October 1900, after dinner at the Eiffel Tower, we watched the illuminations and saw the flood-lit fountains at the Château d'Eau, which were then something new in the city.'[21] Earlier that same year Zola took his children to the Exposition Universelle in the Champs de Mars. Zola was fascinated by a display of new electrical machines: 'We spent several hours there. My father watched and listened, obviously very interested; as for me, I must admit those steel masses and huge wheels making a terrible noise did not interest me in the least, although Jacques followed our father step by step, asking question after question.'[22]

The last apartment in which Jeanne Rozerot and the children lived during Zola's lifetime was at 3, rue du Havre, across the way from Jacques's school. 'The house was always tranquil and happy,' Zola's daughter remembered, and Jeanne continued to lead a quiet, unobtrusive existence. Years before Zola had given her a duplicate of the necklace Clotilde (the heroine of *Le Docteur Pascal*) had been given by Pascal, a necklace of seven pearls. She wore it 'beneath the collar of her dress and never took it off, that tender chain of love which accompanied her even in her death.'[23]

That last summer in the countryside was typical and happy, not only for Jeanne and the children, but for Zola as well. And although he never mentioned his second family in his correspondence to Alfred Bruneau —

no doubt for fear of Alexandrine's prying eyes — it was easy to read between the lines. 'We have dwelt in perfect serenity during the nearly three weeks we have been here,' he wrote early in July 1902. 'My wife is better, now that we've had some good weather. I have worked well, but won't finish *Vérité* before the end of the month.'[24] He did have to admit, however, that the long continuous hours at his desk required to meet the publication deadline had left him really exhausted. Occasionally, when rising from his labours, he would pick up the seven-inch gold medal with his effigy on it, bestowed on him by the Legion of the Rights of Man in Yves Guyot's office at *Le Siècle* upon his return from exile. Perhaps he smiled as he reread its inscription, which seemed particularly appropriate to the novel he was now completing: 'Truth is on the march and nothing shall deter it'.

Despite the stresses and strains of recent years, Zola still enjoyed excellent health, and his success had brought him certain rights and comforts which he indulged whenever he could. 'I spend delicious afternoons in my garden [in fact, at Verneuil] watching everything live round me,' he told Bruneau, then adding in a more pensive vein, 'With the passage of years I sense all escaping me and thus I love everything all the more passionately.'[25] The black moods which had plagued him during the Dreyfus Affair no longer intruded so frequently, but he still received death threats which troubled his peace of mind:

Where is the Charlotte Corday who will rid France of your putrid presence? There is a price on your head!

Dirty pig who sold out to the Jews. I've just left a meeting where it was decided to do you in. Therefore I'm warning you that within six months' time a second Caserio will take care of you; France will be rid of an infamous personage.[26]

With the arrival of the Charpentiers in mid-August and the completion of *Vérité,* Zola could indeed enjoy the fruits of his decades of labour and the warmth of this rich valley with old friends and his own family.

The month of September was spent in the countryside, as usual. My father seemed sad at the idea of having to return soon [to Paris], and frequent nightmares troubled his sleep. On 22 September he had agreed to take us for a ride on the Seine in his new boat, *L'Enfant-roi* [the name of Bruneau's new opera for which he had prepared the libretto]. We went by bicycle to wait for him at the Triel bridge. Once there we put our bikes to one side and greeted him gaily, as we had never been in a boat before. It was not long before we were between the two islands off Médan. I thought my job, to leap out on to the bank and attach the chain to a tree, a simple one, but my foot slipped and I fell into the shallow water, calling out to my father for help . . . he immediately came to my rescue, pulling me out of the mud . . . The outing was spoilt because of me, for I had to remain in the sun to dry out. We were to have visited the pavilion on his island, 'Le Paradou', but there was no question of that now.[27]

That was as close as the children ever got to Paradou during Zola's lifetime. Then came their last day in the countryside.

On 27 September, he [Zola] came to Verneuil to kiss us goodbye, and we were all to return [separately] to Paris the following day. I no longer remember why, but we did not accompany him, as we usually did, to within a few hundred feet of his house, going via the village streets where, so often during the [Dreyfus] Affair, women would throw their dirty dish water over us as we were passing. Now, instead, we stood at the front door, watching him walk away, turning to look at us once more, and then continuing, finally disappearing round the corner.[28]

That was the last time Jeanne and the children were to see him alive.

While Zola was preparing to close up Médan for the season and return to Paris, it seems that an unidentified group of men were making their own final preparations for the assassination of the novelist. It is not yet clear whether it was the same group which had planned the attempt on Labori's life three years earlier, or the one on Dreyfus, but it seems highly likely that the series of assassination plots with which French history was so liberally littered for several decades right up to World War I (usually attributed to isolated individuals or anarchists), were the product of one or two politically motivated groups of the extreme-nationalist-clerical-right. In Zola's case the assassins had a relatively straightforward plan, namely to block up the chimney connecting with the fireplace in Zola's bedroom. To do that, however, the perpetrators needed to know several details. Which of the dozens of chimney-pots connected with Zola's room, and on which day would he return to Paris? It now seems likely that one of Zola's servants — perhaps the young *valet de chambre*, Léon — must have been in league with the plotters, and if not a servant, then one of the police, who kept Zola under nearly continuous surveillance and who also had easy access to architectural plans of the building. At any rate, while Zola was still *en route* to Paris, two or three men gained access to the roof of 19, rue de Bruxelles, the house next to Zola's, where workmen had for some days been repairing the roof. Acting as if they were repairing Zola's chimney, it would seem that they knocked a considerable amount of loose soot down it, added sand and gravel from the street, and then completely blocked it (probably with a weighted cloth or newspaper). They left, intending to return the following morning to clear the chimney, removing all obvious evidence of their crime.

The Zolas returned to their Paris apartment on 28 September. Finding the bedchamber damp and cold as the central heating had not yet been put on, Alexandrine asked the *valet de chambre* to light a coal fire in their bedroom. (It is not clear whether it was old Jules Delahaye, who had been with them for many years, or the younger man, Léon, who actually lit the fire.) Apparently the mechanism regulating the opening into the flue, was left almost entirely closed ('in error') and that is how it was found the next morning. Zola and his wife retired after dinner and fell asleep. Madame Zola was awakened in the middle of the night, feeling nauseous, as she later related. After being sick, she returned to bed. Zola then got out of bed and stumbled to the floor. His wife called out to him but was soon unconscious. Zola, now unconscious himself, remained on the floor halfway towards the window, which he had probably wanted to open.

At about nine o'clock the following morning (29 September), the servants, not seeing the Zolas up, and getting no reply to their persistent knocking at the bedroom, got help to break the door in. A physician by the name of Marc Berman, who happened to be in a nearby pharmacy, was summoned by a servant. Alexandrine was still alive, though unconscious. Both she and Zola's dog, Fanfan, had survived because they were several feet above floor level, she on the bed, which was itself on a high dais, and the dog on the armchair next to the bed. Zola had collapsed on the floor, inhaling the densest layer of the poisonous gas. Dr Berman tried artificial respiration on Zola and had bottled oxygen brought in as well, and batteries for conducting electric shocks to the heart. He did this for at least twenty minutes, but Zola, who had apparently died about an hour earlier and whose body was still warm, could not be revived. Alexandrine was taken to a clinic at Neuilly-sur-Seine where she recuperated over the next few days, while the police began very slowly to investigate the strange circumstances surrounding her husband's death. It was rather like an episode out of one of the novelist's own books.

Denise Le Blond-Zola later related how she, her mother and brother had heard the news:

All three of us were ready to go out to do some urgent shopping, for things needed after our holiday and for school. We were rushing in order not to keep my father waiting who was due to arrive at about four o'clock . . . The doorbell took us by surprise. Eugène Fasquelle and Fernand Desmoulin, sent by Mme Emile-Zola, stepped in . . . Oh! my mother's shriek, that agonized cry . . . her arms extended to us, then clasping us to her . . . her grief and ours! I still do not know how we managed to live through the week which followed . . . but if I still cry [today] when thinking about it, it is because that 29 September, the source of our tears, revealed to us our immense, irreparable loss, the death of that father so good, so just and so tender.[29]

Several hours later Alfred Bruneau, who was spending his annual holiday on the Atlantic coast at Sainte-Margueritte, was informed of Zola's death by a friend of his, Etienne Destranges (editor of *Le Phare de la Loire*). Bruneau and his family left by train for Paris that same evening. 'My wife, my daughter and I, without losing a minute, went directly to the lugubrious residence. On the divan in his study where we had seen him so alive, talking about his splendid projects, Zola now lay stretched out, his eyes closed. Death had not altered him.'[30]

The Prefect of Police had sent Police Commissioner Cornette to investigate. Meanwhile, Bruneau and Fernand Desmoulin arranged for the vigil; they and other friends, Georges Charpentier, Eugène Fasquelle, Frantz Jourdain, Dr Larat, Théodore Duret, Saint-Georges de Bouhélier, Octave Mirbeau, Alfred Dreyfus, Colonel Picquart and Maurice Le Blond remained with Zola. Recovering at the clinic in Neuilly, Madame Zola insisted upon seeing her husband before the burial and ordered that his body be embalmed. 'The cold had increased sharply,' noted Bruneau during the vigil, 'and, as Commissioner Cornette forbade the use of the central heating and the fireplaces because of his investigation, we all huddled together in the sitting-room, wrapped up in heavy blankets, warming our feet on hot-water bottles, while in the study (the door of which remained open), Zola reposed.'[31] A few days later, after a conversation with Octave Mirbeau, 'I left the sitting-room for a moment and went into the study where I stopped, startled. For lying side by side, next to Zola's remains were his little dogs, Pinpin [II] and Fanfan, though I don't know how they got there.'[32] Just before the funeral Alexandrine finally permitted Jeanne, Denise and Jacques to pay their last respects. All three broke down.

Monsieur Bourouillou, the examining magistrate assigned to deal with the Zola inquest, ordered that two architects (M. Brunel, who worked for the office of the Prefect of Police, and M. Georges Debrie, a government employee), and two chemists (M. Charles Girard, Director of the Municipal Laboratory, and M. Jules Ogier, head of the Toxicology Laboratory), be brought in to carry out the technical side of the investigation. However, these experts only really got down to work a few days *after* the funeral. Given the highly suspicious and unusual nature of the situation, as well as the great number of death threats Zola had continued to receive, one wonders why the experts delayed their investigation until ten full days after the catastrophe. Out of respect for the vigil? Or was there some other reason?

The chemists lit fires in the fireplace in Zola's bedroom on two separate occasions (8 and 11 October), followed by the architects' investigation. The chemists and police brought in three guinea-pigs and three small birds during both tests and they were placed on the floor where Zola's body had been found. On each occasion they were left in the closed room overnight, as Zola had been. The results were both astonishing and disquieting — three guinea-pigs and one bird survived. Air samples from the room revealed only a trace of carbon monoxide fumes, while almost none showed up in the blood samples taken from the dead birds. How then, did they die? Did the 'experts' or the police kill them? If the carefully simulated conditions were found to generate barely enough poisonous air to kill two tiny birds, how on earth could Zola have died under similar conditions? The police autopsy had revealed that he had inhaled large enough amounts of carbon monoxide to kill an otherwise robust and perfectly healthy man — a finding that was quite at odds with the test situation and a paradox which the police chose not to pursue. Why?

Meanwhile, the architects continued with their work and learnt that the neighbours (on the other side of the bedroom wall), last had the chimney swept in October 1901, meeting the legal municipal requirements for an annual sweep. Investigating the chimney of the neighbours at 19, rue de Bruxelles, the experts reported that the top of the chimney was clear, but that the large amount of soot found in the flue was 'totally unlike that found during the previous cleaning'.[33] This soot was taken from a large accumulation in the bend of the flue, but not enough to prevent the entire flow of air. The architects assumed that this accumulation had been caused 'by lack of frequent cleaning' and by vibrations from traffic in the street below. (In fact, the street was relatively quiet with no through traffic.)

The police finally announced their conclusions at the end of October: Zola had died by misadventure. But why had the findings of the experts been virtually ignored, thus allowing the examining magistrate to declare such a clear-cut analysis which precluded any doubt? Was the investigation being hushed up and concluded prematurely, and were the experts' findings ignored on orders, or at the suggestion of, a higher official or influential person? Zola's friends apparently did not suspect foul play at the time — even the usually suspicious Joesph Reinach said simply, 'a foolish accident snuffed out his life . . .'[34] and let the matter go at that. Other views were aired publicly, some totally ludicrous, including Henri Rochefort's hysterical claim that Zola had committed suicide.

Many years later Zola's son, Jacques Emile-Zola, now a retired doctor, admitted his feelings about the circumstances of his father's death. 'The story about the guinea-pigs which survived the experiments carried out in the bedroom where the asphyxiation took place, seems quite incredible to me.' As for possible reasons why any other evidence might have been suppressed, or official doubt expressed, Dr Emile-Zola said:

> Had it been possible to demonstrate that Zola had been the victim of a killing, the passions seen at the time of the Dreyfus Affair would have been heard again. One cannot exclude the possibility that the examining magistrate had been asked not to delve any further . . . The hypothesis of a political killing seems more feasible than the official thesis of an accidental poisoning.[35]

Meanwhile, the funeral arrangements went fairly smoothly, but for two problems. Zola had been suspended as an officer of the Legion of Honour as a result of writing *'J'accuse'* and his subsequent condemnation. Although he was technically reinstated following the general amnesty, he had always refused to wear the red rosette thereafter, so there was now some question as to whether he would be entitled to a military escort to Montmartre Cemetery. This was eventually decided in his favour. The second problem was whether or not Captain Alfred Dreyfus should be permitted to attend the ceremony, as Alexandrine Zola said she feared his presence would spark off demonstrations. (To be sure, uncontrolled demonstrations by street gangs attached to, and encouraged by, the League of the French Fatherland, were common enough throughout the country, though the police generally managed to look the other way when they appeared.) Consequently Mme Zola asked Dreyfus not to attend, but he adamantly insisted. In the event, no serious disturbances took place that Sunday, 5 October 1902.

As Zola's coffin was removed from the house and taken to the hearse, Captain Olivier ordered, 'Present arms!' and rifles snapped into place as the dirge of drums filled the narrow street. Three carriages with wreaths led the way, followed by the hearse, and slowly passed before thousands of spectators along the route, via the boulevard Clichy to the cemetery. In addition to the troops, hundreds of police and municipal guards lined the streets to maintain order among the spectators and the estimated 50,000 people following the hearse. Meanwhile, out of sight, two squadrons of cavalry were kept at the ready. Alexandrine Zola, still very weak, remained at home.

The total absence of any serious demonstrations at the funeral was in itself highly suspicious, not to say, unusual. Why this sudden and unique self-restraint by the right wing now? (Large police and army escorts had never hindered their determination in the past, not even in the very courtrooms where Zola and Dreyfus had been on trial.) Could it be that having achieved what they had set out to do — assassinate Zola — they did not wish to draw further attention to themselves, to cause unwanted questions to be raised and new enquiries started?

As the drums continued to roll lugubriously, Jeanne, Denise and Jacques, attended by the eight pall-bearers — Ludovic Halévy, Abel Hermant, Georges Charpentier, Eugène Fasquelle, Théodore Duret, Alfred Bruneau, Octave Mirbeau, and the Secretary of the Labour Exchange, M. Briat — followed the glass-enclosed hearse through the gates of the cemetery.

A sea of faces extended from the makeshift podium all the way back to the entrance of the cemetery as the three eulogies were delivered, first by M. Chaumié, Minister of Public Instruction and Fine Arts, next by the President of the Société des Gens de Lettres, Abel Hermant, and finally by Anatole France, representing the French Academy. Alexandrine had asked France not to mention anything about Zola's role in the Dreyfus case, but he informed her that he would not speak at all if she interfered with him and Madame Zola gave in.[36] France was by far the most important speaker, he who had been a staunch literary foe of Zola's for so many years.

> Gentlemen, when we saw him raise it [his literary monument] stone by stone, we measured its greatness with surprise. We admired it, we were startled by it, we praised it, or we criticized it. Praise and criticism of equal vehemence were heard. Sometimes he was sincerely reproached (and I know because I was among those who did so), but nonetheless unjustly. Invectives and apologies were hurled at him. But his literary greatness grew.
>
> Today now that we can see the colossal form in its entirety, we can see the spirit with which it was imbued. It was a spirit of goodness. Zola was indeed a good soul. There was a candour and simplicity about him that one finds only in the great. He was profoundly moral. He painted life with a virtuous and vivid hand. What appears as pessimism, a sombre humour found on more than one page of his writings, poorly conceals a real optimism, an obstinate faith in the progress of intelligence and justice. In his books, which are really social studies, he pursued with a vigorous hatred a lazy, frivolous society, a base and harmful aristocracy, and he fought the great evil: the power of money. Democrat that he was, he never flattered people but tried instead to show them the results of ignorance, and the dangers of alcohol which leaves them dumb and defenceless, leading them to shameful ways. He fought social illness wherever he encountered it. Such were the things he hated. In his later books he completely revealed his fervent love for humanity. He tried to divine and foretell a better society.

After discussing Zola's role in the Dreyfus case, France concluded:

> The consequences of his act are incalculable. They continue to develop today with great force and majesty; they go on indefinitely; they have shaped a movement of social equality that will not be stopped. A new order is resulting from it, an order of things founded on a better judicial system and a deeper knowledge of the rights of everyone . . . Zola indeed honoured his fatherland by not despairing of justice in France.
>
> Let us not complain about what we have endured or suffered. We are glad of it. Standing up against the most prodigious accumulation of outrages that stupidity, ignorance and cruelty ever raised, his glory has reached an unapproachable stature. We rejoice in it; he has honoured his country and the world by a great literary achievement and by a great act. We rejoice in it; his destiny and his heart gave him the greatest role to play — he was a moment in the human conscience.[37]

NOTES

The following are the major reference sources referred to in the notes.

BCS *Emile Zola: A biography and critical study*, Robert Sherard (London: Chatto and Windus, 1893)

EZC *Emile Zola, Correspondance* (5 volumes), ed. B.H. Bakker (Montréal: Les Presses de l'Université de Montréal; Paris: Editions du Centre Nationale de la Recherche Scientifique, 1978–1985)

EZJ *Emile Zola, journaliste: bibliographie chronologique et analytique (1859–1881)*, Henri Mitterand and Halina Suwala (Paris: Annales Littéraires de l'Université de Besançon, 1968)

EZR *Emile Zola raconté par sa fille*, Denise Le Blond-Zola (Paris: Fasquelle, 1931)

HL *Houghton Library* collection of correspondence, held at Harvard University

JG *Journal des Goncourts: mémoires de la vie littéraire*, Edmond and Jules de Goncourt (Paris: Charpentier, 1891, 1894 and 1913; Fasquelle et Flammarion, 1956; Monaco: Editions de l'Imprimerie Nationale de Monaco, 1956)

LIEZ *Lettres inédites à Emile Zola*, ed. C.A. Burns (Paris: Nizet, 1958)

NA *Emile Zola: notes d'un ami*, Paul Alexis (Paris: Charpentier, 1882)

NAF *Nouvelles Acquisitions Françaises*. A series of unpublished manuscript letters held in the Bibliothèque Nationale

NR *Emile Zola, Novelist and Reformer*, E.A. Vizetelly (London: John Lane and the Bodley Head, 1904)

OC *Oeuvres complètes*, ed. Gilbert Sigaux (Genève: Edito-Service, no date; Paris: Fasquelle, no date)

OCM *Oeuvres complètes*, ed. Henri Mitterand (Paris: Cercle du Livre Precieux, 1966–1970)

OGC *A l'ombre d'un grand cœur: souvenirs d'une collaboration*, Alfred Bruneau (Paris: Fasquelle-Charpentier, 1932)

TAD *Trente années d'amitié, 1872–1902: lettres de l'éditeur Georges Charpentier à Emile Zola*, ed. Colette Becker (Paris: Presses Universitaires de France, 1980)

THA *Trente-huit années près de Zola: vie d'Alexandrine Méley*, Albert Laborde (Paris: Editeurs Français Réunis, 1963)

Chapter 1

1 Doumergue's speech appeared in *Le Temps*, 5 June 1908.

Chapter 2

1 *EZC I*, p.91, letter 1: Zola to Cézanne, 14 June 1858.
2 Ibid.
3 Ibid., p.110, letter 4: Zola to Louis Marguery, 9 March 1859.
4 Ibid.
5 Ibid., p.133, letter 12: Zola to Cézanne, 9 February 1860.
6 Ibid., p.104, letter 2: Zola to Jean-Baptistin Baille, 23 January 1859.
7 Ibid., p.159, letter 18: Zola to Cézanne, 5 May 1860.
8 Ibid., p.144, letter 15: Zola to Cézanne, 16 April 1860, and p.160, letter 18: Zola to Cézanne, 5 May 1860.
9 Ibid., p.160, letter 18: Zola to Cézanne, 5 May 1860.
10 Ibid., p.126, letter 9: Zola to Cézanne, 5 January 1860.
11 Ibid., p.278, letter 42: Zola to Baille, 17 March 1861.
12 Ibid.
13 Ibid., p.274.
14 Ibid.
15 Ibid., p.138, letter 13: Zola to Baille, 14 February 1860.
16 Ibid., p.136.
17 Ibid., p.143, letter 15: Zola to Cézanne, 16 April 1860.
18 Ibid., p.263, letter 39: Zola to Baille, c.10 February 1861.
19 Ibid., p.265.
20 Ibid., p.266.
21 Ibid.
22 Ibid.
23 Ibid., p.259, letter 38: Zola to Cézanne, 5 February 1861.
24 Ibid.
25 Ibid.
26 Ibid., p.258.
27 Ibid., pp.323-34, letter 52: Zola to Cézanne, 29 September 1862.
28 Ibid., p.324.
29 Ibid., pp.384-85, letter 91: Zola to Valabrègue, 4 November 1864.
30 Ibid.

Chapter 3

1 *NA*, p.50.
2 *NR*, p.58: interview in *Revue Bleue*, 'Célébrités contemporaines I*, 10 March 1883.
3 Ibid., p.64.
4 *BCS*, p.44.
5 Roger Bellet, *Presse et journalisme sous le Second Empire* (Paris: Colin, 1967) p.14.
6 Ibid.
7 Ibid., p.13.
8 Ibid.
9 Ibid., p.16.
10 Ibid., p.19.
11 *OC, Correspondance I*, p.287: Zola to Valabrègue, 6 February 1865.
12 Ibid., p.288.

Chapter 4

1 *OC, Correspondance I*, p.289.
2 Ibid., Zola to A. Duchesne, 11 April 1865.
3 Ibid., pp.302-04: Zola to Boudin, 22 January 1866.
4 Henri Mitterand, *Zola journaliste: de l'affaire Manet à l'affaire Dreyfus* (Paris: Colin, 1962) p.54.
5 *L'Evénement*, 31 January 1866.
6 For further information on Zola's articles, see *EZJ*.
7 Manet later rewarded Zola for his support by painting portraits of the author and Gabrielle.
8 *L'Evénement*, 20 May 1866.
9 *EZJ*, pp.48-49.
10 The preface to this work was first published in *Le Figaro*, 27 May 1866.
11 Emile Zola, *Mes Haines* (Paris: Faure, 1866).
12 1793: the year the First Republic was founded.
13 Place de la Grève was the site of King Louis XVI's execution by guillotine during the French Revolution.

14 *THA*, p.23.
15 Ibid., p.35.
16 Ibid., p.36.
17 *NR*. According to Vizetelly, Zola complained more and more about rheumatism, as well as heart and bladder trouble, but following his death nearly four decades later, the autopsy established him to have been in perfect health (organically).
18 Eugène Sue's earlier *Les Mystères de Paris* had done exceptionally well, and it is likely that Zola based his ideas for *Les Mystères de Marseille* on this.
19 *Feuilletons* were printed as detachable supplements to newspapers, and novels were first serialized in this form around 1830. The success of many newspapers depended on the *feuilletons*, many of which were written from day to day with no preconceived plot.
20 *NR*, p.103.
21 *OC, Correspondance I*, p.359: Zola to Manet, 7 April 1868.
22 From Zola's article on the Goncourt brothers, which appeared in *Le Gaulois*, 22 September 1868.
23 *OC, Correspondance I*, p.312: Zola to Valabrègue, 10 December 1866.
24 *EZJ*, p.90: Eugène Pelletan to Zola, May 1868.
25 Ibid., p.94.
26 Ibid., p.106.
27 Ibid., p.119.
28 Ibid., p.120.
29 From Zola's preface to *Nouveaux contes à Ninon* (Paris: Charpentier, 1874).

Chapter 5

1 Zola announced the founding of *La Marseillaise* by Roux and himself (omitting Arnaud's name) in a letter to Paul Alexis dated 21 September 1870. See *OC, Correspondance II*, pp.390-91.
2 *OC, Correspondance I*, p.389: Zola to Edmond de Goncourt, 7 September 1870.
3 *NR*, p.89.
4 Ibid., p.90.
5 Ibid.
6 Emile Zola, *L'Œuvre* (Paris: Charpentier, 1886) p.208.
7 Ibid.
8 Ibid.
9 *La Marseillaise* appeared for the first time on 27 September 1870 and folded on 16 December of the same year.
10 *OCM*, p.344.
11 *OC, Correspondance I*, p.397: Zola to Valabrègue, 29 December 1870.
12 Ibid., p.406: Zola to Alexis, 17 February 1871.
13 Ibid.
14 Ibid., p.407: Zola to Alexis, 2 March 1871.
15 *NA*, p.173.
16 *EZR*, p.71.
17 Ibid.
18 *OC, Correspondance I*, p.413: Zola to Louis Ulbach, 6 November 1871.
19 Ibid.
20 Ibid.
21 Ibid.
22 *NR*, p.135.
23 Ibid.
24 *JG*, Vol. II (1891 edn) p.44: 3 June 1872.
25 Ibid.
26 Matthew Josephson, *Zola and his Times* (New York: Garden City Publising Co., 1928) p. 187.
27 Ibid.
28 *NR*, p.278.
29 Among the psychological works Zola read for research were Dr Jacques Moreau's *La Psychologie morbide dans ses rapports avec la philosophie de l'histoire, ou de l'influence des névropathies sur le dynamisme intellectuel*, and Dr Ulysse Trélat's *La Follie lucide, étudiée et considerée au point de vue de la société*.

Chapter 6

1 *OC, Correspondance II*, p.29: Zola to Charpentier, 28 July 1874.
2 According to Zola's contract with Charpentier, dated 8 May 1877, each volume from *L'Assommoir* onwards was to sell for 3F50, of which Zola was to receive 50 centimes in royalties (about 14 per cent). On earlier works he would receive 40 centimes (about 11 per cent). When Eugène Fasquelle officially bought out Charpentier's publishing house on 1 July 1897, a new contract was drawn up with Zola, maintaining the price per volume, but increasing his royalties to 60 centimes (about 17 per cent) for the *Rougon-Macquart* series, but maintaining the rate of 50 centimes for *Les Trois villes*. These contracts were published by Colette Becker — see *TAD*.

3 *OC, Correspondance II*, pp.30-31: Zola to Alexis, 20 March 1875.
4 Ibid., p.39: Zola to Roux, 5 August 1875.
5 Ibid., p.40: Zola to Alexis, 7 August 1875.
6 Ibid., p.40: Zola to Edmond de Goncourt, 9 August 1875.
7 Ibid., p.43: Zola to Charpentier, 14 August 1875.
8 Ibid., p.43: Zola to Stassulewitch, 8 September 1875.
9 Ibid., p.46: Zola to Alexis, 17 September 1875.
10 Ibid.
11 Ibid., p.50: Zola to Alexis, 20 October 1875.
12 *NR*, p.157.
13 Ibid., p.168.
14 *NR*, p.160.
15 Barbara Beaumont ed. and trans., *Flaubert and Turgenev: A Friendship in Letters — The Complete Correspondence* (New York: W.W. Norton, 1985). Flaubert to Turgenev, 28 October 1876; Turgenev to Flaubert, 2-9 December 1876.
16 Ibid., p.161.
17 *BCS*, pp. 134-35, 136.
18 Ibid., p.155.
19 Ibid., p.156.
20 *OC, Correspondance II*, p.68: Zola to Albert Millaud, 9 September 1876.
21 Ibid., pp.81-82: Zola to Yves Guyot, 13 February 1877.
22 Ibid., p.86: Zola to Alexis, 26 July 1877.
23 Ibid., p.110: Zola to Théo. Duret, 2 September 1877.
24 Ibid. Zola to Mme Charpentier, 21 August 1877.
25 Pierre Cogny ed., *Les Rougon-Macquart* (Paris: Seuil, 1970), Vol.3, p.17.

Chapter 7

1 Although he was also from Aix, Alexis only met Zola for the first time in Paris.
2 John Rewald ed., *Paul Cézanne, Correspondance* (Paris: Grasset, 1933) p.139: Cézanne to Zola, May 1878.
3 Ibid., p. 141: Cézanne to Zola, 1 June 1878. (See also letters of May 1878, p.141; 29 July 1878, p.145; 27 August 1878, p.141; and 4 November 1878, p.149.)
4 It appears possible that it was Cézanne who introduced Gabrielle to Zola. In Cézanne's letters to Zola during the mid-1860s he refers to her as Gabrielle.
5 *NA*, p.184.
6 Ibid., p.91.
7 *BCS*, pp.134-35, 136.
8 Pierre Cogny, *Le Huysmans intime de Henry Céard et Jean de Caldain* (Paris: Nizet, 1957) pp.126-27.
9 Ibid., p.138.
10 Ibid., p.141.
11 Ibid., p.146.
12 Guy Chastel, *J.-K. Huysmans et ses amis* (Paris: Grasset, 1957) p.343.
13 Ibid.

Chapter 8

1 *EZC I*, p.447, letter 147: Zola to Adolphe Lemoigne-Montigny, 29 March 1866.
2 *OCM*, Vol.XI, p.291.
3 *EZC III*, p.113, letter 21: Zola to Léon Hennique, 2 September 1877.
4 *EZC II*, pp.337-38, letter 168: Zola to Edmond de Goncourt, 7 July 1873.
5 Louis Dore, *L'Avenir National*.
6 *OC, Correspondance II*, p.338, footnote 2: Goncourt to Zola, n.d.
7 Ibid., p.340, footnote 3: Marie Laurent to Zola, 26 July 1873.
8 Ibid., p.338, letter 170: Zola to Marie Laurent, end July 1873.
9 Ibid., p.360, letter 186, footnote 2: Lemoigne-Montigny to Zola, 17 July 1874.
10 Ibid. Zola to Charpentier, 23 July 1874.
11 Ibid., pp.361-362, letter 187: Zola to Antoine Guillemet, 23 July 1874.
12 Ibid., p.364, letter 190: Zola to Turgenev, 1 October 1874.
13 Ibid., p.366, letter 191: Zola to Flaubert, 9 October 1874.
14 Ibid., pp.359-60, letter 186: Zola to Charpentier, 23 July 1874.
15 Ibid., p.361: Flaubert to Edmond de Goncourt, 22 September 1874.
16 Ibid., p.373, letter 202: Zola to Daudet, 9 November 1874.
17 Ibid., p.374, letter 203: Zola to Flaubert, 12 November 1874.
18 Ibid., p.373, letter 202: Zola to Daudet, 9 November 1874.
19 Ibid., pp.370-71, letter 197: Zola to Alexis, 2 November 1874.
20 *EZC III*, p.176, footnote 1.
21 Edmond Le Pelletier, *Emile Zola, sa vie et ses œuvres* (Paris: Mercure de France, 1908) p. 183.
22 *JG*, Vol.II (1892 edn) pp.21-22. Also see *EZC III*, p.176, footnote 4.

23 Francisque Sarcey, *Le Temps*, 4 May 1878.
24 *EZC III*, p.177, footnote 2.
25 *JG*, Vol.II (1956 Monaco edn) p.123.
26 *EZC III*, p.177, footnote 3: Flaubert to Edmond de Goncourt, 5 May 1878.
27 *OC, Correspondance II*, p.93: Zola to Huysmans, 3 August 1877.
28 Francisque Sarcey, *Le Temps*, 6 May 1889.
29 Charles Darcours, *Le Figaro*, 19 January 1879.
30 *La Lanterne*, 20 January 1879.
31 *Le Siècle*, 20 January 1879.
32 *JG*, Vol.XII (1956 Monaco edn) p.9.
33 Jules Prével, *Le Figaro*, 1 May 1879.
34 *NAF* 24513, fos 32-33: Busnach to Zola, 11 July 1879.
35 Ibid., fos 584-85: Busnach to Zola, 17 June?
36 Ibid., fos 340-41: Busnach to Zola, 9 September 1892.
37 Ibid., fos 386-89: Busnach to Zola, 1 September 1900.
38 Ibid., fos 254-55: Busnach to Zola, 31 March 1881.
39 Ibid.
40 Ibid., fos 641-42: Busnach to Zola, 19 July 1885?
41 Ibid., fos 392-95: Busnach to Zola, n.d.
42 Ibid., fos 378-79: Busnach to Zola, 30 January 1900.
43 James B. Sanders, *'Antoine et Zola'* from *Les Cahiers Naturalistes*, no.50 (1976) pp.9-18: Zola to Antoine, 18 July 1887.
44 André Antoine, *Bulletin de la Société Littéraire des Amis d'Emile Zola*, no.2 (1923) p.120.
45 *NAF* 24513, fos 201-02: Busnach to Zola, 30 November 1889.
46 Ibid., fo.318: Busnach to Zola, 4 January 1890.
47 Ibid., fos 592-93: Busnach to Zola, 21 June 1892?
48 Ibid., fos 678-79: Busnach to Zola, 1893?
49 Ibid., fos 620-21: Busnach to Zola, 5 May 1892?
50 Ibid., fos 32-33: Busnach to Zola, n.d. (1890 or later).
51 Ibid., fo. 636: Busnach to Zola, 15 July?
52 Ibid., fos 387-88: Busnach to Zola, 18 July 1880.
53 *JG*, Vol.XII (1956 Monaco edn) pp.100-01.
54 Ibid., p.102.
55 Francisque Sarcey, *'Chroniques théâtrales'*, *Le Temps*, 31 January 1881.
56 Auguste Vitu, *Le Figaro*, 30 January 1881.
57 *NAF* 24515, fos 281-82: Busnach to Zola, January 1882?
58 *JG*, Vol.XII (1956 Monaco edn) p.72, and Vol.XIX, p.209.
59 *NAF* 24513, fos 158-59: Busnach to Zola, 1 February 1882.
60 Ibid.
61 Ibid., fos 160-61: Busnach to Zola, 1 March 1882.
62 Ibid., fo. 116: Busnach to Zola, 6 August 1882.
63 Ibid., fos 184-85: Busnach to Zola, 9 August 1883.
64 Ibid., fos 194-96: Busnach to Zola, 6 September 1883.
65 Ibid., fos 184-85: Busnach to Zola, 9 August 1883.
66 Ibid., fo. 206: Busnach to Zola, 6 November 1883.
67 Ibid., fos 211-12: Busnach to Zola, 18 December 1883.
68 Eugène Hubert, *Gil Blas*, 15 December 1883.
69 *JG*, Vol.XIII (1956 Monaco edn) p.69.
70 *NAF* 24515. fos 55-56. p.216: Busnach to Zola, n.d.
71 *NAF* 24514. fos 32-33: Busnach to Zola, n.d.
72 *NAF* 24513. fos 522-23: Busnach to Zola, n.d.
73 Ibid.
74 Ibid., fos 32-33: Busnach to Zola, n.d.
75 Ibid., fos 81-82: Busnach to Zola, 20 October 1880.
76 Ibid., fos 330-331: Busnach to Zola, 18 October 1880.
77 *JG*, Vol.XIV (1956 Monaco edn) p.202.
78 *Gil Blas*, 23 April 1888.
79 Fernand Bourgeat, *'Premières représentations'*, *Gil Blas*, 23 April 1888.
80 Albert Wolff, *Le Figaro*, 24 April 1888.
81 Ibid.
82 *Le Figaro*, 25 April 1888.
83 *JG*, Vol.XIV (1956 Monaco edn) p.164.
84 *NAF* 24513, fos 329-330: Busnach to Zola, 2 December 1890.
85 Ibid., fos 384-85: Busnach to Zola, 29 August 1900.
86 Ibid., fos 665-66: Busnach to Zola, 30 July 1900.
87 Ibid., fos 378-79: Busnach to Zola, 30 January 1900.
88 Ibid., fos 569-70: Busnach to Zola, 10 June 1900?

Chapter 9

1 *La Cloche*, 19 July 1871.
2 Ibid., 21 July 1871.
3 Ibid., 14 July 1872.
4 Ibid., 20 July 1872.
5 Ibid., 20 February 1871.
6 Ibid., 19 June 1871.
7 Ibid., 31 July 1871.
8 Ibid., 22 July 1871.
9 *Le Voltaire*, 17 August 1880.
10 *OC, Correspondance II*, p.165: Zola to Magnard, 16 September 1880.
11 *Une Campagne* was published by Charpentier in 1882.
12 *OC, Correspondance II*, p.165: Zola to Magnard, 16 September 1880.
13 Ibid.
14 Ibid.

Chapter 10

1 *EZR*, p.115.
2 *NAF* 24516, fos 172-86: Céard to Zola, 15 October 1879.
3 Ibid.
4 *Le Voltaire*, 8 October 1879.
5 *BCS*, p.168.
6 Ibid., pp.166-67: Zola to unknown party, 3 December 1879.
7 Pierre Cogny ed., *Les Rougon-Macquart* (Paris: Seuil, 1970) Vol. 3, p.184: Unknown person to Zola, 28 October 1879.
8 *NR*, p.145.
9 *JG*, Vol.VI (1913 edn) pp.101-02.
10 *BCS*, p.196: Zola to Sherard, October 1882.
11 *JG*, Vol.VI (1913 edn) p.112.
12 Ibid., p.127.
13 Ibid., p.192.
14 Ibid., p.194: 8 April 1882.
15 Ibid., pp.209-10.

Chapter 11

1 *OC, Correspondance II*, pp.243-44: Zola to Céard, 12 August 1884.
2 Ibid.
3 Ibid., pp.247-48; Zola to Céard, 25 August 1884.
4 Ibid., p.245: Zola to Céard, 12 August 1884.
5 Ibid., p.251: Zola to Céard, 25 August 1884.
6 Henri Guillemin, *Zola légende et vérité* (Paris: Julliard, 1969) pp.147, 156.
7 Ibid.
8 Legislation was passed on 22 March 1884. See Jacques Chastenet, *Histoire de la Troisième République* (Paris: Hachette, 1954) Vol.II, p.132.
9 Ibid., p.135: 14 October 1883.
10 Gordon Wright, *France in Modern Times* (Chicago: Rand McNally & Co., 1966) pp.364-65.
11 Chastenet, op.cit., p.138.
12 Wright, op.cit., p.363; Chastenet, op.cit., p.133.
13 Richard H. Zakarian, *Zola's Germinal: A Critical Study of its Primary Sources* (Genève: Droz, 1972) p.36.
14 Ibid., p.32.
15 Among Zola's background reading were Emile Dormoy's *Topographie souterraine du bassin Houiller de Valenciennes*, Lavelaye's *Le Socialisme contemporaine*, Oscar Testut's *L'Internationale*, Paul Leroy-Beaulieu's *La Question ouvrière au XIXe siècle*, and Guyot's *La Science économique*. He also read dozens of mining journals.
16 Pierre Cogny ed., *Les Rougon-Macquart* (Paris: Seuil, 1970) Vol.4, p.414: Zola to Kolff, 6 October 1889.
17 *OC, Correspondance II*, p.243: Zola to Céard, 14 June 1884.
18 Ibid.
19 Ibid., p.258: Zola to Charpentier, 25 January 1885.
20 Cogny, op.cit., p.409.
21 Ibid., pp.266-67: Zola to Magnard, 4 April 1885.
22 *OC, Correspondance II*, p.279: Zola to an acquaintance, December 1885.

Chapter 12

1 *NR*, p.264.
2 Ibid., p.267.

3 Ibid.
4 Ibid., p.268.
5 *Le Matin*, 7 March 1885.
6 *OC, Correspondance II*, pp.291-93: Zola to Kolff, 29 July 1886.
7 *Le Temps*, 28 August 1887.
8 *OC, Correspondance II*, p.365: Zola to Octave Mirbeau, 23 September 1883.
9 Pierre Cogny ed., *Les Rougon-Macquart* (Paris: Seuil, 1970) Vol.5, p.220: Goncourt to Zola, 23 November 1887.
10 Ibid., p.221: Huysmans to Zola, 15 November 1887.
11 Lucien Daudet, *Vie d'Alphonse Daudet* (Paris: Gallimard, 1941) p.112.
12 *NAF* 24517, fo. 73?: Daudet to Zola, 26 April 1886.
13 *OC, Correspondance II*, p.285: Zola to Daudet, 27 April 1886.
14 *JG*, Vol.I (1894 edn) pp.206-07: entries dated 2 May 1889, and 18 August 1887.
15 Goncourt's hatred of Zola took many forms. For example, he called Zola the 'most wily' of modern French writers (*JG* [1956 Monaco edn] p.70, 2 May 1889). He also complained of Zola stealing his ideas and glory: 'If no one in the press wants to recognize that I am the procreator and the one plagiarized by Zola, if no one can see that it is the enlargement, the caricature, the cheap popularization of my earlier works which have made his success for him . . . ' (Ibid., 3 May 1889).
16 *JG*, Vol.XV (1956 Monaco edn) p.21, 18 August 1887.
17 Pierre Cogny, op.cit., p.219: Zola to Goncourt, 14 October 1887.
18 *Les Cahiers Naturalistes*, no.13, '*Les Lettres inédités d'Edmond de Goncourt à Emile Zola*': Goncourt to Zola, 14 October 1887.
19 *JG*, Vol.XIV (1956 Monaco edn) p.121, 26 April 1886.
20 Ibid.
21 *OC, Correspondance II*, p.335: Zola to Goncourt, August 1888.
22 *NAF* 24519, fo.88?: Goncourt to Zola, August 1888.
23 Pierre Cogny, op.cit., p.440: Zola to Kolff, 14 November 1887.
24 *JG*, Vol.XVI (1956 Monaco edn) p.177, 21 November 1889.
25 *La Revue Bleue*, 27 October 1888.
26 *Le Temps*, 21 October 1888.
27 Pierre Cogny, op.cit., p.548: Zola to Kolff, 6 June 1889.
28 Jules Lemaître, *Le Figaro*, March 1890.
29 Anatole France, *Le Temps*, 9 March 1890.

Chapter 13

1 *OC, Correspondance II*, p.351: Zola to Charpentier, 27 August 1889.
2 Ibid.
3 *NR*, p.505.
4 *OC, Correspondance II*, pp.356-57: Zola to Goncourt, 21 April 1890.
5 Among the books Zola read for research were: *La Bourse, ses abus et ses mystères, La Quintessence du socialisme, Histoire des Français depuis le temps gaulois jusqu'à nos jours*, and *Mémoires d'un coulissier*.
6 *OC, Correspondance II*, p.357: Zola to Kolff, 9 July 1890.
7 Ibid., p.361: Zola to Daudet, 6 November 1890.
8 Ibid., p.369: Zola to Decroix, 1890.
9 Ibid., pp.365-66: Zola to Daudet, 27 January 1891.
10 Anatole France, *Le Temps*, 22 March 1891.
11 Ibid., pp.398-99: Zola to Kaminsky, 10 September 1893.
12 Ibid., p.276: Zola to Jean Volders, 15 November 1885.
13 Ibid., p.382: Margueritte to Zola, 9 March 1892.
14 Ibid., pp.382-83: Zola to Margueritte, 12 March 1892.
15 Ibid., p.355: Zola to Huysmans, 5 January 1890.
16 Ibid., p.368: Zola to Clément-Janin, 27 May 1891.
17 Ibid., p.375: Zola to Kolff, 4 September 1891.
18 Ibid., p.379: Zola to Kolff, 26 January 1896.
19 Ibid., p.373: Zola to Céard, 8 July 1891.
20 Ibid., pp.393-94: Zola to Kolff, 4 September 1891.
21 Ibid.
22 Ibid., p.382: Zola to Alexis, 21 June 1892.
23 Ibid., p.379: Zola to Kolff, 26 January 1892.
24 Ibid., p.388: Zola to Bruneau, 8 July 1892.
25 De Vogüé, *Revue des Deux Mondes*.
26 Pierre Cogny ed., *Les Rougon-Macquart*, (Paris: Seuil, 1970) Vol. 6, p.664: Céard to Zola, 30 June 1892.
27 Ibid., p.665: Huysmans to Zola, n.d.

Chapter 14

1 *BCS*, pp.258-62.
2 René Peter, *'Zola et l' Académie'* published in *Mercure de France* (CCXCVI), pp.572-73, 1 March 1940.
3 *BCS*, p.277.
4 *BCS*, p.279.
5 *OCM*, Vol.6, p.1405.
6 Manuscript in Bibliothèque Bodmer: Zola to Kolff, 25 January 1893.
7 *OC, Correspondance II*, pp.393-94: Zola to Kolff, 22 February 1893.
8 *NR*, p.324.
9 Ibid., p.325.
10 Ibid., p.334.
11 Ibid., pp.336-37.

Chapter 15

1 Jeanne Rozerot later moved to 8, rue Taitbout, and finally had a flat at 3, rue du Havre. In the countryside she stayed at Cheverchemont and Verneuil, near Médan.
2 *OC, Correspondance II*, p.547: Zola to Marguelitte, 1900.
3 Bruneau did mention the children *following* Zola's death, and they occasionally visited his house to play with his daughter, Suzanne. See *NAF* 24512, fos 288-89: letter from Bruneau to *'Chère grande amie'*.
4 *THA*, p.96.
5 *OGC*, pp.101-02. Céard used this occasion to break with Zola permanently. He cemented the rift at the end of November 1893 by giving a pathetic interview to Jules Huret in *Le Figaro*, in which he likened Zola to Pope Sixtus V: 'Zola is indeed that same Italian with his false expressions and papal hands — you have no doubt noticed those soft and nervous hands — who wants to conquer everything in sight, who so readily changes from one opinion to another, like some character out of the pages of Augier . . . ' (See *OGC*, p.67.)

    Céard was a jealous and bitter man, rankled by Zola's continuing success. But his relations with other friends had long been tumultuous, and he gradually fell out with each and every one of the Médan set. In short, the excuse given by Céard for not attending Zola's dinner was quite irrelevant, for he would not have been welcome there.
6 *THA*, pp.92-93.
7 Ibid., p.104.
8 *EZR*, p.168.
9 Ibid., p.169.
10 Ibid., p.190.

Chapter 16

1 *'Pour les Juifs'*, *Le Figaro*, 16 May 1896.
2 For centuries Catholics, in their bidding prayers on Good Friday, prayed for the 'perfidious Jews' — a practice recently stopped.
3 The French Protestants were accused of similar things in the sixteenth and seventeenth centuries when they literally held their own cities and fortresses within the country.
4 *'Pour les Juifs'*, op.cit.
5 Ibid.
6 Ibid.
7 Ibid.
8 Ibid.

Chapter 17

1 One businessman, a certain M. Bourgeois, later sued Zola for defamation of character as a result of a description in *Lourdes*. Zola was spared an appearance in court when his lawyer reached an out-of-court settlement in February 1895, by the terms of which Zola agreed to change a few phrases of the next edition of the book. *'Voyage à Lourdes'* was published by René Ternois in *Mes Voyages* (Paris: Fasquelle, 1958). See pp.108-09.
2 *NR*, p.409.
3 Colette Becker gives a date of May 1894. See *TAD*, p.137.
4 *NR*, p.410.
5 *'Voyage à Rome'* — see *Mes Voyages*, op.cit.
6 Ibid., pp.237-38.
7 Ibid., pp.237-50.
8 *OCM*, Vol.7, p.1143.
9 Ibid., p.1566.
10 *Le Figaro*, December 1895.
11 Ibid.
12 *Le Figaro*, January (?) 1896.

Chapter 18

1 Alfred Cobban, *A History of Modern France II*, (Baltimore: Penguin Books, 1963) p.236.
2 *NAF* 24521, fo.2: Zadoc Kahn to Zola, 5 December 1897.
3 *Le Figaro, 'Le Procès-verbal'*, 5 December 1897.
4 *NAF* 24517, fo.91: Armand Charpentier to Zola, 8 January 1898.
5 *L'Aurore, 'J'accuse'*, 13 January 1898.
6 Ibid.
7 *NAF* 24517, fo.246: François Coppée to Zola, 2 May 1898.
8 *TAD*, p.129: Georges Charpentier to Zola, 9 April 1898.
9 *'J'accuse'*, op.cit.
10 *NAF* 24521, fo.8: Labori to Zola, 20 January 1898.
11 Jean Jaurès, 24 January 1898. See Jacques Chastenet, *Histoire de la Troisième République* (Paris: Hachette, 1954) Vol.III.
12 *Le Temps*, 6 February 1898.
13 Ibid., 5 February 1898.
14 Ibid., 21 January 1898.
15 Ibid., 6 February 1898.
16 Ibid.
17 Ibid., 16 January 1898.
18 Ibid., 23 January 1898.
19 Ibid.
20 Ibid., 8 February 1898.
21 *Le Matin*, 7 February 1898.
22 *Le Temps*, 8 February 1898.

Chapter 19

1 Jean France, *Autour de l'affaire Dreyfus: souvenirs de la Sûreté Générale* (Paris: Rieder, 1936) p.85.
2 *Journal des Débats*, 22–24 January 1898. See also accounts in *Le Temps* and *Le Figaro*.
3 Ibid.
4 Ibid. Also quoted by Jean Denis Bredin, *L'Affaire* (Paris: Julliard, 1983). Bredin's work is the most recent study, and an excellent one.
5 *EZR*, p.211. Also mentioned by Jean France, op.cit.
6 *OGC*, p.12.
7 *NAF* 13190, pp.269 and 365.
8 This and all further quoted matter pertaining to the trial can be found in *L'Affaire Dreyfus: le procès Zola devant la Cour d'Assises de la Seine de la Cour de Cassation (7 fevrier/31 mars - 2 avril 1898). Compte-rendu sténographique 'in extenso' et documents annexes* (2 volumes), (Paris: *Le Siècle* et P.V. Stock, 1898.)
9 Van Cassel's notes and summary of the trial can be found in *NAF* 13190.
10 Jean France, op.cit., p.110.

Chapter 20

1 *NAF* 24521, fos 32-33: Labori to Zola, 11 July 1898. At this stage, Labori was still hesitating whether or not to appeal against the verdict.
2 *HL*, bMS Judaica 1.3, fos 158-85: Zola to Labori, 12 July 1898. In the same letter, Zola discussed the possibility of appealing the results of the trial set for 18 July.
3 *OC, Correspondance II*, p.442: Zola to Desmoulin, 28 June 1898.
4 *HL*, bMS Judaica 1.3, fos 158-85: Zola to Labori, 12 July 1898.
5 Ibid.
6 Colin Burns ed., *'Emile Zola: Pages d'exile'* from *Nottingham French Studies*, Vol.III, 1 (May 1964) pp.21-46, and 2 (October 1964) pp.48-62. Most of the information for this chapter comes from a manuscript prepared by Zola, but not published during his lifetime. His family finally allowed Colin Burns to publish it in the magazine cited.
7 Burns, op.cit., pp.25-27. See also E.A. Vizetelly, *With Zola in England* (London: Chatto and Windus, 1899).
8 Vizetelly, op.cit., pp.16-17.
9 Ibid., Chapter IV.
10 *NAF* 24521, fos 33-40: Labori to Zola, 24 July 1898.
11 Ibid., fos 34-40.
12 Ibid.
13 Ibid. Zola was informed about the change of address to rue de la Paix in a letter dated 26 July 1898 — see fos 41-42.
14 Ibid., fos 35-40.
15 Vizetelly, op.cit., p.95.

Chapter 21

1 In September 1898 Captain J.B. Marchand, who had arrived at Fashoda in the southern Sudan earlier that year, claiming it for France, was confronted by the recently victorious General Sir Herbert Kitchener. When Kitchener ordered him out of the country, Marchand refused to budge, and eventually both countries mobilized their navies. War was threatened before the French finally gave in, greatly humiliated, and evacuated the Sudan.

2 Colin Burns, ed. *'Emile Zola: Pages d'exile'* from *Nottingham French Studies*, Vol.III, 1 (May 1964) p.28.

3 *OC, Correspondance II*, p.454: Zola to Desmoulin, 6 August 1898.

4 This article appeared on 24 July 1898, and is referred to in Burns, op.cit., p.35.

5 Burns, op.cit., p.50.

6 Ibid., p.38.

7 Ibid., p.50.

8 Ibid., p.38.

9 Ibid., p.51.

10 Ibid., p.61.

11 Ibid.

12 Ibid., p.57.

13 Ibid.

14 Ibid.

15 *NAF* 24521, fos 64-65: Labori to Zola, 7 October 1898.

16 Burns, op.cit., pp.36, 39 and 41.

17 *NAF* 24517, fos 223-26: Clemenceau to Zola, January 1899?

18 E.A. Vizetelly, *Zola in England: A Story of Exile* (London: Chatto and Windus, 1899) pp.118-19.

Chapter 22

1 Colin Burns ed., *'Emile Zola: Pages d'exile'* from *Nottingham French Studies*, Vol.III, 2 (October 1964) p.60.

2 Mirbeau's article, *'Trop'* appeared in *L'Aurore* on 2 August 1898.

3 *OC, Correspondance II*, p.457: Zola to Desmoulin, 12 August 1898 and *HL*, bMS Judaica 1.3, fos 158-85: Zola to Labori, 19 August 1898.

4 *OC, Correspondance II*, p.459: Zola to Labori, 19 August 1898.

5 *NAF* 24521, fos 34-40: Labori to Zola, 24 July 1898.

6 *OC, Correspondance II*, p.470: Zola to Alexis, 11 December 1898.

7 Ibid., p.472.

8 Ibid., p.452: Zola to Reinach, August 1898.

9 *HL*, bMS Judaica 1.3, fos 158-85: Zola to Labori, 19 August 1898.

10 *OC, Correspondance II*, p.460: Zola to Mirbeau, 19 August 1898.

11 *NAF* 24521, fos 47-53: Labori to Zola, 16 August 1898.

12 *OC, Correspondance II*, p.453: Zola to Labori, 8 September 1898.

13 *HL*, bMS Judaica 1, fos 82-95: Zola to Vaughan, 8 September 1898.

14 *NAF* 24521, fos 69-76: Labori to Zola, 11 November 1898.

15 *OC, Correspondance II*, pp.465-66: Zola to Labori, 30 October 1898.

16 *HL*, bMS Judaica 1.3, fos 158-85: Zola to Labori, 11 August 1898.

17 *OC, Correspondance II*, p.507: Zola to Reinach, 30 April 1899.

18 *NAF* 24521, fos 69-73: Labori to Zola, 11 November 1898.

19 Ibid., fos 87-88: Labori to Zola, 16 March 1899.

20 Ibid., fos 69-76: Labori to Zola, 11 November 1898.

21 Ibid., fos 87-90: Labori to Zola, 11 March 1899.

22 *HL*, bMS Judaica 1.3, fos 158-85: Zola to Labori, originally attached to a letter, probably dated the first week of April.

23 Ibid. Zola to Labori, 11 April 1899 — the note called *'Amnestie'* was attached to a letter.

24 *OC, Correspondance II*, p.485: Zola to Mirbeau, 12 February 1899.

25 Ibid., p.486: Zola to Reinach, 16 February 1899.

26 *HL*, bMS Judaica 1.4 (no fos): Zola to Fasquelle, 19 February 1899.

27 Ibid.

28 *NR*, p.490.

29 *HL*, bMS Judaica 1.4: Zola to Fasquelle, 25 March 1899.

30 Ibid. Zola to Fasquelle, 9 April 1899.

31 Ibid. Zola to unknown person, 14 March 1899.

32 *NAF* 24521, fos 96-100: Labori to Zola, 31 May 1898.

33 Ibid.

34 *OC, Correspondance II*, p.510: Zola to Labori, 3 June 1899.

35 *HL*, bMS Judaica 1, fos 82-95: Zola to Vaughan, 1 June 1899.

36 Burns, op.cit., p.60.

37 Ibid.

38 *NAF* 24521, fos 101-04: Labori to Zola, 2 June 1898.

39 This article only appeared after long discussion with Clemenceau, Vaughan and Labori. See *NAF* 24521, fos 96-100 and 101-04: Labori to Zola, 31 May 1898 and 2 June 1898.

Chapter 23

1 *'La Féerie et l'opérette'* appeared in *Le Bien Public* on 15 May 1876, 5 November 1877 and 28 May 1878. These articles were republished in *Naturalisme au théâtre* in 1881.
2 *NAF* 24512, fos 158-447 bis for Bruneau-Zola correspondence.
3 *OGC*, p.13.
4 Ibid., p.20.
5 *NAF* 24512, fo. 169: Bruneau to Zola, 15 July 1889.
6 Ibid., fo. 167: Bruneau to Zola, 31 December 1889.
7 Ibid., fo. 327: Bruneau to Zola, n.d. (*c.* 1890).
8 *OGC*, p.32: Zola to Bruneau, June 1891.
9 Ibid., pp.33-34.
10 Ibid., p.39.
11 *OGC*, pp.49-50: Zola to Bruneau, 6 June 1892.
12 *NAF* 24512, fo.186: Bruneau to Zola, 16 May 1892.
13 Ibid., fos 189-91: Bruneau to Zola, 5 August 1892.
14 Ibid., fo. 192: Bruneau to Zola, 9 August 1892.
15 *OGC*, pp.60-63.
16 Ibid.
17 *OGC*, pp.71-72.
18 *NAF* 24512, fos 197-98: Bruneau to Zola, 21 September 1892.
19 Ibid., fos 310-11: Bruneau to Zola, 27 September 1892.
20 *OGC*, p.48.
21 *NAF* 24512, fos 348-49: Bruneau to Zola, n.d. (*c.* August 1895).
22 Ibid., fos 232-33: Bruneau to Zola, 1 September 1895.
23 Ibid., fo.213: Bruneau to Zola, 30 December 1893.
24 *OGC*, p.111.
25 Ibid., pp.89-90: Zola to Bruneau, 22 July 1896.
26 Ibid., pp.104-05.
27 Ibid., p.108.
28 *NAF* 24512, fos 348-49: Bruneau to Zola, n.d. (*c.* August 1895).
29 Ibid., fo.213: Bruneau to Zola, 30 December 1893.
30 Ibid., fos 328-29: Bruneau to Zola, n.d. (*c.* 19 July 1898).
31 *OGC*, p.114.
32 Ibid., p.119.
33 Ibid., p.144: Zola to Bruneau, 18 October 1898.
34 Ibid., p.147: Zola to Bruneau, 6 January 1899.
35 *NAF* 24512, fos 256-57: Bruneau to Zola, 24 August 1898.
36 Ibid., fos 260-61: Bruneau to Zola, 12 October 1898.
37 Ibid., fos 264-65: Bruneau to Zola, 17 March 1899.
38 Ibid.
39 Ibid., fos 266-67: Madame Bruneau to Zola, 5 May 1899.
40 *Le Figaro*, 7 October 1900.
41 *NAF* 24512, fos 330-31: Bruneau to Zola, n.d. (*c.* May 1901).
42 Ibid., fos 377-78: Bruneau to Zola, n.d. (*c.* May 1901).
43 Ibid., fos 274-75: Bruneau to Zola, 28 August 1899.
44 Ibid., fos 343-44: Bruneau to Zola, n.d. (*c.* September 1901).
45 Ibid., fos 285-87: Bruneau to Zola, 16 September 1902.
46 *OGC*, pp.182-83: Bruneau to Zola, 25 September 1902.
47 Ibid., p.200.
48 Ibid., p.201.
49 For a complete list of Zola's operatic works, see Appendix A.

Chapter 24

1 Waldeck-Rousseau had served as Zola's legal counsel in 1894-95, representing him in the matter regarding M. Bourgeois, who claimed that he had been libellously portrayed in the novel *Lourdes*.
2 Alfred Dreyfus, *Cinq années de ma vie, 1894-99* (Paris: Fasquelle, 1901) p.317.
3 Henry Céard, *Le Temps*, 2 July 1899.
4 Ibid.
5 *NAF* 24521, fos 108-09: Labori to Zola, 8 September 1899.
6 *'Le Cinquième acte'*, *L'Aurore*, 12 September 1898.
7 Ibid.
8 *NAF* 24521, fos 110-11: Labori to Zola, 12 September 1899.
9 *OC. Correspondance II*, p.523: Zola to Bruneau, 13 September 1899.
10 *'Lettre à Madame Dreyfus'*, *L'Aurore*, 23 September 1899.

11 *'Lettre au sénat'*, *L'Aurore*, 29 May 1900.
12 Ibid.
13 *'Lettre à M. Emile Loubet, Président de la République'*, *L'Aurore*, 22 December 1900.

Chapter 25

1 *La Patrie*, 29 April 1898.
2 *'François Zola'*, *L'Aurore*, 23 January 1900. This was the first of three articles, all entitled *'François Zola'*, which Zola later republished, together with related articles on the Dreyfus Affair, in a single volume called *Vérité en marche* (Paris: Fasquelle-Charpentier, 1901).
3 Ibid.
4 *NAF* 24521, fos 42-44: Labori to Zola, 29 July 1898.
5 Ibid., fos 47-53: Labori to Zola, 16 August 1898.
6 Ibid., fos 57-58: Labori to Zola, 28 September 1898.
7 Ibid., fos 59-60: Labori to Zola, 5 October 1898.
8 Ibid., fos 62-63: Labori to Zola, 5 October 1898. See also further correspondence in *NAF* 24521, fos 59-60, 61, 64-65, 67-68, 69-76, 78-79, 80-81, 105, 106-07, 143-44.
9 *'François Zola'*, op. cit.
10 Ibid.
11 Ibid.
12 Ibid.
13 Ibid.
14 Ibid.
15 *'François Zola - II'*, *L'Aurore*, 31 January 1900.
16 Ibid.
17 Ibid.
18 Ibid.
19 Ibid.
20 *'François Zola - III'*, *L'Aurore*, 8 March 1901.

Chapter 26

1 Jean Jaurès published this with Zola's permission in *La Petite République*, 23 April 1901.
2 Zola, who had no time for Victor Hugo and the Romantic School, stood surprisingly close to many of Hugo's basic social values, and Hugo's words before the newly-formed Assembly in 1848 could well have been uttered by Zola himself: 'Socialism is based on sad realities that hold true for our times and all times; the *malaise* of human frailty; the aspiration to a better fate . . . '
3 *NAF* 10034.
4 Zola read many of Fourier's works, but his background reading also included *La Conquête de pain* by Kropotkin, *La Société du futur* and *L'Anarchie* by Jean Grave, *Solidarité* by Hippolyte Renaud, and the then popular writings of Edward Bellamy, an American socialist.
5 Josiane Naumont, *'Enquête sur une visite de Zola à Unieux'*, *Les Cahiers Naturalistes*, no.48 (1974), pp.182-204.
6 *NAF* 10034, fo. 330.
7 Ibid., fos 387-94.
8 Ibid.
9 Ibid.
10 *NAF* 10334, fos 355 *et seq.*
11 *NAF* 10335, fos 355 *et seq.*
12 *OC, Correspondance II*, pp.557-58: Zola to Laboustière, 5 June 1901.
13 Ibid., p.560: Zola to Le Grandais, 14 October 1901.
14 *OCM*, Vol.14, p.1535: Zola to unknown student, 25 November 1901.
15 Maurice Le Blond, *La Revue Naturaliste*, May 1901.
16 Marcel Théaux, *La Grande Revue*, May 1901.
17 Jean Jaurès, *La Petite République*, April 1901.
18 *NR*, pp.497-98.
19 Ibid., p.498.
20 The debate in the National Assembly over the transfer of Zola's remains is quoted in *Le Journal Officiel*, 20 March 1908, pp.658 *et seq.*
21 Léon Deffoux published correspondence between Loewenstein and Zola in *'Emile Zola et l'édition illustrée allemande de "La Débâcle"'*, *Mercure de France*, no.209 (1 January - 1 February 1929) pp.108-17. Zola to Lowenstein, 22 March 1900.
22 Deffoux, op.cit., pp.110-12: Loewenstein to Zola, 28 March 1900.
23 Ibid., pp.112-13: Zola to Loewenstein, 30 March 1900.
24 Ibid., pp.114-15: Loewenstein and Mayer to Zola, 4 April 1900.
25 Ibid.
26 Ibid., pp.115-16: Zola to Mayer, 9 April 1900.
27 Ibid., pp.116-17: Loewenstein to Zola, 28 April 1900.
28 Ibid., p.117: Zola to Loewenstein, 4 May 1900.

Chapter 27

1 *LIEZ*, p.21.
2 Ibid., pp.42-43: Céard to Zola, July 1877.
3 Ibid., pp.53-54: Céard to Zola, 12 November 1878.
4 Ibid. Zola to Céard, November 1878.
5 Ibid., p.55: Zola to Céard, 17 November 1878.
6 Ibid., pp.55-56: Céard to Zola, 21 December 1878.
7 *EZC III*, pp.78-79, letter 7: Zola to Céard, 16 July 1877.
8 Jules Claretie in *La Presse*, 20 January 1879.
9 *EZC II*, p.318, letter 153: Zola to Ulbach, 9 September 1872.
10 *LIEZ*, pp.57-58: Céard to Zola, 23 December 1878.
11 *OC, Correspondance II*, p.175: Zola to Claretie, 28 March 1881.
12 *LIEZ*, p.90: Céard to Zola, 2 July 1879 (regarding the play, *Voyage en Suisse* by Ernest Blum and Raoul Toché.)
13 Ibid.
14 Ibid., p.130: Céard to Zola, 13 January 1880.
15 *NAF* 24516, fos 451-55: Céard's notes to Zola.
16 *LIEZ*, pp.87-89: Céard to Zola, September 1879.
17 Ibid., pp.113-14: Céard to Zola, 25 November 1879.
18 Ibid., p.107: Céard to Zola, 28 October 1879.
19 Ibid., pp.118-20: Céard to Zola, 14 December 1879.
20 *EZC III*, p.416, letter 332: Zola to Céard, 13 December 1879.
21 *LIEZ*, pp.118-20 and 122-23: Céard to Zola, 14 and 16 December 1879.
22 Ibid.
23 Ibid., pp.408-09: Céard to Zola, 23 May 1893.
24 Armand Lanoux, *Bonjour, Monsieur Zola* (Paris: Amiot-Dumont, 1954) p.122: Zola to Céard, 11 November 1891.
25 *LIEZ*, p.27.
26 Ibid., pp.410-11.
27 Ibid.
28 *OC, Correspondance II*, p.383: Zola to Alexis, 30 March 1892.
29 Ibid., pp.426-27: Zola to Alexis, 30 December 1896.
30 B.H. Bakker, 'Vingt-cinq lettres inédités de Paul Alexis à Emile Zola et à Jeanne Rozerot (1890-1900)', *Les Cahiers Naturalistes*, no.49 (1975), p.38: Alexis to Zola, 31 December 1895.
31 Ibid., p.40: Alexis to Zola, 5 January 1896. It will be noted that Zola rarely referred to his own works as '*œuvres*'.
32 Ibid. Albert Carré was one of the directors of the Vaudeville Theatre, and Jules Claretie was then a director of the Théâtre Français.
33 Ibid., p.46: Alexis to Jeanne Rozerot, 4 August 1897.
34 Ibid., pp.62-63: Alexis to Zola, 10 September 1900.
35 *OC, Correspondance II*, p.399: Zola to Alexis, 4 December 1893.
36 Originally Goncourt had named Zola as a member of his Academy, but when he learnt that Zola was applying for the Academie Française, he was furious and jealous and withdrew his name. At this stage the members of the Goncourt Academy were Daudet, Huysmans, Mirbeau, Margueritte, Gustave Geoffroy, the two Rosnys and Hennique.
37 Bakker, op.cit., p.42: Alexis to Zola, 21 July 1896. Alexis was nearly blind and required a secretary to write everything for him. He had been interviewed by J. Huret — together with Huysmans, Céard and Hennique — for what proved to be a scathing article in *Le Journal* on 24 November 1893.
38 Ibid., p.46: Alexis to Zola, 1 October 1897.
39 Ibid., pp.49-50: Alexis to Zola, 22 October 1897.
40 Ibid., p.51: Alexis to Zola, 29 October 1897.
41 Ibid., pp.59-60: Alexis to Zola, 9 April 1900.
42 *OC, Correspondance II*, p.542: Zola to Alexis, 1 June 1900.
43 Ibid., p.559: Zola to E. Séménoff, 6 August 1901.

Chapter 28

1 On the development of *La Croix*, see Pierre Sorlin's interesting work, *La Croix et les Juifs (1880-99)*, (Paris: Grasset, 1967). See also Eugen Weber, *Action Française: Royalism and Reaction in Twentieth-century France* (Stanford: Stanford University Press, 1969).
2 *OCM*, p.1492: Jean-Louis Bory's notes on *Vérité*. At the turn of the century there were 90,000 students in French secondary schools run by religious orders (fewer than that number in state schools), and 1,600,000 pupils in Catholic primary schools.
3 *NAF* 10343, fos 305-06.
4 *OCM*, pp.1493-95: Jean-Louis Bory's notes.
5 *OC, Correspondance II*, p.569: Zola to Bruneau, 8 August 1902.
6 'Rachilde', *Mercure de France* XLVI (April - June 1903) p.185.
7 *Le Temps*, 22 February 1903.

8 Emile Combes was a strongly anti-clerical former prime minister (1902-05), who introduced legislation separating Church and State.

9 *Le Figaro*, May 1896.

10 *Athenaeum*, no. 3930, 21 February 1903, p.232.

11 *La Revue Socialiste*, no.220, April 1903, p.505.

12 Ibid., pp.505-09.

13 *La Revue*, 15 February 1903.

Chapter 29

1 *EZR*, p.173.

2 Ibid., p.169.

3 Ibid., p.254.

4 Ibid.

5 Ibid., p.172.

6 Ibid., p.173.

7 Ibid., p.169.

8 Ibid., pp.254-55.

9 Ibid., p.170.

10 Ibid., p.171-72.

11 Ibid., pp.170-71.

12 Ibid., p.193.

13 Ibid., pp.255-56.

14 Ibid., p.170.

15 Ibid., pp.255-56.

16 Ibid., p.256.

17 Ibid., p.183.

18 Ibid., p.184. Among the dramas Zola proposed to write were *Violaine la chevelue*, *Sylvanire*, *L'Eau qui passe*, *L'Eternité d'amour*, *Pourquoi l'on aime*, *Jeunesse*, *Belle-maman* and *Madame*.

19 Ibid., p.245.

20 Ibid., pp.201-02.

21 Ibid., p.256.

22 Ibid., p.250.

23 Ibid., p.172.

24 *OGC*, p.179: Zola to Bruneau, 2 July 1902.

25 Ibid., p.180.

26 Armand Lanoux, *Bonjour, Monsieur Zola* (Paris: Amiot-Dumont, 1954) p.374. Quoted from notes in the possession of Dr François Emile-Zola.

27 *EZR*, pp.256-57.

28 Ibid., p.257.

29 Ibid., p.258.

30 *OGC*, pp.186-87.

31 Ibid., p.188.

32 Ibid., p.189.

33 In an article in *Libération* (29 September - 7 October 1953), journalist Jean Bedel recorded some information he had received from one P. Haquin of Tessy-sur-Vire (Manche), regarding an unnamed friend — a chimney-builder — dating from April 1927, just before the latter's death: 'Haquin, I am going to tell you how Zola died.' He explained how he and a couple of men had gone to locate the chimney belonging to Zola's bedroom and then blocked it up. 'We cleared it very early the next morning. Nobody saw us there. Zola was simply asphyxiated accidentally. It was we who blocked the chimney to his apartment.' See Lanoux, op.cit., pp.372-75 and 386. This was the first work to advance the hypothesis that Zola was murdered.

34 Joseph Reinach, *Histoire de l'affaire Dreyfus*, (Paris: Charpentier et Fasquelle, 1908) Vol. 6, p.198.

35 Dr Jacques Emile-Zola gave these views in an interview recorded by Lanoux, op.cit., p.375.

36 Ibid., p.391.

37 Eulogy by Anatole France, *Le Temps*, 5 October 1902.

APPENDICES

APPENDIX A

Major plays, and collaborative works with William Busnach.

Major Plays

Madeleine, written 1865; first performed 1 May 1889, Théâtre Libre. *Thérèse Raquin*, completed 1873; first performed 11 July 1873, Théâtre de la Renaissance. *Les Héritiers Rabourdin*, written 1872; first performed 3 November 1874, Théâtre de Cluny. *Le Bouton de Rose*, completed 1878; first performed 7 May 1878, Palais-Royal. *Renée*, completed 1881; first performed 16 April 1887, Théâtre du Vaudeville.

Collaborative Works with William Busnach

L'Assommoir (with O. Gastineau), completed 1878; first performed 18 January 1879, Théâtre de l'Ambigu. *Nana*, completed 1880; first performed 29 January 1881, Ambigu. *Pot-bouille*, completed 1883; first performed 13 December 1883, Ambigu. *Le Ventre de Paris*, completed 1886; first performed 18 February 1887, Théâtre de Paris. *Germinal*, written 1885; first performed 21 April 1888, Châtelet. *La Bête humaine*, final version c. 1900; never performed.

APPENDIX B

Novels

La Confession de Claude, 1865; *Thérèse Raquin*, 1867; *Madeleine Férat*, 1868. Rougon-Macquart series: *La Fortune des Rougon*, 1871, vol. 1; *La Curée*, 1872, vol. 2; *Le Ventre de Paris*, 1873, vol. 3; *La Conquête de Plassans*, 1874, vol. 4; *La Faute de l'abbé Mouret*, 1875, vol. 5; *Son Excellence Eugène Rougon*, 1876, vol. 6; *L'Assommoir*, 1877, vol. 7; *Une Page d'amour*, 1878, vol. 8; *Nana*, 1880, vol. 9; *Pot-bouille*, 1882, vol. 10; *Au Bonheur des dames*, 1883, vol. 11; *La Joie de vivre*, 1884, vol. 12; *Germinal*, 1885, vol. 13; *L'Œuvre*, 1886, vol. 14; *La Terre*, 1887, vol. 15; *Le Rêve*, 1888, vol. 16; *La Bête humaine*, 1890, vol. 17; *L'Argent*, 1891, vol. 18; *La Débâcle*, 1892, vol. 19; *Le Docteur Pascal*, 1893, vol. 20. Trois villes series: *Lourdes*, 1894, vol. 1; *Rome*, 1896, vol. 2; *Paris*, 1898, vol. 3. Quatre Evangiles series: *Fécondité*, 1899, vol. 1; *Travail*, 1901, vol. 2; *Vérité*, 1902, vol. 3; vol. 4, *Justice*, was planned but never written.

APPENDIX C

Collaborative works with Alfred Bruneau

Le Rêve, libretto by Louis Gallet and Zola, completed 1890; first performed 18 June 1891, Opéra-Comique. *L'Attaque du moulin*, libretto by Louis Gallet and Zola, completed 1892; first performed 23 November 1893, Opéra-Comique. *Lazare*, libretto by Zola, completed January 1894; first performed 1957 by Radio-Diffusion Française. *Messidor*, libretto by Zola, completed c. 1893; first performed 19 February 1897, Académie Nationale de Musique (by the Paris Opéra). *Ouragan*, libretto by Zola, completed November 1896; first performed 29 April 1901, Opéra Comique. *L'Enfant-Roi*, libretto by Zola, completed c. 1900 (Bruneau completed the score in August 1902); first performed 3 March 1905, Opéra-Comique.

In addition to the above works, Bruneau wrote three subsequent operas (including libretto) based on works by Zola: *Naïs Micoulin*, first performed on 2 February 1907, at the Théâtre du Monte Carlo; *La Faute de l'abbé Mouret*, first performed at the Odéon on 1 March 1907; and *Les Quatre journées*, first performed at the Opéra-Comique on 19 December 1916.

SELECT BIBLIOGRAPHY

Published Works and Correspondence

Zola's novels and plays are listed in Appendices A and B. The author's complete works, including plays, pamphlets and important critical articles, have been published in various editions, including that edited by Gilbert Sigaux, *Œuvres Complètes*, in 42 volumes, under the imprint Cercle du Bibliophile (Paris: Fasquelle; Genève: Edito-Service, no date), and Henri Mitterand's edition, *Œuvres Complètes*, in 15 volumes (Paris: Cercle du Livre Précieux, 1966 1970). Pierre Cogny has also provided a useful annotated six-volume edition of *Les Rougon-Macquart* (Paris: Seuil, 1969 70). In addition Colin Burns published Zola's autobiographical notes, 'Pages d'Exile,' in *Nottingham French Studies*, vol. III (May 1964), pp. 21-46, and in the October issue of the same year, pp. 48-62. Two other autobiographical sketches were edited by René Ternois in *Mes Voyages* (Paris: Fasquelle, 1958), including 'Voyage à Lourdes' and 'Voyage à Rome'. Zola's correspondence is currently being compiled and published in a superb work edited by B.H. Bakker, *Emile Zola, Correspondance* (Montréal: Les Presses de L'Université de Montréal; Paris: Editions du Centre Nationale de la Recherche Scientifique, 1978-1985), of which the first five volumes have appeared, up to the year 1886. This work is fully annotated and comprehensive.

Memoirs and Biographies on Zola

The following are probably amongst the better known in this field: Paul Alexis, *Emile Zola: notes d'un ami* (Paris: Charpentier, 1882); Alfred Bruneau, *A L'ombre d'un grand cœur, souvenirs d'une collaboration* (Paris: Charpentier, 1932); F.W.S. Hemmings, *Emile Zola* (Oxford: Oxford University Press, 1953); Matthew Josephson, *Zola and His Times* (Garden City, N.Y.: Garden City Publishing Co., 1928); Albert Laborde, *Trente-huit années près de Zola: vie d'Alexandrine Méley* (Paris: Editeurs Français Réunis, 1963); Armand Lanoux, *Bonjour, Monsieur Zola* (Paris: Amiot-Dumont, 1954); Denise Le Blond-Zola, *Emile Zola raconté par sa fille* (Paris: Fasquelle, 1931); Edmond Le Pelletier, *Emile Zola; sa vie et ses œuvres* (Paris: Mercure de France, 1908); Joanna Richardson, *Zola* (London: Weidenfeld and Nicolson, 1978); Robert Sherard, *Emile Zola: A Biography and Critical Study* (London: Chatto and Windus, 1893); E.A. Vizetelly's two works, *Emile Zola, Novelist and Reformer* (London: John Lane and the Bodley Head, 1904), and *With Zola in England* (London: Chatto and Windus), 1899; and Philip Walker, *Zola* (London: Routledge and Kegan Paul, 1985). For a variety of academic studies of Zola, see the most useful *Cahiers Naturalistes*.

Manuscripts

The main holdings are in the Bibliothèque Nationale. One of the richest sources is the massive correspondence to the novelist, particularly NAF 24510 to 24523. See also the following manuscript sources: NAF 15385, 15439, 15682, 15737 for Alexandrine Zola; NAF 13005-140061 for Georges Clemenceau; NAF 14378 for Mathieu Dreyfus; NAF 13582 and 24897-8 for Joseph Reinach; NAF 12711 and 23819 for Scheurer-Kestner, and NAF 13190 and 13191 for notes by Van Cassel during Zola's trial. The Bibliothèque Nationale also possesses many of the manuscript notes and texts of Zola's works.

Other manuscript holdings include the University of Toronto, which has a large variety of Zola letters and manuscripts, and Brown University, which owns several dozen letters, most of which have been published by Professor Albert Salvan. Houghton Library, Harvard University holds a few dozen choice letters by Zola to Fasquelle, Labori and Vaughan (bMS Judaica 1, 1.3 and 1.4) concerning the Dreyfus Affair and his own trials. Various judicial sources have been consulted at the Archives Départementales de la Seine and des Yvelines, in addition to the Archives du Ministère de la Justice, Cour de Cassation, and the Archives Nationales.

Other Works

Antoine, *Mes souvenirs sur le Théâtre-Libre* (Paris: Fayard, 1921); Baguley, David, *Bibliographie de la Critique*, 2 vols (Toronto: University of Toronto Press, 1976-1982); Beaumont, Barbara, ed., *Flaubert and Turgenev: A Friendship in Letters — The Complete Correspondence* (New York: Norton, 1985); Bernhardt, Sarah, *Ma Double vie: mémoires*, 2 vols (Paris: Charpentier - Fasquelle, 1907); Bredin, Jean Denis, *L'Affaire* (Paris: Julliard, 1983); Carter, Lawson A., *Zola and the Theater* (New Haven: Yale University Press; Paris: Presses Universitaires de France, 1963); Céard, Henry, *Lettres inédites à Emile Zola* (Paris: Nizet, 1958); Rewald, John, ed., *Paul Cézanne, Correspondance* (Paris: Grasset, 1933); Charpentier, Georges, ed. Colette Becker, *Trente années d'amitié, 1872 1902* (Paris: Presses Universitaires de France, 1980); Chastel, Guy, *J.K. Huysmans et ses amis* (Paris: Grasset, 1957); Cogny, Pierre, *Le Huysmans intime de Henry Céard et Jean de Caldain* (Paris: Nizet, 1957); Daudet,

Lucien, *Vie d'Alphonse Daudet* (Paris: Gallimard, 1941); Dreyfus, Alfred, *Cinq années de ma vie, 1894–1899* (Paris: Fasquelle, 1901); France, Jean, *Autour de l'affaire Dreyfus, souvenirs de la Sûreté Générale* (Paris: Rieder, 1936); Goncourt, Edmond et Jules de, *Journal, Mémoires de la vie littéraire*, 22 vols (Paris: Fasquelle et Flammarion, 1956); Guillemin, Henri, *Zola, légende et vérité* (Paris: Julliard, 1969); Mitterand, Henri, *Zola journaliste, de l'affaire Manet à l'affaire Dreyfus* (Paris: Colin, 1962); Mitterand, Henri and Suwala, Halina, *Emile Zola journaliste: bibliographie chronologique et analytique (1859–1881)*, (Paris: Annales Littéraires de l'Université de Besançon, 1968); Reinach, Joseph, *Histoire de l'Affaire Dreyfus*, 6 vols (Paris: Charpentier et Fasquelle, 1908); Sarcey, Francisque, *Quarante ans de théâtre*, 8 vols (Paris: Bibliothèque des Annales Politiques et Littéraires, 1900). For the transcript of Zola's trial, see *L'Affaire Dreyfus: le procès Zola devant la Cour d'Assises de la Seine et la Cour de Cassation (7 février–23 février/31 mars–2 avril 1898). Compte-rendu sténographique 'in extenso' et documents annexes*, 2 vols (Paris: Le Siècle et P.V. Stock, 1898).

INDEX